R.K. NARAYAN

R.K. NARAYAN

Soundarya Apartments
164 A-1 Eldams Road
Alwarpet
Madras-600018
Tel. (044) 455440, 457856

21st Oct. 1992

My dear Ranga Rao,

Many thanks for your note and the Times piece, which I appreciate immensely. Your Survey of my writing shows a deep study and an abiding interest. I was not aware till you pointed it out that Sex had been dormant and blossomed through successive works, in a kind of evolution, although it died, as a personal element of love, with the death of my wife.

Thanks again for your offering at 86 & still cannot reconcile myself to this number or take it seriously, although the mechanisms of the body have slowed down and begun to creak.

Best wishes
R K Narayan

R.K. NARAYAN

THE NOVELIST AND HIS ART

RANGA RAO

OXFORD
UNIVERSITY PRESS

OXFORD
UNIVERSITY PRESS

Oxford University Press is a department of the University of Oxford.
It furthers the University's objective of excellence in research, scholarship,
and education by publishing worldwide. Oxford is a registered trademark of
Oxford University Press in the UK and in certain other countries

Published in India by
Oxford University Press
YMCA Library Building, 1 Jai Singh Road, New Delhi 110001, India

© V.P. Ranga Rao 2017

The moral rights of the authors have been asserted

First Edition published in 2017

All rights reserved. No part of this publication may be reproduced, stored in
a retrieval system, or transmitted, in any form or by any means, without the
prior permission in writing of Oxford University Press, or as expressly permitted
by law, by licence, or under terms agreed with the appropriate reprographics
rights organization. Enquiries concerning reproduction outside the scope of the
above should be sent to the Rights Department, Oxford University Press, at the
address above

You must not circulate this work in any other form
and you must impose this same condition on any acquirer

ISBN-13: 978-0-19-947075-4
ISBN-10: 0-19-947075-8

Typeset in Berling LT Std 10/13
by The Graphics Solution, New Delhi 110092
Printed in India by Replika Press Pvt. Ltd

For Vijayalakshmi, who has supported the obsession; and in memory of Professor K.R. Srinivasa Iyengar and 'AVK'

More than all else, do I cherish at heart that love which makes me to live a limitless life in this world.
—Sant Kabir quoted by Ananda Coomaraswamy in
The Dance of Siva (1918: 27)

You become a writer by writing. It's a yoga.
—R.K. Narayan in Ram and Ram (1996b: 21)

Contents

Foreword by Shyamala A. Narayan ix
Acknowledgements xiii
Introduction xvii

I HOME-GROWN: BACKGROUND

1 Mixed Sap: A Life 3
2 I Had Not Been False: A Career 14
3 Profundity with a Light Touch: A Style 22

II THE PRE-INDEPENDENCE NOVELS

4 In a World Dominated by Adults: *Swami and Friends* 29
5 Live a Man's Life: *The Bachelor of Arts* 37
6 Sacral Space: No Trespassing!—*The Dark Room* 50
7 Purify the Mind and Clarify the Vision: Ordeal and Aftermath 65
8 Some Eternal Scheme: *The English Teacher* and the Partitive Parallax 71
9 Enchantment in Life: *Mr. Sampath* and the Naipaul Enigma 89

III VICE-FECTION: THE POST-INDEPENDENCE NOVELS AND NOVELLAS

10 A Wizard for Malgudi: *The Financial Expert* 123
11 The Moth and the Mahatma: *Waiting for the Mahatma* 136

12	Grateful to Love and Death: *The Guide*	144
13	For God, Country—and Comedy! *The Man-Eater of Malgudi*	158
14	Private Sorrows, Indian Remedy: *The Vendor of Sweets*	197
15	First Love Again! *The Painter of Signs*	205
16	Caution! Masterful Male! *Talkative Man*	211
17	Guru and Chela: *A Tiger for Malgudi*	215
18	Mettle Fatigue: *The World of Nagaraj*	218
19	Gunas Horror: *Grandmother's Tale*	223

IV SUMMING UP

20	Cosmic Comedy: R.K. Narayan's Gunas Comedy	241

Notes	255
Bibliography	293
Index	311
About the Author	321

Foreword

Ranga Rao (Dr V. Panduranga Rao) is one of the first scholars to conduct research on R.K. Narayan's fiction; his doctoral thesis, submitted to Andhra University under the supervision of Professor K.R. Srinivasa Iyengar (the 'father' of Indian writing in English) in 1964, was the first in any Indian university—and the second the world over, after Nirmal Mukherji's 'The World of Malgudi' submitted to Louisiana State University in 1960.

R.K. Narayan is the most significant Indian English writer of the twentieth century, with fifteen novels and novellas and more than half-a-dozen collections of short stories to his credit. He was the first Indian writer in English to win the Sahitya Akademi Award. More than eighty books on R.K. Narayan's writings have been published in the last fifty years; many of these have been thematic studies, or routine analyses of his novels and short stories. Ranga Rao's work stands out for his original approach; his reading is with reference to the Indian philosophical concept of the three gunas.

R.K. Narayan: The Novelist and His Art is as much about the man as it is about the writer. Ranga Rao presents an intimate picture of R.K. Narayan the man, based on the novelist's memoirs like *My Dateless Diary* (1960) and *My Days: A Memoir* (1974); Susan and N. Ram's biography *R.K. Narayan: The Early Years, 1906–1945* (1996); and interviews. Certain incidents in the novelist's life are brought to public notice for the first time. The first three chapters of the book provide the background—a chapter each is devoted to R.K. Narayan's life, his career, and his style. Ranga Rao next takes up the three novels of Narayan written before his wife's death: *Swami and Friends* (1935), *The Bachelor of Arts* (1937), and *The Dark Room* (1938). Chapter 7, 'Purify the Mind and Clarify the Vision: Ordeal and Aftermath', is a sensitive account of the way Narayan coped with the sudden death of his wife, just five years after their marriage. Narayan had married the girl, eleven years younger than him, in spite of the opposition of their families. He was completely shattered and never married again; he loved her so much. The next two chapters analyse the 'post-ordeal' novels, *The English Teacher* (1945) and *Mr. Sampath* (1949), published in the USA as *The Printer of Malgudi* in 1957.

The third part of the book is devoted to R.K. Narayan's later fiction; it traces the development of his fiction through the remaining ten novels and novellas, from *The Financial Expert* (1952) to *Grandmother's Tale* (1992). These novels and novellas reveal a movement from the sattvic comedy of the pre-Independence novels to rajasic and tamasic comedy. Ranga Rao shows how each protagonist of this period suffers from some vice—avarice in the case of Margayya in *The Financial Expert*; sloth of Sriram in *Waiting for the Mahatma* (1955); and lust in the Sahitya Akademi Award winning novel *The Guide* (1958). Vasu in *The Man-Eater of Malgudi* (1961) is an embodiment of tamasic qualities, like the rakshasas of Hindu mythology.

The last part, the summing up, reveals a new approach to R.K. Narayan's work. The three gunas—sattva, rajas, and tamas—are qualities of human nature, a blend of which determines the potentialities of human personality. Ranga Rao shows how sattva is the dominant guna of the protagonists in the early, pre-Independence novels—they are sensitive and creative, with a certain innocence. In the novels written after his wife Rajam's death, the protagonists are more outgoing and passionate, dominated by rajas. Narayan's emphasis is on the possibilities of spiritual evolution of the characters: they are all, consciously or unconsciously, moving towards self-development.

Ranga Rao points out that Narayan's fiction falls into three broad groups: the first five novels with *Mr. Sampath* marking the transition to the second group of four novels, *The Financial Expert, Waiting for the Mahatma, The Guide,* and *The Man-Eater of Malgudi;* the third phase comprises two novels, *The Vendor of Sweets* (1967) and *The Painter of Signs* (1976); and the four shorter works: *A Tiger for Malgudi* (1983), *Talkative Man* (1977), *The World of Nagaraj* (1990), and *Grandmother's Tale* (1992). All the characters have rajasic and tamasic tendencies, and their approach to others is marked by deviousness, a contrast to the innocence of the early works; however, the possibility of spiritual regeneration is always present. The later fiction reveals the changing social world of Malgudi. The critic shows that the darker world of the later novels is marked by violence and the breakdown of the father–child relationship; these novels also reveal changing sexual mores. Ranga Rao's study highlights new aspects of Narayan's later work; the detailed commentaries on *The Guide* and *The Man-Eater of Malgudi* are outstanding.

The bibliography, painstakingly compiled from varied sources (newspapers, journals, books, and correspondence with people close to R.K. Narayan), lists the author's own works as well as studies of his work. The section on interviews (which includes Ranga Rao's personal interaction with the novelist) is particularly useful—Ranga Rao takes care to preface the thirty-three interviews with Sharada Prasad's caution: 'With journalists, especially interviewers, he likes to play little games' (*The Hindu*, 29 August 1988).

This book is the fruit of fifty years of study. R.K. Narayan himself acknowledges in his letter to the critic, 'Your survey of my writing shows a deep study and an abiding interest'. It is relevant to note that Ranga Rao is the author of three novels, *Fowl Filcher* (1987), *Drunk Tantra* (1994), and *The River Is Three-Quarters Full* (2001), and a collection of short stories, *An Indian Idyll and Other Stories* (1989). He has also translated two volumes of short stories from Telugu into English. His own experience as a creative writer enables him to analyse R.K. Narayan's craft as an insider, thereby providing a fresh perspective. He also brings to the study the insights he has gained from five decades of teaching.

This book will be useful for both researchers and lay readers; and anyone who has not read R.K. Narayan's novels will be moved to do so if he reads Ranga Rao's jargon-free analyses.

SHYAMALA A. NARAYAN
20 October 2015

Acknowledgements

At Andhra University, Professor K.R. Srinivasa Iyengar changed the course of my life when he accepted me as a doctoral candidate in 1961: his gracious guidance set me in Narayan's orbit.

The Hindu (Madras/Chennai) and the Frontline (Madras/Chennai) have always kept open house to Indian literatures, eminently to Narayan and to critics on Narayan. The Miscellany, edited by P. Lal and his Writer's Workshop (Calcutta), first published many of our writers; as did to some extent the Illustrated Weekly of India (Bombay), now defunct and receding fast from our memory.

Susan Ram and N. Ram know Narayan and his work intimately; their retrieval of 'The Psychic Journal', especially, is a landmark in Narayan studies; R.K. Narayan: The Early Years, 1906–1945, their authoritative biography, prescribed reading for all Narayan readers and critics, has filled large gaps in my narrative. For their update and more on Narayan, see the 18 October 1996 issue of Frontline. Ram has always responded promptly and positively to my requests for critical materials. I am indebted to the chief librarian of the Hindu's Central Library in Chennai for prompt follow-up.

Parts of this book have appeared in some form in journals and periodicals: Indian Literature (Sahitya Akademi, New Delhi); The Times of India (Bombay/Mumbai); The Hindu (Madras/Chennai); Frontline (Madras); The Indian Express (New Delhi); Biblio (New Delhi); Outlook (New Delhi); The Book Review (New Delhi); The Journal of Commonwealth Literature (Leeds and London); and London Magazine. I thank the editors: D.S. Rao and K. Satchidanandan; Nirmala Lakshman; N. Ram; Adil Jussawalla; Dileep Padgaonkar; Sheela Reddy; Arthur Ravenscroft and John Thieme; and Chandra Chari and Uma Iyengar. And Alan Ross—meeting with the poet-editor in his tiny office in London, after absorbing the shock of his landlady's discarnate voice, was a Dickensian experience. The British Council tour also helped me meet with Alastair Niven and John Thieme; they have been generous with their critical and moral support.

Down the decades, many have read portions of this book at various stages of its evolution and offered suggestions: from lay readers to undergraduates to colleagues in the University of Delhi and Sri Sathya Sai Institute of Higher Learning (deemed to be a university), Prasanthi Nilayam, as well as distinguished academics and critics and friends in India and abroad.

Narayan himself read some of my published articles; as did four of his friends, S. Krishnan, Professor M.N. Srinivas, H.Y. Sharada Prasad, and T.S. Satyan; Narayan's younger brother R.K. Laxman, the brilliant cartoonist; and Narayan's soft-spoken niece Mrs Anandaram; and my friends. Those still around, I am sure, will feel somewhat relieved now. I also thank my wife Vijayalakshmi and our children—the grandchildren were too young to suffer the trial.

The Sahitya Akademi (India's National Academy of Letters) published the Indian edition of my monograph *R.K. Narayan* in their 'Makers of Indian Literature' series in 2004. They also supported my work on Narayan with a fellowship for six months. I also thank the secretary and the Akademi for granting permission to use some material from my monograph in this book. The Akademi's assistant librarian, Mr Padmanabhan, has helped me with some rare citations. I am in his debt for quick follow-up.

'DS', Dr D.S. Rao (former editor of *Indian Literature*), has been a wise counsellor in my Narayan journey. He was the first to appreciate the concept of 'gunas comedy'.

Professor Shyamala A. Narayan has been heroic: she closely read through the entire manuscript and offered several corrections, and helped me trace references. She even convinced me of the value of a veteran—and extremely generous—research guide as a friend.

My elder son Shiva helped me reach OUP India: working with their teams processing the manuscript—and its difficult author—has reminded me that publishing decencies are rooted in human values.

Digital assistance has come from Jai Kumar and Bhasha of Sri Venkateswara Off-set Press, Puttaparthi, who have helped me prepare soft copies of the numerous drafts of the manuscript.

Bhagavan Sri Sathya Sai Baba's Prasanthi Nilayam and his university have been, since June 2002, just right for concluding life's continuities.

Introduction

What would have happened, I often wondered, if the travel-weary manuscript of R.K. Narayan's first novel had not reached Graham Greene? 'Weight the manuscript with a stone and drown it in the Thames', the frustrated novelist had decreed (Ram and Ram 1996b: 8). Kittu Purna, Narayan's hometown friend, did not carry out the author's bidding, but took the typescript to Graham Greene—'by some instinct', Narayan said decades later (Ram 1991: 118). Greene's intervention averted the calamity, literary and environmental.

As early as 1938, Somerset Maugham could foresee the future of Indian literatures: 'I am hoping that, with all the national aspiration of India, you will give rise to a great school of writers and artists [...]' (Ram and Ram 1996a: 200). Prescience, or prophecy!—it has come about. Following India's Independence in 1947, with liberation sweeping through Asia and Africa—something like the post-Armada mood and spirit in Shakespeare's England—the 1950s and the 1960s witnessed yet another rise of the novel in English.

In India, after the Gandhian surge of the 1930s, we experienced a second flowering of the novel in English: Sudhin Ghose published four novels between 1949 and 1955; Jhabvala, eight novels between 1955 and 1968, including *Esmond in India* (1955); Khushwant Singh, *Train to Pakistan* (1956) and *I Shall Not Hear the Nightingale* (1961); Narayan's five novels, including *The Guide* (1958) which won the first Sahitya Akademi Award for English in 1960; Raja Rao, *The Serpent and the Rope* (1960); Manohar Malgonkar published four novels between 1960 and 1964; Anantanarayanan, *The Silver Pilgrimage* (1961); and Anita Desai, *Voices in the City* (1965) and *Cry, the Peacock* (1968).

Elsewhere, Chinua Achebe published *Things Fall Apart* in 1958 and V.S. Naipaul, *A House for Mr Biswas* in 1961. A cloudburst of African—prominently, Nigerian—fiction in English prompted a British publisher to launch a series exclusively for African writers. 'Sometime during the 1950s our perspective on English literature changed' (King 1974: 2).[1]

R.K. Narayan played a central role in this saga.

When Professor K.R. Srinivasa Iyengar suggested 'The Art of R.K. Narayan' for my doctoral dissertation in 1961, he had just returned from Britain after delivering a series of pioneering talks on Indian Writing in English at Leeds University; with critics like Norman Jeffares and William Walsh, Leeds had set out on its catalytic role in postcolonial literatures.[2] Over the decades, the reception accorded to this New Literature has been as satisfying as Narayan's steady progression to centre stage.

Henry Reed observed as early as 1945 that '[Narayan] may be building up a series of novels which will give us a really complete and convincing and touching picture of a land and a society quite different from—though invaded and overshadowed by—our own [...] he writes like no English or Indian writer I've ever come across' (Ram and Ram 1996a: 405). Walsh (1982: 163) noted that Narayan had won 'at least the appreciation of novelists as different from one another as Somerset Maugham and E.M. Forster'.[3] Graham Greene, a great admirer of Henry James, declared: 'Since the death of Evelyn Waugh, Narayan is the novelist I most admire in the English language' (Ram and Ram 1996b: 5).[4] E.M. Forster commended Narayan to an Indian writer, 'Read him. High-class comedy, without any isms' (Singh 1997: 13). Richard Cronin (1989: 34) was categorical: 'It was Narayan who invented what I have called the Indian English novel, the novel that can be written in English because it makes of English an Indian language.' John Updike (1975: 38) referred to Narayan as 'the foremost Indian writer of fiction in English'. Anthony Spaeth (1992: 50) paid a definitive tribute: 'He is that rare literary figure who satisfies both the high-brows and the page turners [...]'. Vikram Seth remarked at a gathering of academics and scholars: 'R.K. Narayan is a supreme writer. I am moved by his characters, I laugh with them, love them. As I have often said, and I am saying it again, if he had written about North India, I would not have—I would not have dared to' (Mukherjee 2004: n.p.). Warren French declared: '[Narayan is] one of the few profoundly humanistic writers of our time' (Atma Ram 1981: xv). In a forceful demonstration of Narayan's appeal to the new generation of writers, Jhumpa Lahiri (2006: ix) declared: 'Narayan firmly occupies a seat in the pantheon of 19th- and 20th-century short-story geniuses [...].'

For decades R.K. Narayan had been the only Indian writer known all over the English-reading world after Rabindranath Tagore. He remains global.[5] At the international conference in Mysore in 2006, the paper presented by Dr Alastair Niven was titled 'Why Can't Englishmen Write Like R.K. Narayan?' The periphery had reached the centre.[6]

By Narayan's pre-Independence novels I refer to the following: *Swami and Friends* (1935); *The Bachelor of Arts* (1937); *The Dark Room* (1938); *The English Teacher* (as *Grateful to Life and Death* in the USA) (1945); and though published in 1949, *Mr. Sampath* (as *The Printer of Malgudi* in the USA): all of these books, as Naipaul (1979, 227) noted, 'written in the days of the British'.[7] Narayan's post-Independence novels and novellas were ushered by *The Financial Expert* (1952).

Over R.K. Narayan's pre-Independence novels, especially, has settled, extensively, stubbornly, a cloud of critical unknowing; the list of scholars and critics who have put down the unpretentious early works is formidable: it includes Williams, Hemenway, Naik, even Walsh.[8] The critical injustice excels itself in their dismissal by Naipaul in *India: A Wounded Civilization* (1979); Naipaul picks in particular on *Mr. Sampath*—and the post-Independence novel *The Vendor of Sweets*—to support his thesis of 'Hindu withdrawal'. As No-Nonsense Naipaul arrives at his inferences and assertions through a seminal infringement; and gifts a shibboleth—'Narayan's small men'—to a generation of academics and critics, time we called Vidia's no-balls.[9]

We shall, however, breathe the centennial spirit, practise critical sobriety; not just avoid ritualism, bread-and-butter criticism: for our author has warned: 'I do not write for professors and do not appreciate their trying to analyze me' (Kalhan 1973: 1). To match our subject, we shall attempt simple textual analysis: without any ismic bias. Old-fashioned respect for facts of the fiction, its 'given'atomy—sort of bare-foot criticism—tackles entrenched embolism.[10]

With untypical flamboyance Narayan announced to Ved Mehta (1962: 153): 'Like true reality, I am many things to many men.' Narayan to me is a novelist of inclusive vision and exclusive art. Narayan's fifteen novels and novellas confirm that Narayan had mastered early, like Chekhov, the art of distancing. Predisposition of the protagonists for 'freedom' as well as 'self-discipline' elevates these novels and novellas to 'high-class comedy'. Realizing the need for controlling the mind to achieve the highest form of human happiness, Narayan's heroes seek self-emancipation. The 'inward' journey carries rare appeal. These 'heroes' are, at the same time, no sanyasins; far from it, they are, like most of us, open to joys of everyday experience; they are also active participants in the lives of their families and society, zealous seekers of life, here and now.[11] Thus, balance is the mantra of Narayan's 'heroes', especially, of the pre-Independence phase, a subtle balance of freedom and discipline; for Narayan, their creator, it is subtle balance again: of art and acumen.

Lit up by his rare range of humour, Narayan's novels and novellas also present and develop a unique species of comedy. We may hypothesize it as gunas comedy. In common Indian parlance, the three gunas—sattva, rajas, and tamas—are qualities of human nature, a blend of which determines the disposition of human personality. In the first five novels, the protagonists are all of one dominant type, sattvic: gentle, introspective, questing, conscionable; in contrast, rajasic and tamasic types, obsessive, passionate, or violent, dominate Narayan's post-Independence novels. Such a range is possible only to a major novelist; for few have the talent, and the stamina.

Fewer still enjoy Narayan's pure gift: love for people as people. 'Almost half the day he spends rambling in and around the city' (Libra 1952: 27). The novelist's daily stroll—eight to ten miles— was more than a fiction writer's recce; the writer loved to join common folk in the streets of Mysore. 'Narayan genuinely enjoys people and derives emotional and artistic sustenance from his contacts' (Krishnan 1975: 42). In his conversation with Ved Mehta (1962: 150) in New York, Narayan confirmed his fondness for mankind: 'Yeveryday [sic] I like to meet a new person', for, 'novels may bore me, but never people'. Narayan makes it clear that this interest is not casual: 'Once I meet a person I always like to keep in touch' (Mehta 1962: 151): a statement that must outrage writers fostering privacy. Narayan affirms his faith in common humanity: '[The] writer does not live in a vacuum; he seldom enjoys a hermit's isolated life [...] there is action and reaction, though it is true that everything becomes transformed in the actual process of writing' ('Interview with R.K. Narayan' 1961: 50). This is, as Updike said, 'no less than a genuine belief in the significance of humanity [...]'.[12]

We know now where the novelist found the models for his ambience characters as well as his action characters.

Narayan has deceived critics: he has done his work so unselfconsciously. '[H]e walks quietly among us' (Mojtabai 1981: 25). For, 'Narayan has been around for so long, and his books are written with such grace, that it takes an effort to recognize the unlikeliness of his success, both artistic and commercial' (Spaeth 1992: 50).

As Narayan's achievement was at once personal and national, moral and literary, I begin my study with a brief life and profile of the man; for proper perspective I relate the novelist in substance and style to his precursors in south India. In Part II, after a chapter each for the first three novels, I look at the catastrophe that struck the novelist when his wife passed away prematurely; and, with inputs from Ram and Ram's 1996 book *R.K. Narayan*—my sourcebook— assess the aftermath of that blow. I go on to analyse the later two novels of the early period, *The English Teacher* and *Mr. Sampath*. In Part III, I take up readings of Narayan's post-Independence novels and novellas. I conclude my appraisal with a summing up in Part IV.

This book is a bi-text; the notes at the end of the book are more comprehensive than customary in a conventional study.[13] Gathered over five decades from various sources—newspapers, journals, mostly Indian; books and critical anthologies on Narayan, including the three books on Narayan that have appeared after our author's death; Narayan's works; thirty-five interviews and profiles, most of them Indian; and my own interviews and correspondence with people close to Narayan—these notes are a magpie collection. Most readers of Narayan abroad, and even in India, may not be aware of several of these secondary sources—unless they, too, are Narayan addicts. As these notes also touch upon topics of tangential interest, academic scholars as well as students of literature might find them complementary, supplementary, or extensive. Thus, the notes are best read again at the end, as a sort of review and expansion of the main text. With the rising tide of popularity of R.K. Narayan all over the world in this century, even the lay reader might dip into them.

I
HOME-GROWN
Background

1

Mixed Sap

A Life[1]

The intellectual history of modern India was formally inaugurated by Macaulay's *Minute* submitted to the East India Company in 1833. Accepting the recommendation, the British 'kumpini', now the suzerain over the best part of India, decided to impart to their subcontinental subjects Western education in English medium. The University of Calcutta was founded in 1857; two more universities, Bombay and Madras, came up a few months later in the same year: with unanticipated results, predictable in retrospect.[2] Western education quickened Indian Renaissance and led, among other things, to the founding of the Indian National Congress; the very first graduate of Calcutta University, Bankim Chandra Chatterjee, wrote the first Indian novel in English, *Rajmohan's Wife* (1864). Encouraged by British power and policy in India, and stimulated by British presence, the early progeny of Macaulay's *Minute*, the first two generations, had prepared the ground for Narayan and the Indian intelligentsia of the tertiary generation.[3]

On his father's side, Narayan's ancestors had been mirasidars, landowners, in Rasipuram (the 'R' in his name), a remote village in the Tamil country in south India. Though they were orthodox Iyer Brahmins, Narayan's father, Krishnaswami Iyer (the 'K' in his name) joined the rising English-educated middle class of India, cut himself off from his father's family after his marriage, was practically a rationalist, and went out always immaculately dressed in a three-piece suit, walking stick in hand—Macaulay's dream come true: almost! 'My father was very puritanical [...] he was a teetotaler [...]' (Narayan 1974: 122).[4]

Krishnaswami was also a lover of Carnatic music and offered hospitality to visiting musicians, gifting our novelist a cultivated taste for classical music. The elder also passed on his love for English language and literature to his family. While mistakes in Tamil or Kannada would be viewed lightly, Narayan's younger brother Laxman, the celebrated cartoonist, said 'a grammatical lapse in English was frowned upon in no small way' (Ram and Ram 1996a: 69); Narayan clarified later: 'Proficiency in English being a social hallmark [...]' (Narayan 1974: 71-2). Krishnaswami's library included the standard classics of the period: Carlyle, Ruskin, Pater.... He recommended them to his sons. But Narayan could not go beyond a few pages of these writers; in contrast, double-column editions of Wordsworth, Byron, Browning, and Shakespeare—and Marie Corelli—seized the imagination of young Narayan: the Romantics and Corelli overwhelmed his youthful sensibility. The collection of books in his father's library represented 'the cultural history of our country for half a century or more; the root and branches of our cultural growth and the mixed sap coursing through them' (1988: 140).

'Mixed sap' sums up the post-Macaulay generations of India. Narayan himself is a product of the Indo-British encounter, of the *mixed sap*—of the Macaulayasa *gothra*, clan.

Acculturation proved more colourful on Narayan's maternal side. Narayan's maternal grandfather was a middle-level revenue official in the British administration, a Brahmin westernized with a vengeance: with a partiality for gin and meatballs. He was also famous for his venality, though we cannot be sure this feature, too, was a British gift.[5] The gentleman was distinguished by an endearing nickname: 'Kuthupatta'—'one who has been stabbed'.

Not he, fortunately (though Narayan was named after him), but his wife Parvati, Narayan's maternal grandmother, turned out to be, more than anyone else, the most enduring influence. Little Narayan was raised by Parvati, popularly known as 'Ammani' (respected madam) in Madras. After his birth on 10 October 1906—slightly premature—at his maternal grandmother's home in Madras, his mother grew too busy and, in the early years, enervated after a quick succession of childbirths—Narayan was the third of eight— to find time and energy for all her children. So, away from his parents domiciled in the princely state of Mysore where his father was appointed headmaster, Kunjappa—'little fellow', Narayan's pet name—was nourished by a wet nurse in Madras, who would later embarrass little Narayan by turning up at his school in Madras and comment on how big the boy had grown.

Narayan spoke of his grandmother's regime of 'high principle and purposeful activity' (Ram and Ram 1996a: 16ff). An extremely energetic woman, self-educated, conversant with Sanskrit and able to follow English, the grand lady served the neighbourhood in various ways: she educated its deprived children—'People from the street would come to learn from her' (Ram and Ram 1996a: 19); she kept an open home: anyone who would eat could eat there; anyone who wanted to perform a marriage could do so at her home; any relative whose term had come could use one of the rooms upstairs as delivery chamber. She also wielded medical prowess, with a range of homemade remedies: 'She was a key figure in the lives of many' (Ram and Ram 1996a: 36). Ammani was also fond of gardening.[6] Decades later Narayan described her to his biographers as an 'extraordinary character—absolutely principled' and 'deserving of a book in her own right': and regretted, '[w]e don't have that kind of granny nowadays' (Ram and Ram 1996a: 17).[7]

Narayan's social activism, a sense of neighbourly engagement may have derived from his mother's side. The writer's involvement extended to non-governmental institutions. 'He is connected with several organizations: AIR, ICCR and the Sahitya Akademi' (Kalhan 1973: 1); he presided over the national convention of authors, sponsored by the Authors' Guild of India, in late 1974: 'I am not very fond of participating in affairs of this kind but I felt I owed it to my fellow-writers' (Updike 1975: 39). Narayan was, in Updike's phrase, 'writer as citizen'.[8]

Little Kunjappa received from Ammani a parallel non-formal education, which included an introduction to the various ragas of Carnatic music.[9] Music was the novelist's chief form of recreation. Narayan enjoyed playing on the veena; though his friend and veena maestro Doreswamy Iyengar gave him lessons, Narayan practised his own style, resisting 'scientific music'. Narayan played well, Iyengar told Susan Ram and N. Ram (1996: 303-4), 'as a non-professional' and that he had 'an effective style'.[10] During this first formative period—'urchin days at Ammani's', in Ved Mehta's words (1962: 140),[11] little Narayan may have also received a special gift from his maternal grandmother: humour. Towards the end of her life, Ammani was unable to eat due to oesophageal cancer and was fed through an opening in her stomach. She responded cheerfully: 'You can give me anything. Whether it is honey or castor oil, it's all the same to me' (Ram and Ram 1996a: 113).

'Kunjappa'—with 'such large eyes and all those curls falling down to [his] cheeks!' (Narayan 1996: 2)—went to school in Madras, under dual care and tutelage: of his maternal grandmother and of her elder son, Seshachalam, Narayan's elder maternal uncle, the 'Senior' Uncle—'who brought me up' (1996: 2). Seshachalam was an idealist lawyer, Narayan recalled to Ram, 'who would not talk of reforming the world but he did that without any fuss' (Ram and Ram 1996a: 25).[12]

On the top panel of the little bureau he had been given to keep his books at his grandmother's, Kunjappa inscribed a legend: *R.K. Narayanaswami, B.A.B.L., Engine Driver.*[13] Though little Narayan's ambition would remain unfulfilled, the aspiration suggested a refinement of his uncle's professional idealism; for one day Seshachalam returned home in disgust with the corruption in the legal profession and cast off the lawyer's gown for good.

'Kunjappa' was influenced later by his own mother Gnanambal. 'Gnana' was lively and spirited; regaining her energy after several childbirths, she grew as active as her own mother Ammani.[14] Wrapped in a nine-yard sari, with seven Blue Jager diamonds in each earring, and a single-diamond nose stud, she played tennis at the Ladies Club of Mysore and was rated high; she also played badminton and putting, and chess and cards, and she rarely missed a Tamil movie. Gnanambal was a modern Hindu woman of her times. Gnanambal also enjoyed a sense of humour; she combined it with considerable narrative skill.[15] Sitting up and talking till late in the night, the children reviewed the day's happenings with her; she 'could always be counted upon to be sympathetic' (Narayan 1974: 113).[16]

Narayan said to Ram: 'Grandmother, Seshachalam, and mother were of one type—principled' (Ram and Ram 1996a: 72).

Happy family relationships were the very foundation of R.K. Narayan's life. The writer described later what he considered to be distinctively Indian: 'I would say our attachment to the family and its background' (S.V.V. 1963: 44).[17] Narayan made a claim: 'To be a good writer anywhere, you must have roots, both in religion and in family. [...] I have these things' (Mehta 1962: 148).[18] V.S. Naipaul (1964: 227-8), 'a writer without a country', conceded that Narayan 'operates from deep within his society'.

The younger maternal uncle, Venkataraman, inherited his own father's weakness for liquor ('four gins before lunch'); and meatballs, besides all kinds of meat and fish; and 'he was very devoted to my mother' (Narayan 1974: 121).[19] This 'Junior' uncle goaded his talented nephew later to write 'better' to satisfy the current fashion. Though young Narayan did not think much of his advice, Junior Uncle helped the struggling author-nephew scout around for possible publishers and hospitable editors; and he became a handy source of humour for Narayan the novelist.

Destiny had taken a hand in the affairs of the family. Arbuthnot and Company, a prestigious British-managed financial institution of Madras collapsed and almost ruined Narayan's forefathers on his mother's side. In search of employment, in the typical manner of Tamil Brahmins, they migrated around the time of Narayan's birth to the city of Madras.[20] 'By the time I came into the family, my kinsmen were happily urbanized' (Mehta 1962: 139).

And Madras proved to be an early and enduring influence on Narayan. 'I will meet you at Madras,' Narayan wrote to Greene in 1953, 'and try to give you glimpses of the components of my Malgudi' (Ram and Ram 1996a: 6). Purasawalkam, a sleepy suburb of Madras city, provided the future author with seeds of an imaginary landscape. The sociologist M.N. Srinivas observed: 'Narayan's formative years were in Madras, a middle-class family. And he remained that throughout his life. At heart he sees it all through a Tamil prism' (Ram and Ram 1996a: 92).[21]

In 1922, at the age of sixteen, Narayan left Madras, when he finally rejoined his parents and the family in Mysore, the capital city of one of the better-administered princely states of the raj in south India. After his early years in Madras, the youthful period in Mysore turned out to be the second formative phase in Narayan's life. 'I feel thankful to Heavens for placing me there. [...] The quality of life that Mysore offers is unique' (Ram and Ram 1996a: 232).[22] It was not just the 'Hellenic' ambience of Mysore; as much as his own minutized Tamil joint family, shaping 'the Tamil prism', the warmth of Mysoreans sustained Narayan throughout his early struggle;[23] the city offered him lifelong friendships.[24] Narayan at the same time sorted out his professional priorities: 'Mysore was an excellent place to write in, but Madras was my market' (Narayan 1974: 130).[25]

In a letter to Graham Greene in 1936 Narayan described the early period in Mysore as 'a sort of Dark Ages in my life history' (Ram and Ram 1996a: 181). Narayan had failed two years in a row in Mysore University entrance examination (first in English and then in Tamil); passed the test in 1926; failed in BA exam once. Narayan passed BA, along with his younger brother, in 1930; and he narrowly missed registering for his MA.[26] In retrospect, however, not quite 'the Dark Ages'. The two years of enforced leisure preceding his entry into college in Mysore Narayan had devoted to voracious and planned reading: 'I read everything with the utmost enjoyment' (Narayan 1974: 79).

And Narayan started writing. 'I have been writing since 1924' (Ram and Ram 1996a: 78–9); this was the year he had first failed in the entrance test.[27] By 1930, when he graduated, Narayan had made up his mind: he would be a writer. When he won the first prize in a short story competition held by *Merry Magazine* in the early 1930s, the editor asked him about his future plans. Narayan replied: 'I hope to write till my fingers come off' (Srinivas 1996: 26). The uncertainty, the insecurity, continued for decades; for Narayan refused to tread the beaten path and dropped the idea of a conventional job.

Narayan recalled to Geeta Doctor:

'It was terrible. [...] You cannot imagine the humiliation. It was hell for years and years. I was in the position of a hanger-on in the family. When my first cheque arrived. [...] I took the cheque to my father and gave it to him. It was a cheque for thirty rupees. [...]

'How can you make a living from this?' he asked me.

'How are you equipped to be a writer?'

'What are you going to write about?'

I asked him to give me back some part of it, part of the cheque and he said again, '[T]his is your first cheque and it will also be your last cheque'. At this I picked up my courage. I would never have dared to speak to my father, but I could not help but ask him, 'Why did you say the last cheque?' I did not know why I said that, but he kept quiet.[28]

Narayan eventually overcame the hurt. '"My father was very disappointed, of course, but […]." [Narayan] raises his hands helplessly. "Since then I've been unemployed"' (Murari 1990). That's a good one! At eighty-five!

An emotional development further complicated Narayan's early professional struggle. Narayan fell in love. '[T]he real thing occurred' (Narayan 1974: 139).[29] One day Narayan spotted a young woman drawing water at a street tap and fell in love with her. When the young man insisted on marrying her, the pundits discovered that the horoscopes did not match; and even the non-astrological odds were heavy—the impulsive involvement was a clear violation of subcaste and convention.[30]

But Narayan had his way—that he did, always.

The wedding took place in 1934. Narayan was twenty-eight and Rajam seventeen; Narayan was five-foot-four, Rajam an inch or two taller. 'The unconventionality of my love'—Narayan remarked to Mehta (1962: 144).

Narayan was a devoted husband. He noted in his journal: 'She was a delight […] looked an angel' (Ram and Ram 1996a: 231).[31] In a letter to Graham Greene in 1936 Narayan said: 'I married a girl from Heaven three years ago.' Decades later Narayan reminisced about his wife Rajam to his biographers as 'very sensitive'. She would easily cry—and 'just as easily regain her sunniness' (Ram and Ram 1996a: 127). Rajam herself carried a stubborn streak. As a child she had quit school early because her Maths teacher had called her a donkey in the classroom. 'If I am a donkey, what about the donkey's father?' the girl demanded to know: an acute ontological doubt—the teacher was her own father. Rajam never went back to school.

Their daughter Hema was born in 1936. Narayan agonized over the welfare of both; and was never comfortable being away from them even for a few days.[32] Yet even Rajam could not appreciate Narayan's reason for not taking up a proper job: 'What is the connexion between writing stories and not taking up a job?' (Ram and Ram 1996a: 128).[33]

After only five years of rapturous marriage, Rajam caught typhoid and on 6 June 1939, around midnight, passed away.[34]

Narayan considered joining his wife on the funeral pyre (Mehta 1962: 147): this sentiment alone should redefine Narayan 'the Hindu' for us. Mehta (1962: 144) mentions: 'As he spoke her name, tears came into his eyes'—over two decades after Rajam's death! Decades later Narayan recalled: 'I lost my anchorage' (Narayan 1974: 179). His younger brother Laxman remembered: 'He couldn't write, he couldn't think, he couldn't sit, he cried' (Ram and Ram 1996a: 254). Much later, Gowri Ramnarayan (1990: ix) brings up the matter with the celebrity author:

Once I asked him why he had never remarried. Instead of brushing the question aside as I had half thought he would do, he said very slowly that he had no choice in the matter. 'Once you are married, it is for life. The death of the partner cannot alter the bond, can it?' I felt a prickling sensation all over, and a lump in the throat. The speaker was then well past 80.

Narayan's daughter, little Hema, the very likeness of his wife, restored him slowly back to life and the living. With support and guidance from the British mystic Paul Brunton visiting Mysore at the time, Narayan cultivated psychic powers: he could now sight a 'ghost' (Narayan 1974: 193). Later, with the help of a medium, in a series of seances—'Table tilted four times to mark the arrival of spirits' (Ram and Ram 1996a: 264)—he established contact with his wife's spirit.[35] Narayan drew from the moral reserves he shared with his heroes; life always wins.[36] However, the catastrophe and its aftermath—'a perpetual unrelenting climate of loneliness' (Narayan 1974: 179)—left a permanent mark on his mind. 'Since that time, I have lost all distinction between life and death' (Mehta 1962: 147).[37]

Narayan sustained his professional struggle through the personal calamity and over several decades. Speaking at a symposium in Delhi on 'Living by Writing', the successful novelist recalled that while his wife had been alive, he could not buy her a single sari. By the early 1960s, however, following his success in the USA, Narayan was driving down from his spacious bungalow in Mysore to his daughter in Coimbatore—Rajam's hometown—in his own blue Mercedes.[38]

The early adversity firmed up Narayan's professionalism. Narayan learnt, as we can see in *My Dateless Diary*, to be 'ruthlessly professional'; Rajagopal notes that when his essay for the *Atlantic* exceeded the original limit by 250 words, Narayan demanded and received $250 more.[39] The early battles had only toughened the man: refined the writer and strengthened his writing.[40] The achievement of R.K. Narayan was as much moral as literary.[41]

Vimala Anandaram, Narayan's niece, told me that her uncle had little tolerance for the pretentious: in fact all the brothers and sisters of Narayan were known to be devastatingly candid, with a wry humour, inherited from his mother's side.[42] I witnessed this side of Narayan when I interviewed him in 1966. He drew my attention to a discussion on BBC Radio among three participants, two Indians, a novelist, and a poet; and the moderator, a British novelist. The Indians had run down Narayan, while the hapless Englishman defended Narayan. It was not an uncommon sight in those days, especially, among Eng-Lit circles in India.[43] Walsh (1979: 11) noted: 'R.K. Narayan is not at all a fashionable writer.' Narayan's foreign fame could not penetrate even Mysore; a long-time Mysorean friend of the novelist confirms the problem: 'Foreign fame was adventitious. In his own town, Mysore, many were not impressed by it. There were teachers who discouraged their students from reading Narayan because his English was too Indian.[44] However, it is true that if Narayan had not been published abroad, he would not have come to be known in the rest of the country' (Sharada Prasad 1988: 8).[45]

In the BBC discussion, Narayan resented, particularly, the observations and adverse comments of the Indian poet in English; and he added that he did not care for what 'a tenth-rate poet' said about him. During Narayan's next visit to Delhi not much later, I took the transcript to him. Stretching himself on the sofa, he listened to me attentively. When I came to the 'tenth-rate poet', Narayan asked me to hold on, paused for just a second or two, and said: 'Promote him to third-rate.'[46]

Three non-academics have been more perceptive than India's English teachers. As early as 1935, the reviewer in *Morning Post* (Ram and Ram 1996a: 163) praised Narayan for being 'unpretentious and extremely charming'; and he characterized Narayan's art as 'one of omission and selection'—a perspicacious observation—and for that time—on Narayan's art of exclusion.[47] R.K. Laxman observed: '[T]hings dissolve into some sort of a word. That is why his writing is so lucid. Language almost disappears: what remains is the idea' (Philipose 1990: n.p.).[48] Updike (1975: 39) offers a rare insight into Narayan's success: 'But Narayan's fertility would be tedious without his control and economy [...].' The debate was settled, nearly two decades after *Swami and Friends*: by the Americans, when a university press, Michigan State University, republished his novels.

Narayan grew gracefully old.

After a life of daring—a fulfilled life and career—Narayan moved to Madras in 1990. 'Visiting my granddaughter and her child is my sole occupation these days, six to eight every evening' (Narayan 1996: vii).[49] This granddaughter, Mrs Bhuvaneswari, now manages Narayan's estate.[50]

He mused; he reflected: he wrote on old age and death.[51] 'Nature seems to have arranged it all with great forethought. That receding forehead, that greyness at the temple, that filled-in shape are all divinely ordained, and succeed in producing a wonderful picture of serenity and wisdom, and lend weight to the personality' (Narayan 1988: 58). He wrote with amusement (1988: 58):

It seems to me from the questions asked of me that I look decrepit and pitiful, stooping and ambling and shuffling along somehow, leaving others to marvel at the feat. I have continuously to dodge enquiries after my health. [...] Sub-consciously everyone is keyed up and apprehensive and naturally view those advanced in years as freaks of nature if they are seen moving about freely [...] must be ready to meet his Maker.

A character in a novel of the late period says: 'Beautiful old age, when faculties are dimmed one by one, so that we may be restful, very much like extinguishing lights in a home, one by one, before one goes to sleep' (Narayan 1983: 174). Narayan uses another image for his friend S. Krishnan (1975: 42) to define old age: '[N]ature's way of warning you to slow down, you know, it just pulls off a few fuses.' With uncommon serenity he goes further: 'At this point, however, [Narayan] feels less bewildered by death than by life' (Narayan 1988: 156).

Narayan had accepted God and Life; old age and death were just stages in the journey. He said to Spaeth (1992: 51): 'I don't believe that death really is death. [...] It is a continuation of personality in a different medium. [...] It's like casting off your old clothes and getting new ones.' That image of garments is of course from the Gita. Narayan told Greta Garbo in the USA 'we believe in a sequence of births' (1974: 190). When his daughter Hema, his only child, died of cancer at the age of fifty-eight in 1994, Narayan remarked to his friend N. Ram: 'We are all in the queue. She has jumped the queue' (Ram and Ram 1996b: 13). The ability to accept death is a blessing of temperament and tradition, or religion. Narayan's own battle with life and death had given him poise of true strength, transcendent faith. After a life of discipline and uncommon professional verve, Narayan received a final reward, a quick end.[52] One of India's much-loved writers passed away on 14 May 2001: 'being old and full of days'.

In the journal Narayan maintained during his psychic training after Rajam's death, he had assured Rajam's spirit: 'When all our Karmas are spent we shall never again be separated and [shall] journey together to that fountainhead of creation' (27 May 1942). This is a startling prayer; a stunning vow. 'Once you are married, it is for life. The death of the partner cannot alter the bond, can it?' Still, Narayan's resolve is extraordinary. The closest we can get in English literature to the first half of Narayan's prayer, cutting through the critical thicket surrounding it and contextual disparity duly considered, is Shakespeare's song, 'The Phoenix and the Turtle'. The Renaissance phrases resonate even in the distant and modern Indian context: 'Two distincts, division none'; 'Single nature's double name'; and 'Grace in all simplicity.' The second half of Narayan's assertion, however, is hard to fit into our religious belief: the soul's final journey for the Hindu is perfectly solitary.[53] Thus, to Hindus, Narayan is aiming in the prayer, to his credit, at an impossible joint moksha. After all, 'religion', etymologically, is 'reunion'. Death for R.K. Narayan is reunion; and reunion for him is Re-Union: of, uniquely, an *atmic* binary.

'Love has reason, Reason none.'

2

I Had Not Been False

A Career

Narayan's early hardships as an Indian novelist in English were aggravated by his resolve to do something different.

In south India, Narayan's home base—catchment area—three novelists writing in English had made a name for themselves much before our Malgudi man: B. Rajam Iyer (1872–1898), A. Madhaviah (1872–1925), and K.S. Venkataramani (1891–1951). All three were, like most educated Indians of their time, bilingual. Though they wrote and published in English, they addressed themselves, like Bankim Chandra Chatterjee of Bengal before them, to their regional audience, as the large number of Indianisms in their work reveal, sharing their attention with the vernacular colleagues. Writing on serious themes in English, they were, to their credit, didactic; the Indian nation was taking shape, and the Indian novelists in English, like their colleagues in the Indian languages, played their patriotic part. Gowda (1967: 55) quotes Venkataramani: 'I develop a didactic tail which my compassion for all life refuses to clip.'[1]

By the time Narayan began writing, nationalism had taken root in India under Gandhi's leadership; Narayan did not carry on his back, like Venkataramani and others of his time, a patriotic burden.[2] Narayan's admiration for the British authors he had read avidly led him to aspire for their public; London had a magic literary ring for this ambitious youth in distant Mysore.[3]

Besides, aspiring for creative expression in a second tongue—and achieving it—is nothing new to writers in India. While Islamic culture dominated north India, as Krishna Kripalani (1982 [1968]: 92) points out, we wrote in Persian; and much earlier, in Sanskrit. Kripalani also mentions modern writers who were born to one Indian language but excelled in another. 'It might be more appropriate to say that if not necessarily the mother tongue proper, the language of one's cultural upbringing and environment is the best medium for creative expression.'[4]

The Indian writer in English, however, is a creature of a more complex ecology. With literatures in our Indian languages often a thousand years old, the pull of the lively Indian tongues works against the Indian English writer's hold on the 'alien' medium, which in most cases is the writer's second tongue. The Indian novelist in English can take off only by countering the homely tug of his mother tongue. Creative displacement seems to be one way, if not the norm: Mulk Raj Anand and Desani wrote in England, and Raja Rao in France; R.K. Narayan first went abroad only when he was past fifty, but early in life he had moved from his native Tamil-speaking Madras to the Kannada-speaking Mysore, in time for his later formative years. In the anomalous ethos of the Indian novelist in English, following a cross-cultural shift of any degree, the first tongue recedes: the mother tongue is lost as a potential literary medium—if it is not already lost, like the umbilical cord, at birth. The translocation works to the advantage of the writer's primary filiation with the secondary medium; English becomes the writer's replacement language; the foster medium becomes the creative tongue; loss with affinity achieves linguistic facility, an organic bonding: the writer takes wing. Vikram Seth said to a Punjabi friend of mine: 'I hardly know any Punjabi.' Narayan said: 'I might have found it harder writing in my own language' (*Hindustan Times* 1968: 9); two decades later Narayan disclosed to David Davidar (1988a: 72) that he had never written in his mother tongue, Tamil: 'I read and write Tamil laboriously.' Indian fiction in English is literature by the 'dispossessed'.

An alien language can, at the same time, alienate. 'The confusion or conflict of Indian and Anglian elements in the authorial personality can produce expatriate artificiality or result in the disintegration of sensibility' (Harrex 1977: 12, vol. 1). The achievement of the Indian novelist in English lies in his exceptional gift to filter away the incongruous elements that seep through his second tongue: we can sojourn 'too long in the west'; the Westward voyager still needs to be warned of the Sirens. That is probably why Bankim Chandra Chatterjee, after writing and publishing our first novel in English, switched to his mother tongue, Bangla. With English as the sole language of his literary life, however, Narayan succeeded in yoking the provincial to the cosmopolitan without hurting his roots in family, religion, and society: keeping at bay crippling dysculturation. Our Malgudi man had the right instincts.

In one of the more engaging episodes in his memoir, Narayan recounted how he had 'worked' for a living, as a teacher, for three days; when Narayan returned home and declared his resolve to be a writer, his family and friends were shocked. 'They seemed to suspect my sanity' (Narayan 1974: 112). And 'they' well might: it was nothing short of madness to have thought of making a livelihood of creative writing in mofussil India, and in English, and in the early 1930s—before R.K. Narayan. Narayan recalled to Ved Mehta (1962: 145): 'It was the most penniless thing one could do!'[5] Narayan confesses elsewhere: 'I thought I would throw myself into this gamble of a writer's life' (Ram and Ram 1996a: 104).[6] He later remarked to N. Ram (2006: 10): 'I wonder how I had the foolhardiness to make such a crazy decision! I don't think I could do it again if I had to make a choice.'

A precious gadget represents in retrospect the primitive conditions under which the young writer worked: Narayan's huge Underwood typewriter. Laxman (1992: 100) recalls that it 'resembled a vintage T-model Ford and nearly matched it in size'. This behemoth had separate keys for capital and lower cases; its carriage moved with a big boom. As Narayan worked on the landing of their home, the entire staircase rocked and boomed: when occasionally his father protested, young Narayan had to 'haul the machine over to the roof of the house and type there' (Narayan 1974: 102–3).

This *makhana*, or primitive contrivance, is an icon of our postcolonial spirit.

Every adult male in the middle-class south-Indian Iyer Brahmin home—Narayan's sociological slot, a 'mixed sap' of orthodoxy and modernity—had to contribute his share to the family kitty; especially, after the death of the father. And so, from the beginning, Narayan (1974: 103) wrote with a purpose: 'All this amount of desperate composition was to allow me to earn money and help the family.' A Shavian commitment sustained the young writer. From the beginning, '[he] regularly wrote a few pages each day' (1974: 79). Narayan mentioned 'daily discipline', 'fear of missing [his] daily schedule'; even, 'this weekly grind' (1974: 125, 132, 199). Besides that 'thousand-word literary clowning week after week' (1974: 118), Narayan's career in the journalistic crucible is also significant: Narayan, a Brahmin, worked as a correspondent for a non-Brahmin newspaper in those days, and on a precarious remuneration; but the job gave him the opportunity to go around socially sensitive places like courts, police stations, and so on.

Looking back, a definitive feature of R.K. Narayan's career is its amplitude: journalism, causeries, columns, short stories, novels, radio programmes, film scripts.... Professionalism was his mantra.[7] One of the earliest assignments Narayan accepted elsewhere and carried out with zeal was the review of a book on maritime laws. He was not paid for it; decades later Narayan still remembered the complete title: *Development of Maritime Laws in 17th-Century England*: 'The title stuck to me like a thorn' (Ram and Ram 1996a: 115).[8] He wrote a government-sponsored tourist brochure on his domicile state; *Mysore: A Travel Record* (1939) will be remembered for the writer's unsuccessful attempt to claim his honorarium from the office of the dewan (prime minister) of the Mysore maharaja; Rajam's scepticism about the fee proved justified, Narayan's hopes of buying something special for his daughter and his wife remained unfulfilled (Narayan 1974: 157ff).

Narayan's attempts to publish his first novel illustrate the gritty campaign of the periphery to reach the centre. Living here in India in those remote times, working here, Narayan nursed an absurd dream. Mulk Raj Anand, too, had to overcome tremendous initial resistance, but during that corresponding critical period Anand lived in London, in close touch with the Bloomsbury group. For young Narayan, domiciled in provincial Mysore, to keep trying to publish his first novel across the seven seas needed moral strength of a different—religious—order. 'I had got used to getting back my manuscript with unfailing regularity once every 6 weeks—two weeks onward journey, two weeks on the editor's table, and two weeks' homeward journey with a rejection slip pinned to it. [...] All in all it provided me with six weeks of hope!' (Narayan 1974: 151).[9]

The punch line, sourced in moral strength, is the hallmark of Narayan's creativity; for he talks elsewhere of 'hundreds of rejection slips' (Mehta 1962: 146).[10] Narayan was an unemployed Indian young man of the period, that outrage—a dependant in a middle-class family—drawing ridicule from his father's friends. In his mid-twenties, Narayan had not so much as a rupee at his command (Ram and Ram 1996a: 112). His daily budget was two annas (an eighth of a rupee); a couple of cigarettes during his evening walk were his sole luxury. For the aspiring writer, the expenditure on special stationery and foreign postage was subsidized by his mother.

In a final bid to get his first novel published in England, young Narayan sent the manuscript to Kittu Purna, 'my neighbour, a very warm-hearted friend' (Narayan 1974: 20), who had been highly appreciative of Narayan's first novel back home even as it was being written in 1931. Now a student in Oxford and socialistically inclined, Purna, with faith in his own opinion, left the manuscript with Graham Greene, also residing in Oxford, and also socialistically inclined (Ram and Ram 1996a: 148–9); Purna had earlier been encouraged by Greene's response to some of Narayan's short stories he had shown him. When Greene found the time to read the novel in manuscript form, he was delighted: '[A]n excellent piece of work,' he wrote to Purna. 'If I were a publisher myself, I should publish it with no hesitation' (Ram and Ram 1996a: 152). *Swami* appealed to Greene, who was already dissatisfied with the subjectivity of contemporaneous British novelists.[11] Kittu Purna sent the prized cable: 'Novel taken Graham Greene responsible.'[12] Young Narayan in distant Mysore was jubilant: 'I can hardly believe,' he wrote to Graham Greene, 'that I am in a real world now […]' (Ram and Ram 1996a: 155). Narayan dropped his newspaper job.

Swami and Friends was published in London in 1935.[13] Though Greene had said, '*Swami* to me is a book in ten thousand' (Ram and Ram 1996a: 151, 397), and *Swami* received good reviews, the young Indian novelist's trials did not end there.[14] The publisher was disappointed with its sales; he rejected Narayan's second novel. Greene intervened again, and the second novel, *The Bachelor of Arts*, with an introduction by Greene, came out in 1937 from a second publisher. Following its commercial failure, Narayan's second publisher turned down his third novel, *The Dark Room*.[15]

The Greene-ing of Narayan continued: Narayan's third novel was taken up by a third publisher.[16]

Narayan's professional life spanned almost eight decades. If you do not know privation, you cannot appreciate this career, this success; if you do not know the mofussil, the non-metro ambience, you cannot assess the true magnitude of R.K. Narayan's achievement.

When the Second World War broke out, cutting off Narayan from his British publishers, British sustenance, Narayan's early professional struggle reached another crisis. To fill the vacuum Narayan ran a journal of his own, *Indian Thought: A Miscellany*; but it was short-lived. Even then Narayan did not give up. He turned to his countrymen. The editor of the *Hindu* (Madras), Kasturi Srinivasan, supported him with three things: a regular slot in his reputed newspaper; a generous honorarium of thirty rupees per piece; and a medium to build for himself a second audience, the Indian reading public. Another Srinivasan ('two saviours', as Narayan described them), the proprietor of the newly established Gemini film studio, who had serialized the Tamil translation of *Swami and Friends* in his popular magazine *Ananda Vikatan* in 1939, gave him work in the story department of his studio and supported him with 'a few thousands of rupees during the war years' (Ram and Ram 1996a: 324);[17] but the assignment was on a part-time basis because, as Narayan said later, 'My principle in life was never having to ask anybody for leave'.[18] Narayan even wrote an exclusive film story which was produced as *Miss Malini* (1947) in Tamil. Narayan had turned adversity to advantage.[19]

The same moral blend, of self-respect with drive and direction, took Narayan to freelancing for All India Radio, travelling from Mysore to Madras each time. One of the projects he planned and researched for AIR was a documentary on the Madras Sappers and Miners—with as much professionalism as he had reviewed earlier a crusty book on the maritime laws of seventeenth-century England. (And never paid for it!)

Narayan described Graham Greene's support as 'even, sustained and sustaining'.[20] Again and again during the early years—in every way, the most stressful time of Narayan's life—the period, more or less, during which he produced the five novels of his early comedy—and during the war years, Narayan shares his financial worries with his friend Graham Greene. He writes to Greene on 25 March 1936: 'I am terribly hard up and I don't know what to do' (Ram and Ram 1996a: 174).[21] Throughout this trough season, Greene was totally supportive. He read every manuscript Narayan sent him; he vetted every manuscript Narayan sent him. '[Graham Greene] gave most of the titles—only recently I started giving them' (Rao 1971: 80). Greene recommended the manuscript to a publisher; he proofread the manuscript, not once, but thrice; he negotiated with the editors and agents and publishers on behalf of Narayan: he was Narayan's literary editor and literary agent in one; and during wartime with chronic paper shortage, 'Greene managed to find the quota of paper for a first edition of 3800 copies of *The English Teacher*' (Narayan 1974: 194). Greene's commitment to Narayan is unparalleled; literary agent, editor, publicist—giving copies of Narayan's novels to his literary friends and conveying their enthusiastic response to Narayan—friend, guide, admirer, psychiatrist, fan. Helping the young Indian writer at every stage and level—material, psychological, and moral—Greene zealously tended, incubatored, Narayan's literary presence in the West.[22] The nub of this unique Indo-British compact of letters is Greene's 'critical' support: for example, after Greene's first introduction, few critics of Narayan failed to see the Chekhovian analogy. And Graham Greene showed strength of true character in his prediction: 'the finest promise too'. Praising a manuscript before you is one thing, prophesying a positive career is quite another.[23] Greene's wife Vivien, too, wrote to Narayan: what really mattered was that Narayan was getting known and was 'preparing an audience [...] reading public' (Ram and Ram 1996a: 187). 'Preparing an audience' for this Indian writer in English took the best part of three decades.

Creative writing in developing countries can be as hazardous as a career of arms in unsettled societies; a successful artist like R.K. Narayan, however, combines the grit of a samurai with the endurance of a homesteader: fickle fortune has to fall in line. Narayan's commitment and physical discipline and spiritual stamina more than matched his professional challenges; with refinement, of sentiment and style, never flashy, never strident; his narrative lucidity foregrounded the ethical deliberation of his heroes. In the professional struggle and success of R.K. Narayan we also see the development of a literary genre, and history in the making as well.[24]

R.K. Narayan could look back with modest satisfaction: 'The great gods who could view the past, the present, and the future as one block would have realized I had not been false!' (Narayan 1974: 154).

3

Profundity with a Light Touch
A Style

Looking back on his literary adolescence (Narayan 1974: 86), Narayan says that his early writings have derived from his reading. Two features seem common to all his early (unpublished) works: they were plays or verse—'Prose' is too plebeian! And they were all tragedies—or, 'all about the stars'. For young Narayan had also ravenously fed on tragic works in English. 'I loved tragic endings in novels. I looked for books that would leave me crushed at the end' (1974: 80).[1] He wrote an 'outpouring' entitled 'Friendship', very nearly echoing the lamentations of 'Adonais', but in a flamboyant poetic prose. On another piece of a similar inspiration, he (1974: 85–6) said: 'I composed it in a state of total abstraction. [...] What did it all mean? I don't know. But I was terribly moved and impressed and had no doubt that this was going to add to the world's literary treasure.'[2] Narayan (1974: 86) added: 'These efforts were totally unclassifiable—neither poetry, nor prose, nor fiction. Prose in physical form, sound and echo of poetry, and flights of utmost fiction. Odd combinations of moods and methods.' The conclusive phrase breathes Narayan's classical temper as we know it today.

Why young Narayan dropped his early preoccupation with tragic form to become the kind of writer who could not stand even a single performance of a tragedy (Narayan 1960: 201) will probably remain inexplicable: aesthetic endocrinology works mysteriously. The metamorphosis had occurred even before his introduction to Graham Greene. Thanks to his biographers (Ram and Ram 1996a: 88), we know that the critical shift in Narayan's style from mushy mysticism to controlled realism occurred in the summer of 1930. After his BA examination, Narayan went to Vizagapatam, a port city in the north Coromandel, for a vacation at an uncle's home.

Every day, early in the morning, Narayan took a walk on the beach. Inspired by the Bay of Bengal and the clouds which wanted to 'make you do something', he sat down to write a story. The result was 'A Night of Cyclone' (included in *Lawley Road and Other Stories* [1956a: 127–32]). The pre-Malgudi piece already carried the hallmark of a Narayan product: simplicity of style.

Not much later, in September 1930, Narayan began writing his first novel, during a visit this time to his grandmother Ammani in Bangalore (now Bengaluru). On a day chosen by her, the popular Indian festival of Vijaya Dasami, the young man sat down before a notebook, pen in hand. And 'Malgudi with its little railway station swam into view, all ready-made, with a character called Swaminathan running down the platform peering into the faces of the passengers [...]' (Narayan 1974: 104). It was a magical moment, the emergence of a butterfly from its chrysalis. Young Narayan had found what for him through the fruitful decades that followed was 'the right track of writing'. The poetic prose had disappeared along with the tragic preoccupation, like adolescent acne.

We may pick up a clue to Narayan's new stylistic approach from his experience much later with his short-lived literary journal *Indian Thought*.[3] The journal was 'devoted to literature, philosophy, and culture' (Narayan 1974: 198ff). As though the intellectual ambition of the periodical was not adequately represented by its title and the prospectus, Narayan defined its goal: 'profundity with a light touch'.[4] The literary ideal of course is unimpeachable; it also puts Narayan in proper historical perspective.

All the three novelists before Narayan in south India were stylistically heavy. Rajam Iyer and Venkataramani, particularly, brought in scholarly allusions to Shakespeare, Virgil, and the Bible, besides the Indian classics. Venkataramani admired Edmund Burke; Madhaviah was influenced by Tyndale and Huxley and Spencer. All the three novelists were scholars attempting fiction in English: it showed, inevitably, in their diction, syntax, and imagery. Narayan seems to allude to them in a paper he presented at a seminar at the University of Leeds in 1964.[5] 'Passing, inevitably, through phases of symbolic, didactic, or over-dramatic writing, one arrived at the stage of valuing realism, psychological and technical explorations, and technical virtuosity' (see Narayan's chapter 'English in India' in

John Press 1965).[6] As Narayan summed up his own development at the Leeds seminar he seemed to be commenting on the evolution of the novel in English in south India. He added categorically: 'We are still experimentalists'; and: 'We are not attempting to write Anglo-Saxon.'[7] The literature produced, Narayan continued, 'was perhaps not first-rate, as often the writing seemed imitative, halting, inept, or an awkward translation of a vernacular rhetoric, mode or idiom.'[8] He added: '[O]ccasionally it was brilliant.'[9]

What had been missing in the novelists before Narayan, though, was not 'seriousness of theme' or 'purpose', but a consistently applied *light touch*.[10] Venkataramani (1927: 163) says of one of his characters in *Murugan the Tiller* that he tries to 'pack more allusions and suggestion than the language could bear'. Later Narayan asserted to Mehta (1962: 149): 'There were no Indian novelists to speak of Indian writers were either too "westernized" or too "deliberate". [...] I can't like any writing that's deliberate.' In that sense, too, '[t]he way for [R.K. Narayan] was prepared by K.S. Venkataramani and people like him' (Sharada Prasad 1988: 8).[11]

Narayan's goals were as serious as those of the novelists before him in south India: he achieved his results with a delicate touch. To a tradition of thematic gravity, he brought a transparent and deliberately 'unstudied' voice—a low-cholesterol style—and humour. The restraint and the art of poise were not adventitious: Narayan cultivated them. His temperament helped, circumstances took a hand; but he had learnt, from the south-Indian example, performance.[12] Narayan mentioned the sources of his inspiration: elements that would normally 'stimulate one to write'; and for him they are 'curiosity, *interest in people or one's surroundings*, desire for achievement of any sort, or for a future' (Narayan 1974: 139; emphasis mine): elements, we may note, very much of this world. Such a drastic change in theme, form, and style—originality—was bound to put off some people. 'The general criticism was that my stories lacked "plot". There was no appreciation of my literary values, and I had nothing else to offer' (Narayan 1974: 132). The young novelist attempted to deal with subjects other than love; he consciously set himself up as a 'realistic fiction writer in English' (1974: 134).[13] Greene admired Narayan, we recall, for '[his] own individual style of realism' (Ram and Ram 1996a: 160).[14]

In the larger Indian context—not just south Indian—Narayan's style was also in harmony with the Gandhian revolution in prose, 'from the elaborate to the simple, from the ornate to the plain, from the opulent to the pointed' (Iyengar 1962: 275).[15] Not just Narayan, the Indian English novel itself was changing tracks around this time. Narayan, Anand, and Raja Rao—the tertiary three—represent the take-off generation in Indian fiction in English. The Indian novel in English had achieved its emancipation years before India attained her Independence; the Indian novel in English had become swadeshi before the nation achieved its Swaraj. The genre has not looked back since. The arrival in Malgudi, rather tortuous, even mysterious, was ultimately historic. The nation itself was on the move. 'Malgudi was inescapable as the sky overhead' (Narayan 1974: 30).

II
THE PRE-INDEPENDENCE NOVELS

4
In a World Dominated by Adults
Swami and Friends

Some years ago, my younger son, home for holidays from his postgraduate studies in surgery, helped me unearth from our family cache a favourite novel of mine: with the casual remark—one of those revelations which make parents wonder at the private lives of their children—that he had read the book as a schoolboy, five times in five successive summers. A half-century earlier the slim volume had captivated a more professional reader, Graham Greene: '*Swami* to me is a book in ten thousand' (Ram and Ram 1996a: 427). If we recall that Greene was also a great admirer of another novelist so different from Narayan—Henry James—we might give the unpretentious first novel the attention it deserves.[1]

In electing to write about a boy who is around ten years old, no more than a child—'who did not really stand over four feet' (Narayan 1935: 29)—and that in his very first novel, Narayan is in select and unlikely company. In his early twenties, Tolstoy had written a short novel, *Childhood, Boyhood, Youth* (1852: 62): 'Happy, happy childhood! That blissful time never to be recalled. [...] Those memories refresh and elevate my soul, they are source of never-ending joy to me.' Young Narayan, more familiar with English literature than Russian or American, is more likely to have read *Tom Brown's School Days* and Richard Llewellyn's *How Green Was My Valley*. Yet Tom is as English as Huw Morgan is Welsh or Nikolenka Russian. Narayan's Swami is unmistakably a south-Indian, middle-class Brahmin. And *Swami* appealed to Greene: '[A] book in ten thousand.'

Narayan observes: 'In childhood, fears and secrecies and furtive acts happen to be the natural state of life, adopted instinctively for survival in a world dominated by adults' (Narayan 1974:

21).[2] The young novelist presents the child's world without adult condescension, as an entirely complete and valid human experience. Take for example the vision of a cricket field, the kind you may find in countless small towns of India even today: '[A] dun field sparsely covered with scorched grass, lit into a blaze by the slant rays of the evening sun, enveloped in a flimsy cloud of dust, *alive with the shouts of players stamping about*' (1935: 123; emphasis mine). The emotion captured here, especially, 'alive' with the shouts of players, is not normally available to adult imagination: without rare empathy. The 'Tail' episode, similarly, can only be amusing to 'adult' minds; but '[t]his was probably Swaminathan's first shock in life' (31); Swami goes home and is soon lost in watching with total absorption the progress of an ant he has dropped in a paper boat for a journey down the rapids of the street gutter. The fights; the quarrels: 'the peace-making efforts'; the doubts ('How did they find out that Europe was like a camel's head?'); the exam ordeal and the relief thereafter—'the spirit of liberty that was abroad' (66)—are all authentic, universal. Narayan has realized the child's world with a child's engagement and focus. He brings to his presentation of a child's world a poet's empathy.

The first eleven chapters show that these boys are no 'heroes': they are human. '"How many days is it since you have touched your books?" father asked. [...] Swaminathan viewed this question as a gross breach of promise' (83); the solid adult phrase accurately conveys the boy's feelings; it is only amusing to us if we view it with the superior airs of the adult world; but Narayan is speaking from within the child's world where breach of promise is traumatic. Rajam keeps his friends waiting before coming to receive them 'because he had seen his father doing it' (26). The adult world shows itself up more directly in the Kesavan episode. 'Swaminathan shuddered as he realized what a deep-dyed villain Dr Kesavan was behind that genial smile. He would teach that villain a lesson; put a snake into his table drawer; he would not allow that villain to feel his pulse even if he [Swaminathan] should be dying of fever' (144). Little Swami's experiences in the adult jungle, his frustrations and confusions, are paralleled towards the end in the forest scene; he cannot find his way out in the jungle: he is lost. 'The strangeness of the hour, so silent indeed that even the drop of a leaf resounded through the place, *oppressed* him with a *sense of inhumanity*. Its *remoteness* gave him a feeling that he was walking into a *world of horrors, subhuman and supernatural*' (164; emphasis mine). The pathless jungle is a trope for the adult world.

Samuel the Pea is described by the novelist in a full paragraph: Samuel is 'just ordinary, no outstanding virtue of muscle or intellect'. Narayan concludes: 'The bond between them was laughter' (9). Still in his early twenties, the novelist has discovered a rare value: humour—the gift of laughter is a great positive: humour redeems. The bond of laughter makes the Pea very special, as it distinguishes Swami: and Narayan, a writer of first-rate comedy.

The child's world is in flux. When the school is reopened, the Pea is missing; returns late by three months, 'quite full up with medical certificates, explanations, and exemptions. […] He was a man of hundred worries now, and passed his old friends like a stranger' (107). That sounds more like the first intimation of mortality for the child, Swami. The realism of subdued pathos—'the faint discoloration of ivory' in Greene's words (as quoted in the introduction to *The Bachelor of Arts*) is evident again in the final parting of friends at the end of the novel, when the train arrives at the Malgudi station to 'leave four minutes later, carrying away Rajam, forever' (174).

'Father's Help', included in *Malgudi Days*, a short story by Narayan which Iyengar (1962: 365) believes 'belongs to an earlier period than that described in the novel' anticipates Swami's 'peculiar nature'. With a few changes, the same story is incorporated early into *Swami and Friends*. Now note the opening of the short story: 'Lying in bed, Swami realized with a shudder that it was Monday morning. It looked as though only a moment ago it had been the last period on Friday; already Monday was there' (Narayan 1947: 125). The novel opens: 'It was Monday morning. Swaminathan was reluctant to open his eyes. He considered Monday especially unpleasant in the calendar.'

A unique feature of 'Father's Help' is the part played by Swami's conscience, his 'peculiar nature'; conscience plays an equally important role in the novel. In the same chapter of the novel, Swami takes a letter from his father to the headmaster complaining of the brutal treatment that Ebenezar, the fanatical Bible teacher, meted out to Swami the previous day; and Swami shows the familiar pattern of behaviour: '[H]e sat apart, sunk in thought. He had a thick letter in his pocket. He felt guilty when he touched its edge with his fingers' (Narayan 1935: 6). The hallmark of Narayan's comedy, especially of the pre-Independence novels, is his focus on 'the internal culture of the individual'.[3] Conscience sets apart the protagonists of the pre-Independence novels; it plays a critical role even in Raju's life (in *The Guide*). Now in *Swami and Friends*, conscionability is only one aspect of little Swami's engaging humanity. He is 'apprehensive, weak, and nervous' about things (9); a snob who panics when the upper-class Rajam is to be received in his middle-class home (36–7); a backbencher, to begin with (49); no leader, but a happy follower (66); and a reluctant participant in heroics (76). Yet there is early evidence of a rebel in this little man; a rebel reluctant, acting on just human impulse. The Bible teacher comes up against this streak in Swami and reacts predictably. Much later, when the headmaster sends for the peon, Swaminathan is shocked: 'What, is he going to ask the peon to thrash me? If he does any such thing I will bite everybody dead' (106). When whacked, '[h]e had a sudden flood of courage, the courage that comes of desperation' (106) and rushes out of the school, muttering, 'I don't care for your dirty school'. The manner of this exit, described as 'theatrical' (107), is characteristic.[4] Swami's trial scenes, here and later, are true to character.

Swami is no 'ordinary' boy, however; as his friend Rajam tells him: he is 'peculiar' (149). Swami cannot be called an average boy either: he is not ordinary in the cricket field: he is honoured by his colleagues with the title of 'Tate' (121). Besides, 'Swaminathan seemed to be an expert in thinking out difficulties' (112). From the backbencher habit in Albert Mission School (49), he moves to the second row in Board High School, and takes a studious turn (123). Swami's friends range from the highly brainy to the purely brawny. A good human blend: consider his anti-academic rage, the 'mango maze' (86); also 'considered to be bit of a heretic' (114); his sarcasm at things holy (128); his sense of humour, his sense of honour; and an active, diligent conscience. Narayan's little hero is a unique individual. '[A] character who has a more individual and spontaneous existence than the orthodox schoolboy in the ordinary school story' (Walsh 1982: 29). In common Hindu parlance, Swami's gentle, peace-loving personality is sattvic, as are the 'heroes' to come of the pre-Independence novels.

Not just personality traits, even themes bind Narayan's pre-Independence novels. The central theme is introduced in the slim first novel itself and in the very first paragraph, and so unobtrusively that we need to take a second look: 'It was Monday morning. Swaminathan was reluctant to open his eyes. He considered Monday especially unpleasant in the calendar. After the delicious *freedom* of Saturday and Sunday, it was difficult to get into the Monday mood of work and *discipline* [...]' (Narayan 1935: 1; emphasis mine). At home or at school, we see Swami throughout resisting 'discipline', asserting 'freedom'. His rejection of two schools is more than mere impulsive action: each time it is an assertion of his spirit of freedom. Now compare the opening paragraph of the short story: the critical words are missing. In the novels to come of the early comedy, we see a similar conflict between the individual urge to be free and society's demands of discipline; between the freedom impulse and the societal constraint. Freedom and discipline are both integral to human aspiration and growth; all the heroes of Narayan's early phase realize or demonstrate this truth at some stage.

The ethical binary, freedom–discipline, relates to another theme in *Swami and Friends*: the family. As the hero of Narayan's pre-Independence novels struggles to come to terms with himself, with his society; while the 'freedom' instinct is refined to some social purpose, subjected to 'discipline', he gets salutary support and guidance from his family. More than any other character in *Swami and Friends*, it is Granny who symbolizes the enduring family ties. Swami's bond with his grandmother lends much grace to the novel. 'What did it matter? [...] Granny's presence nearby was reassuring' (49). The attachments that keep Swami secure are evident again soon after his disappearance; a whole chapter, chapter 16, foregrounds the strength and beauty of family ties. The father–son relationship, delicately and realistically portrayed, is truly engaging. In spite of the abrasive encounters, Swami remembers his father in the final crisis when he is lost in the forest, 'because father could be depended upon to get him out of any trouble' (156). However, the same father can be unthinking, a domineering 'adult' (169). Granny, too, is not romanticized; she feels lonely and left out at times; even with Swami she has to be wary (125). The working grace and daily concern of the joint family is quietly conveyed by Narayan; Granny comes to Swami's rescue when the boy is teased by his father (128). The passage brings the entire family together, with the bonds, the tendrils, of affection, of eating together, of living together; all of it at the same time is down-to-earth, for Granny complains that she has the company of Swami alone.

Even as there are three teachers specifically mentioned, there are four 'friends'; each, unlike every other, has a particular attraction for Swami; each throwing light on Swami's mind and temperament, his eager natural warmth and conviviality, all contribute to the theme of childhood. Narayan's craft wisdom is evident even in his first novel.

A quiet confidence marks Narayan's handling of the language in his first novel. Swami is in bed after the harrowing brush with the law: '[T]hree or four falls that he had had that day. One was—when—yes, when Rajam got down from his car and came to the school, and Swaminathan had wanted to hide himself. [...] And he had been called a monkey! He was no monkey. Only they—the policemen—looked like monkeys, and they behaved like monkeys too' (103).

We must put this medley of physical pain and mortification of spirit alongside a dramatic monologue.

Good. But you must also try and get marks like him … you know, Swami, your grandfather used to frighten the examiners with his answers sometimes. When he answered a question, he did it in a tenth of the time that others took to do it. And then, his answers would be so powerful that his teachers would give him two hundred marks sometimes. [...] When he passed his F.A. he got such a big medal! I wore it as a pendant for years till—when did I remove it? Yes, when your aunt was born. [...] No, it wasn't your aunt. [...] It was when your father was born. [...] I remember on the tenth day of confinement. [...] No, no. I was right. It was when your aunt was born. Where is that medal now? I gave it away to your aunt—and she melted it and made four bangles out of it. The fool! And such flimsy bangles too! I have always maintained that she is the worst fool in our family. [...] (22)

With the candour of a child, Swami calls such rambles 'old unnecessary stories', and Granny readily agrees they are. But the cheerful backtracking, one spontaneous detour leading to more—the confusions—competently reveal Granny's mind; offering, at the same time, a peep into a whole ethos. Senility will be too harsh a word for it in Narayan's world. We also know that Swami is the only one she can 'socialize' with, the others are too busy. In contrast we have the father. He is in one of his pedagogic moods, which Swami finds so trying: and gives us another monologue (59), of an irate adult now, the putative head of the family, who, at the same time, one suspects, in the light of earlier experience, would not want to give that message himself. The unobtrusive adequacy is evident even when Narayan describes action (100–1). Or a scene: 'The river's mild rumble, the rustling of the "peepul" leaves, the half-light of the late evening, and the three friends eating, and glowing with new friendship—Swaminathan felt at perfect peace with the world' (20): the restoration of 'normalcy', of inner peace, lately disturbed, the tranquillity of children in sync once again, in harmony once again, shared by nature around them in the hour of amity—the whole brief season of childhood—is quietly conveyed in this succinct sunset, *sandhya*, to chapter 2.[5] The same plasticity and pliancy of style and point of view—are evident in the three letters in the novel. Already, as a writer of fiction, Narayan is a natural.

Among the virtues of *Swami and Friends* as a first novel, its unpretentiousness comes first. The very simplicity of the story signals thrifty talent and daring originality of theme. Narayan's first novel also establishes the character of Malgudi, a 'small town located in a corner of south India'.[6] *Swami and Friends* also presents a basic plan common to so many of Narayan's novels: 'a flight, an uprooting, a disturbance of order—followed by a return, a renewal, a restoration of normalcy' (Iyengar 1962: 30l); 'return'—but as a different, a transformed individual, personality; even little Swami has earned a new stature and status in his limited circle of family and friends; he is not likely to be messed with as earlier; this dialectic of human experience gives to so many of Narayan's novels to come later their structure of action, a fictive algorithm. Swami also establishes the sattvic temper, the truth-searching mind, the conscionability, which are the hallmarks of Narayan's 'heroes', especially of the pre-Independence novels; and as their matrix the novel first presents evolved family relationships.[7] The slim novel is also epochal in the history of the Indian novel in English: one of the three novels—with Anand's *Untouchable* and Raja Rao's *Kanthapura*—in the 1930s, launching a new phase in the development of the Indian novel in English; in south India, particularly, the little novel signified a shift from rhetoric to realism.[8] *Swami and Friends* announces, quietly, the future preoccupation of Narayan. Public things are not for him; not as yet; as of now, his genius was for private matter, the focus of the early comedy. Narayan affirms the private throughout. Talking of his editorial concerns during the war, he says, '[n]either politics nor the war was of any interest to me' (1974: 151). A half-century later he had not changed his mind: 'I am only interested in ordinary people. If I find a character I like, I tell his story, that's all. The larger sociological issues, politics and what not do not interest me' (Davidar 1988a).[9] Although Narayan spoke too soon—his own fiction presents serious social engagement, the novelist's remarks offer as much insight into his own approach to fiction: in Mojtabai's (1981) words, 'a combination of moral appeal and direct writing'. In the story Narayan wrote on Gandhi, titled 'Gandhi's Appeal' (see Ram and Ram 1996a: 179),[10] the stress is on the moral stature of the Mahatma.[11]

R.K. Narayan was twenty-four.[12]

5

Live a Man's Life
The Bachelor of Arts

Within weeks of a British publisher's acceptance of *Swami and Friends*, Narayan began work on a new novel, once again on the auspicious Vijaya Dasami day, in late 1935; he completed *The Bachelor of Arts* in less than six months, by March 1936. Almost synchronizing with the professional success, his daughter Hema was born on 3 February 1936.

Narayan takes up the story of Chandran at a formative stage, while the youth is in his final year at college: the story follows him through to his marriage and initiation in life. At the beginning of the novel Chandran is twenty-one: full of hopes, plans, prejudices, dreams. By the end he is twenty-five: he has had his rub with life, has had his share of antics and hysterics, wiser now, more able to order his life, with a 'philosophy' of his own. These critical years also present a panorama of youth, with other young people appearing in his life and disappearing, in their own directed or misdirected energies and courses. The centre of the book is Chandran's emotional collapse following the betrothal of the girl he loves to someone else. Given Narayan's hero, however, a comedic conclusion is inevitable.

In the Hindu scheme of things, youth is an integral phase of man's life. Life itself, no doubt, is a preparation for the fulfilment to come *here*, when Self-Realization is achieved *here*. This philosophical outlook attracts, at times, the clichéd conclusion that life here for the Hindu is a burden to be patiently borne; a 'Medieval' gloom is invoked. Not for the Hindu. Not for R.K. Narayan. While the end of the existential cycle is Self-Realization, the Hindu believes that life itself is not to be despised or neglected. Life is a worthy end: the journey has equal importance. Life must be fulfilled, fullfilled. This attitude lies behind the Hindu doctrine of the four asramas or stages of life: *brahmacharya* (bachelorhood, devoted to seeking *brahmagnana*, knowledge, wisdom of Self); *grahasthya* (the stage of the householder, fulfilling one's duties to self and society); *vanaprasthya* (retirement from active life in society); and *sanyasa* (renunciation). Few are qualified to go straight to the final asrama of sanyasa without realizing the first three.[1] The cycle of physical, emotional, and moral life must be experienced in full; if life is not properly and fully lived, it leads to afflictions, physical, psychological, and spiritual. Coomaraswamy (1918: 29) affirms that 'desires suppressed breed pestilence'. The scholar quotes Kabir, the saint-singer: 'More than all else, do I cherish at heart that love which makes me to *live a limitless life in this world*' (1918: 27; emphasis mine). The perspective is just. To set right a dog-eared misconception again, Hinduism is not synonymous with withdrawal from society.[2] Life is a preparation, a progressive passage, a graduation, starting with the very first stage, to attain the ultimate goal of complete human experience, of Self-Realization. 'This inseparable unity of the material and the spiritual world is made the foundation of the Indian culture, and determines the whole character of her social ideals' (1918: 29). This is the essence of the Hindu way of life that Narayan's pre-Independence novels affirm. As a creative writer, who has quietly assimilated his ethos, our novelist's world view happens to identify unselfconsciously with this vision of life shared by eminent compatriots. Narayan makes the Hindu way of life real; with wit and joy, natural, humane, he makes it lively, makes it contemporary. We have a preview of this vision in Narayan's fluent sketch titled 'Uncle's Letters' in *Lawley Road* (1956a: 55–9). A narrower focus on a single phase of 'man's estate' offers us in *The Bachelor of Arts* youth viewed against the background of time; the tone of the narrative recalls the same comic contemplation, as in the short story, totally without condescension as in *Swami and Friends*, naturally without a trace of cynicism.

The Bachelor of Arts is an engaging absorption in the world of youth, as *Swami and Friends* is in childhood. In Narayan's first novel, childhood is presented in dynamic and subtle transience; in his second novel we witness youth in full flow, a young man on the move. The theme is more than the education of a young man; it is Chandran's 'educare'; for Chandran graduates at college, at home, and in the world at large; develops psychologically and morally. Chandran educares himself, does a Bachelor's in human values.

This modest book is elegantly structured in four parts. In the first part, Chandran attends his last year at college; already there is awareness of his years and their significance: 'He was not eighteen but twenty-one. At twenty-one to be afraid of one's parents and adopt sneaky ways!' (Narayan 1937: 11). The second part of the book presents the world of Chandran's love, first love. A glimpse, a glance—Chandran is in love. 'No one can explain the attraction between two human beings. It happens' (59). Who better than the novelist to speak on the subject! Early in the third part of the book, his impulsive youthful love frustrated, Chandran quits home; scorched by failure, moving from one extreme to the other, from an unabashed assertion and proclamation of love the young man swings to an impetuous renunciation of love, even of family and home—collaterals; he 'becomes' a sanyasin. Ochre robes, however, do not make a sanyasin. Eight months on the road, as a 'sanyasin', provides him with the best education of his life. Squatting in the shade of a banyan in a remote village, buffeted by the overwhelming faith of the villagers—anticipating *The Guide*—enlightenment dawns on him. He realizes he has been in love with love: 'It was scorching madness [...]' (120). And this, tongue-in-cheek, from young Narayan, married for love and radiantly happy! Chandran's educare is continued in the fourth part. Now he has decided what 'his greatest striving ought to be' (132). He perceives the pathos in the passage of Time that makes all human relationships so vulnerable. He accepts life at its current value; drops his grand plans for studies in England, and takes up the dealership of a newspaper distribution. When he marries, after all his romantic dreams, Chandran is completely reclaimed by life, like the majority of young people. Staple attractions of life are sovereign in Narayan.

Swami was no ordinary schoolboy; Chandran is no average college student. Studious, alert in the lecture hall, sought after as a prime mover in college debates. The intellect, however, is never dissociated from the body in Narayan's early comedy.[3] Chandran goes to a movie to celebrate the day's triumph. Narayan accords this little excursion the special place due to it in youth. 'It was an aesthetic experience to be approached with due preparation [...]'

(13–14). Far from any 'Hindu' withdrawal, this is physical enjoyment raised to a sacred rite.[4] A little further in the novel, we have the same body–mind team on track. 'Every day as he went through one item he eagerly looked forward to the next, and then the next, till he looked forward to the delicious surge of sleep as he put away his book for the night' (57). The book and 'delicious surge of sleep' sum up the point adequately.[5] But now in the first chapter, we have a third attraction of youth: friendship. 'Ramu's company was most important to him. It was his presence that gave a sense of completion to things [...]' (13).[6] A good friend is a psychological complement, foil, support. Susan Ram quotes Narayan:

Friendship, it's such a rare commodity. [...] But just friendship by itself, people coming together without any purpose, that is an achievement. I value it. That's one thing I feel for, you know: we are so close at some point in our lives, and then we lose everything. It's like a spray, a spray of water—it'll just disappear. That is a thing that puzzles me. (Ram and Ram 1996a: xxiv–xxv)[7]

Little Swami could not live without friends. Unlike the gregarious schoolboy, Chandran has only a few friends. Ramu's special position as a friend is made obvious just further in the passage above: 'He too smoked, chewed, drank coffee, *laughed (he was the greatest laugher in the world)*' (Narayan 1937: 13; emphasis mine). This is homogeneity of humour; the comic sense affirmed as a sovereign value. We recall the 'bond of laughter' between little Swami and his tiny class-fellow, nicknamed the Pea. In Narayan's second novel laughter is more significant: the gift of laughter relates harmoniously to both the body and the mind: it is the expression of a zestful growing mind in a vigorous youthful body. To appreciate Narayan's unobtrusive art, let us proceed further in the same passage: 'He too smoked, chewed, drank coffee, laughed (he was the greatest laugher in the world), *admired Chandran* [...] breathed delicious scandal over the names of his professors and friends and *unknown people*' (13; emphasis mine). With 'delicious scandal' Narayan also evokes the authentic atmosphere of youth at college: the targets are not only 'his professors and friends', but also 'unknown people'. The total impact is that of lively youth thriving naturally at a totally human level.

THE BACHELOR OF ARTS | 41

The professor Chandran admires most is not an Indian, but an Englishman, Principal Brown. Brown is distinguished by his sense of humour; it wins him the admiration of his students (40–1). Later at the history function, after Chandran has finished with his own speech, his attention lights on Brown; and his mind wanders off in a solo 'colloquium'. 'All Europeans are like this. [...] Sheer colour arrogance. [...] Why not give the poor devils—so far away from their home—[...] Anyway who invited them here?' (5–6). This passage throws more light on Chandran than on Brown: and incidentally, that is the closest perhaps we get in Narayan's early novels to the nationalist sentiment of the turbulent 1930s in India. Far from romanticizing this Englishman, we are given another view of Brown: he is 'the custodian of British prestige' (49); Mohan, a friend of Chandran's and aspiring poet, ridicules him as '[G]randmother Brown' (51).[8] As a foil to Brown, Narayan presents Gajapathi the assistant professor: 'He earned the hatred of the students by his teaching and of his colleagues by his conceit' (26); comparison is inevitable; the Indian suffers. Narayan balances the faculty, as in *Swami and Friends*, by showing presently the kind of professor deserving of Chandran's respect among the Indians: Raghavachar, serious, dignified, and scholarly, though without Brown's humour. Gajapathi however surprises Chandran when he visits him towards the end of the novel. 'Gajapathi put his arm round Chandran's shoulders and patted him' (157).

Narayan notes in his psychic journal: 'Any fetish, fanaticism, rigidity or rigour, by their very nature make living harsh, hard and dried up, while the positive values of existence all along lie in suppleness, harmony and joy' (Ram and Ram 1996a: 378). That of course is our novelist's manifesto. Chandran, like Narayan, is temperamentally averse to fanatics and fanaticisms.[9] Among the three friends, Chandran finds Veeraswami incompatible: 'Veeraswami bristled with prejudices and violence' (Narayan 1937: 49).[10] Veeraswami drops out of Chandran's life; he is an example of what is to be shunned: as much as, in a different way, Kailas, the rake he encounters in Madras, who exemplifies a way of life that is unworthy of Chandran. 'I am fifty-one. I shall be good enough for this kind of life for another twenty years at least. After that it doesn't matter what happens; I shall have lived a man's life'

(104).[11] Thanks in part to the examples of Veeraswami and Kailas, Chandran discovers now how not to live a 'man's life'. Neither intellectual, nor emotional extremism, nor coarse sensuality is Narayan's norm; Chandran moves away from both.[12] Ramu, in contrast, is Chandran's alter ego.

Chandran's friendship with Ramu should prepare us for his first love episode. 'He would have willingly settled there and spent the rest of his life watching her dig her hands into the sand' (59). The quiet indulgence carries us with its utter authenticity of, not just love, but first love of youth—dramatized by a novelist of the same age group. From its initial impact; through its burgeoning ('as if drawn by a rope' [63]); with its delicacy so natural and absurd ('and was quite thrilled at the sight of the green sari in the distance' [64]); the humour ('and he had also some doubts about her nose' [68]); the predicament ('Chandran realized that friends and acquaintances were likely to prove a nuisance to him by the river' [68]); and finally—in the circumstances—its inevitable conclusion, Narayan's treatment of Chandran's first love establishes him as a novelist of pure comedy. Experiences in love, first and subsequent, bring out prominently for us the rich human mettle of all Narayan's heroes: their resilience and vitality: they all bounce back—and move ahead.[13]

Love and friendship, the two attractions of youth, both come under review. One of the first things Chandran does on getting back home after his eight-month unplanned and non-academic outsourced course in self-education is to enquire about his friend Ramu. He learns from his father that Ramu has disappeared without a trace: 'Ramu was dead as far as Chandran was concerned' (125). And he is hurt that his friend has not informed him. As he has reacted to love, so does he to friendship: 'Friendship was another illusion like Love […]' (126). Unlike the earlier dismissal of romantic love, this disenchantment with friendship, with the undermining exaggeration, especially of the last definitive exclamation, is touched by a whiff of mutability: recalling the concluding episode of a dear departure in *Swami and Friends*. On enquiry from Chandran, his father tells him about the state of his own friendships: 'Each of us has to go his own way' (127). The statement comes to Chandran as 'a depressing revelation' (127). In *The Bachelor of Arts* awareness of mutability develops into realistic acceptance of the transience of human relationships, and of human aloneness. In a tale of youth bubbling with physical and intellectual verve, the 'callousness of Time' provides an undercurrent of pathos.

Chandran's moral profile is somewhat familiar to us; a grown-up Swaminathan. For the first time we hear articulations of inward concerns which characterize most protagonists of Narayan's novels. Swami's 'peculiar nature' was, even at that age, marked by conscionability. In *The Bachelor of Arts*, we hear of the same inner voice: 'July, August, September, and October were months that glided past without touching the conscience' (19). But Narayan quickly suggests that his hero here is 'a young man of normal indifference' (19). 'Normal' is the epithet, as with Swami: normal, not 'average'.[14] Conscionability, like any moral feature, can yield in the hands of R.K. Narayan, a harvest of humour; it leads us to the comedy of human resolves and resolutions. 'He also resolved not to smoke because it was bad for the heart, and a very sound heart was necessary for the examination' (19). Now the 'very sound heart' is comic inflation; just out of Chandran's age group, the novelist quietly chuckles at the trials of his hero, a young man of 'normal indifference'. Chandran draws up a study-plan, 'an intricate document', notes the novelist, 'as complicated as a railway time-table' (22). The call of conscience at the same time does not go in vain: 'He felt an immense satisfaction at having made a beginning' (32): he has read 'five pages'! In the evening his father asks him: 'Your plan of study not come into force yet?' We now see a grown-up Swaminathan: 'The question hurt Chandran's conscience. [...] He went to bed and his conscience gnawed at him in the dark till about eleven' (32). This is further evidence of growing seriousness; and the trend is kept up. 'In March Chandran lost about six pounds in weight. He hardly thought of anything, saw anybody or did anything, except study' (53). Young men of 'normal indifference' are also capable of 'normal' seriousness. Narayan's comedy focuses on 'normal' human nature.

The true value of human experience is found in the moral dividend. As Chandran drifts about after his first love fiasco, he reaches a hamlet where villagers bring gifts for him. 'The sight of the gifts sent a *spear through his heart*. [...] Sitting in the dark, he subjected his soul to a *remorseless vivisection*. [...] *He was in no mood for self-deception*' (119; emphasis mine). The unusual violence and force of the images is evidence that conscionability is no longer simply comical; striving towards self-education, it now belongs to the realms of moral comedy. The momentum is kept up even after Chandran returns home. He holds his own conduct responsible for '[his] mother's extra wrinkles and grey hairs, for [his] father's neglect of the garden; and a poor postmaster is a shirt and dhoti less on account of [his] Love' (133). The allusion to the poor postmaster is again a typical Narayan ploy to keep seriousness from going up like a helium balloon.

The family plays a more significant role in Narayan's second novel. The charm of the novel in part arises from the abundant domestic affections, the fine family harmonies of Chandran's home. In the first chapter of *The Bachelor of Arts*, we see Chandran in his proper milieu, which comprises not only his college and friendships, but also, more prominently, his family relationships. He has a secure moral base, a home: father, mother, and his younger brother—who sounds most of the time like another Swaminathan—completes the family. In just over one page Narayan presents almost the entire family at home, a rapid exposition of family vitalities. From the very beginning, we are struck by the robust family bonds. Chandran has been held up at the college; while the mother has not eaten, waiting for her son to join her at dinner, the father is waiting on the veranda: 'Late-coming was one of the few things that upset him' (11). Chandran belongs to a home that cares. And the youth responds: when his mother is irritable, Chandran empathizes: 'Not unusual at this hour ... attending to all the eccentricities and wants of her husband and children' (23–4). The 'eccentricities and wants' suggests Chandran's own self-understanding.

The flower thief episode, especially, while throwing light on each of its members, brings out the fine filiations of the family. Mother taunts Father into action. 'Father was very indignant. He behaved like a medieval warrior goaded by his ladylove into slaying a dragon' (43). The idea of the elderly gentleman playing the chivalrous knight is urbanely amusing; but the charm of the passage issues essentially from the point of view; it is Chandran's; tales of chivalry are very much part of his intellectual background, of the *mixed sap*. The subtle strengths of family affections could not have been better expressed; the point of view and the style are just right, blending effortlessly, perfectly. This is equalitarian humour. The father and the children jointly attempt an elaborate ambush in the early hours. The imagery, once again, delights: 'There was the light of a hunter in Father's eyes' (44). We remember that Swami's father, too, had been made to take the joke in the first novel; and now, as Chandran sees it, both father and Seenu are equal partners—comrades in arms! With a subtle manipulation of the point of view, Narayan turns the focus on the hero himself; and the imagery is now definitely—deflatively—martial: 'Chandran found the tactics weak. He took command [...] he himself would be here and there and everywhere, moving with panther-like steps from cover to cover' (45). The comic genius is now focusing on Chandran who has caught the spirit, which he found amusing in his father but a minute back. The humour is also created by the confident delicacy of language: comic exaggeration and euphemism are finely tempered by the context. The 'thief' turns out to be a sanyasin. Though 'Chandran was cynical', the debate that follows on the merits of poaching flowers for worship suggests at this very early stage the possibility of a higher value system.

The family does exercise restraint on the young man, a fine, loving, moral influence, though not enough initially to keep the young man in Malgudi, the scene of his Mars-crossed drama. When he reaches Madras, however, away from his family, the strength of his family ties alone keeps him intact, the care and the human warmth and moral security of home; in contrast the city is so remote, so aloof: Chandran suffers from a 'feeling of being neglected' (102) and concludes 'anything was possible in this impersonal place' (102). Madras is a metaphor as much as the jungle in *Swami and Friends*. Now Chandran refuses to drink with the rake: 'Chandran was firm. In his opinion, he was being asked to commit the darkest crime' (105). He tells Kailas: 'Excuse me, I made a vow never to touch alcohol in my life, before my mother.' Chandran's mother represents traditional values. The rudderless Kailas's response is more than a drunk's blabber: 'Then don't. Mother is a sacred object [...]' (105). Mother represents for both Chandran and Kailas a complex of moral values; though Chandran has earlier identified his mother with heartless orthodoxy. The fine texture of parental affinity and attachment is best illustrated by Narayan in the impact of Chandran's truancy on his family. Father and mother look very care-worn. Seenu, the little brother, confirms: 'Father and Mother were worried about you, brother. Nobody would talk to me in this house. They were all very ill-tempered and morose all these months' (124). Narayan presents two images of parental concern: mother has kept his room neat and clean, dusting the books, etc., every day; father gives her secret away to Chandran: 'She swept and cleaned it with great care every day' (125). Mother has her revenge when Chandran discovers that the garden has been neglected. 'Mother said mischievously: "He was busy searching for a missing son"' (127–8). Chandran's mother is presented first as a pious, traditional woman; and then as a member of her family, not simply the mother of her immediate home, but a member of a larger unit. Her traditional piety and outlook prepare us for the problem Chandran faces; but a complementary factor is her well-rounded attachments to 'husband, home, children, and relatives', all touched with the beauty of her sensibility. She breaks custom to satisfy Chandran. Still, in the exchanges between mother and son (90), we witness the clash of generations, which takes a central place in Narayan's post-Independence novels.[15] Father offers the liberal counterpoint: of Macaulayasa gothra—though anything but a copy of the novelist's father, Krishnaswami. It is an endearing portrait here, the best of its kind in Narayan. When Chandran is in doubt he turns to his father, his mentor, even on such a simple matter as his study schedule. And father, in his dealings with his elder son, can get into a 'puckish, teasing mood' (43). If father were to have his way, the horoscopes would not come in the way.[16] Once the horoscope processing begins he suggests to Chandran: 'Look here, you will never be qualified to marry unless you cultivate a lot of patience. It is the only power that you will be allowed to exercise when you are married' (86). The anti-feminist jibe here puts father in his class–caste configuration. When the marriage proposal falls through, 'Chandran's father knew that it would be perfectly useless to reason things with Chandran' (97). Tact and decency characterize the father–son relationship; the sage counsellor also consoles; father is a friend. Such understanding makes its impact; after his return

Chandran learns to be more sensitive to his father's sensibility, to his views, opinions, and feelings. Chandran's eight-month vagrancy makes, all the same, a lasting impact on father: 'He felt nervous when Chandran came and proposed anything' (136). With a quiet caring home, a well-knit family, the bachelor graduates.[17]

We should think that the gravity of these themes were sufficient for a slim volume. But Narayan opens chapter 14 with: 'Chandran settled down to a life of quiet and sobriety. He felt that his greatest striving ought to be for a life freed from distracting illusions and hysterics' (132).[18] Very few statements in Narayan's novels startle us as much as this quiet observation the young novelist makes in the course of a youth's struggle to come to terms with life and society. Chandran's 'education' fulfils an ethical syllabus, educare; he learns the distinction in life between right and wrong; he learns to find his rightful role in society; and plays it with youthful zest. And now this statement is made soon after Chandran's return to his family-fold: it marks an extraordinary extension to Chandran's interests and inclinations, a new dimension to the novel's central theme. It defines R.K. Narayan's early comedy. The vital verb of action in the statement is 'freed'. It recalls and relates to Swami's nascent impulse and instinct for freedom and his struggle against imposed discipline. Now in a novel purporting to be the story of a young man, the central theme is elevated simultaneously to a higher reality. A typically Hindu touch, and more, is given to the meaning of growing up, graduation: in Narayan's early comedy, thematic interests go beyond one's accountability to family and society: one is answerable to one's self. At this stage it is only natural—and 'normal' in a Narayan novel—that the hero should focus his attention on his relationships in the family and the society: and simultaneously on his inner persona, the life within, the inner world, the inward interest, and the spiritual energies of the self and the paramount need to satisfy the innermost self. This dual focus is typical of a Hindu view of life; it comes to Narayan naturally, instinctively, and he offers it to us naturally, unpretentiously, artistically. While nurturing one's external bonds, one fulfils the needs of the spirit. In the former task one depends for guidance on his family and friends, on society; in the latter journey, one seeks the aid of a guru or one is all on one's own; the heroes of Narayan's pre-Independence novels, engaged in a spiritual quest, are mostly all on their own. Mostly; because they do get valuable instruction from their family and from a section of Indian society, rural India. *The Bachelor of Arts* initiates the idea. We can see that the protagonist's 'flight' in Narayan's novels serves a definite artistic purpose: Chandran's rambles for eight months in rural India are actually an unpremeditated tryst with the land and its people, a spiritual encounter, a face-off with his innermost self. The villagers' faith deeply disturbs Chandran—anticipating Raju (*The Guide*)—sets off ultimately the cycle of rethinking and revaluation resulting in his final induction in society. This is a distinctive pattern in some of Narayan's novels; each time the hero has his brush with rural India, he comes out a chastened man. The 'flight' is rewarded not with a 'return to normalcy', but with psychological and moral development we associate with high comedy. We see towards the end of the novel—post rural graduation!—the hero is no longer the earlier Chandran: he has grown up. When a letter he knows to be important for him arrives Chandran would 'at other times' have taken it himself from the postman, but now he curbs that impulse: 'He did not go before Father at all [...] till Father himself called Chandran and gave him the letter' (138–9). The training of the mind has yielded results; Chandran has gone through a self-devised schedule, of self-education: 'With an iron will he chased away *distracting illusions*, and *conscientiously* avoided *hysterics*, with the care of one *walking on a tightrope. He decided not to give his mind a moment of freedom. All the mischief started there.* [...] *The training of the mind was done feverishly and unsparingly* (132; emphasis mine): this young man could be a novitiate in a monastery cutting himself off with a will from the world; Chandran's self-training is self-launched. He has come a long way: from an assertion of 'freedom' to a voluntary control of freedom, even to a determined self-regulation of it. The moral dividend is a spiritual poise, though a balance achieved by youth, precarious; when his father nervously brings up the marriage proposal towards the end: 'It violently shook a poise that was delicate and attained with infinite trouble and discipline' (162). Chandran's achievement cannot be self-assured and unambiguous at this stage; but the self-awareness and the striving are both initiated, and both are key features, especially, of Narayan's early comedy. The concept of 'freedom' attains a higher gravity in *The Bachelor of Arts*: not just freedom from discipline imposed arbitrarily by school, college, home, or society; but self-liberation, freedom from one's mind, 'the mad monkey'. This is the meaning of a 'man's life': human life.

6

Sacral Space: No Trespassing!
The Dark Room[1]

The Dark Room jolts the reader like a cross-country detour off the Narayan highway.

The central character is no latter-day Chandran fulfilling our expectations after *The Bachelor of Arts*, but a woman: married for fifteen years—a middle-aged mother with three children at school. The human instinct for individual freedom, no doubt, plays a key role even in this novel; however, more than the spirit of liberty in a milieu of untenable tradition, the family as a 'matrix' becomes a dominant feature in *The Dark Room*. After the delicate weave of family rapport of the first two novels, we witness in *The Dark Room* a spectacle of ripping domestic discord ending in violence unique in Narayan's early comedy. *The Bachelor of Arts* ends on a note of conjugal harmony of engaging youth; the crisis in *The Dark Room* is built on adultery. To cap it all, having quit her home in protest against her husband's infidelity, Savitri returns 'home' in a dismal compromise that makes the resolution of the novel far from 'happy' or 'comedic'. Savitri is left trapped in an unrequited moral struggle, close to life in death: 'A part of me is dead' (Narayan 1938: 208).[2]

Even the novelist seems unable to explain his interest in the theme. 'I was somehow obsessed with a philosophy of Woman as opposed to Man, her constant oppressor. This must have been an early testament of the "Women's Lib" movement' (Narayan 1974: 119). The champion of the child is also a feminist.

For an explanation of this 'fixation' we have to go back to the period of the novelist's 'apprenticeship'. Struggling to find his feet, looking for hospitable editors in Madras, Narayan had been introduced by his 'Junior' uncle to a man planning to start a magazine, the *Matrimonial Gazette*.[3] After this fateful meeting, Narayan went home and worked hard on the theme of matrimony. In every story he wrote: 'The tone, for some reason, emphasized misery—if not tragedy. It seemed so hard to find a happy couple in this world' (1974: 99). This, from a happily married young man! Here, perhaps, is the inspiration and genesis of Narayan's third novel. For the novelist at this stage, a self-consciously 'Realistic fiction writer in English', the theme and the tone—if not an original or embryonic version—was probably ready to hand when he thumbed through his notebooks for his third novel in three years.

Narayan tells the story of Savitri and Ramani with economy and impressive psychological and social realism. After *The Bachelor of Arts*, the technique in *The Dark Room* is tersely dramatic; the stress is on 'showing'; the narrative moves with simple, mostly, linear momentum. The workman-like simplicity is seen in the dramatic opening. The structure of the novel, too, attracts our notice; such formal austerity we associate with drama. Two other features of the novel confirm this impression. Narayan reveals here, once again, a talent for building up a variety of dramatic 'scenes': whether it is a serious scene with Savitri and Ramani; or lighter ones with Pereira, or between Kantaiengar and Shanta Bai; or that delectable scene in the later part of the novel when the village priest interviews Savitri for a job. All these episodes in the novel conclude with a crisp finish. The dialogue also matches this terse treatment with fluency and spontaneity; relaxed, tense, or comic; see the children in their kid talk (1938: 56–7), or wary Ramani handling wily Pereira, or Pereira rallying glum colleague Kantiengar (75), or coy Shanta Bai (86). Even when Narayan moves out of the urban environment into the Indian countryside, a challenge to a writer in English, the dialogue does not lose its point or charm; consider the encounter between Ponni and Mari (159); or the delicious exchange between the senescent priest and Mari (164). From serious confrontation to light banter (Holmström 1973: 43),[4] Narayan's dialogue in *The Dark Room* impresses with practised ease (Harrex 1977: 56–7, vol. 1). The result of this level of dramatic presentation, of scene and dialogue, is a distancing warranted by a theme of marital discord and dark despair. The narrative technique makes sense for the best part of the book; however, where youthful Narayan's compassion overwhelms aesthetic instinct, art suffers.

Let us go back for a moment to Narayan's comments in *My Days* (1974: 119; emphasis mine): 'I was somehow *obsessed* with a philosophy of Woman as opposed to Man, her constant oppressor. This must have been an early testament of the "Women's Lib" movement. [...] *A wife in an orthodox milieu of Indian society was an ideal victim of such circumstances.*'[5] 'Obsession' and R.K. Narayan don't go together; subtle balance shuns it; sanity and sobriety are his characteristic values; these are appreciated and shared to some degree even by young Chandran. Still, looking back on *The Dark Room*, Narayan finds an obsession. We shall see the full meaning of this presently; however, while in all his other novels of the early comedy, any 'obsession' of the heroes and others around them is an aberration, and Narayan stands apart and follows its course with good humour, *The Dark Room* is the only novel in which we find Narayan obsessed. To break away from routine tedium, the urge to be free, to liberate oneself ultimately is natural to all 'heroes', especially, of the early comedy; Savitri is no exception. Moral strength marks the typical protagonist of the pre-Independence novels. What characterizes Savitri alone is the extraordinary stress on her 'orthodox milieu of Indian society'; here is 'Woman as opposed to Man, her constant oppressor'. In keeping with Narayan's narrative pace in this novel, the central theme is suggested on the very first page of the novel. 'It is none of a woman's business', says Ramani, ticking off his wife Savitri. And almost every character in the novel says something on woman 'as opposed to man'. Savitri's friend Janamma represents the orthodox school: 'What he does is right. It is a wife's duty to feel so' (1938: 59). This view is part of the tradition; Savitri's daughters have already imbibed it; at the time of Navaratri, a festival celebrated especially by women, Sumati and Kamala make fun of their brother Babu. 'Are you a girl to take a hand in the doll business? Go and play cricket. *You are a man*' (37; emphasis mine). The conventional view can take a harsher anti-feminist stance. 'Women are terrible', says Ranga, the domestic servant (51). His colleague the cook boasts: 'Only once has my wife tried to interfere, and then I nearly broke her bones. She has learnt to leave me alone now. Women must be taught their place' (51). The attitude has little to do with class or caste; the priest of the village also advises Mari: 'If she won't let you rest, thrash her; that is the way to keep women sane' (167); Savitri's husband Ramani, as we are going to see, cannot agree more.

What appears to be a more accommodative view is simply sexist. It is suavely represented by Ramani's subordinate Pereira; when the boss, Ramani, employs the modern girl Shanta Bai and asks Pereira to find some office space for her, Pereira goes to his conservative colleague Kantaiengar and observes, 'I shall have to fix up a nuptial chamber in the office' (69). Sexism is not confined to the town. As Mari desperately looks for some work for Savitri so she can subsist on her own hard-earned money, a customer at his shop shows interest. 'And he made a ribald suggestion' (160). Even champions of women's rights, of women's individuality, appear to be of little consequence. Gangu, the other friend of Savitri's, apparently enjoys a more liberated life, especially because her husband '[b]elieved he was serving the women's cause by constantly talking about votes and divorce' (19). The derision, rare in Narayan's fiction, is unmistakable. While the cause is real, the solutions are liable to be illusory, self-deceptive, or shallow.

Narayan's 'hero' of course is no effigy of social protest. The opening chapter presents Savitri during the course of one day, from early morning to late evening; taking her through routine tensions: by quick turns the novelist presents her as mother, wife, mistress of the household: none of the roles is to Savitri's satisfaction. At the same time we see Savitri in her traditional milieu: 'Now Savitri had before her a little business with her god [...] and muttered *all the sacred chants she had learnt from her mother years ago*' (4–5; emphasis mine).[6] Here is a hint of continuity of tradition; and more than a hint of the religious ballast of that tradition. Chapter 1 also shows this wife is married to a 'modern' husband. Chapter 2 has notable simplicity: it poises Savitri precisely in her milieu—between Savitri's neighbours, Gangu and Janamma, two poles of 'modernity' and orthodoxy. Savitri may be traditional, but she is not orthodox; and though traditional she enjoys the company of a 'progressive' neighbour with whom she also enjoys 'the bond of humour' (18). (That bond again, in the third successive novel.) Savitri is at home in the company of both. Savitri is neither naively 'modern' nor staidly orthodox. 'Between these two implacable enemies Savitri maintained a subtle balance' (20).[7] Tradition is a value in Narayan;

orthodoxy is not; tradition contributes to togetherness, sanity, and sobriety; orthodoxy enervates.

In the earlier novels, especially in *The Bachelor of Arts*, the relationship between Father and Mother is vibrant with warmth and wisdom: without sentimentalism, practical. The third novel is a startling contrast; thanks to Ramani. Ramani is the first 'foreigner' in the world of Narayan. His attitude to his wife (15-16), after fifteen years of marriage, is unnatural, 'superior'. Ramani's domestic style is alien to the world of Narayan. In the first novel, Swami's father can see through Swami's stratagem to avoid going to the school, but gives in to the mother's plea and Swami stays home. The shared joy in children in the first two novels is missing in *The Dark Room*. From the first page to the last, Savitri's attachment and indulgence are contrasted with Ramani's inflexibility. The novelist presents these features of Savitri early (chapter 3) through the movie episode; completing the novel's exposition.

Savitri can now be expected to go to the rescue of Babu when Ramani slaps him; and she retires to the dark room in protest.[8] When Janamma is fetched by the girls to get their mother out of the dark room, Savitri tells her: 'I don't mind any treatment personally, but when a child—' (50). 'Any treatment', too, shall have its limits: no trespassing on sacral space. But now Janamma's final argument moves Savitri out of her protest: 'You are spoiling the happiness of these two girls' (61). Later, harassed by thoughts of her husband's affair with Shanta Bai, Savitri finds the children the only solace: 'Their presence was a check on Savitri's gloom' (107). Even when she decides to walk out of her home in a rage of protest, she attempts—vainly—to take the children along. Looking back at the house she worries: 'Will the children sleep there in the dark without me?' (114). As she enters the river in her suicide bid, she prays to her God on the Hill 'to protect the children' (121). After her chance rescue, she wonders if her husband has brought the other woman into the house: 'Would she be ill-treating the children?' (134). In the village, passionately resolved to live on her own, Savitri tells Ponni: 'If you don't want me to starve, give me some work. I can cook, scrub, sew. *I know a little gardening too. I had a beautiful garden once. I can look after children*' (103; emphasis mine). Juxtaposition of gardening with child-rearing and other professional skills is not casual; as we have seen in *The Bachelor of Arts*, good gardening and congenial family environment go together in Narayan.[9] But not all can understand this attachment, and some men, never. The lowly servant-maid ticks off her male colleagues: 'What do you know of the fire in a mother's belly when her child is suffering?' (51).[10] The most caustic thing the old priest can say to Mari is: '[N]o wonder your wife is barren' (164). Soon after securing a menial job in the village temple Savitri feels the absence of the children and asks herself: 'What was this foolish yearning for children, this *dragging attachment?*' (170; emphasis mine). Her only prayer to the deity in the temple is: 'Protect Sumati, Babu, and Kamala. Let them all eat well and grow' (186–7). It builds up, this human need. 'What a void they create!' Savitri's bonding with her children is conclusively demonstrated when she takes the desperate decision to return home. 'I must see them; I must see Babu, I must see Sumati and I must see Kamala. Oh ...' (189–90). It speaks of both Savitri's sensibility and the society that has shaped her that while bidding farewell to her 'great friend Ponni', Savitri blesses her: 'God will reward you for your goodness. May He bless you with a child soon!' (191).

The Dark Room is not a story of a love triangle; it is a 'family drama'. While the children mean so much to her, Savitri has other filiations. The family, as well as family relationships, is a significant theme in the first two novels; in *The Dark Room*, so different from the earlier novels, both play a critical role; and much value is attached to them by the various characters. If the family serves as a moral matrix for Chandran, a secure base from which he can launch himself into the world outside, for Savitri, the Indian wife in her orthodox milieu, her family is everything. Early in the novel, Sumati appears to her '[a]s my mother must have looked about forty years ago' (9). Later, 'a rosy-cheeked auburn-haired doll was eloquent with memories of her father' (35). Advancing the family as a human need her bitterest cry is: 'Everybody forgets me' (108). Later still, under extraordinary psychological strain, on the verge of attempting suicide: 'Not a husband but one's parents—theirs was the true affection, *not even one's children's*' (117; emphasis mine). The dismissal of 'one's children's' affections' reflects the extreme isolation she feels in the situation. Family attachments are not exclusive to class or age. Ranga and Mari are in their own way family men. When Ranga breaks the elephant doll accidentally, he accepts the reprimand and requests Savitri to give him the broken doll: 'My little boy will tie a string round its neck, drag it about, and call it his dog' (36–7). Mari turns burglar occasionally because 'he did it to please his wife. He was intensely devoted to her […]' (122). Savitri's children cannot do without her. In the dark room episode, even with Savitri in the house, the children feel her absence: 'Mother's absence gave the house a still and gloomy appearance' (5). Ramani knows it: 'They were not to miss their mother' (143). They do; with their mother absent, things soon become difficult for the children (147).

With such focus on the family and family relationships goes sensitivity to houses and habitations in the novel. Regaining consciousness, recalling the shameful hurt, filled with bitterness again, Savitri makes an attempt to renew her rejection of home. 'She must go on with her back to *that cluster of roofs* […]' (133–4; emphasis mine). Home is just a 'roof' now, a metonymic loss of character and status. Savitri goes with Ponni to her village: the alternative is unthinkable—going back home. And that clinches the matter. 'I will come with you,' she said, 'on condition that *you don't trouble me to come under your roof or any other roof. I will remain only under the sky*' (138; emphasis mine). 'Roof' signifies enslavement; 'sky', emancipation.

The Dark Room underscores the difficulty of finding a home for a 'single' woman. Commended by the priest, a shelter—a roof—is found for her at last by Mari after prodigious effort: 'It was very dark, light and air being admitted only by the chinks in the joints of the iron sheets. Rats jumped about, startled, and there was some flapping of wings above, which might be bats or sparrows. […] Savitri withdrew her head and breathed again' (179–80). Rebelling, raising the banner of emancipation, looking for a home away from home, a haven of dignity and self-respect, Savitri has only entered another dark room, worse than the first.

The coherence and completeness, the plenitude of Savitri's world view is suggested by the Navaratri dolls 'in their yellowing newspaper wrappings' (33). Ranga who takes out the dolls looks like 'an intoxicated conjurer giving a wild performance' (33). For '[i]n an hour a fantastic world was raised. [...] *Here and there out of the company of animals and vegetables and mortals emerged the gods*— [...] their *serenity unaffected by the company about them* [...]' (39–40; emphasis mine). Here is God's plenty; and Himself. The inclusiveness of Narayan's pure Hinduism—equalitarian, of a god's eye-view—emerges as living faith in divinity of humanity—a sacral view of life, of creation. This of course is Narayan's world view, too, established with characteristic consistency from *Swami and Friends* to *Grandmother's Tale*. William Walsh (1982: 167) was ahead of his time: 'What one can say about Narayan without qualification is that he embodies the pure spirit of Hinduism. [...] Again, one must say that there is deeply in Narayan the profound Hindu conviction, or instinct for, the fundamental oneness of existence.' Savitri represents this culture. Not just Savitri: the story of the mythological movie Ramani takes Savitri to watch is familiar to most of the spectators in the hall.

Ramani does not belong here. While Savitri remembers her parents with particular warmth, Ramani knows better: 'He had never tolerated any advice from anyone—not even from his father [...].' He knows his mind. 'I know better what I must do' (Narayan 1938: 140).[11] We hear little about Ramani's parents besides this dismissive allusion. It is probably because 'Ramani was self-made'; not inheriting tradition, but self-made. Now in Narayan, 'self-made' is generally anything but complimentary, though the novelist's own life demonstrates its merit; years later, Narayan gives us the most destructive character ever, Vasu of *The Man-Eater of Malgudi*: and Vasu is 'self-made'; Vasu is the eponymous 'man-eater'. Ramani also acknowledges tradition, selectively. Pointing to Kuchela's wife in the movie, Ramani advises Savitri to '[n]ote how patient she is, and how uncomplaining' (29). All the same Ramani himself is the foreigner. He has already suggested this. '[Y]ou'd have to write a new epic if you wanted anyone like me in an epic' (14–15). The classical Savitri in the epic pursues God of Death, Yama Himself, as He carries away her husband's life; she so moves Yama with her devotion that He grants her various boons and finally restores her husband's life. Other 'women in our ancient books' also invite comparison; especially Sita, consort of Rama. When her husband prepares to go to the forests without her, she remonstrates with him: 'That a woman cannot live without her husband is a dharma which you have yourself pointed out to me [...].' Sita lays down for all times to come the Hindu wife's primary duty. And when her mother-in-law compliments her, Sita replies that she has been taught as a girl: '[A] wife apart from her husband was a stringless lyre, a wheel-less chariot, and that son, father, mother, everyone else gave only a little, compared to what the husband gave the woman' (Raghavan 1980: 173). Against this ancient complex of beliefs, Narayan's heroine revolts. A new epic is written by Narayan: not about a new hero, but about the trials and transformation of a woman in a traditional milieu subjected to 'modernity'. 'Malgudi in 1935 suddenly came into line with the modern age' (26). For Narayan, having assimilated the traditional milieu himself, the revolt of Savitri, is a defiant departure from tradition. John Thieme (2008: 194) observes: 'Malgudi is a trope for uncertainty, openness and ongoing secular struggle.'

Narayan uses the same movie to emphasize Shanta Bai's contrasting background. To this 'stirring episode from the Ramayana', her response is 'modern': '"What rubbish the whole thing is!" she said' (Narayan 1938: 90–1). Savitri, too, has earlier watched 'mythological nonsense' and 'a wretched Indian film'. '[T]he whole picture swept her mind clear of mundane debris and filled it with *superhuman splendours. Unnoticed by her passed* [...] *all the exaggeration, emphasis, and noise* [...].[12] Savitri brought her palms together and prayed' (29–30; emphasis mine). Savitri's strength of inherited tradition, her native intellectual vitality nurtured on the ancient lore and in the mother tongue, and, above all, her emotional and moral maturity which cares selflessly for the family, the children: these are set off against the ideological pretence and emotional self-indulgence of a populist version of 'modernity': against this humbug, the reality of women's cause is presented in Savitri's predicament, though Narayan presents the Shanta–Ramani drama with uncharacteristic sarcasm (88). The psychological realism with which Narayan develops his heroine's story and proceeds with her characterization more than makes up for the weakness. The fire inside her is not the same as 'the fire inside a mother's belly' (61): 'the fire inside' characterizes all the 'heroes' of Narayan's early comedy.

Savitri's moral features are familiar to us; they distinguish the central characters of Narayan's early comedy: conscience, introspection, self-criticism, the freedom impulse; an urge to liberate oneself from constraints on personality; selflessness as opposed to fatal self-centred existence exemplified by Shanta Bai: 'I'm rather mad tonight,' says Shanta Bai to Ramani, 'You have a mad woman beside you tonight' (91). Mari considers Savitri mad: 'There is a mad woman in there, who won't touch food unless she is given work' (160): and he conveys the assessment to the temple priest: 'She is resolved to work and earn. It has grown in her as madness' (160). Two mad women, then. Savitri's 'madness' is a revolt triggered by a complex of factors including violation of tradition and related values; above all, there is one, a key factor—violation of personality. For Savitri is not any housewife, no more than Chandran is an average young man. 'Was there nothing else for one to do than attend to this miserable business of the stomach from morning till night?' (10). Narayan's heroes—especially of the early comedy—are aware of a higher life; their striving for a life of humane value constitutes the central interest of Narayan's comedy. The urge to break free from mechanical life, the need to assert one's human dignity cannot be ignored for long. Savitri's 'innermost self' longs for independence; and it is 'madness' in the world of 'orthodox Indian milieu'. This homemaker-heroine is special, though traditional: she is a protagonist of Narayan's early comedy. For Savitri, as for other heroes of Narayan's early comedy, self-criticism comes naturally. Balance, moderation, modesty, warmth without show are some of the characteristics of Narayan's early 'heroes'. And consideration for others: 'Savitri laughed. [Ramani] would have been hurt if she hadn't' (16). Going through throes of suspicion, Savitri retains a sense of fairness. Savitri throws a different light on Ramani, remembering the very early days of their married life and what he confided to her: '[T]hat the moment he saw her he decided to marry her, and that he would have taken his life if he hadn't got her' (118). Conscience is an alert presence. An emotional maturity, a cultured outlook even in intimate personal relationships; and self-effacing—almost, not quite, because self-respecting—tolerating provocation, absorbing hurt only up to a point: keep off sacral space. Ramani provokes her by violating the domestic sanctities, especially her love for the children; and more seriously, outraging her self-respect, her inner-most self, her sacral space: 'I'm a human being. You men will never grant that. For you we are playthings when you feel like hugging, and slaves at other times. Don't think that you can fondle us when you like and kick us when you choose' (110). Savitri's traditional sense of matrimonial sanctity and purity—deeply ingrained in her by the 'ancient books'—is of course a staple: 'Don't touch me!' she cried, moving away from him. 'You are dirty, you are impure. Even if I burn my skin I can't cleanse myself of the impurity of your touch' (112). A sacrament for the Christian: marriage is a samskara for the Hindu. Savitri retains this resolve even beyond the river: 'She was an individual with pride and with a soul and she wasn't going to submit to everything hereafter' (133). No trespassing!

Narayan charts the course of the crisis with fine psychological touches. When Savitri dresses up in competition with 'these strumpets with their powder and paint!' (104), the novelist takes his time to describe her preparations: 'The glass clouded with the moisture of her breath. [...] She felt a little shy to dress so well for the home' (104–5). The effort and its unnaturalness are disturbing to the reader. A showdown is deferred, thanks to Savitri's natural accommodation and native dignity. But she takes it out on her servants: 'A set of useless, blundering wasteful parasites in this house' (95): she includes herself among her targets.

When she walks out of her home of fifteen years, leaving behind everything, economic independence gains conscious form. 'What possession can a woman call her own except her body? [...]' (112–13). From youthful Narayan, inspired by his fulfilled love, that is another telling feminist salvo—as early as the mid-1930s of the century.[13]

Savitri carries the fierce resolve beyond her suicide bid. The traditional Indian woman—and mother of three—takes the extreme step: towards economic independence; she gives up her children. Not just the children, but her own father whom she so dearly loves; she renounces him: he is a man (114). Soon enough, however, Savitri realizes the truth: economic independence for a traditional Indian woman without 'education' is impossible. And '[n]o one who could not live by herself should be allowed to exist' (119). Marriage as an institution, the very foundation of Narayan's beloved family, is questioned. 'What is the difference between a prostitute and a married woman?—the prostitute changes her men, but a married woman doesn't; that's all, but both earn their food and shelter in the same manner' (80). Even considering the youthful humanism of young Narayan, the sentiments were revolutionary. 'This must have been an early testament of the "Women's Lib" movement' (Narayan 1974: 119). It certainly was.[14] 'I have *slaved* for him all these years', Savitri says to Ponni (136; emphasis mine). The metaphor has more than idiomatic force: economic dependence is slavery—the children, the home, included. Now, to clarify further the concept's content, the novelist shifts focus at the peak of Savitri's struggle, to the town, to Ramani and Shanta Bai. Narayan presents to us one of the earliest portraits of an Indian male chauvinist: the sanctimonious Indian. What compounds its repugnance is the sanctity Ramani seeks to give it, in the tradition of hypocrites down the centuries, by citing the sacred books, taking the reader back to chapter 1 where Savitri is compared to women in our ancient epics; breaking into the trials of Savitri, Shanta's philosophy shows itself up as sheer sham. Narayan cuts back, cinematically, to Savitri's ordeal.

Savitri refuses food and shelter from Ponni, not because of her caste: Savitri's reasons are progressive; she is determined to earn her own food. Radical is such a resolve for this Tamil Brahmin housewife of those days. Savitri accepts food, though bananas and coconut milk, from Ponni without being the least conscious of Ponni's caste; the higher goal matters. 'If you don't want me to starve, give me some work' (158). Even a menial job is welcome: it is a new life of economic independence, a life devoid of charity: for 'eating food that was her own had grown into a perfect obsession [...]' (171); and '[s]he mentioned her hunger as the least urgent of the reasons' (172). In Narayan, when the focus is on the spirit, the 'innermost self', the body can be ignored. The 'lesser charity' is the shanty offered by the priest. Eating the cooked rice, without even a pinch of salt for relish, uneatable, she exults: '"This is nobody's charity to me." She felt triumphant, and a great peace descended on her [...] it was worth it because it enhanced one's sense of victory' (185).[15] Soon, though, the truth must be faced. 'I am like a bamboo pole which cannot stand without a wall to support it [...].' That recalls

Sita quoted earlier from the Ramayana. Economic independence is still out of reach for Savitri.

Savitri's other objective of achieving liberation from fear within is far less feasible. 'One definite thing in life is Fear. [...] Afraid of one's father, teachers, and everybody in early life, afraid of one's husband, children, and neighbours in later life—fear, fear, in one's heart till the funeral pyre was lit and then fear of being sentenced by Yama [...]' (115–16).

It is a universal predicament: '[W]as there no escape from fear and charity?' (188). Charity she can avoid, but not fear. 'Everything terrified her. [...] As the hours advanced her fears also increased' (189). The proximity of God only serves to underscore her orthodox upbringing, which has instilled the timidity, the fear-complex. The struggle for economic independence has a chance of success; but the moral struggle, for true emancipation, liberation from fear, ends in crushing defeat: '[S]he couldn't help contrasting the comfort, security, and un-loneliness of her home' (189).

So unlike our 'women in our ancient books' in her defiance of convention, Savitri is also like them in undertaking a moral struggle. The classical Savitri takes on death; her latter-day counterpart engages in a contest that is no less awesome—a struggle to emancipate herself from 'fear and charity'. Her obsession with avoiding 'charity' gives her revolt an economic dimension. Emancipation from fear and charity, her twin concerns, defined the women's liberation movement decades before it came to be recognized as an authentic social reform campaign. But the very attempt to break free, the astonishing drive towards emancipation, moral and economic, presents absorbing drama.[16]

The supportive cast and world of Mari and Ponni, the low-class/ caste couple who go to the heroine's rescue is meticulously realized. Narayan begins early by noting that in the heroine's establishment the cook 'lived in a state of protracted hunger' (5). Introducing Mari, the novelist discloses that 'there was a predatory strain in his nature, perhaps handed down to him by his ancestors' (122); the heroine finds him a 'dark hefty man' (134). The skin colour ('the dark face' [133]), and class ('You are so fair and you look rich' [135]), and caste ('I see you are a Brahmin' [137]) are relevant in this early novel as belonging to the social context of the heroine's struggle.

The world of Mari itself is presented with sensitive attention to detail. 'There was an old woman squatting on the narrow pavement at the Market gateway selling fried groundnut, coloured edibles, and cucumber slices, arranged on a gunny-sack spread on the ground' (124). When Mari pleads for credit from this old woman, she replies, truthfully enough: 'I am a poor wretch who has to add pie on pie; what can I do?' (125). The little that Mari manages to buy from the old woman makes no impression on his hunger, for there is 'a fire-like hunger inside me and this is just a pinch in some corner' (126); he begs her: 'I shall go raving mad if I don't get a little piece of tobacco now.' The old woman reveals more charity than members of the upper castes. The novelist notes attentively:

> The old woman took out her *greasy cloth purse*, peered into it by the light of the *smoky flare*, picked up a piece of tobacco and *a crumpled betel leaf*, and flung them at Mari, grumbling, 'You are the biggest scoundrel God ever made. You spend *half an anna* but take *goods for three-quarters of an anna.*' 'Let me be smitten with *leprosy* if I have a pie more about me,' said Mari, receiving the gift and putting it in his mouth. (126–7; emphasis mine)

From the 'greasy cloth purse' to 'leprosy' the details form a coherent world that lies normally outside the central purview of Narayan's pre-Independence novels, his early comedy, focusing on inner struggles of middle-class heroes.[17] The 'spacious rest house before the market' strengthens the picture with 'travellers, adventurers, and mendicants', one or two among them 'sitting and sucking an enchanted clay pipe filled with opium leaf, the pipe glowing in the dark!' (127). And soon we are given glimpses of new depths of human misery rare in Narayan's early novels. As Mari is engaged in exploring the house he has broken into, his labours are brought to a premature end. 'At this moment a noise like that of a terraced roof crashing down came through the darkness. [...] And then he heard groans, and a weak voice calling someone; and again another cascade of falling bricks, groans, and further sounds of choking. [...] A young boy was administering medicine to an old man who was sitting up, choking and wheezing' (130). This level of human distress, too, jells with the heroine's tale of suffering. The stark approach is extended, reaching into nooks of contemporary reality, as in Narayan's description of the village shrine 'which smelt of burnt lamp-oil, flowers, incense and *bats*' (186; emphasis mine); the shrine is serviced by an old priest with 'webbed, shrunken hands' (165): 'the bats' and 'the webbed, shrunken hands' realize the shrine and its priest harmoniously. The naturalistic attention to societal detail establishes a matrix of reality for Savitri's tale of heroic effort. This is precisely what V.S. Naipaul missed out during his travels through India; this India is outside the itinerary of a foreign tourist. The fringe world also provides the ballast of humour and humanity in *The Dark Room*, enacts relief and support that is once again extraordinary in Narayan's novels. When the next novel comes, it will be another surprise.

7
Purify the Mind and Clarify the Vision
Ordeal and Aftermath*

> *One may learn to walk on water, mesmerize a mad elephant, muzzle a tiger or a lion, walk on fire, and perform other feats, but yet the real feat would be to still the restless mind and understand one's real self.*
> —Narayan (1974: 149)

In Narayan's life 1939 turned out to be the disaster year; and the beginning of a period of over five years—'a perpetual unrelenting climate of loneliness' (Narayan 1974: 179)—the most critical formative period, that resulted in a 'new kind of life and outlook and vision' (1974: 366). His wife's death and its aftermath further shaped R.K. Narayan's spiritual as well as social and literary values. It was mind control above all that Narayan aimed at and achieved through exercises in psychic training. He even succeeded in controlling his sexuality. Narayan's attitude towards work also changed during this crucial period. The self-education did not lead to any withdrawal from life; it resulted in greater social participation, 'working for a common good'.

Yet Narayan's professionalism was evident throughout: even as his wife's body lay in the house the writer took notes of his experiences (1974: 259); he also met his weekly deadline for the *Hindu*. Later, following his fateful meeting with the medium and the seances, he started a diary of his psychic experiences. Susan

---

* Parts of this chapter appear in the chapter titled 'A Life' in Ranga Rao's *Makers of Indian Literature: R.K. Narayan* published by Sahitya Akademi, New Delhi, in 2004. Reprinted here with permission from Sahitya Akademi.

Ram and N. Ram have done a critical service to the literary world by discovering and quoting extensively from the Psychic Journal.[1]

Narayan received help in this struggle from practitioners of theosophy and books on the subject.[2] The mystic, Paul Brunton, also played a major role.[3] Brunton taught Narayan the significance of memory and dreams as well as techniques of memory retrieval; and trained Narayan in yogic exercises for conquest of time—'because the separation existed only in time and time is an illusion'. The overhaul of personality and psychic reorientation culminated in his meeting with the discarnate spirit of his wife, Rajam.

The process of self-training was not smooth; the bereaved man hit several lows; at times it was as though he was back in June 1939. The commercial failure of his first three novels, which Narayan equated with professional failure, joined forces with his personal loss, the dear departure. A mortal mix of self-doubt and bereavement wrenched his heart: 'Living becomes less attractive every day. Perhaps it is meant to be so; so that we may envy those who die and not become too attached to this existence. *The unrelieved monotony of a life full of interest* is perhaps not the best means of attaining a true perspective [...] at least so far as this world is concerned' (emphasis mine). The pathos of 'unrelieved monotony' in 'a life of full of interest' is hard to comprehend; it perhaps underscores Narayan's commitment to work, the desolation of his creative mind.[4] This hardy spirit, his self-faith under relentless siege, his rare professionalism breaking down, tottered on the precipice. 'God help me. Oh, God, you can best help me by striking me down. The burden of life and failure becomes unendurable [...].'

Even after he had fought his way out of the Pit, it was still a toboggan run, moving from elation of yogic success and psychic discovery to deadly frustration and back; and 'a torment of longing, inescapable and hopeless'. Narayan's physical and moral reserves—which he shared with his heroes—helped: 'I must pull myself together.' He did. During the turbulent period Narayan stubbornly stuck to his main interests in life, 'personal relationships and self-development': the central interests of his heroes, especially, of the two novels to come of the early comedy. Recovery began on a trip to Madras. 'Gradually, memories of funerals and details of the sickroom began to fade and in their place I tried to catch and retain the moments of elation I felt at the touch, sight and sound of the sea' (Narayan 1974: 138). The rich earthy springs of R.K. Narayan, his basic artistic strength was revived—'touch, sight and sound'. Professionalism holding firm, Paul Brunton and the family—and life—helped: R.K. Narayan pulled back from the abyss.[5]

Life had dealt Narayan a crushing blow: he turned it into an opportunity for a yogic quest, towards a philosophic understanding of life and psychic contact with his wife's spirit. Narayan noted in his journal: 'The positive aspect of one's life mainly consists in doing one's duties, following one's lights, and leaving at that. The results are inconsequential [...]': that is the Gita again.

Narayan also made several discoveries relevant to his career; for example: 'Full efficiency of mental life, powers and work is necessary for a harmonious existence. This is to be obtained only by intelligent conservation and direction of energy [...].' The key goal, 'Harmonious existence', recalls, especially, Chandran's aspiration in *The Bachelor of Arts* (1937: 132); which predates the psychic training following his wife's death. It was essential, Narayan noted in his journal, that if the self was to function fully in all the planes there should be 'no confusions and frictions'—confirmation of Chandran's 'illusions and hysterics' again. The mind must be one of 'absolute purity'. The attitude of the individual should be one of 'humility of a receiver of gifts', the gifts being 'experience and the moods and emotions and the knowledge they create'. Narayan's instruction to himself: receive the gifts, pray, and keep the mind 'so resilient that it glides from plane to plane without effort' and 'so pointed that it forgets the rest when it is concentrated on one object'. This would help to extract from each plane 'the finest essence' and also attain 'the finest synthesis of all planes and varieties of experience'. In this way, he would gain 'a glimpse of Reality according to God'.

Narayan further widened his ethical philosophy: 'As a general rule it is best to view with respect all matters and affairs which occupy other people's thoughts. [...] The matter is given value not for itself, but because it takes place in another human being's mind and emotion.' Narayan concluded: 'Every human activity from breadwinning to self-realization has a right to that work, if each at the particular moment absorbs the mind.' Far from distancing, dissociating, himself from life, Narayan's psychic training took him closer to common humanity.

Narayan gave himself three instructions. First, watch himself and economize attention. Second, allow his mind to 'lapse into its natural state of calm and rest without feeling obliged to set it working [...] which pathological habit is responsible for most of the weaknesses and exhaustion now felt.' Third, plan intelligently a programme for the mind and 'try to stick to it as far as possible'. One goal of Narayan's spiritual life had been achieved: purifying the mind.

Narayan also refined his professional goals: 'The thing to do as it seems to me is to write, whether it be for an hour or ten hours, when the impulse goads you, and at other times keep yourself in readiness to get the impulse.' Narayan noted another human problem. As he put it: 'There had been constant disturbance from erotic causes.' For the problem of his sexual need Narayan found a doctrinal way out, typical of his maidenliness: avoid looking at women altogether; and, second, aim at sublimation. 'The properly balanced can have the act only for this purpose (as Gandhi says). The merest attraction of it at other times is a misuse, and is a result of passion and desire.' Narayan argued for an absolute monogamous loyalty. He aimed at a fundamentalism of sexual morality we associate with religiouses. Narayan evolved a solution: every time he looked at a beautiful woman, he would say to himself: 'Oh, Divine Mother, who sustains all Creation, I see now a passing glimpse of your radiant form [...]' (see Naik 1985: 24). On this personal problem also Narayan expresses super-human hope: 'In course of time, when I have established the most perfect contact with my wife's spirit, I shall have risen above even this need of precaution. For when our hearts are perfectly united, I shall not be feeling any want in life.' Applying this perspective to himself, he noted that his life had had its fulfilment 'to the degree defined by God's will'. And he assured himself that he would be able to reach out to Rajam. The past—his wife Rajam—he was convinced now, was retrievable.[6] Narayan's fidelity to his wife in life and after her death was unequivocal.

The high points of Narayan's psychic evolution during the period included three visions. First, a vision of himself much later in life, as an old man who had attained that 'final understanding'. Weeks later Narayan experienced a dream-like state in which he had a vision of a God-like personage: '[T]he influence of the Presence was very soothing.' The vision ended with promise of further help; it also instructed him to locate and follow a variant of Gayatri mantra which contained a hidden part.[7] Paul Brunton had suggested a deliberate cultivation, whether one was awake or asleep, of 'the Universal Spirit and Vision of all matters big or small', for the prayer which enabled one to link up with 'the universal power' would bring 'power, peace and a vision of reality according to God'. This is spiritual surrender we are familiar with in the Gita, as well as in every religion; and memorably in the *Book of Job*. The third vision, the finale, a meeting with his wife Rajam, took more effort and time. Under Brunton's guidance, Narayan grew actively interested in dreams and memory. He formed an idea of the function of dreams. Dream and memory, argued Narayan, are the means by which humans reach immortality. Narayan further explains the concept: 'The preserving is done by memory. The re-taking must be done by dream and the subconscious, the most pervasive of faculties and the most neglected, too.' After two years of yogic practice, Narayan attempted yogic contact with Rajam. He succeeded: Narayan's mind was now 'clean and bare and a mere chamber of fragrance' (Ram and Ram 1996a: 385).

Mental and psychic training brought him closer to the two institutions of family and society; and this is the philosophy evolved by the protagonists of the two books to come of his early comedy. Narayan's single-minded search was aimed at accomplishing the right mental training which would yield 'a generally harmonious state of mind *in family and social life*' (emphasis mine). Second, a 'long view' of things (Ram and Ram 1996a: 369): how often we hear Narayan talk of 'true perspective' and his implied belief in 'some eternal scheme' of things![8] And third, conservation of mental energy and the cultivation of calm and rest: 'The normal existence of mind should consist in great spaces of calm and rest—and all those things that contribute to this calm.' When 'a final understanding' brought greater joy, personal tragedies would keep a person 'in trim in the relations between himself and God'. The practical outcome of Narayan's psychic training, however, was creative. In all his efforts, he reminded himself: 'Any fetish, fanaticism, rigidity or rigour, by their very nature make living harsh, hard and dried up, while the positive values of existence all along lie in *suppleness, harmony and joy*. This is, according to my outlook, what God intends it to be' (emphasis mine). This is quintessential Narayan, the sanity, the wholesomeness of human life. A delight in the here and the now, accompanying a refined awareness of the hereafter, beyond the boundaries of mere reason. Narayan makes a remarkable discovery for Mehta (1962: 161): 'I find I write best when I have no burden on my mind, when I am absolutely at peace with myself.' The exclusive temperament ('absolutely at peace with myself') leads to no self-centred withdrawal. His at-oneness results in a surprising level of social participation (see Chapter 1 of this book). By the end of 1942, Narayan had come out of the ordeal. He was now able to concentrate on writing his fourth novel. Narayan turned the war constraints to his benefit. Writing to newspaper deadlines, doing freelance radio and film work, bringing out a journal, and trying his hand at the business of publishing—all this further contributed to the healing, and helped him reconnect with the world. The personality of R.K. Narayan had now acquired fullness and fine balance.[9]

He owed it all to Rajam. We owe it all to Susan Ram and N. Ram.

8

Some Eternal Scheme

The English Teacher and the Partitive Parallax[1]

To Narayan's letter of 20 June 1939 informing him of Rajam's death, Graham Greene replied promptly on 4 July. 'I don't suppose you'll write again for months, but eventually you will, not because you are just a good writer (there are hundreds), but because you are one of the finest' (Greene 2007: 97).[2] Narayan did write: *The English Teacher*.

One of the most popular of Narayan's novels, *The English Teacher* is also a victim of lopsided reception. When the novelist toured the USA, *The English Teacher* gained him a visit to Greta Garbo who, in Ved Mehta's words (1962: 152), 'took him to be a specimen of the mystic East'; as probably did Aldous Huxley, and others in the West. In contrast, the Indian response, first voiced by Srinivasa Iyengar (1962: 369–70), has generally found the 'second half' disappointing: 'Nevertheless it is difficult to feel that the first and second halves of *The English Teacher* blend naturally and make an artistic whole.'[3] Narayan responded to this 'Indian' reaction: 'That book falls in two parts [...]' (Narayan 1974: 134–5). Some novelists do feel drawn to 'explain' their own work. For Narayan, though, it was unusual; as two reports confirm: 'The first thing that became evident was that Mr Narayan belongs to that admirable company of writers who do not particularly care to talk about writing; they just get down to work' (Sio 1961: 44); and: 'Narayan does not easily enter into a discussion of motives and meaning. He is quite satisfied in having accomplished a work, without questioning the reason for its existence or expecting rewards' (S.V.V. 1963: 45). And wisely so; when a novelist attempts explanations, he may not always do justice to his own work. Narayan himself realized this difficulty later in an interview. 'He refused to admit to a connection between his own experience and that of Krishna, although the details of his marriage as recounted in his autobiography *My Days* show a clear parallel' (Croft 1983: 26). A sensible retraction; and of course only what every creative writer is entitled to.[4] Later Narayan affirms to Gowri Ramnarayan (1990: ix): '[E]very book, once written, acquired a value and integrity of its own, an organic substance and meaning, for which the author was not responsible!' With *The English Teacher* such revisionism is entirely in order.

The English Teacher is fiction, not autobiography; it is autobiographical fiction, but written some years after the experiences depicted. Consider, for example, the fact that Narayan the novelist had lived, even during the brief happy years with his wife, in a joint family. Narayan recalls in *My Days* the special attention and care received by his daughter Hema after his wife's death (1974: 136–7): that is the autobiography. Turning to the fiction, Krishna of *The English Teacher* lives in a nuclear family; and—more remarkably, after his wife's death, he stubbornly rejects any help from his family in taking care of his daughter Leela, and except for the cook, provides all the company himself.[5] Again, in real life, Narayan sensed the presence of his wife's spirit during the very first psychic sitting; Krishna of *The English Teacher* takes several sessions and much time to reach this stage. Narayan asserts (1974: 144): 'All that factual side seemed to me immaterial'; Krishna frantically looks for material evidence to support the psychic communications. All these disparities and more can be explained: by the fictional character of the English Teacher. And the fiction of the novel makes sense only when the novel's structure is analysed, not as the first half and the second, but as presenting the story of a sensitive man's self-development: linking *The English Teacher* with *The Bachelor of Arts*, a precursor, and more substantively with *Mr. Sampath* which followed.

For a novel cherished by many for its celebration of wedded love, the opening passage of *The English Teacher* is remarkable: without a trace of wife, marriage, wedded love.

I was on the whole very pleased with my day—not many conflicts and worries, above all not too much self-criticism. I had done almost all the things I wanted to do, and as a result I felt heroic and satisfied. The urge had been upon me for some days past to take myself in hand. What was wrong with me? I couldn't say, some sort of vague disaffection, a self-rebellion I might call it. The feeling again and again came upon me that as I was nearing thirty I should cease to live like a cow (perhaps, a cow, with justice, might feel hurt at the comparison), eating, working in a manner of speaking, walking, talking, etc.—all done to perfection, I was sure, but always leaving behind a sense of something missing. [...] One ought, of course, to be thankful and rest content. But such repose was not in my nature, perhaps because I was a poet, and I was constantly nagged by the feeling that I was doing the wrong work. This was responsible for a perpetual self-criticism and all kinds of things aggravated it. [...] (Narayan 1945: 1)

A fluent opening; the first-person singular narrative strikes vibrant notes at the very beginning: blending introspection and good humour with deflative rhetoric. For the first time as a novelist, Narayan is narrating the story in the first-person singular; as the focus is solely on the self, the very first word of the novel is 'I'.

The passage at once recalls *The Bachelor of Arts* and goes beyond. 'Conflicts and worries' brings up at once Chandran's 'illusions and hysterics'; and this kinship is confirmed immediately: 'The urge had been upon me for some days past to take myself in hand [...] some sort of vague disaffection, a self-rebellion I might call it [...].' We are familiar with Chandran's rebellion: from rebellion Chandran moves to self-rebellion: now, in *The English Teacher*, the hero at the very outset advances the need for self-rebellion. The novel opens with an inward movement, a marked 'self' preoccupation. 'Conscience'—a staple, especially, of Narayan's early comedy—is more articulate in this novel, stirring 'self-criticism', urging, as we shall see, for 'a remorseless self-analysis', leading gradually to an awareness, 'a sense of something missing'; and finally 'saw illumination'—the inflation, the religiosity of 'illumination' carrying just that much self-ironic exaggeration, a good-humoured undercutting, to keep our Narayan hero tethered to his worldly moorings. In the fourth novel of Narayan's early comedy, the crucial task is more than ever 'to take oneself in hand' so that one can 'cease to live like a cow'. We have thus no hint here in the opening passage of wife, marriage, or family.

A further analysis of chapter 1 only confirms this view. Krishna's priorities are: the self, his work, his family, *and* a prominent member of the family, his wife; chapter 1 introduces these: in this order.

In the first section, after the two significant opening paragraphs, there is a smooth shift of focus to his work. Krishna is a college teacher and he is not happy with his vocation ('a vague disaffection' of the first paragraph). The first section concludes with a resolve to take himself in hand, a central concern, to correct his course of routinized life devoid so far of drive and direction, marking a beginning, a move towards the ultimate self-development. The second section of the same chapter sets Krishna apart even among his colleagues, contrasting him with his fellows in the hostel, even as the first section has marked him out in English department. Krishna says, 'I want to cultivate new habits' (Narayan 1945: 4). He has already referred to himself as a poet; now giving a reason for rising early, he says: 'I want to see the sunrise.' Already and briskly underway is an elaboration of the earlier sketch of Krishna's personality. Immediately after the exhilaration of the early morning outing, the novelist takes us into Krishna's classroom. Krishna does not enjoy his work, his heart is not in it; he has no calling for this kind of teaching; and the theme of right vocation is vital in this tale of Krishna's self-development. The second section is the longest; and it presents to us Krishna implementing his resolve to take himself in hand, a restless self, openly exhibiting contempt for his job. The brewing rebellion against work for which he does not feel a vocation is again reflected in the way he stirs a rambling discussion in the staff common room. The third section of the first chapter introduces other important forces that will shape Krishna's future: his family; and a member of that family, his wife. There has been a reference to his wife (7), a casual mention; and now of the two letters here, Krishna chooses to read first the letter from his father: for the family is still the central force; besides, Krishna has not really known his wife, and the actual development of understanding and harmony of wedded love, so hypnotic—distracting to many—is yet to come. As soon as Krishna picks up his father's letter, it sets off memories of his childhood and establishes that rapport with tradition, which is achieved in Narayan's novels, especially of the early comedy, through the institution of the family. Next, the jasmine creeper in the compound of the hostel—receiving extra attention— also goes with Krishna's personality;[6] as does the humour at the expense of himself in the mirror: 'This is how, I suppose, I appear to that girl and the little one. Yet they have confidence that I shall be able to look after them and run a home!' (20). The conclusion of this section initiates action, which culminates only in the very last lines of the novel.

Krishna is a more mature Chandran. The bachelor (brahmachari) Chandran and now the householder (grihastha) Krishna: representing the first two asramas of the Hindu way of life are already introduced to us as a moral continuum. An alert restive conscience marks them. Krishna reveals its presence early enough, with characteristic good humour (7). Conscience keeps Krishna in a state of perpetual dissatisfaction with his teaching work: 'The words rang hollow in my ears [...]' (10). Conscience also keeps a tab on the progress of his vocation: poetry (47). His notebook, so lovingly made, contains, on the authority of the 'poet', a long unfinished poem on an epic scale 'to which [he] added a few dozen lines whenever [his] conscience stirred in [him]' (47–8).[7] Krishna also shares a restive temperament with Swami and Chandran—a family group with a striking genetic likeness to their author (Narayan 1974: 175): Krishna reveals a tendency to indulge in wild conjectures; his search for a house to set up his family shows this early (1945: 22–3). Krishna is prone to great agitation; he is also looking for a 'great peace' (103); he is at the same time capable of the simple joys of life: smoking a cigarette while taking an outing during the height of Susila's illness, Krishna feels, 'All this seemed to restore the *old glow of life*—its peace and tranquility' (78; emphasis mine). The 'old glow of life': of this world: not the next, not 'the other world'. The jolly rotund medium says it: 'But first rest and refreshment and then the other things of life' (123–4).

When disaster strikes, after the shock and the agony, Krishna reveals faith and resilience: 'God has given me some novel situation in life. I shall live it out alone, face the problems alone, never drag in another to do the job for me. [...] I found a peculiar satisfaction in making this resolve' (109). 'God' offers the support to carry out one's duties, personal or social, all by oneself: 'God intends me to learn these things and do them efficiently. I can't shirk it' (109). There is little religiosity, though, in this Indian novelist: 'Religion is [...] like one's underwear' (Narayan 1960: 118).[8] At the same time Krishna moves on to a more conscious philosophical awareness than Chandran: '[F]or in the contemplation of those sad scenes and hapless hours, I seemed to acquire a new peace, a new outlook; *a view of life with a place for everything*' (1945: 112; emphasis mine). Not defeatist philosophy, nor resignation: this is plenary acceptance of life—*and* death.

Though Krishna is not an 'achieved' poet, he is one by temperament. Krishna's poetic sensibility is revealed in his sensitivity and sensuousness. Pressed to explain why he wants to rise early, he says, 'I want to see the sunrise' (5): pitying his fellows still slumbering in their cozy beds he 'felt triumphant [...] when there was such glory awaiting them outside' (6).[9] Morning magic is made palpable:

The sand was damp with the morning dew, but as I buried my feet, they felt deep down the warmth of the previous day's sun. [...] I felt I was really in a new world. [...] I felt I had a new lease of life [...] but at no other time could I remember such a glow of joy as filled me now. How could I account for it? There was something in the deliberate effort, and the hour and the air, and surroundings. [...] Nature, nature, all our poets repeat till they are hoarse. There are subtle, invisible emanations in nature's surroundings: with them the deepest in us merges and harmonizes. I think it is the highest form of joy and peace we can ever comprehend. (6–7)

As of now Krishna is taken up with 'the cold water's touch on the skin, the cold air blowing on chest and face, the rumble of the river, cries of birds, magic of the morning light' (7)—involving various of the senses, these images vividly confirm the hero's resonance. Coming early in the novel this passage suggests a singular urge to integrate man and nature; developing later into acceptance of life, death, and beyond.[10]

The novelist has also planted early the jasmine creeper. 'Just to remind us that there are better things in the world, that is all [...]' (19). While 'better things in life' relates to the theme of the novel, the jasmine here is specially favoured, and not just for its fragrance: the flower is a symbol of human beauty and human striving in difficult circumstances: '[T]he only object of any beauty hereabouts. The rest of the quadrangle was mere mud, scorched by Malgudi sun' (19). The flower also anticipates the climactic reunion; for the olfactory is the operative sense in Krishna's description of his wife's place of worship in their home: 'There hung about this alcove a perpetual smell of burnt camphor and faded flowers' (37). After his wife's death, Krishna opens her phials now dried up.

These tiny phials had compressed in them the essence of her personality, and the light in her eyes, the perfume of her presence. The bottles were empty now but *the lingering scent in them covered for a brief moment the gulf between the present and the past*. I shut my eyes and dwelt in that ecstasy; and I reflected: 'Of all the senses it is smell which is the subtlest; it takes you back to the core of your existence.' (145–6)

The sense of smell can dissolve the barrier between life and the beyond. It is a piece of the jasmine garland which Krishna offers the discarnate spirit of his wife.

With this sensuous distinction goes a refined appreciation of the material world. Krishna takes to the new locality because it has 'a most satisfactory outlook aesthetically, the corn fields, which were receding in the face of the buildings, waving in sunlight [...]' (60–1). Krishna yearns to be close to nature, away from the hustle of the town: 'I had watched through this window the play of clouds and their mutation for a decade' (21). He rejects a house with 'a narrow suffocating veranda' (63). He cherishes seclusion, respects the privacy of others (24); loves a garden, even a small one, or the possibility of one (65–6). Sensitivity to places extends to the cremation ground, 'an extremely tranquil place' (106). Krishna is also alert to atmosphere. After making progress with his mind training, he observes: 'The softness of night was essentially psychic, I felt' (181). The effect is palpable even in ugly places; for example, the dirty Anderson Lane: 'Even this street looked soft in the morning light' (188). Still later, Krishna remarks at the spirit medium's place, 'the hour was as beautiful as ever' (193). When Krishna sets out with his wife on the lookout for a house: 'I was highly elated. The fresh sun, morning light, the breeze, and my wife's presence' (57); his wife is equally nature's bounty. It is not surprising that Krishna enjoys, like his creator, a flair for the veena (148); music is not functional in *The English Teacher*, as the jasmine is; music goes with Krishna's poetic sensibility.

With this kind of personality Krishna attaches much importance to letters: 'Letters are very exciting things for me' (15).[11] His diary, his memories—and mementos: memory vehicles—and material things hallowed by time—like the old clock—are precious personal effects in *The English Teacher*. But letters above all: 'It was an unwritten law existing between us; whenever we were parted we wrote to each other on alternate days, and when we met again, I took back from her all the letters, bundled them up and offered to destroy them, but she always protested and I just kept them with me' (132). In real life Rajam was a negligent letter-writer; in the novel, however, Susila not only maintains the contract meticulously, she values the records.

The intensities of *The English Teacher* in general impress us; for no other novel of Narayan's, except *The Dark Room*, presents as starkly the plight of 'helpless humanity'. The lyrical temper is reflected in the language of the novel, its astonishing abundance, for Narayan, of imagery; Narayan casts aside his characteristic restraint, pulls out all the stops: readers in India and abroad have loved it. Apart from 'joy', the unique ideals for Krishna are 'peace' and 'harmony'. The poetry of this 'poet' culminates ultimately in his 'aspiration, striving and joy' (147), a fulfilment of the promise of the opening paragraphs of the novel. The exquisite climax of the novel is entirely in character: 'It was a moment of rare, immutable joy [...]' (213); the final movement is definitive, comedic.

The point is made on the very first page, in the very first paragraph of the novel: 'I was constantly nagged by the feeling that I was doing the wrong work.'[12] The 'right vocation' for Krishna is writing poetry, while living his life, like all early heroes, to the brim of one's personality and personal relationships. Not enough poetry gets written, but the preoccupation sets Krishna apart from the beginning from such other teachers as the logic lecturer whom Krishna pities for having 'a straight-forward literal mind', and Gajapathy 'with his loyalty of a lifetime to English language and literature' (13–14).

Writing 'about fifty lines of verse' on nature to his satisfaction, Krishna feels he has 'discharged a duty assigned to [him] in *some eternal scheme*' (8; emphasis mine). Earlier the need for affinity with nature has been affirmed, and its reality; now the scope of this affinity is defined: 'some eternal scheme'. Poetry, too, fits into the macro scheme. An awareness of its true magnitude, man's place and

THE ENGLISH TEACHER AND THE PARTITIVE PARALLAX | 79

role in Narayan's universe, will be further defined in Narayan's next novel *Mr. Sampath*; meanwhile, poetry in this novel represents the urge to make serious sense of one's life; it leads to disaffection with one's routinized work. This aspiration propels, in tandem with the dynamic of wedded love, self-development of Krishna.

Krishna at work is an unhappy spirit, until his wife's death makes his job unbearable. Krishna's professional disaffection leads to discovery of his vocation.

Krishna meets with a curious character, the headmaster. Vividly described (141), an idealist of such eccentricity, he surprises us by appearing in Narayan—until we remember that Narayan himself was an 'eccentric'—a rebel refusing to take up a routine job because he held dear the literary ideal. Krishna knows from the beginning: 'I had a feeling that I was about to make a profound contact in life' (142).[13] The headmaster 'had the abstraction of a mystic rather than of a maniac' (184). The new influence is soon felt; Krishna talks to his senior teacher Gajapathy more openly about literary studies (171). The headmaster asks what, for Krishna, is *the* question: 'But do you think you are happy in your work there?' (184). The discovery of vocation is a slow, gradual, but sure process for this Narayan hero. Watching the tiny tots, 'all sense of loneliness ceased to oppress, and I felt a deep joy and contentment stirring within me. I felt there was nothing more for me to demand of life' (203–4). To the puzzled Englishman he explains: 'It doesn't please my innermost self' (207); and adds: 'Of all persons on earth, I can afford to do what seems to me work, something which satisfies my innermost aspiration […]' (207–8).[14] That sounds of course like Narayan himself.

A proper alignment, at last, of the private and the public is achieved in Krishna's search for the right vocation. Krishna has discovered what he wants from life; not turning away from society, life, but discovering both afresh; not disillusioned dissociation, but elementary engagement. Krishna gives up his job,

> not with a feeling of sacrifice for a national cause, but with a very selfish purpose. I'm seeking a great inner peace. I find I can't attain it unless I withdraw from the adult world and adult work into the world of children. And there, let me assure you, is a vast storehouse of peace and harmony. I have not had in mind anything more than that […]. (211)

Wedded love is the other dynamic in Krishna's life. This theme of love in marriage has contributed greatly to the popularity of *The English Teacher*, and not just in India (see Somerset Maugham in Ram and Ram 1996a: 409). When we view the matter a little more closely, we realize the need to further deglamorize this theme: in *The English Teacher* wedded love is more meaningful as a family relationship; that is, wedded love without a show of sexuality; and that should have been one more factor operating against the novel's popularity; but it has not: obviously because of the uncommon beauty of family relationships in the novel—matrimony being one among them—all lit up by human warmth and restrained grace.

Krishna gets an early hint of his own importance in the family structure from his father's letter (1945: 17).[15] 'I felt I was someone whose plans and determinations were of the utmost importance to others' (19). Krishna himself looks forward to it: 'My dear wife will see that the proper light comes at the proper angle' (20). The quip does not diminish Krishna's longing for his family; this yearning is entirely justified in the context of the family values realized in the novel. For others in the family, too, are responsive. Mother's attention to father, parents' concern for the daughter—we are of course familiar by now with the strength of personal and family relationships in Narayan's early comedy. In *The English Teacher* family relationships inspire and support the hero's own inner development.

The father-in-law, 'rather unorthodox in his speech and habits' (91), also plays the role of a father (91). This family elder also has a role natural to him as a grandparent: 'I believe in spoiling children; who should be spoilt if not children?' (91). (That again sounds more like Narayan himself.) Certain attachments in this world call for special deference. Krishna's mother-in-law calls in an exorcist to cure Susila: Krishna says: '[He] had to be silent because [he] couldn't argue with [his] mother-in-law, and [he] was uncertain how it would be viewed by Swamiji' (93).[16] Urged by Krishna, even the headmaster, in spite of his pronounced disaffection for his wife, says: '[My] last night. I should like to spend it with my wife and children' (186). Krishna returns home from his farewell function: 'Carrying a garland to a lonely house—a dreadful job' (211). The loneliness of course is caused not by the absence of one, but two dear ones: his wife first, and his daughter as well.

Family ties make inevitable the comedic conclusion of Krishna's tale of loneliness; the roles played, especially, by three members of his family who sustain, inspire, and keep him on course.

Krishna's mother represents wholesome tradition we are familiar with by now in *The Bachelor of Arts* and *The Dark Room*. Though the mother in *The Bachelor of Arts* is traditional, she is still a resident of Malgudi, a townswoman: Krishna's mother is rooted in the village, with a pronounced rural authenticity to her traditional way of life. In the first chapter Narayan evokes her milieu: '[A]ll the facts—home, coconut-garden, harvest, "revenue demand"' (17); 'revenue demand' is a typical Narayan touch, balancing the evocation: but that is the wellspring of her values and a tradition of housekeeping, even 'a house-keeping philosophy'. Mother is the homemaker. 'The essence of her existence consisted in the thrills and pangs and the satisfaction that she derived in running *a well-ordered household*' (28–9; emphasis mine). Krishna recollects his mother's indispensable role in taking care of the children in the family (18). Such memories help Krishna accept with assurance his own role as the father of a motherless child—because his mother will be there to support.[17] Presently, Krishna's mother lays the 'foundation' for his home. 'A well-ordered household' is of primary importance in the world of R.K. Narayan's early comedy, a positive life-supporting base, somewhat like the International Space Station to the astronaut 'taking a walk' in deep space. The 'house-keeping philosophy' is of course unmodern (29); and his wife Susila benefits. Of course 'the elder daughter-in-law does not fancy this kind of expert or expertise (30); Narayan thus slips in a contrast to the more traditional Susila. Krishna's own approval of Susila, more so his approval of his mother's traditional strengths and value, are made obvious. 'They had constant contact after that, and with every effort Susila came out better burnished than before [...]' (30). The image is rather solid, but the sentiment is palpable; for the mother's traditionalism is radiant with warmth. Her reception of her daughter-in-law and the baby is a blend of custom and spontaneity: 'After that she held out her arms, and the baby vanished in her embrace' (35). The remark is suggestive: the tradition will be passed on. 'I was moved by the extraordinary tenderness which appeared in her face' (35). All three—Susila, Krishna, and the child Leela—benefit from

Krishna's mother. Susila even adopts certain tricks of economy from her mother-in-law.[18] His mother's care and aid, readily given, help Krishna bear up the bereavement. After Susila's death Krishna's mother plays a critical role; she takes over the care and responsibility of the child.

Krishna's mother means more than her maternal instincts: she seems to restore for a moment 'one's sense of security, the solid factors of life, and its warmth and interests' (197). This is a key passage in *The English Teacher*, a novel that dramatizes human loss, grief, and loneliness; the mother, however conservative and tradition bound, represents one of the positive factors, even a recuperative force. The 'solid' factors of life signify life's attractions before his wife's death, chief among them being family relationships; overflowing into 'its warmth and interests' they also represent the impact of Krishna's recent discoveries in the psychic realm: Krishna's mother embodies for him all that life means, past, present, and future, all that makes life not just tolerable, keeping at bay human loneliness, bereavement; the old lady makes his life enjoyable once again. Krishna's response to his mother is a clear indication of his emotional recovery. And: '[T]he child bloomed with a new life, under her handling. She ceased to approach me for company or help' (200). The child can 'have her own life' if she lives with her grandmother in her traditional milieu in the village; that is the ultimate tribute to this tradition-bound old lady. Now Krishna can turn to his psychic development.[19] Harrex (1977: 56–7, vol. 1) has observed perceptively: '[I]t appears that the most accomplished novelists to date are essentially tradition-oriented sensibilities, and that even among the committed writers tradition, artistically speaking, need not be destructively incompatible with social realism.'

The outstanding influence in Krishna's life is Susila. Presented through the eyes of the poet-husband, her personality comes through vividly and with irresistible charm. She is introduced in the first chapter, though in absentia; we sense her before we see her. 'I smelt my wife's letter before opening it. It carried with it the fragrance of her trunk [...]' (18). A sensuous entry, which places Susila on a level of high refinement. Krishna's preference for the jasmine, we know, predates his marriage; and when Susila comes, she is surrounded by a mild jasmine smell. The very first glimpse of

Susila makes the point. 'I saw her sitting serenely in her seat with the baby lying on her lap' (33). The portrait is touched up later, when Susila offers to be the subject of a poem: 'Just move a little to your left please. [...] Don't drop your lovely eyelashes so much. You make me forget my task. Ah, now, don't grin please [...]' (48–9). A cameo of elegance, refined sentiment: from Narayan, a love poet of rare delicacy.[20] Coming through the lover's eyes, her feminine charm still makes its impact: '[L]ike a vision, clad in her indigo sari, and hair gleaming and jasmine covered' (55). Later we also see an extraordinary team spirit: 'She took sides with me in all my discussions and partisanships, and hated everyone I hated and respected anyone I respected' (38). The world of these 'lovers', complete and whole, is hermetically closed; and this mutual sufficiency is threatened by Susila's illness. Krishna's reports are insistent (74, 77, 84, 89); with love's affirmation, even in sickness: 'It kept me so close to my wife that it produced an immense satisfaction in my mind' (89).

Death only results in love's renewal. During the first meeting with his wife's spirit, Krishna confesses: 'My heart choked with the questions still unasked [...]' (131). That is a verb too vehement for Narayan; Krishna–Narayan is made for it. At a later sitting he tells her: 'I can't throw out the tiniest speck that belongs to you' (134). He protests: 'How can I help having you as the background to my thoughts?' (176): that again sounds like the primacy of first love. The psychic communion is arranged by Susila: 'She is eager to communicate with her husband' (129). The helpers report at their 'first meeting' with Krishna: 'She is very much excited and she is also not able to recollect her thoughts easily [...]' (130). At once Krishna recalls their 'first viewing', the girl-viewing customary in traditional families before the alliance is finalized. The flashback is well timed. Though Krishna is only in the presence of his wife's spirit, it is bride-viewing all over again. Susila's discarnate spirit confides with love's empathy: 'Perhaps it may look like selfishness for me to be so happy here when there you are so sorrow-filled and unhappy [...]' (147). Shared joy, shared sorrow; mutuality is all this extraordinary love story is about: for consideration and concern for the other continues to the end of the story; when finally Krishna manages to realize a 'reunion' with his wife Susila, she comes to him thoughtfully dressed: '"Yes, I always wear this when I come to you. I know you like it very much," she said' (212–13).

The reunion at the end is in fact their marriage all over again—now of the 'lovers': 'The boundaries of our personalities suddenly dissolved' (213). They are married for eternity. And are in love. Krishna offers the garland to her spirit: 'For you as ever' (213). That is the motto of this love story.

The appeal of *The English Teacher*, especially to Indian readers, lies elsewhere as well: it presents a middle-class paradise. The very daily routine (36–8) is the staple of middle-class lives; Krishna discovers 'an autocratic strain in her nature in these matters and unsuspected depths of rage' (39). The dreams and plans, too, are middle class (60); even thrift. Krishna teaches her; he also learns from her. There are other joys of middle-class husbandry. 'She was very proud of her list. It was precise' (42). When the groceries arrive, '[s]he always waited for them at the door with unconcealed enthusiasm' (42). As the month progresses she keeps an expert eye on the containers: '[L]ike a technician watching an all-important meter at a power house' (42–3). Krishna pays attention to his wife's philosophy of housekeeping: and practice: 'She kept a watch over every rupee as it arrived, and never let it depart lightly, and as far as possible tried to end its career in the savings bank' (46).[21] Susila makes sense to every middle-class wife: 'We must live within our means, and save enough'; reflecting a middleclass concern, she cautions her husband: 'And remember there is a daughter for whose marriage we must save' (46). The image of Susila as a woman, too, is middle class. We have already seen Krishna's mother taking to Susila and training her. When Krishna tells Susila, 'I don't like you to spend all your time cooking either tiffin or food,' she retorts, '[b]ut I like it. What is wrong in it?' (44). Even after her death Susila sends, at the very first meeting, a familiar message: 'The lady wants to say that she is as deeply devoted to her husband and child and the family as ever' (131). At another meeting, Susila's spirit says: 'I come to meet my lord and I dress myself as befits the occasion' (149).[22] In one respect alone, Susila is surprisingly ahead of her time—in opting for the small family norm (46).[23]

Religion is integral to the ethos. The religious spirit may be an expression of something deeper: 'She seemed to have a deep secret

THE ENGLISH TEACHER AND THE PARTITIVE PARALLAX | 85

life' (37): anticipating her astral phase later. On the fateful day of their house hunting, the trip—their last—is concluded satisfactorily with a visit to a temple.

In this flickering light the image acquired strange shadows and seemed to stir, and make a movement to bless—I watched my wife. She opened her eyes for a moment. They caught the light of the camphor flame, and shone with an unearthly brilliance. Her cheeks glowed, the rest of her person was lost in the shadows of the temple hall. Her lips were moving in prayer. I felt transported at the sight of it. (70)[24]

The chiaroscuro and high close-up had probably come from Narayan's stint in Gemini Studios; but the scene foregrounds the writer's faith.[25]

After her death, the Helpers convey a message: 'The lady sends her love and prayers for her husband and child' (143). It is a world of 'love' *and* 'prayers'. In a seance Susila sums it up: 'Worshipping and wondering, how much life's journey is made easier for one who can see nature and God every moment!' (175). Life is poetry and piety, wonder and worship, nature and God. That is the essence of *The English Teacher*; and of post-Rajam R.K. Narayan.

After Susila's death, all the members of the family play their respective roles, but none more fetching than his little daughter, Leela. When we first hear of Susila we also hear of the child; the only time we see the couple together and alone, without the child's presence, is at the end: a unique feature of a novel popular for its tale of wedded love; but by then the child's role has been fulfilled.

Krishna's first feelings for the infant are mixed. 'I no doubt felt a mild affection for it, but there was nothing compelling or indispensable about it' (18). A realistic beginning to a unique bonding; the relationship between a young father and his only child, this familial affection is just one ascending curve, without 'first' and 'second' parts. In the first letter Susila writes to her husband more about the child than about anything else. The child is already and naturally the medium of the message Susila is sending to her husband: establish our home. When Susila arrives, she 'talk[s] incessantly about the habits of the infant' (35). Soon the child shows results: she brings the daughter-in-law and the mother-in-law together:

'The child seemed to be their meeting point, and immediately established a great understanding and harmony between them' (35). The child is a catalyst of harmony; she occupies a special place in the family. Children make all the difference in Narayan's early comedy. Witness the drama of *The Dark Room*; they are the driving force in Savitri's life and pull her back from exile. In *The English Teacher* the child keeps Krishna from succumbing to grief after his wife's death. The child's therapeutic role begins even during her mother's illness. As the illness distances Susila, the child Leela moves closer to her father. Susila's sickness foregrounds Leela's normality (90). Leela, like any normal child, manages an easy natural transference of affections from mother to father and later to grandmother. Now life's recuperative force sets to work. The very opening paragraph of the next chapter makes this clear. Krishna opts for sole charge of his daughter, a deliberate and meaningful decision. Life's resiliencies are ever at work in Narayan's novels: '[B]ut our nature adapts itself to circumstances with wonderful speed' (108). We have just seen the first suggestion of the healing process in which the child plays a critical role. 'I slipped into my double role with great expertness' (108). The results show: 'I had to keep her cheerful and keep myself cheerful too lest she should feel unhappy' (108). The child takes Krishna out of his grief-stricken self: 'I made it a point to take the child wherever I went, except the college' (109). Instead of declining into self-centred morbidity, debilitated by grief, Krishna now takes the child in hand. 'Her eyes looked like a pair of dark butterflies dancing with independent life [...]' (114). Leela is a natural phenomenon to her father: she wields nature's magical healing. Life's autonomy or value could not have been conveyed better to the reader: 'dancing with independent life'. The chapter, mainly devoted to Krishna's spiritual convalescence, focuses on the father–child relationship because it is the child who is mainly responsible for Krishna's initial recovery. Family triumphs once again in Narayan. The chapter ends as it begins: with the child. 'It seemed a noble and exciting occupation—*the sole responsibility for a growing creature*' (115–16; emphasis mine). Leela not only keeps her father afloat; like her mother, she tacks him on to the mainstream of life again. After all, she is 'a miniature version of her mother' (140). A stage comes when the father confesses: 'I had never been separated from her; the thought appalled me' (201).

The English Teacher is a classic comedy involving universals like aspiration, sorrow, happiness won and lost, and joy achieved: of triumph over death and grief and loneliness. All elements relate to the centre of the fiction: Krishna's self-development. Integration, not reconciliation, is the ultimate goal in this novel. The reaching out takes the form of a dual development here: the discovery of right vocation is simultaneous with mind training for psychic reunion with his wife's spirit. Krishna's search from the very beginning is for 'a harmonious existence'; for life here and now. Ultimately harmony is quite simply a life devoid of 'illusions and hysterics'. The novelist takes particular care to focus on the here while presenting the hereafter: Krishna seeks meaning, purpose in life, in this life. And he achieves it.

The mind is the central interest in the early comedy, collateral with the self. Krishna's psychic success is the culmination of his mind training. Though the beginning is notionally made in the very first chapter of the novel, the best part of it is achieved only after Susila's death. The necessary guidance is given by his wife; we witness a role reversal; throughout the early years of their wedded life Krishna treats her as a 'child' and teaches her—even poetry; now after her death Krishna becomes and even feels like a pupil, 'felt really like a child' (133), and even notices a 'touch of reprimand' (178). A point comes when Susila's spirit cautions him that his attitude now 'borders on worship' (183). Then there is the yogic practice, sadhana. Though the terms are not used Krishna goes through a course of psychic training: dharana, dhyana, and samadhi (concentration, meditation, and the highest level of meditation). The struggle is long and agonizing, but human spirit triumphs and the goal is reached. Susila's spirit trains the pupil, first in cleansing his mind of the grief, a corrosive emotion; and second, in overcoming rigidity and achieving resiliency of the mind. It is a thorough reorientation involving a new 'attitude to death', a 'new habit of thinking' (199). The English Teacher is a miracle story: the miracle is of the human spirit, learning to 'embrace life as a whole', integrating life, death, and thereafter.

The stylistic conduct of *The English Teacher*, too, merits notice. No other novel of Narayan's employs imagery as much as *The English Teacher*; we note an unusual frequency of images in the early happy chord, followed by a dry spell, before the imagery is revived with the psychic contact, climaxing on the last page in a cloudburst.[26]

The ultimate dividend of this extraordinary book Narayan himself identifies: '[A]nd literature as usual enriches life, so that after being written about even death appears somewhat softened' (Narayan 1997: 210).

9
Enchantment in Life
Mr. Sampath[1] and the Naipaul Enigma

> *Only for the Gita improvement in the individual nature
> is the way to social betterment.*
> — S. Radhakrishnan (1993: 96)
>
> *Because we take to novels our own ideas of what we feel they must offer,
> we often find, in unusual or original work, only what we expect to find,
> and we reject or miss what we aren't looking for.*
> —V.S. Naipaul (1979: 25)

The first critical question on *Mr. Sampath* is: does Narayan identify totally with Srinivas? And, the second: what is the novelist up to in *Mr. Sampath*? Facts of the fiction offer surprising answers; for *Mr. Sampath* is the culmination of Narayan's pre-Independence novels.

After the death of his wife Narayan received psychic and spiritual guidance from Dr Paul Brunton; Narayan fictionalized his psychic development from the training in *The English Teacher* (see Chapter 7 in this book). However, psychic powers—even union with the spirit of one's beloved—are ultimately unimportant in the larger context of the self: to 'still the restless mind' is only a means; for the supreme goal is to 'understand one's real self' (Narayan 1974: 149); a consistent engagement in yogic training could have no other goal. Thematically, the early comedy has been progressing towards this central interest; this perennial priority culminates in *Mr. Sampath*.

Mr. Sampath is the story of Srinivas: Srinivas comes to Malgudi, gets involved with various people and matters, and when enough is enough, devotes himself to what he now realizes to be his proper goals. Though the narrative focus generally follows Srinivas's fortunes, Mr Sampath, too, appeals to our imagination, like Falstaff in *Henry IV*. *Mr. Sampath* presents two foci, with different degrees of intellectual and emotional appeal. Narayan's narrative technique achieves a complex authorial attitude to both the central characters. This dualism is suggested at the very beginning of the novel. After *The English Teacher*, the opening passage of *Mr. Sampath* presents a remarkably different style.

Unless you had an expert knowledge of the locality you would not reach the offices of *The Banner*. The Market Road was the lifeline of Malgudi, *but* it had a tendency to take abrupt turns and disrupt itself into side-streets, which wove a network of crazy lanes behind the facade of buildings on the main road.

Kabir Lane was one such; *if* you took an inadvertent turn off the Market Road you entered it, *though* you might not if you intended to reach it. And then it split itself further into a first lane, a second lane and so on; *if* you kept turning left and right you were suddenly assailed by the groans of the treadle in the Truth Printing Works; and from its top floor a stove-enamelled blue board shot out over the street bearing the sign 'The Banner.'

It was the home of truth and vision, *though* you might take time to accept the claim. You climbed a flight of wooden stairs (more a ladder), and its last rung was the threshold of *The Banner*. It was a good deal better than most garrets: you wouldn't knock your head on roof-tiles *unless* you hoisted yourself on a table; you could still see something of the sky through the northern window and hear the far-off rustle of the river, although the other three windows opened on the courtyards of tenement houses below. [...] (1949: 5; emphasis mine)

We may begin with two stylistic features of the first three paragraphs of *Mr. Sampath*, which set up the 'scene'. First, we are struck by the complex syntactical choice, so different from the direct and open earnestness of the first paragraph of *The English Teacher*; this point will be discussed later. Second, a minor stylistic element is the verbs in the passage; we note that nearly all of them are transitive, of energetic action and mostly in the active voice: 'take' (abrupt turns); 'disrupt'; 'wove'; 'split'; 'were assailed'; 'shot out' (phrasal verb); 'climbed'; (to) 'knock'; 'hoisted'. Their family likeness attracts us; they present a forceful similarity—and we realize only later they are all in a way premonitory: the palpable animation of the verbs anticipates the rare energies that the main characters in the novel display, their misdirected activities, wasteful, self-destructive. *Mr. Sampath* dramatizes rampant guna energies, largely blighted.

The other major stylistic feature we note is the syntactical choice: a good proportion of the sentences in the opening passage are complex, and with subordinate adverbial clauses. The adverbial clause is grammatically more sophisticated than the other kinds; here in the opening passage we 'experience' the subtler kinds: the conditional and the concessional clauses; and in the third paragraph quoted earlier, in a uniform position following the main clause. Looking back we realize that the syntactic strategy achieves an engaging rhetoric: a fairly factual statement of the main clause, which would remain straightforward if left alone, is tactically undermined by the conditional or concessional clause: the result of such structuring is a soft-spoken, gently witty undercutting of the main predication. When the construction is repeated several times in succession, the overall effect is of a stylistic twinkle in the authorial eye, forewarning ambiguity, unpredictability; and it is the central character of the novel who is introduced in the passage.

This device of identification squared up by authorial disengagement soon establishes itself as a narrative tactic in the novel. The narrator's presence becomes so palpable, and so pervasively established that we sense the significance of the author-narrator in *Mr. Sampath* who makes sufficiently clear at the very outset his liberty to commit himself or not commit himself to the ways and values of the hero. Unlike in a first-person narrative, there is to be little confusion of subject and object. In *The English Teacher*, the authorial voice formally merges with the narrator's; in *Mr. Sampath* there is a dual presence, of the hero and of the narrator. The pliable point of view in *Mr. Sampath* achieves detachment or identification as the fictive need arises; it is a variable point of view, landing unwary readers in confusion.

This creative ambivalence points to a moral pluralism in *Mr. Sampath*. The narrative focus is the intellectual Srinivas; but the emotional centre of the novel is Mr Sampath: Srinivas, the sadhaka, may not regret the departure of Sampath at the end, but we do.

As the narrator of *Mr. Sampath* forewarns us at the very beginning, neither Srinivas nor Sampath monopolizes the values dramatized by its fiction; neither is rejected at the same time, because each represents more than himself; they are two different psychological types, the introvert and the extrovert; in Hindu parlance, two strands of human quality, the sattvic and the rajasic; two worlds of man, the idealistic and the worldly: already introducing to us Narayan's post-Independence comedy rich with the 'hectic' gunas, the rajasic and the tamasic. As the title of the novel confirms, however, the heart has reasons unsuspected by the intellect; Sampath turns out to be the creative writer's delight, the 'discovery' of the novel. Not Sampath, but Mr Sampath.

While the opening passage of *Mr. Sampath* suggests a subtle authorial distancing to the central character, its images present the two worlds of the novel, of Srinivas and of Mr Sampath; and more, a contraposition is implied that is apparently irreconcilable.

The very location of Srinivas's office is significant. Beginning with the Market Road, 'the life-line of Malgudi', we are led into its side streets 'which wove a network of crazy lanes behind the facade of buildings on the main road' (5). The Market Road and the 'crazy lanes'—in sync with the energetic abundance of the verbs—have already launched one of the two worlds: the world of Sampath. Besides the shenanigans of the miserly landlord, and of Sampath and the 'zany' world of the cinema studio, one of its residents will suffer a mental breakdown before the end of the novel: the Market Road is the *life line* of Malgudi, its *side streets* weave a network of *crazy lanes*. The elevation of the *Banner*, too, is remarkable: it is a garret, high above the madding lanes and you have to climb a flight of wooden stairs which the novelist parenthetically and reductively describes as 'more a ladder'; and equally: 'its last rung was the threshold of *The Banner*', a distinction of some dubiousness.

This is not all.

We are now offered redeeming features of the cramped premises: '[Y]ou could still see something of the sky through the northern window and hear the far-off rustle of the river' (5). Aligned for us here are three more images—the garret, the sky, and the river: representing the world of the *Banner*, the world of Srinivas. And almost in the same breath, the novelist offers another striking image of the 'other' world: '[T]he other three windows opened on the courtyards of tenement houses below'; the residents of these tenements are described as 'the dwellers below' (5). At the same time segregation is suggested: '[N]o one would open these windows and volunteer to behold the spectacle below' (5–6). The world of Srinivas considers the world below too low for its notice. Thus, we already have two groups of images arrayed differentially: the elevated office of the *Banner* which is the garret with, at a distance, the sky and the river, as against the courtyard of tenement houses 'below' and the 'dwellers below' as well as the Market Road, with its crazy lanes.

Srinivas himself regrets the divide. Back home, surrounded by the 'dwellers below', our hero muses: '"I wish I could do all my writing here," he said to himself again and looked forlornly about him [...] all the nerve-racked neighbours and their children were asleep' (7). The earlier 'dwellers below' are now identified as the residents of Anderson Lane, one of the 'crazy lanes'; and more specifically, 'all the nerve-racked neighbours and their children'. Srinivas, of the world of the garret, the values of which are associated with the two striking images of 'sky' and 'river', is growing aware of the limitations of his world, distanced from the world 'below', of his neighbours, fellow citizens, fellows; he longs now to be closer to the earth, than be nearer the sky.

The images recur at the beginning of chapter 2. After a hard bout of work, Srinivas rises, throws the proofs below to the printer, and: '[Srinivas] paused for a moment at the northern window, looking at a patch of blue sky, and turned away' (30). This seeker-editor is attempting to present a spiritual message 'in terms of actual experience' (31). Looking for the right thoughts:

[H]e roamed his little attic, round and round *like a sleep-walker*, paused at the farthest window to listen to *the rumble of Sarayu*. It seemed ages since he had gone to the river. He resolved to remedy this lapse very soon. When he came to the window he could hear *the uproar emanating from the tenements below*—he always spent a few minutes listening to *the medley of voices*. He wished he could open the window and take a look at *the strife below, just to see what exactly was troubling them* [...]. (31; emphasis mine)[2]

From contraposition—rather derisory—at the beginning we have moved to juxtaposition, natural, fairly wistful, in sympathetic coexistence: the sky, the river, *and* the tenements below with their medley of voices; the rumble of Sarayu *and* the uproar emanating from the tenements below. The wish of the editor of the lofty *Banner* is going to be more than fulfilled: not only is the 'sleep-walker' going to wake up and 'see' the world below, he will be drawn into its 'maze'.

Mr. Sampath is the drama of interaction between the worlds represented by two human groups, two configurations of gunas; the thematic ambivalence affirms that neither the Market Road and its crazy lanes alone nor the river alone matters. But together they make sense; from a contraposition at the beginning we move to, not juxtaposition, but a yearning for allied values: even a coalescence. This is confirmed by the progression of the imagery through the novel.

Consider first the Market Road: a tiny restaurant on the Market Road opens early enough for Srinivas to get his first cup of coffee (18). After the closure of the *Banner* it is at the big square in the Market Road that Srinivas as editor and Sampath as printer part ways. Soon the landmark unfolds fine value: liberated from his editorial duties after the collapse of the *Banner,* Srinivas 'discovers' that the Market Road offers him something more nourishing than a cup of coffee. What for Narayan is an 'extensive' description follows; but it is not a set piece: coming through the eyes of Srinivas it is a revelation—of what, we are told next: 'It was as if he were breathing in *the free air of the town* for the first time, *for the first time opening his eyes to its atmosphere.* He suddenly realized what *a lot he had missed in life and for so long, cooped up in that room.* "The death of a journal has compensations," he reflected' (79–80; emphasis mine).

Srinivas identifies the Market Road with life—and not just 'life at this hour'; and the humble details of the description make sense as representing life of the mundane world, 'the free air of the town'. 'Free' is 'emancipated': a critical change is already taking place in Srinivas's outlook. Consider his very next thoughts: 'He toyed with the idea of going to the river. "I had nearly forgotten the existence of the river"' (80). No longer contraposed, the two images cohere. Life in the Market Road, 'free air', is as attractive as the river.

A major development takes place now. Srinivas hails a jutka. The novelist devotes almost three pages to the commonplace act of hiring and travelling in a humble horse carriage. The episode, no doubt, reveals Srinivas's inability to cope with a common dweller from the world below; it also helps self-discovery: 'He felt surprised at his own indignation' (81). More remarkable is the jutka man himself. With the realism that characterizes Narayan's treatment of the world below in the pre-Independence novels, the humble creature is closely observed (80). The lowly animal 'limping along' and its master 'with nothing over his brown body' are both caught in the heat of the noonday sun—one cannot think of a better evocation of the world of the 'dwellers below'. But the novelist develops a revealing association. 'Somehow the sight of the hirsute, rough-looking driver gave him a feeling of permanence and stability in life—the sort of sensation engendered by the sight of an old banyan tree or a rock' (82).

Realism and poetry are allied again. We recall that in the previous novel, *The English Teacher*, it is the mother who evokes similar feelings in the sensitive hero: the old lady symbolizes the 'solid factors of life' (Narayan 1945: 197). Srinivas has descended from the lofty heights of the *Banner* and entered the world of 'dwellers below', a world now discovered to be rich with value. The realignment, the reorientation continues. As Srinivas approaches Sampath's locality: '[O]ne seemed able to see the blue sky for the first time here. "What a lovely area!" Srinivas exclaimed' (Narayan 1949: 83). Of course Sampath lives here 'in the backyard in an outhouse'. The association of an image of the other world with Sampath himself is not accidental. The river, too, gets its turn. Srinivas is put in a car by Sampath and driven to the studio for the first time, opening a new, fateful, chapter in the life of the two major characters. On the way, at this crucial juncture, Srinivas observes the river:

People were relaxing on the sands, children played about, the evening sun threw slanting rays on the water. A few bullock wagons and villagers were crowding at the crossing [...] and the wheels of the taxi splashed up the water and drenched them. Srinivas peeped out and wished that his friend would put them down there and go forward. He was seized with a longing to sit down on the edge of the river, dip his feet in it, and listen to its rumble in the fading evening light. But the Chevrolet carried him relentlessly on. [...] (90)

The Chevrolet carries him 'relentlessly on', however, to the studio; but the river is now hallowed by the association of common everyday life, children, pedestrians, and bullock carts; the focus is on bustling life of the Market Road as well as on the 'rumble in the fading evening light'.

'The tenements below' cannot be ignored either. Srinivas reads out his story of the Burning of Kama to the studio bosses, Sampath, Somu, and De Mello. 'As darkness gathered around his room and voices rose from the tenements below he became lost in his own narration; his listeners seemed to him just shadows' (129). Now 'the voices from the tenements below' are no chance presence. Srinivas's vision has to fulfil itself and make sense only in the context of the 'tenements below' and the world they represent, this world.

The images are gathered together only after the studio debacle; but we are recalled, from time to time, to the river and the sky and Market Road. Sitting in the studio for the rehearsals to begin, Srinivas waits. 'Through the window he could see far off Sarayu winding its way, glimmering in the sun, the leaves of trees on its bank throwing off tiny reflections of the sun, and a blue sky beyond, and further away the tower of the municipal office, which reminded him of his *Banner*' (137). The 'medley' of sounds and voices, river and the sky, as also the *Banner* will have to, not just coexist, but ally, and coalesce: Srinivas realizes, now, that the trouble with his journal lies in its having been removed too far from this world; Srinivas's wife confirms it later.

Market Road, already representing the attractions of life, makes its presence felt more and more now. It is on this busy thoroughfare, but at a quiet late hour (160) that Srinivas takes the decision to refrain from warning Ravi: the road is almost deserted on this occasion, but '[t]he sky was full of stars'. After Ravi is locked up in a cell in the Market Road police station, Srinivas tries to feed him, 'as the Market Road babble continued outside' (194). The 'babble' is a constant, an elevated 'medley'. When Sampath comes to visit him at the same police station they sit in Sampath's car parked in the Market Road and talk. 'The babble of the market place kept

MR. SAMPATH AND THE NAIPAUL ENIGMA | 97

a continuous background to their talk' (194). Srinivas appeals to Sampath to withdraw the case against Ravi; and Sampath obliges. But that is not the end of the episode.

> The inspector followed them to the door. He said: 'I used to read your *Banner* with great interest. What has happened to it?' This was a piece of encouragement from a most unexpected quarter. Srinivas stood arrested like a man recovering a lost memory. Traffic was passing, policemen were walking in and out with their boot-nails clanking on the hard stone floor. [...] Srinivas stood looking at the point of light in the inspector's belt-buckle, which caught a ray of light from the shop opposite. [...] The groan of a man in custody was feebly heard [...]. (196)

Especially attractive is the 'point of light in the inspector's belt-buckle'; it is a glimmer of great hope for Srinivas: from a most unexpected source. And that 'groan' there—quietly resonant with terror—tempers the optimism. Now perhaps it is apt that the journal should get a break through a police inspector—and against the babble of the Market Road. For, not the least of the *Banner*'s attractions is its social relevance, arising out of a concern with this world here and now, of fellow, fallible, humans. Srinivas is delighted. 'Srinivas felt that he had got back his enchantment in life' (197).[3] It is 'enchantment in life', not fascination with the next; this life, made richer by this world, that makes sense for Srinivas—and for R.K. Narayan.

Now 'Srinivas turned his back on Kabir Lane without a sigh' (199). And 'no life stirred there'; from the loftiness of the garret in Kabir Lane, the *Banner* '[n]ow emerged from an office in Market Road itself' (197). When Srinivas meets with Sampath for a final chat, they pass through the Market Road—'Traffic flowed past them'—and they reach the river. 'Srinivas left [Sampath] alone and listened to the murmur of the river and the distant, muffled roar of the town' (216). In one smooth stroke the novelist indicates the change that has come about in his hero's vision: the river and the town, the murmur and the muffled roar, together make sense, make for a full life: the muffled roar certainly sounds conclusive. Srinivas does not withdraw to a hermetic world; Srinivas goes back to his *Banner*—'Tomorrow is press day' (219). *The Banner* and its editor make sense: both are richer for the acceptance of the world and engagement with their society. This is the ambience and spirit of R.K. Narayan's early comedy.

Distancing has been a notable aspect of Narayan's art from his very first novel; in *Mr. Sampath* distancing is the key to a proper appreciation of the complex central character, Srinivas. Some elements in the hero's character and his preoccupations recall his cognates of the early comedy: Srinivas's aptitude for self-analysis is a staple; then he desires to be 'both truthful and tactful' (55)— a sattvic blend, reminding us of even little Swami's tribulations; good humour marks Srinivas's interaction with characters like the landlord and Somu; his sense of duty reflects a lively conscience. In his acute awareness of Time; and in his preoccupation with self-training, Srinivas reminds us of Krishna and Chandran; Srinivas is the latest and the most mature—and ambiguous—hero.

Even in *Mr. Sampath*, we find autobiographical elements; for example, the novelist modelled Mr Sampath after a special friend of his, affectionately known all over Karnataka as Sampath.[4] Srinivas's experiences with the editing of a journal are very close to his reformist elder uncle's in Madras; and of Narayan's own experience with *Indian Thought*. The manner in which copies of the *Banner* are rushed to catch the last train before the deadline recalls Narayan's own hectic time with his weekly contributions to the *Hindu*. Srinivas's dissatisfaction with his first drafts recalls Narayan's own rigorous recursive practice (see this chapter's notes at the end of the book). Above all, Narayan has given Srinivas his own work ethic: '[Srinivas] doesn't seem to have cared for anything else except his work' (36).

Yet Srinivas is not Narayan.

In fact from the way the novelist positions himself in the narrative, he makes it amply, subtly clear: here is a hero who is different from his precursors in the early comedy. Narayan suggests this in the opening passage itself; and through the imagery. Now let us consider two further devices the novelist uses in presenting Srinivas.

First, in the domestic perspective of the early comedy, Srinivas falls short. From *Swami and Friends* to *The English Teacher*, Narayan has presented the family—the joint family—as an institution of tremendous value and appeal. After our experience of *The English*

Teacher, Srinivas's conduct of his family relationships is shocking; early in the novel, Srinivas even talks and behaves like Ramani of *The Dark Room*, and the headmaster in *The English Teacher*; and the novelist puts both in 'back of Anderson Lane'; while the headmaster has an excuse in incompatibility, Srinivas is denied any such concession. In general, *Mr. Sampath* presents a spectacle of domestic discord. Other than *The Dark Room*, no novel of Narayan's early comedy shocks us with domestic misery on such a scale; the old landlord, Ravi, and Sampath, besides Srinivas himself, are all creators or victims of family strife, foreshadowing a bleak post-Independence development in the world of Narayan novels; already we are around 1947. Yet *Mr. Sampath* upholds the family norm: Srinivas's wife, their son, and Srinivas's brother, all represent the secure harmonies of the joint family; even in the depths of personal misery, Ravi thinks kindly of his old mother and brothers and sisters; the only emotion that seems to humanize the old miser is concern for his granddaughter: 'At the mention of the granddaughter his eyes glittered with joy' (56).

We are alerted early about Srinivas: 'He felt depressed at the sight of his son' (11). Such a reaction is abnormal in the world of Narayan's pre-Independence novels. 'His wife had to put up with endless misery at home through his ways, and his little son looked ragged. They put up with his ways for a considerable time' (12). And Srinivas leaves their 'ancient sprawling house' (12); one reason given for his departure—the only reason as it turns out—is that he 'always felt suffocated in the atmosphere of that small town' (12). Srinivas's conduct draws a gentle reminder from his elder brother, more harmonious with the world of Narayan. 'They must not feel they are unwanted by you' (12). The delicacy of the admonition reminds us of the principles and practice of the family in Narayan's pre-Independence novels, reaffirming the ground rules. And these are egregiously violated by Srinivas: 'He had not written home ever since he came to Malgudi' (24). In contrast with the headmaster's wife in *The English Teacher*, Srinivas's spouse is an unselfconscious upholder of family ties. '"[W]hat have I done that I should be treated like this?" Her voice was cracked with sorrow. Srinivas was baffled' (32–3). Srinivas senses his failure: '[H]e had neglected his family' (33). Typically, he attempts to rationalize his failure in the name of 'deeper conviction' and hopes: '[O]ther things like this will adjust themselves' (33). And he rushes to make notes on the topic in the spirit of the early Srinivas. 'Did the philosopher mean family life's all-absorbing nature when he cried for relief from its nightmare? [...] Man is condemned to be charged with neglect either here or in the heavens. Let him choose where he would rather face the calumny' (34). Coming immediately after our experience of *The English Teacher*, the otherworldly earnestness here in solemn style—which he himself has just deprecated—is nothing short of sacrilege. It is left to Sampath, Srinivas's 'brother' in Malgudi, to administer a gentle rebuke: 'I say, Srinivas, you are trying them too much, I fear, keeping them waiting!' (34). Philosophical predilections do not explain Srinivas's want of delicacy in compelling his orthodox wife to eat food she does not wish to. Equally strange is the tone Srinivas employs with his wife (35). It follows: 'Srinivas found domestic duties an extra burden' (36). And worse, after the conjugal relationship of *The English Teacher*, we have an indifferent husband: 'He himself wondered that he had observed so little of her in their years of married life' (37). Srinivas admires the domestic ideal, though; he even 'secretly admired those hundreds and hundreds of people who did so much in the world, in spite of a domestic life, even with many more to make demands upon them' (36); and blames himself for his failure; and, significantly, links it with the deficiencies in his journal: 'I don't know the art of family life. There is something lacking in me as in the journal, which leaves a feeling of dissatisfaction in people's minds' (48).

Thus, in the domestic sphere the collapse of the *Banner* makes for a change. Srinivas starts the process of readjustment and even thinks nostalgically of his ancient home; and learns to remember that his wife has a temper. There has already been 'a lot of readjustment on his part' (95); still, by the standards of Narayan's early comedy he continues to be harsh (138). The domestic ideal is foregrounded, once again, by Srinivas's elder brother; in a letter he urges Srinivas to keep the ancestral property for the children: '[I]t really belongs to our children and their children.' Srinivas's response is characteristic: '"[C]hildren and their children": it produced a lovely picture on the mind like the vista of an endless colonnade' (199). Srinivas at the same time is offended by the advice rendered. To some extent the *domestication* of this metaphysical hero is achieved by the end of the novel; and that is one more reason he does not object to the exorcism towards the end. Appropriately in this set up of devalued domestic harmony, where the hero is 'self'-occupied, Srinivas's wife remains unnamed, anticipating the series of nameless wives in the post-Independence novels.

Another device of authorial distancing in *Mr. Sampath* is more engaging: playful, comic, and definitive. When, from time to time, Srinivas gets too solemn the novelist steps away from his hero. Narayan's artistic cast-off, dissociation—dumping!—takes the form of landing the grand and the sublime on its posterior; when the hero begins to fly too high on his gossamer wings Narayan takes the wind out of them. The novelist engages again and again in a purposeful course-correction; he keeps his 'self'-centred hero tethered to this here and now, this world. To interpret this process as a mere comic device is to miss the fictional art. One may be preoccupied with the self in search of self-knowledge; self-realization may be a worthy aim in the Hindu way of life; all the same, one is best anchored, at a certain stage in one's life, in one's family, personal relationships, his society. 'Service to mankind is service to God': that is the principal tenet of our seers, the central Hindu tradition.

Early in the novel Srinivas himself laments his weakness. 'In 1938, when the papers were full of anticipation of a world war, he wrote: *The Banner* has nothing special to note about any war, past or future. It is only concerned with the war that is always going on— between man's inside and outside. Till the forces are equalized the struggle will always go on' (6). This passage attracted Vidia Naipaul; and he responded with outrage—identifying Srinivas with Narayan. If only Vidia had waited a second![5] The very next paragraph puts it in its formal perspective.

Reading it over a couple of weeks later, Srinivas smiled to himself. There was a touch of comicality in that bombast. It struck him as an odd mixture of the sublime and the ridiculous. [...] 'I wish I could write all that stuff here,' he reflected lying on his mat at home. [...] 'I wish I could do all my writing here,' he said to himself again and looked forlornly about him. (7)

Srinivas wishes—twice in that passage—that he could write all that stuff *here*; this 'here' defines itself soon enough as part of the squalid world, 'of the dwellers below', harsh, stupid, ludicrous, human. Srinivas is not aware of it: even *here* he is capable of grand flights: and Narayan hauls him down, promptly, purposely, comically.

Let us turn to the text again to see if we can be a little more attentive to a major novelist's fifth novel. Out of touch with reality, Srinivas plans a superb format for his journal: only to be told by his printer that all that his press can offer is but 12-point in English—'a type that looks like the headings in a Government of India Gazette' (20); and when his journal is finally printed, 'his heart sank. It was nowhere near what he had imagined. He had hoped that it would look like an auctioneer's list, but now he found that it looked like the handbill of a wrestling tournament' (20). Srinivas's imagination is quelled by ground realities.

We cannot ignore facts of the fiction.

Take another example. Srinivas is engaged with his characteristic earnestness in exploring a vexing philosophic question: 'Why really bother?' As this is again a speculation Naipaul identifies the novelist himself with—ignoring the ample fictive signals already provided by the text—let us see again how attentive Naipaul's second-time repeat reading—done over months—in snatches—is to the text before him.

He suddenly flung out his arm and cried: 'I have got it, just the right and—' turned towards his table in a rush. He picked up his pen; the sentence was shaping so very delicately; he felt he had to wait upon it carefully, tenderly, lest it should elude him once again; it was something like the very first moment when a face emerges on the printing paper in the developing tray—something tender and fluid, one had to be very careful if one were not to lose it forever.[6] [...] He poised his pen as if he were listening to some faint voice and taking dictation. He held his breath, for fear that he might lose the thread, and concentrated all his being on the sentence, when he heard a terrific clatter up the stairs. He gnashed his teeth. 'The demons are always waiting around to create a disturbance; they are terrified of any mental concentration.' (31)

Incidentally, as pointed out elsewhere (in my 2003 article 'Naipaul's Nobel Poise?'), the meticulous craftsman that he is— 'Master of the English sentence'—Naipaul devotes a uniquely long paragraph (of more than 200 words) to assure the readers that he took great trouble with *Mr. Sampath*, reading the novel over months. Sadly Naipaul's textual scanning misses out on vital data, again.[7] Now the 'demons' in this scene of the novel turn out to be his own family; despite his prolonged neglect of them, Srinivas's loving wife and son arrive to join him: a timely reminder to Srinivas of his comprehensive obligations on which he has defaulted; and a reminder to the reader as well that beyond a point Narayan steps aside and allows his hero to puncture his high-flying balloon. The whole passage nicely illustrates Narayan's craft-wit in *Mr. Sampath*.

Besides, the mundane image from photography evokes the mystery of creativity; and Srinivas as a metaphysician merges with the creative writer. The elaborate stage setting suggests a holy ritual; prepares for the visitation of the 'demons' to disturb his tapas.

Now let us look at another scene: '[H]e felt, with an extravagant seriousness, that a whole civilization had come to an abrupt stalemate because its men had no better basis of living than public opinion. He raved against their upbringing' (37). For anyone familiar with Narayan's work, extravagance in any form—and 'raving', especially—is unnatural:[8] in the world of Narayan's pre-Independence novels the sole purpose it can serve is create comedy of 'illusions and hysterics'. Srinivas's 'extravagant seriousness' is offset by his wife, who, among other things, offers him a salutary view of her husband's journal: 'That *Banner* was so dull!' (96): the truth Srinivas realizes only later.

Naipaul cites the 'brinjal' philosophy to support his thesis of Hindu withdrawal and idle speculation. Srinivas is relaxing on his mat at home, having given himself a holiday.

Mixed sounds reached him—his wife in the kitchen, his son's voice far off, arguing with a friend, the clamour of assertions and appeals at the water-tap, a pedlar woman crying 'brinjals and greens' in the street—all these sounds mingled and wove into each other. Following each one to its root and source, one could trace it to a human aspiration and outlook. 'The vegetable seller is crying because in her background is her home and children whose welfare is moulded by the amount of brinjals she is able to scatter into society [...].' The vastness and infiniteness of it stirred Srinivas deeply. 'That's clearly too big, even for contemplation,' he remarked to himself 'because it is in that total picture we perceive God.' (49–50)

Naipaul does not take the passage to its dramatic finale, the way the novelist Narayan does; for Narayan lets it build up. But the passage does not end there:

At this moment he heard over everything else a woman's voice saying: 'I will kill that dirty dog if he comes near the tap again.'

'If you speak about my son's dog I will break your pot,' another voice cried. 'Get away both—I've been here for half an hour for a glass of water.' (49–50)

Immediately follows the novelist's punch line: 'Now they formed to him a very different picture' (49–50).

Here we have a neat illustration of Narayan's delightful face-off, of metaphysical speculation with solid—sordid—reality. Nothing can be more obvious than this of what the novelist thinks about his hero: 'extravagant seriousness'. Srinivas, the intellectual, is addicted to disproportionate perspective. 'A very different picture' is what matters in *Mr. Sampath*. Naipaul could have moved with the tempo of the passage to its logical conclusion, allowed it to fulfil its rhetorical rhythm.

Naipaul calls such passages idle and half-comic. Just the opposite: they are, as we have seen in their dramatic context, set off against harsh reality, and fully comic. Naipaul ignores such creative movements, their definitive formal rhetoric as well as frequency. (Recall his quote in the epigraph to this chapter.)

Let us take yet another passage cited by Naipaul, concerning the hero's philosophy of noninterference which Naipaul, now predictably—too readily—attributes to Narayan. Srinivas decides not to disclose to Sampath that the artist Ravi does not want to do a portrait of Sampath's child because he does not feel inspired enough by the child's features. 'There's no sense in interfering in other people's lives [...] he felt thrilled by the thought that he stood on the threshold of some *revolutionary discoveries in the realm of human existence* [...]' (63–4; emphasis mine).

By now we should have learnt from our experience of Narayan's craft play in his early comedy to suspect anything *revolutionary*: the only exception is in *The English Teacher*, where the spirits promise Krishna one and the hero does achieve extraordinary results, but then the point of view in that novel and its relatively straightforward handling make it patent. Here in *Mr. Sampath* the narrative strategy is altogether different; what we have is a highly pliable point of view: we totally identify the novelist with Srinivas only at our peril.

For, in this episode all that the reader needs to do is move just a wee step further in the text: to the very next sentence: 'The expected revolution in *The Banner* came in another way.'

Srinivas's journal has collapsed! And because of Srinivas's own financial mismanagement. The quiet tone of Narayan's tongue-in-cheek thrust in the crucial statement is characteristic: we are familiar with it by now.

When Srinivas's imagination catches fire it is doused by a domestic confrontation. His wife brings him face to face with himself. 'And he smiled weakly realizing at once *what a hopeless confusion his whole outlook was. He could not define what he wanted*' (96; emphasis mine). Srinivas's comic flaw could not have been stated more explicitly. In his project of demolishing India, Naipaul ends up performing a Procrustean procedure on *Mr. Sampath*.[9]

Sampath proves more successful in assessing Srinivas. When Srinivas demands that Sampath induct Ravi into the film company, Sampath expresses his fears: 'But I hope he will not create complexities here' (157). Srinivas, however, is confident—as usual: 'Well, I don't think he will do anything of the kind' (159). Later in the studio though 'somewhat taken aback by [Ravi's] frenzy', '[h]e felt a pity for Sampath and his clumsy fears' (161); we come to know only later who is being clumsy. Srinivas continues to assure the apprehensive Sampath: 'Things will be all right; don't worry' (161). Soon he finds 'some dark, irresponsible mood' seemed to be coming over Ravi; but Srinivas doesn't bother about it. '"It's all in the artist's make-up," he told himself' (163–4), once again losing touch with reality. When Ravi does suffer a breakdown and runs amok, Srinivas is totally helpless: 'He was blindly running along with the rest of them, catching the mood of the mob [...]' (190).

The next major critical question is: after the studio debacle, does Srinivas withdraw from social participation as Naipaul alleges? For, as per Naipaul's conviction Srinivas returns home from the studio, leaving Ravi in the lurch, and sits down for another vacuous philosophic speculation and 'non-doing'.

Does he?

Srinivas does nothing of the sort. Far from it. Srinivas engages in action and plenty of it. And—sadly for Naipaul!—dharmic action at that.

Let us turn to Narayan's text again and look at the conclusion of the farcical studio scene: 'The lights were ablaze once again at 5 a.m. The police arrived in a van soon after' (193). The curtain comes down on the studio activity.

What we witness now in Narayan's text is wholesome, comprehensive dharmic action.

The very next para of the novel opens: 'The major part of the next four days, Srinivas spent in running between the Market Road Police Station and his home' (193). In Narayan's novel, Ravi is arrested and put in the lock-up at the police station. Srinivas takes care of him; Srinivas aids even Ravi's helpless family. Srinivas is engaged in taking care of the deranged youth; even feeding him with his own hands. For, the young artist is a fit case for an asylum.

> Srinivas carried food for him every day in a brass vessel. He had the lock-up opened, went in, sat beside Ravi and persuaded him to eat the food. Ravi seemed to have forgotten the art of eating. Srinivas attempted to feed him with a spoon, but even that was difficult. He kept a morsel on his tongue and swallowed only when he was persistently told to do so. It was an odd spectacle—Srinivas sitting there in that dark corner beyond the bars, coaxing Ravi to eat, as the Market Road babble continued outside.

This, according to Vidia Naipaul, is Srinivas's 'non-doing'.

Now for some more of Naipaul's non-readings (especially, of pages 249–76 of the novel).

When Sampath arrives to call on him Srinivas persuades him to withdraw his complaint against the deranged youngman; from the police station Srinivas takes him, not to Ravi's home, but to his own home and installs him there and takes over the responsibility of the mentally disturbed young man. This egregious 'non-doing' is, actually, dharma in action.

Not just this. Unbelievably Srinivas's 'non-doing' goes limitless: 'Srinivas kept Ravi in his own house. He had more or less the task of running both the households on his means. Ravi's little sister came in several times a day with a petition for a rupee or two, and Srinivas

MR. SAMPATH AND THE NAIPAUL ENIGMA | 107

ungrudgingly parted with them and advised his wife to do so in his absence' (203).

And Srinivas has to do all this—and more—against fierce hostility from Ravi's father. When Ravi's mother decides to take Ravi to a temple away from Malgudi, Srinivas's wife gives her twenty-five rupees, a considerable sum in those days, for her expenses; and Srinivas supports her action. Finally the most challenging act of charity Srinivas and his wife take on is looking after Ravi's aged, grumpy father in the absence of his family.

When 'Srinivas [finds] himself facing, for the first time, financial problems as a reality', he writes to his brother in their village and manages to get an emergency grant from him; moves out of the old premises to a more affordable office. And '[o]ut of all the welter of paper he was carrying away he took care not to miss the little sketch of Ravi's in the cardboard file' (199).

There is more 'non-doing' to come. With the help of the police inspector Srinivas revives the *Banner*, the vehicle and symbol of his social commitment: dharma in action again. For Srinivas according to Naipaul is, memorably, among Narayan's 'small men, small schemes, big talk, little means'! A 'Contemplative idler'![10] All this activity, according to Naipaul, amounts to Hindu calm, 'the killer'. In the idiom of our media, these Naipaul quotes have 'gone viral'. Fortunately for us Naipaul himself offers an explanation for such a critical enormity. (See the epigraphs to this chapter.)[11] Poor—unsuspecting—Srinivas!

Such a hero fails to stop the exorcist; for the exorcism is an extension of the studio ceremony; the image once again is of primitive ritual; and Srinivas is ritual weary. After *The English Teacher* we realize again that certain attachments in India have a ballast of deference. In *The English Teacher* when Krishna's mother-in-law calls in an exorcist to cure Susila: '[Krishna] watched it all from the doorway in fury, but [he] had to be silent because [he] couldn't argue with [his] mother-in-law, and [he] was uncertain how it would be viewed by Swamiji' (93).

And at the end of it all, in addition to shouldering the responsibility of nursing back Ravi, supporting his family and accepting the invidious duty of putting up with Ravi's father, Srinivas indulges in more non-doing: he goes back to editing and publishing the *Banner*. It holds the key to Srinivas's personality.[12] 'Distancing' does not mean that Srinivas can be dismissed; for, the values he strives for are relevant to life in society. There is no *Mr. Sampath* without Srinivas's philosophical pursuit; and still less without its medium, the *Banner*.

The philosophical aspect of the novel may be approached through Ananda Coomaraswamy (1918: 28–9):

The life or lives of man may be regarded as constituting a curve—an arc of time-experience subtended by the duration of the individual Will to Life. The outward movement on this curve—Evolution, the Path of Pursuit—the *Pravritti Marga*—is characterized by self-assertion. The inward movement—Involution, the Path of Return—the *Nivritti Marga*—is characterized by increasing Self-Realization. The religion of men on the outward path is the Religion of Time; the religion of those who return is the Religion of Eternity. If we consider life as one whole, certainly Self-Realization must be regarded as its essential purpose from the beginning; all our forgetting is but that we may remember the more vividly. But though it is true that in most men the two phases of experience interpenetrate, we shall best understand the soul of man—drawn as it is in the two opposite, or seeming opposite, directions of Affirmation and Denial, Will and Will-Surrender—by separate consideration of the outward and the inward tendencies. Brahmans [Brahmins, rishis here] avoid the theological use of the terms 'good' and 'evil', and prefer to speak of 'knowledge' and 'ignorance' (*vidya* and *avidya*), and of the three qualities of *satva*, *rajas*, and *tamas*. As knowledge increases, so much more will a man of his own motion, and not from any sense of duty, tend to return, and his character and actions will be more purely *satvic*. But we need not on that account condemn the Self-assertion of the ignorant as sin; for could Self-Realization be where self-assertion had never been? It is not sin, but youth, and to forbid the satisfaction of the thirst of youth is not a cure: rather, as we realize more clearly every day *desires suppressed breed pestilence* [emphasis mine]. The Brahmans therefore, notwithstanding the austere role appointed for themselves, held that an ideal human society must provide for the enjoyment of all pleasures by those who wish for them; they would say, perhaps, that those who have risen above the mere gratification of the senses, are just those who have already tasted pleasure to the full.

For the reasons of this kind it was held that the acquisition of wealth (*artha*) and the enjoyment of sense-pleasure (*kama*), subject to the law (*dharma*) as may protect the weak against the strong are legitimate preoccupations of those on the outward path. This is the stage attained by modern western society, of which the norm is competition regulated by ethical restraint. Beyond this stage no society can progress unless it is subjected to the creative will of those who have passed beyond the stage of most extreme egoism, whether we call them heroes, guardians, Brahmans, Samurai, or simply men of genius.

Narayan is not a 'studied' writer; it is not difficult, however, to see that the metaphysical drama—the bare bones of *Mr. Sampath*—consists of the sattvic hero's ('Who am I?' is Srinivas's famous query) interaction with the rajasic and the tamasic individuals: 'The scales of value in this world amazed him' (1949: 98); as a result, he achieves yet another stage in his quest for self-realization. A unique feature of Narayan's narrative is that the rajasic and the tamasic alone do not monopolize the comedy of life; even the sattvic Srinivas, as we have already seen, can be absurd and comic; while the rajasic is equally capable of sublime experience—anticipating Narayan's post-Independence novels.

The comedy of *Mr. Sampath* results from the acquisition and pursuit of wealth (artha) by the old landlord; and the hunt for sense-pleasure (kama) by Sampath and Ravi: illicit passion enters the world of Narayan extensively in *Mr. Sampath*; all three transgress righteous conduct (dharma). With Narayan, however, metaphysics can be fun; for *Mr. Sampath* will be remembered for its 'people'—their gunas comedy—human comedy.

As a man of sattvic nature, however, Srinivas is 'truth'-seeking. And sattvic nature cannot be 'conformist'; Srinivas is a 'rebel'. 'But what can I do? I have a different notion of human beings. I have given their notions a fair trial' (11). For him 'the extensive property' of his father is not good enough to hold him in 'an ancient sprawling house' (12). Tolerance and spiritual striving mark the sattvic truth seeker—not 'intellectual depletion'. Srinivas is different from the majority of his society; he is above conventions and traditional norms; the passage of time oppresses him (11). A little later the novelist brings it out forcefully: 'The question of a career seemed to him as embarrassing as a physiological detail' (11). (That also sounds more like Narayan himself.) Srinivas may have 'a different notion of human beings'; but the sattvic hero is also healthily sensitive, like his creator, to feminine beauty (139–40); and even the sattvic hero has occasional rajasic feelings.[13]

Like his creator, Srinivas is a believer, and consistently so; he can also, to some extent, appreciate the higher appeal of his favourite god's symbolism. We cannot think of a better, a more beautiful trope of Srinivas's aspiration than the little image, rich with detail, of Nataraja ('Dancing Siva') that he has received, aptly, from his grandmother. Srinivas may grasp 'the symbol but vaguely', but we can do a little better, thanks again to Coomaraswamy. The Princeton scholar devotes a complete essay to the significance of the various images of the dancing Siva. This particular dance form of Siva is known as Nadanta. Coomaraswamy (1918: 93) calls attention to 'the grandeur of this conception itself as a synthesis of science, religion and art'. Quoting extensively from ancient texts, the scholar sums up the significance of the dance of Siva (1918: 87):

The dance, in fact, represents His five activities (Panchkritya), viz.: Shrishti (overlooking creation, evolution); Sthiti (preservation, support); Samhara (destruction, evolution); Tirobhava (veiling, embodiment, illusion, and also, giving rest); and Anugraha (release, salvation, grace). These separately considered, are the activities of the deities Brahma, Vishnu, Rudra, Maheshvara and Sadhashiva. This cosmic activity is the central motif of the dance. [...] 'Creation arises from the drum: protection proceeds from the hand of hope: from fire proceeds destruction: the foot held aloft gives release.' It will be observed that the fourth hand points to this lifted foot, the refuge of the soul.

Coomaraswamy (1918: 89) quotes from other texts and adds:

Its deepest significance is felt when it is realized that it takes place within the heart and the self. Everywhere is God; that Everywhere is the heart. [...] Siva is a destroyer and loves the burning ground. But what does He destroy? Not merely the heavens and earth at the close of a world-cycle, but the fetters that bind each separate soul. [...] The place where the ego is destroyed signifies the state where illusion and deeds are burnt away: that is the crematorium, the burning-ground where Shri Nataraja dances.

The adoration of such an image is appropriate to Srinivas, a truth seeker.

Adoration of the beautiful image of Nataraja leads us to another aspect of Srinivas's sensibility: his interest in art and music. In fact his support for Ravi is chiefly aesthetic; when Ravi shows him a sketch of the girl, 'Srinivas became breathless at the sight of it' (Narayan 1949: 40). He declares: '*The Banner* can justify its existence only if it saves a man like Ravi and shows the world something of his creative powers' (138). After the collapse of the *Banner* Srinivas packs up; and the one thing that he makes it a point to take along with him is a drawing by Srinivas. This is another reason why he attaches so much importance to the *Banner*: Narayan's sattvic hero aims at, besides self-development, an aesthetic-social goal.

Srinivas is a writer seeking expression; he gives convincing evidence of creativity (97).

All night his head seethed with ideas and would not let him snatch even a wink. Half a dozen times he interrupted a possible coming sleep to get up, switch on the light and jot down notes. He got up late next day and rushed to his office. He knew no peace till he was back at his untidy table. He seized his rose-coloured penholder, dipped it in the inkpot, and kept dipping it there, as if excavating something out of its bed. The sheets before him filled up, and he became unconscious of the passing of time […]. (97)

The absorption is authentic. Narayan gives his hero his own familiarity with the creative experience (102). Again and again imagination gains prominence: 'Srinivas's imagination was stirred as he narrated the story' (101). Such a sensibility seeks self-expression. After the collapse of his journal he tries the movie world, concludes that there is no place for it in this crazy world: he is thrilled to find himself back with his *Banner*.

We have been told on the very first page that the offices of the *Banner* are 'the home of truth and vision, though you might take time to accept the claim'. We do take time and so does Narayan; but by the end we appreciate the true significance of the *Banner*: it combines the twin objectives of truth and vision, socio-philosophic truth and creative vision; when of all people in Malgudi the police inspector offers him a chance to revive his *Banner*, Srinivas feels that 'he ha[s] got back his enchantment in life' (197). Enchantment in this world, the here and the now, not the next.

Though the novelist plays games with him Srinivas is the latest link in the evolving series of early comedy heroes; and enjoys some exceptional traits of head and heart. Srinivas is Narayan's intellectual. The imagery associated with him has an appropriate range: human habitation, nature, art, music, photography, pedagogy, etc., associated with this world, and with the higher faculties of man. From the beginning Srinivas also reveals a well-developed social conscience. 'Duty' is a constant with him; rich with social and spiritual connotations; the favourite concept is mentioned five times in the novel (on pages 43, 60, 62, 93, and 159). The story of Srinivas is ultimately the story of development of human personality, self-training. The social purpose of the *Banner* also is made clear from the very beginning: 'In fact it constituted itself an enemy of a great many institutions and conditions. Within twelve pages of foolscap it attempted to set the world right' (6). The undertone of good-humoured criticism of the ambition is unmistakable—'set the world right'. All the same, the journal soon develops a reputation as a social critic—for example, of rapacious landlords (6); and more insistently, of the inept Malgudi municipality. The editor achieves results: 'It was gratifying to the editor of the *Banner* to see the effect of his words' (26–7). Concrete social action elicits positive bureaucratic response; the municipality even sends him the new scheme they have revived. 'He went through it feeling happy that the *Banner* had roused the municipal conscience' (29). At the beginning of chapter 2, we are again given a clear statement of Srinivas's social resolve, now with a striking refinement: he aims to achieve 'subjective value in relation to a social outlook' (30). In other words, our truth seeker is not going to cut himself off from his social matrix. Even if it is a philosophical statement he wishes to 'do his best to word it in an easy manner, in terms of actual experience' (31). This life, here and now, 'actual experience', is what matters: not withdrawal, not indifference; not non-interference, but positive, passionate, insistent, humanitarian intervention in the public domain.

Even during his stint at the studio, away from his journal, Srinivas is true to himself: he offers the movie moguls a story with 'the message of Gandhiji in terms of an experience' (99). Here is no armchair philosopher or recluse. Like any creative writer, 'experience,' 'actual experience', is what Srinivas respects.

To Narayan's heroes of the early comedy 'life' is supreme. Like any creative writer Srinivas is sensitive to suffering; he understands Ravi better than anyone. 'Srinivas knew what silent suffering was going on within that shabby frame [...] Srinivas felt pity for him' (44). Concern for people and insight into human suffering mark Srinivas's social awareness: these values find expression through the *Banner*. The *Banner* combines his marked social commitment with his creative aspiration. The journal becomes everything to Srinivas: 'The clear-cut lines of life are visible only when I'm at my table and turning out *The Banner*' (139).[14] Now Srinivas is not prepared any more to indulge in high-brow talk even on philosophic topics: 'He didn't like to use the word "cosmic" if he could help it' (212). He has realized his weakness, 'putting himself one remove from his public' (47); he has now been educated out of it. He is back with his *Banner*, vehicle and symbol of his social, metaphysical—creative—'innermost aspiration'.[15]

For Naipaul, a global player, to say that the revived *Banner* lacks the humour of its former avatar is to commit the ultimate outrage. The text of *Mr. Sampath*, written by the Indian novelist R.K. Narayan, refers to only one editorial written by Srinivas after the revival of the journal. From its impact on Somu and company we can see that the editor has not lost his touch; and what is more, Srinivas's scene with Somu confirms that the editor enjoys, as much as ever, wit and humour (251–4).

Srinivas's higher quest, however, is unfulfilled even by the end of the novel: 'I am searching for something, trying to make a meaning out of things' (196).

Once again in the pre-Independence novels realism marks the presentation of this world, the world outside, the life of affirmation. *Mr. Sampath* recalls *The Dark Room* at times in its stark realities. We have already seen the prominence given to Market Road and its 'babble'; but the world of the 'dwellers below' is closely observed. Offering a portion of his house to Srinivas, the old miser 'turns the key, flings the door open'; 'darkness seemed to flow out of the room' (13–14).[16] Darkness is a natural element of this world. The novelist points out 'the soft stabs of feeble, flickering light emanating from door chinks and the windows of humble homes, the only light available here' (46). The fiasco in the studio finds all of them plunged in darkness: 'And utter darkness enveloped them again' (191). 'Darkness', after all, is 'tamasa': a quality of the characters within and of their world without. Ravi loves 'the dark, ill-lit lanes'. Narayan goes into more details about Srinivas's tenement. 'The walls were of mud, lime-covered, with an uneven and globular surface; bamboo splinters showed in some places—the skeleton on which the mud had been laid. The lime had turned brown and black with time' (14–15). This of course is the 'world below'. The human inmates of this world cannot be ignored either. Srinivas's neighbour, Ravi, 'paid a rent of two rupees for one room in which his entire family was cooped up' (17). The old miser lived in 'a small room'; elaborately locks up his 'cell' (13) when he goes out. Suffering is endemic. Srinivas's predecessor in the tenement 'had hanged himself', no one knows why (17). Ravi's own father 'was stricken with paralysis' (42). When we do enter Ravi's 'room' (115) human misery touches a new low.

The women are anything but romantic. During his visit to Sampath, Srinivas finds Sampath's non-descript wife 'wearing a saree of faded red, full of smoke and kitchen grime' (85). When Srinivas wishes to make up with his wife after losing his temper with her: 'He put his arm around her and pressed his face against her black saree. A faint aroma of kitchen smoke and damp was about her' (96).

The fitting climax of this novelist's 'own realism' (as Graham Greene put it), we get, appropriately, in the picture of the police station on the Market Road through Srinivas's eyes: 'He saw a policeman pushing in a jutka-driver for some traffic offence; he saw an urchin brought in and sent away with a couple of slaps on his face; he saw a terrified villager brought in for questioning and pushed away *somewhere out of sight*. All the while a sergeant sat at a table, *implacably writing on brown forms* [...]' (193; emphasis mine).

The vagueness of 'somewhere out of sight' is vivid with terror; 'implacably' writing on 'brown forms' compounds it with mindless bureaucratism. After Ravi's release, as Srinivas considers the police inspector's generous offer: 'Traffic was passing, policemen were walking in and out with their boot-nails clanking on the hard stone floor. [...] The groan of a man in custody was feebly heard [...]' (196).

The auditory images resonate with human misery and human viciousness. We know of at least one key socioeconomic factor contributing to this misery: 'Overnight, as it were, Malgudi passed from a semi-agricultural town to a semi-industrial town' (26).

Nowhere in the novel does Narayan hold our interest with greater success than when he deals with select members of this world of 'dwellers below'. They play key roles in the hero's life; thanks to his association with them he realizes the need for constructive social engagement like the *Banner*. The old man and Sampath especially are a true delight, and together with Ravi they form a significant thematic pattern. These three principal characters of 'life below' belong to three different age groups; and what is more, they represent, in Hindu parlance, three different asramas (stages in life): Ravi, of brahmacharya; Sampath, of grahasthya; and the old landlord, of vanaprasthya—though masquerading as sanyasa. None of the three is true to the ideals of his asrama. Intermessing is a natural feature of the 'dwellers below': the old man wants Ravi for his granddaughter; Ravi chases Shanti who becomes Sampath's love; Sampath tries to exploit the old man for his money; even Srinivas, the central node, seeks the art in Ravi. This aspect becomes more blatant of course in the film world: 'Sohan Lal was dogging his steps, and he dogged the steps of Sohan Lal, and Somu went round and round these two [...]' (178).

Srinivas comes away from it all, chastened. No experience is wasteful. For the sattvic hero the darkness that engulfs the whole crew in the studio following the crisis is monitory; it is of the world of darkness, of *avidya*, Ignorance. For him this netherworld is also the 'maze', a metaphysical metaphor: the maze of passions, with their failure to sublimate, to burn Kama. The last word about this world we hear—from Sampath—makes eminent sense: 'And only Kama, the God of Love, is left in the studio' (218).

Narayan introduces the three costars of Srinivas in the very first chapter; an Indian file: and vanish in the same order from the book. The first to appear is the old man. Narayan has already presented an old miser, the village priest in *The Dark Room*; but the old man here has greater thematic relevance. The rajasic man pretends to be sattvic: a spiritual impostor. The first chapter lights up with the humour involving the old miser. Narayan gives him, at the same time, an unexpected depth and very early: 'He had led a happy family life in this house till the death of his wife' (7); a vestige of that joy he reveals in his love for his granddaughter. At the same time he is 'a monstrous old man' (10); he boasts of living in a single room given to him by a 'friend'—but the 'friend', it turns out, is a poor debtor whom the old man had done out of the room. A creature of unfulfilled appetites, the old man's miserly habits are a parody of self-abnegation. The best comment on this old Brahmin is offered by Sampath after his death, when he presides over the conference of the wretched claimants to the miser's will, with a quote from the old man himself: 'When I become a handful of ash what do I care who takes my purse [...]' (170). This verse is at the same time a cryptic comment on the conduct of the greedy crowd bidding for the old man's property and cash; on Sampath as well: he has tried, unsuccessfully, to help himself to the old man's hoard. The suddenness of the old man's death is a reminder to Srinivas of the urgency of his quest.

Ravi and Sampath offer a different lesson for Srinivas: the price of failure to burn Kama is heavy. But the young artist, too, is humanized by Narayan. First, through his hapless family: in his darkest denunciations Ravi exempts his mother, brothers, and sisters (159). Just before the crisis in the studio, Ravi, already tense and peevish, confesses to Srinivas of his attachment to his family: '"But for these young fellows and my mother," he said reflectively, "I should have blasted my so-called home ages ago"' (176). The novelist also gives Ravi the benefit of his own first-love experience (42); sadly, however, in Ravi's story we witness not the refreshing comedy of first love, but tragedy of 'blighted' youth. What makes Ravi's tragedy more poignant is his gift of art. Of all the three principal characters of this world Ravi reminds us most of the vehemence of the verbs in the opening passage. In this world of unabated appetites and unquenchable passions, Ravi is the misguided missile. One of his victims is Sampath himself.

Srinivas's special relationship with Sampath shows him in utterly human light. 'The printer was a vociferous, effusive man. When he took a sheet from the press he handled it with such delicacy, carrying it on his palms, as if it were a new-born infant, saying: "See the finish?" in such a tone that his customers were half hypnotized into agreeing with him' (20-1). What we witness is love for people as they are, for what they are, though the sattvic hero Srinivas tries to reform Sampath and, predictably, fails. Sampath's very first appearance—rather delayed for a character that later attracts so much of the novelist's interest—and his attention—is revealing. He 'sells' the only font he has as the best and with a smile: 'This is very good, you cannot get this finish in the whole of South India' (20). This introduction brings out key elements of Sampath's rhetoric; especially his 'tact', or in plain English, lies ('Truth Printing Works', after all). His rajasic temperament, his nature of passion, is suggested by the lion image on the curtain in the press. In only one relationship he displays honesty: with Srinivas. Sampath's support proves invaluable to Srinivas. Otherwise, Sampath 'dealt with all his customers amiably, but to no purpose' (21). This effusive, carefree man hates solemnity: he fulfils an 'ambition' by cracking nut shells in the court, 'something to foil the terrible gloom of the place' (24). Sampath's energy impresses Srinivas: printer, actor, director, mediator, Sanskrit pupil, musician. He comes under Sampath's spell. He even admires 'usual radiance' of Sampath's face: 'You are a great fellow! People must bow before you for your capacity' (145). Sampath is not destined to be a printer again and for no fault of his own; he can only dream of it. With brilliant timing the novelist introduces a flashback: the first meeting of Sampath and Srinivas. The bustling restaurant is a perfect setting for Sampath's unveiling; no one represents this world better than Sampath. Sampath's rhetoric, his animal spirits, and his special relationship with Srinivas emerge forcefully. At the end the derelict printer does not offer a single word of recrimination; all that he can say is: 'It was an evil hour that brought me and Ravi together' (194). That is Sampath's tact refined to touching decency for his friend Srinivas: in fact, we recall, it is Srinivas who has imposed Ravi on Sampath. And yet Srinivas now responds coolly to Sampath's woes, 'determined to discourage martyrdom at all costs' (194). Sampath's hearty laughter rings often, even at the expense of himself. Sampath's talent, too, is unsupported by character and circumstance. The one chance he gets to prove himself in a public performance is ruined in the studio.

Sampath's downfall is also brought about by his infatuation with a beautiful woman who possesses in the circumstances more dignity than anyone else in the novel. Shanti is a splendid improvement over Shanta of *The Dark Room*; Sampath has already prepared us with his remarks: '[A] girl in the flesh ought to be worth a dozen on paper' (126).

Narayan's success in *Sampath* is complete: a go-getter and adulterer wins our hearts. Once again, as in the case of Srinivas, imagery establishes character. In that remarkable scene in Bombay Anand Bhavan, Srinivas recalls, Sampath holds sway: 'He descended from the counter with great dignity. [...] His voice commanded people hither and thither and *held itself monarch above the din*' (66; emphasis mine). Sampath is the lord of this realm, *this* world; Srinivas gets an advance feel of the fact in his very first meeting. And in the last scene of the novel, when Srinivas turns finally and resolutely away from Sampath the last image of Sampath we get is the very last trope of the novel. 'While turning down Anderson Lane [Srinivas] looked back for a second and saw far off the glow of a cigarette end in the square where he had left Sampath; it was like a ruby set in the night' (219). Darkness still envelops Mr Sampath; but the king cannot be dismissed lightly—recall the lion image on the curtain of his little press; now his jewelled crown goes with him into exile. The ruby in Indian gemology is the royal stone.[17]

Mr. Sampath marks the culmination of Narayan's early comedy. We get a surprising share of ambient suffering in the early novels, especially of the post-ordeal period. How much longer could Narayan retain his sense of comedy? The novel's thematic gravity and craft wisdom distinguish it. And consider, besides, how much Narayan packs into his first chapter, with subtle authorial tints establishing the stylistic distinction of the novel. At the same time *Mr. Sampath* is a watershed. Narayan's thematic preoccupation with sattvic humanity is finally fulfilled with Srinivas opting for self *and* society: for karma yoga, from the self-centrism he is so full of at the beginning of the novel to the social philosophy of the Gita: Service to Man is Service to God. Srinivas's involvement with people recalls to our mind little Swami's eagerness for company—describing a full circle. Simultaneously Narayan discovers rich material for another kind of comedy in the rajasic and tamasic guna. For the novelist the inward journey is done: his interest in the life of assertion grows, focusing on adulterers, hoarders, adventurers, bullies, and 'bad' men.[18] The sattvic hero of his early comedy is 'fulfilled'; but the comedic feast will never end, for we are all richer by this world.[19]

'Would you agree with V.S. Naipaul that your novels are about 'small men, small schemes, big talk, limited means'?
'I suppose so' (Davidar 1988a: 81).

III

VICE-FECTION

The Post-Independence
Novels and Novellas

10
A Wizard for Malgudi
The Financial Expert

R.K. Narayan's post-Independence novels and novellas also challenge the art of the novelist: this procession of malcontents, actually, presents a more formidable challenge: how can these rajasic–tamasic spirits win the reader's sympathy?

Margayya struggles hard to gain material success, graduates from a petty bank loan adviser of rustics to the financial wizard of Malgudi; through his painful comeuppance by the end he presents to the reader a hoary truth. The novel is the first of Narayan's synoptic tales with moral equity; a morality 'play' in five acts, the action builds up to a mythic inevitability.

The Financial Expert shares the spirit of the post-Independence period. A virtual orphan, Margayya is also the first of the post-Independence failed fathers. A trace of anti-feminism in Margayya, too, goes with the rajasic temper of the post-Independence hero. The conclusion of the novel is characteristic of the novelist; as the beating up of Dr Pal was the first step in Margayya's reformation, the reaching out for his grandchild at the end is affirmation of his return to sanity.

Margayya is a phenomenon no less. 'The emergence of Margayya was an unexpected and incalculable effect of a cooperator's zeal' (Narayan 1952: 1). The cooperator's fervour has not been matched by the integrity of his successors and their underlings; and Margayya succeeds with its peasant clientele.

Margayya himself is a victim: 'By the time my father found husbands for them there was nothing left for us to eat at home' (7). The first-person account already gains the reader's sympathy. The division of property has left the brothers and their families alienated: 'It was a relationship essentially thriving on a crisis' (175).

Margayya's twin failures—in his career and in raising his son—are but consequences of his misconceived attempts—surrendering basic values—to adapt himself to a ruthless world: for, 'Life was a terrible affair' (47). Already in his early forties when the novel opens, Margayya is at home among his kind, among the villagers and the peasants; he is helplessly handicapped for want of formal education when exposed to the modern world.

Impecunious Margayya feels helpless even in dealing with the society around him. The Malgudi gutter episode confirms this for him. When Balu throws his precious little account book into the gutter Margayya finds all around him 'this absolutely hostile world' (42); and '[s]ociety was pressing in upon him from all sides' (42); and '[s]ociety seemed to overwhelm him on all sides' (42). He laments: 'No one will let me do what I want' (43). Even later the antipathy is confirmed for him: 'It seemed such a formidable and horrible world that he wondered how he had managed to exist at all' (77).

A serious consequence of the societal rot around him results in his belief: that money is everything in this world. Making money is the only way to counter the ways of the society: 'Money is everything, dignity, self-respect' (77). Insecurity impels him into his early money-making ventures. Later even after he makes money from Pal's book, he is worried: 'I don't want people to say that Balu enjoys all the money earned through *Domestic Harmony*' (118); for the present, however, '[h]e seemed to swell with his goodness, nobility and importance, and the clean plans he was able to make for his son' (118). The 'clean plans' are, it turns out, a further descent into the morass. That he still succeeds in getting the upper hand any time in his struggle is a satire on the society; for, the same society hero-worships the wealthy Margayya. His tainted origins—from a family of corpse bearers—are ever at the back of his mind; and of course his name, 'which seems almost a branding with hot iron' (48). Thus, when he comes to search for an alliance for his son, he can boast: 'I have a certain position in life to keep up [...]' (184). Means do not matter and horoscopes can be fixed, because he can 'dictate to planets what they should do [...] he will stand no nonsense from the planets' (185). It is Dr Pal, an educated citizen, who finds the compliant astrologer for Margayya

(187); the two associates lead each other into progressively deeper mess.

Margayya's rajasic guna would not let him be.

There was probably no other person in the whole country who had meditated so much on the question of interest. Margayya's mind was full of it. Night and day he sat and brooded over it. The more he thought of it the more it seemed to him the greatest wonder of creation. It combined in it the mystery of birth and multiplication. [...] It bordered on mystic perception. (116)

Now avarice sits on Margayya's shoulders like the Old Man of the Sea: 'I want only money, not brick and lime or mud' (183). Logically, in the final stage of Margayya's career, 'Dr Pal's services became indispensable and constant' (188). For, in the terminal stage Margayya moves 'from lending to deposits' (192). Pal's 'contacts' are such that a dozen new clients come to join his scheme every day. For, '[h]e could get anybody through Dr Pal' (140). Margayya has reduced Pal to 'a tout' (192), one more of Margayya's victims. Margayya's climactic financial scheme exposes not just Dr Pal, but the whole society—so many citizens make money illegally. The M-coli infection affects even lesser creatures: 'smaller tradesmen and clerks and workers' (200). It is a pandemic now. 'Margayya accepted any deposit that came to him' (200). And Margayya becomes his own victim. Margayya is self-victimized by avarice; Margayya is vice-fected.

The symptoms show. Margayya's wife, never a priority, now becomes as good as non-existent: 'He hardly noticed that she waited for him: his mind was fully occupied with various calculations.' Soon enough '[i]t became a household where perfect silence reigned' (199).[1] He tells his wife: 'With work ahead, I have no patience for food' (201); for 'a sort of dizziness perpetually hung about his head' (202). Soon he realizes his helplessness: 'He figured himself as being in the centre of a tangled skein. [...] I cannot afford to move even slightly this way or that' (202). Vice-fected Margayya is helpless; he evokes pity in the reader. 'I am virtually a prisoner here' (203). And '[h]e wanted so much to lie down' (204). Finally, Margayya 'resigned himself to whatever might be coming' (204). However, a secret reserve saves him; when the crash overtakes him, '[h]e relaxed completely' (217). Rejoining his family, he looks back: '[M]oney was like a gem which radiated subdued light all round' (217). Now the carbonic 'glow' has gone; sunlight has returned.

That is the arc of experience of our financial wizard of Malgudi: from fear and anxiety and insecurity to arrogance to resignation and resilience—a classic Narayan pattern. In Balzac's classic the reader's sympathy is quietly achieved, not for M. Grandet, the miser, but for his young daughter, Eugene. In *The Financial Expert* Narayan retains the reader's sympathy for the vice-fected Margayya. The early Margayya is so comically naive that everybody he comes across can read his thoughts; eminently, the priest and Dr Pal. Even the peasants can exploit him; before he picks up 'people skills', enough to tackle the Seth and walk away with a handsome cheque in his pocket.

Early in his career, moving in the squalid world of petty finance, Margayya concludes that money is the basis of the world: 'Margayya felt that the world treated him with contempt because he had no money' (14). He moves further down the same philosophic path: 'Money alone is important in this world. Everything else will come to us naturally if we have money in our purse' (21). This is the universal crux: most of us, not just the misers of the world, share it. Margayya's ancient lore supplies him with an adage: 'He that hath not is spurned even by his wife; even the mother that bore him spurns him' (22). This hoary dogma shuts Margayya's eyes to the loyalty and care and concern of his wife. Returning from his 'office' near the Cooperative Bank after an unpleasant encounter with the bank's underling, Margayya begins to believe what he has just told the villagers, that he was trying to help them out of their financial worries. It takes him little time to engage in alarming graduation, from the gullible villagers to the whole society: 'He viewed himself as a saviour of mankind' (28). From missionary to messiah to mystic!

Margayya's obsession with money-making, with indisputable faith in money as a source of universal happiness, develops gradually. The spectacle of people using an unclaimed dead body to collect money, supposedly for its last rites, sets off a chain of thoughts in Margayya. 'It left him admiring the power and dynamism of money, its capacity to make people do strange deeds' (28). The society around him strengthens his belief, and every day: 'If money was absent men came near being beasts. [...] Money was men's greatest need, like air or food. People went to horrifying lengths for its sake, like collecting rent on a dead body [...]' (28). Margayya's *reading* of the world is the same as the world's. Who is worshipped more— Lakshmi or Saraswati? Goddess of Wealth or Goddess of Learning? The reader empathizes with Margayya even at this stage.[2]

Another powerful factor affects Margayya's life and contributes to the reader's support for him: the pull of the family. Margayya is a 'family man': initially his rigorous overtures to Goddess Lakshmi are motivated by the need to support his family: 'If I have money ... I could give those medicines to my wife. The doctor would look at her with more interest and she might look like other women. That son of mine, that Balu—I could give him everything' (29). This concern for his indigent family is familiar and understandable; craft-wise, this makes Margayya human at the very outset of his classic rise. As his money-making gets out of hand, however, his first love—his family—suffers; he neglects and ignores his wife, shows no interest in going in search of his son.

Now Margayya only picks up the ways of the world. 'Margayya, true to his principles, did not wish to show his ignorance' (102). The strategies are extended to his family matters. When Balu fails to do well at school, 'Margayya decided to take charge of the school' (102). His goals are human, but his means are as old as humanity: 'Unless he admitted himself also to the school' (108), his son Balu's academic grades will not improve. At this stage Margayya's approach to life and people is simple and popular: means do not matter. 'He had immense confidence in himself now. He could undertake any plan with ease; he could shape his son's future as if it were so much clay in his hand' (108). This is a clear manifestation of rajasic hubris; and at an early stage of his ascent, anticipating his later excesses. He shows his faith in the miraculous power of money: 'He felt that no expense was too great for a child's future' (108). As his early deprivation spurs him in his financial adventures, his own lack of education demands compensatory action in his son's academic career. His dreams are universal and touch every reader. 'He would give him a separate study. He would buy table lamps with green shades; they said that green was good for the eyes' (111). Unfortunately for the father, '[t]he boy was too wild' (110). Balu may be inapt, but he is perceptive enough to retort: 'I know it is a different Goddess you worshipped.' Lakshmi, he means, not Saraswati; sadly for Margayya both goddesses fail him, one with too much, and the other with too little. But of course the novelist understands: 'No one lost his head so completely over a question of discipline as the parent of an only child' (110); besides, '[h]e was a fond and optimistic father' (142). Margayya will stand no nonsense from the teachers, 'but he dare not even touch our little darling; I would strike off that miserable teacher's head' (116). That sounds like R.K. Narayan (one can refer to Mrs Anandaram's undated transcript quoted in Chapter 1 of this book).

Now Margayya's treatment of his wife contrasts starkly with his mollycoddling of his son. With his confirmed faith in the power of Goddess Lakshmi he offers her money. But she responds wisely: 'What shall I do with Money. I have no use for it.' For Margayya, '[i]t was in the nature of a seditious speech' (146). The vice-fection is starkly evident. The successful financier denies her a servant; and no cook for her either. The lady accepted it meekly because she knew her husband: 'She knew, as he himself did, that he did not employ a cook because he did not like to spend money on one. […] She knew that he viewed money as something to accumulate and not to be spent on increasing one's luxuries in life' (147). Meenakshi knows him better than he does. She knew all his idioms even before he uttered them. There is a flicker of the old love and concern still: 'Sometimes when he saw her sitting at the fireplace, her eyes shrunken and swollen with the kitchen smoke, he felt uneasy and tried to help her with the kitchen work, keeping up the pretence of being newly-weds' (147). After all the miser denies himself too. At this stage Margayya is our own M. Grandet. 'He whitewashed the walls of his house inside only' (145). Mrs Margayya gains our sympathies with her attitude to her husband and her son. When Balu leaves for his new home, 'the house seemed to have become dull and lonely for Margayya's wife without her son' (191). The novelist contrasts this response with Margayya's attitude, 'but Margayya noticed no difference because his mind was busy formulating a new plan which was going to rocket him to undreamt of heights of financial success' (191).

THE FINANCIAL EXPERT | 129

Margayya's materialistic philosophy is defeated by his love for his family; his realization of the truth is confirmed when he goes back to his first love, the family—a new member of the family, his grandson: 'Now get the youngster here. I will play with him. Life has been too dull without him in this house' (218). Margayya is reclaimed by the family and life.

Among Margayya's positive traits that win the reader's sympathy early, his self-respect, and that too of an indigent man, comes first. He reproaches himself sitting idly on the parapet of the fountain on Market Road: 'Here is an adult, sitting on the fountain like a vagrant when he ought to be earning' (81). He carries the conviction to the end that a man has to work, must labour to earn his livelihood. His dealings with Dr Pal, too, throw light on this inner core. Dr Pal is the first of post-Independence series of modern 'intellectuals' who do not merit Narayan's respect. Margayya is ever uneasy with this intellectual, 'associating him with smut' (81). He defends with zeal and conviction his own conjugal privacy; and, typically, he would not suffer Pal to talk lightly of any married woman. 'I don't like anyone to talk of my wife. [...] No—you should not speak lightly about wives [...] but you must not make free reference to another man's wife' (85). Margayya's second meeting with Pal comes about as the culmination of his desperate search for earning a living. As Pal presses the yellow manuscript on him Margayya prays: 'God, why have you put me in the company of this terrible man amidst these wooden boxes!' (90). Margayya's origins undermine his resistance: 'He will probably choke me if I don't agree' (90). This pusillanimity he shakes off when he realizes his folly in allowing Pal free access to his son; he punishes the evil agent: exorcises himself. The irony at the end is Margayya himself has contributed to Pal's further degradation.

Now Margayya's simple faith in god—superstition—also leads him to conclude a deal with Dr Pal. As he hears a bicycle bell ring at the critical moment he decides: 'The sound of the bell was the voice of God. God spoke through his own signs' (90). Margayya conveys the book home 'as if he was trying to secrete a small dead body' (90). This is the second stage in Margayya's career. Feeling 'lonely and isolated and unhappy' (94), he realizes that 'self-assurance is the most important quality to cultivate' (94). When Margayya stumbles into Lal, the printer, the narrative picks up pace. Already Lal sees in him 'a kindred soul' (99). For:

> Being non-committal is the most widely recognized virtue among businessmen and it came to Margayya instinctively, as his other qualities came to him. The musician hums the right note at birth, the writer goes to the precise phrase in the face of an experience, whereas for the businessman the greatest gift is to be able to speak so many words which seem to signify something, but don't, which convey a general attitude but are free from commitment. (99)

This period is a sort of internship. From Lal Margayya also picks up the idiom and airs of big business, 'discovering [things] instinctively' (99).

He concludes that 'he who spoke last gained most' (99). He matches Lal's business tactics: 'They kept talking non-commitally, warmly, discreetly and with many digressions, till late in the evening, but without concluding anything' (101). This is somewhat of a warm-up session: the main bout is just ahead. When Lal certifies '[y]ou are a sharp businessman' (85), and '[y]ou are an uncanny fellow [...] [y]ou seem to understand everything' (105), Margayya has graduated. He has in the process extricated himself from Pal's smut and 'association', just to save his son from any disrepute.

In the third stage, Margayya becomes a fanatical believer: 'Do you know why I succeeded? It was because my mind was concentrated on the Goddess' (113), he tells his son, echoing the instruction of the temple priest. Presently Margayya's adoration of money 'bordered on mystic perception. It gave him the feeling of being part of an infinite existence' (116–17). Margayya now adopts a 'financial pugnacity' (125); from pontificating to his compliant audience that 'money is not everything' (117), he now proclaims that 'money is everything' (117). After all only 'when the profits dwindled he began to view the book in a peculiarly realistic light' (118). He offers a reason for starting his banking business: '[I]t hurt his dignity to be called the publisher of *Domestic Harmony*' (118): and thoughts of Balu incurring censure on this account weigh with him (118). Once again it is Balu who is responsible for a turn in Margayya's career.

The divinization of avarice accelerates: to 'the mystic feeling that money engendered in Margayya' (182). Now Margayya is a financial visionary; he pities the common public. 'He pitied them. He felt that he must do something to enlighten their minds. He would not be a banker to them, but a helper, a sort of money doctor who would help people to use their money properly with the respect due to it. He would educate society anew in all these matters' (123).

Margayya ('the path-man') takes off on the universal trajectory: from need to greed to mania. Vice-fection spreads rapidly, unstoppable; sooner or later, develops secondaries. Margayya now sees himself as 'a financial mystic' (124). Guru Raj, the owner of the building on Market Road that Margayya chooses to locate his new office, himself is a miniature version of Margayya: when asked to install electric lights in his tenant's shop he claims to have 'sent a direct order to the General Electric in America' (150). This Guru Raj, however, reveals better sense when he advises Margayya not to neglect his family.

Margayya works like a demon to satisfy his greed. He is so absorbed in 'the adventure of money-making' that, for the first time, love for his son recedes: 'His affluence, his bank balance, buoyed him up and made him bear the loss of their son' (148). The world does its bit, too, by adoring moneyed Margayya: 'Whatever he said sounded authoritative and mature nowadays, and people listened to him with respectful attention' (149). M. Grandet's neighbours, too, knowing full well his devilish cunning and treachery to members of their community, shamelessly flatter him and pamper his ego.

Nothing now satisfies Margayya's gold lust except liquid cash. 'I want only money, not brick and lime or mud' (183). He is ruthless: '[T]he moment a man signed his bonds, he was more or less finished' (183). And as he approaches the summit of his success, '[h]e no longer believed that man was a victim of circumstances or fate' (185). In Narayan's world this is demoniacal egotism inviting ruin and worse. Hard to believe he is the same Margayya who fasted, feasted pundits for the favour of Goddess Lakshmi. Now he was 'like a financial mountaineer who sets his heart on reaching the summit of Everest' (193).

Margayya takes up the new line to feed on the venality and vice in the society itself; his new customers are largely war-time black marketeers and corrupt officials; who constitute of course the real Malgudi gutter.

Margayya's vice drives him relentlessly on; we recall M. Grandet's last moments, or the central character in Narayan's own short story 'Guru'. Margayya admires the currency notes with as much thrill as M. Grandet enjoys the sight of his gold. However, the family pull gets the better of his madness; he plans to wean away Pal from his son, but the means are flawed; he bribes Pal to keep him away from his son Balu.

The pathos underlying the violence at the end cannot be missed. This man has never been completely happy; he has suffered from poverty and privation, and want has defiled even his relationship with his wife. He takes it out the only way he can; he is a bully at home: 'Once inside his home all his old assertiveness returned' (37). The first time he addresses her it comes as a surprise to us; she has a name given by her parents: Meenakshi. Self-effacing Meenakshi, though less literate than her husband, is self-composed. From the beginning she seems to understand him better than anyone else; that knowledge, however, does not contribute to marital felicity: 'Ever since he could remember she had always shown a sort of uneasiness about Margayya' (48). She pities him more than she fears his temper. As Balu grows up into a family puzzle, and Margayya withdraws into his financial bubble, Meenakshi grows lonelier. Like the other women in Narayan's novels, Mrs Margayya draws from an inner spring; she can instinctively notice it when Margayya develops his maniacal obsession. 'Lately, after he had become affluent [...] he had come to believe that whatever he did was always right. She did her best not to contradict him: she felt that he strained himself too much in his profession, and that she ought not to add to his burden' (137). She leaves the men, father and son, alone. And she 'attained thereby great tranquillity in practical everyday life [...] watched the trouble brewing between the two as if it all happened behind a glass screen' (138).

Balu is the other factor in Margayya's private life. For the boy was born rather late in life, and that too after an elaborate vow, strenuously redeemed later, to Lord Tirupati. Thus, '[w]hen he came home, he could not bear to be kept away from him even for a moment' (10). 'Next to the subject of money, the greatest burden on his mind was his son' (34). Margayya's fondness for Balu—a son-fixation endemic in India—proves to be a source of trouble. And, 'his son misbehaved so much in his presence' (74). With a virtual feast of sweets spread before him by the printer, Lal, in their first meeting, Margayya remembers Balu: 'He was racked with a feeling that he was stealing some delicacy which ought to have gone to his child' (97). Fathers make a mess of their duties in Narayan's post-Independence phase. Even Mrs Margayya recalls her own father: 'People had been afraid to speak to her father even when he was in the sweetest temper, for his face had a severity without any relation to his mood' (137). And later Margayya compounds two injustices with a third: he spoils Balu with overindulgence; the boy is not a victim of Margayya's parsimony, as his mother is, but of Margayya's extravagance.

Two chords to his career and actions: and both lead him into trouble. Along with money Balu is the causal twin in Margayya's career. Balu 'initiates' all critical changes in Margayya's career. The spoilt kid throws Margayya's accounts book into the gutter and as good as sets his father on his later career; this incident is later paralleled in Balu's tearing up his SSLC register and throwing it into the same gutter. The open drain is a handy metaphor for the seamy side of human nature and human society.

When the anonymous postcard arrives from Madras announcing Balu's death, for the first time, Mrs Margayya hurls the truth at him: '[Y]ou ruined him' (155). And when Balu comes back:

> She looked more youthful. A new flush appeared on her shallow cheeks. Her eyes had become very bright and sparkling. She became loquacious and puckish in her comments. She took the trouble to comb her hair with care and stuck jasmine strings in it. She seemed to feel that she was born anew into the world. She spoke light-heartedly and with a trembling joy in her voice. This was a revelation to Balu. (174)

Margayya's dash to Madras comes as an interlude in the episode of Balu's 'death': the second time a Narayan hero goes to Madras, after Chandran's outing in *The Bachelor of Arts*; Margayya dislikes the place as much as young Chandran. Through the train journey the novelist takes the reader right into the heart of India. Narayan enjoys these outings. In this small space and duration, with a compartment meant for twelve accommodating almost twice as many, Narayan presents ambience characters, such as the villager and the bangle seller, as well as an action character: for, the sardine can introduces the police inspector, who volunteers to help Margayya locate his son. Police inspectors come off fairly decently in R.K. Narayan's novels: like the memorable police inspector who comes to the aid of Srinivas in *Mr. Sampath*. For Margayya the inspector turns out to be a saviour.

In 'the mad man of Park Town' the author of the postcard mischief, a Dickensian eccentric, the novelist presents a different derangement, a parallel to Margayya's malady; Margayya is completely crazed in the world of money and money-making, in the grip of avarice: on the train to Madras Margayya 'suddenly felt that he had kept away too long from the thought of money. It was like a tobacco chewer suddenly realizing that he had been away too long from his pouch' (164). In juxtaposition this Park Town version of derangement is too 'otherworldly'. Two species of mania, then.

The humanitarian police inspector is a foil to both; he is the centre that holds.

The novelist's art secures Margayya from our contempt. Control of reader's sympathy for Margayya's shenanigans accounts for the success of *The Financial Expert*. Circumscribed by his own self in his unenviable milieu Margayya earns the sympathy of the reader. The two loves in his life, money and his son, both ruin him. Margayya is equally unsuccessful in his relationship with his wife. And Margayya compounds two injustices with a third: he spoils Balu with overindulgence; the boy is not a victim of Margayya's parsimony, as his mother is, but of Margayya's extravagance. Sadly, 'Margayya felt that at a time when he had a right to have a happy and bright home, he was being denied the privilege unnecessarily' (119). However, in the climactic scene when he beats up Pal, Margayya's clarity in witnessing himself is remarkable. 'He was conscious of a desperation that impelled him on.' Narayan's success lies in winning the reader's understanding for this 'desperation'. 'All the caution and discretion was swept aside' (211).

The novelist ends the tale on a positive note: with Margayya's affirmation of human warmth and human relationships: 'Now get the youngster here. I will play with him. Life has been too dull without him in this house' (177).

Endurance of the human self—spiritual stamina—and its potential for spiritual growth, redeem the heroes to come of the Middle Period.[3]

11

The Moth and the Mahatma
Waiting for the Mahatma

After Margayya's comedy of worldly success, *Waiting for the Mahatma* is a love story. *The Bachelor of Arts*, a pre-Independence novel, is also a love story: *Waiting for the Mahatma* is love story plus; the plus is the Mahatma.[1] The novel presents the education of another young man, Sriram, this time under Gandhian guidance. Like Martin Luther King Jr and Nelson Mandela, Narayan was also an admirer of the Mahatma. In the story Narayan wrote on Gandhi, 'Gandhi's Appeal', where the stress is on the moral stature of the Mahatma.[2]

Sriram is a post-Independence hero; though much younger than Margayya, he belongs to the same guna family. By age and temperament he is in greater need of self-development; even at the end, a much-changed young man, Sriram is still capable of uncontrolled emotions. A typical post-Independence hero suffers from a vice; in *Waiting for the Mahatma* Sriram's sloth is contrasted early with the purposeful energy and self-discipline of his grandmother, Granny; and, later, of the Mahatma and of his disciple Bharati. The central interest of the novel is the development of Sriram: from sloth to selfless action, through the mediation and ministration of his beloved, a spirited girl, a favourite disciple of the Mahatma, aptly named Bharati: 'Bharat' is India.

How credible is the portrait of Mahatma Gandhi? Narayan is interested in, as he puts it in another context, 'not the mystery but the fact': it is Mahatma the man the novelist presents. His speeches, his conversations, and actions and reactions in Narayan's novel build up a portrait of a rare man, a 'great soul'; Mahatma Gandhi as a 'character' comes through vividly.

The opening paragraph, perhaps inspired by Narayan's childhood in Purasawalkam (Madras), recalls *The Financial Expert*. After

Margayya, a virtual orphan, we have now an orphan, Sriram; parentless but not unparented: his strong-minded Granny, yet another avatar of Narayan's grandmother Ammani, plays the role of a foster parent. In his ancient house Sriram also happens to be the first post-Independence character representing the decline of the Brahmin class: for the Kabir Street 'aristocracy' have fallen on evil days.[3]

With a rajasic character at the centre of the story, sexuality is admitted more freely in the human scheme of things; *Waiting for the Mahatma* presents the first 'attempted' rape in Narayan's novels. Jails are a likely ambience for rajasic characters at some point; for the first time a jail appears in a Narayan novel. With the triad of Gandhi, Bharati, and Granny playing decisive roles in shaping Sriram, the novel may also be read as an allegory of India's moral regeneration under Gandhi's leadership.

Waiting for the Mahatma is an ambitious effort: Narayan brings in Mahatma Gandhi. Even for us later generations of Indians— and many others abroad—who went to school in India after Independence and Gandhi's assassination, Gandhi is a pre-eminent national idol. It is very likely that most of us have not seen him in person; Gandhi is a legend to us, a hear-say hero; a page or a chapter from history or a phantom from the past. With the impact of a discovery a young man or woman of today learns that Gandhi was something more, something different, unique. Albert Einstein (1950) said 'Generations to come, it may be, will scarce believe that such a one as this ever in flesh and blood walked upon this earth' on the occasion of Gandhi's seventieth birthday in 1939. Nelson Mandela (1999) called him the 'Sacred Warrior'.

Srinivasa Iyengar (1962: 203) assesses the literary impact of the Mahatma:

The period between the two World Wars and comprising them both was the Gandhian Age in India, our modern 'Heroic Age'. Once Gandhi entered India after the First World War, life could not be the same as before, and every segment of our national life—politics, economics, education, religion, social life, language, and literature—acquired a more or less pronounced Gandhian hue.

Narayan's Gandhian affinities, too, cannot be ruled out. In his fiction as well as in his non-fictional prose, Narayan reveals qualities of heart that were Gandhi's virtues for life: sympathy and support for children, women, and the have-nots and the downtrodden (his focus especially in his short stories); communal harmony; abhorrence of violence, especially in the name of God and religion. Narayan's own preoccupation with the self and its Kurukshetra here on this earth is typically Gandhian. *Mr. Sampath*, especially, is close to the spirit of Gandhi; the hero, Srinivas, practically seeks the path of karma yoga for the amelioration of his fellow citizens of Malgudi. Gandhi for Narayan is not so much a politician or a statesman: he is a Mahatma, a Great Soul. Narayan's contemporaries, Mulk Raj Anand and Raja Rao, take up the theme of Gandhian influence in their first novels. For the villagers in Raja Rao's *Kanthapura*, Gandhi is an avatar in the Hindu tradition. After Gandhi's departure though the atmosphere is polluted by politicians and self-seekers; and the Gandhian spirit appears to flag, as it does midway in *Waiting for the Mahatma* with the advent of the terrorist Jagadish on the scene; even after his departure from Malgudi the Mahatma is a force to reckon; he is a felt absence. 'Though the Mahatma's physical presence was no longer with him, Sriram had a feeling that his movements were being guided' (Narayan 1955: 63).[4]

Gandhi is not a 'character' in the novel, not fictitious, not 'touched up'. Gandhi in the novel is Gandhi as he lived, a historical personage. We witness Gandhi in action in the first two chapters—in his first appearance—in his preoccupation with the principles he stood for in his life. We see him as the 'politician' with a difference, a suave 'diplomat', and the national leader who conducted crowds as coolly as a maestro his symphony orchestra. We see him revealed in his five principles: abolition of untouchability, prohibition of all liquor, achievements of Hindu–Muslim unity, propaganda for hand-spinning khadi and the amelioration of women. Considering the economy with which the novelist builds up the image, this is achievement enough. In his walks with Sriram, in his chat with the outcaste urchin, we see the humorous Gandhi and the compassionate soul. When Gandhi's train leaves Malgudi—'Taking the Mahatma to Trichy, and then to Madras, Bombay, Delhi and out into the universe' (63)—we have seen and experienced Gandhi the Mahatma.

But this is not all. Narayan does something more to Gandhi in the memorable last scene of the novel. We see the Mahatma meeting with Sriram and Bharati and we recognize him; he is familiar as a politician, as a statesman, and as Bapu ('Father' of the Nation). Even his compassionate concern for the orphans is no surprise to us. What comes as a revelation is his 'walking to his Death'. Now, to begin with, there is this 'man with the watch' whom Gandhi facetiously refers to as 'my conscience-keeper'. With Gandhi, that is, he is an overarching force; and the man's anonymity in the light of later incidents promotes him to an embodiment of time itself. After promising to attend the wedding of Sriram and Bharati, the Mahatma moves towards the prayer meeting.

Mahatmaji suddenly stopped, turned round and said, 'Bharati, I have a feeling that I may not attend your wedding tomorrow morning.' 'Why? Why, Bapu?' she asked. 'I don't know.' His voice trailed away. 'I seem to have been too rash in promising to officiate as your priest'. [...] 'If God wills it I shall come'. [...] Mahatmaji took out his watch and said, 'I hate to be late [...].'

Immediately follows the assassination: 'He was dead in a few seconds' (173).

Vincent Sheean (1949: 249) wonders: 'How tranquilly he walked to his death!' We have just heard Gandhi and we are struck by the suggestion of Gandhi's intuitive reception of death. We have witnessed an extraordinary episode of prescience and spiritual calm. We recall parallels from history and mythology, of 'great souls', mahatmas, who 'walked' to their deaths. And then we realize that something magical has been done to the story of Sriram by Narayan through Gandhi; Gandhi has been all along a familiar figure, but now he has joined the ranks of Great Souls, Mahatmas, that have ever been and are now part of our mythology and folk imagination. 'He is another Christ.'[5]

In the course of a mere fifty lines of narrative the story has been raised to the level of a myth. The book was written after Gandhi's death and published in 1955.

Gandhi's story is the story of contemporary India, post First World War; we have in the novel the history of India in more or less connected form from 1920 to 30 January 1948. At the same time it is the story of Sriram from his childhood in the 1920s. Sriram is the hero of the novel; the novel presents mainly his experiences.

It is the story of this young man under the influence of Gandhi, directly and indirectly. At another level it is the story of the cultural regeneration of India under the influence of a Mahatma. India has been waiting for a Mahatma; and he arrives to resuscitate her. Sriram is a representative figure, the hero is an emblem character; he is a representative of the cultural condition of India in his times—even as Jake Barnes in *The Sun Also Rises* represents the rootlessness and the isolation of the post-War world; Hemingway took the title from the Bible. However, there is a difference between the two novels. Though Sriram's father has died in the Middle East, the war has no impact on Sriram's world comparable to its devastation in the West. For Hemingway the so-called Great War is a man-made catastrophe that has destroyed a whole world of values for his generation. For Narayan the story begins with the end of the war because it was the time when, properly speaking, Mahatma Gandhi arrived in India—waiting for the Mahatma. Sriram represents the national condition following the spiritual atrophy of centuries. Narayan makes the issues clear. The very first sentence of the novel tells us that Sriram is an orphan (and Bharati, too, is an orphan). Sriram knows little about his parents; they are remote. He is not satisfied with his mother's picture; in contrast, he covets 'that portrait of a European queen with apple cheeks and wavy coiffure' (Narayan 1955: 1). The fascination this exotic portrait of an alien in Kanni's shop wields on Sriram borders on the abnormal; the young man even offers to buy it. Towards the end when Sriram returns from the prison, mature and wise, educated out of many illusions, he remembers the picture: '[T]he portrait of Maria Theresa was no longer there to brighten up the surroundings' (152).

At the same time the boy does not understand his grandmother. 'Granny was very old, probably eighty, ninety, or a hundred. He had never tried to ascertain her age correctly. And she would not understand new things' (57). Naturally, because Granny has lived all her life in an ancient house full of traditions. This is one of the ancient houses in Kabir Street which is going to play a conspicuous role in Narayan's novels and novellas to come. 'The house was over two hundred years old and looked it. [...] There the family lineage began centuries ago and continued still [...]' (4). Granny belongs to an old order; her sense of duty wins her respect even in the post office. Her love and care for her grandson and attachment to her family mark her out. Sriram finds Granny amusing in the importance she attaches to values that have no meaning for him. Later she comes back from 'death', in all her tenacious life: to die later as she desires, a peaceful and conventionally holy end by the holy Ganges. This is a land and its people in transition, a changing India. And it is time for change of guard in Malgudi; the episode of Granny's resurrection marks the critical point in Sriram's 'rebirth', intellectual, moral: he comes back from a phase of violence and acknowledges boldly his love and debt to Granny; Sriram goes to her funeral knowing well that the police are waiting for him.

Granny and Sriram belong to different worlds. Sriram is a recluse; he is not a success at school; so cut off from his culture, he does not know even the almanac. Granny upbraids him: 'It's going to be your twentieth birthday, although you behave as if you are half that' (3). True to his rajasic nature Sriram is full of instincts and impulses. Narayan presents the only scene in his novels so far where a woman is assaulted by his hero: 'It was a night of absolute darkness' (89). For the American novelist it is impotence; for Narayan it is the obsessive—oppressive—libido of his hero.

Bharati attracts Sriram at first glance; she is the angel from another world, from Gandhi's entourage, of his 'family'; and she leads him towards this beacon. Sriram stumbles into the pool of light; on an impulse he joins Gandhi's followers: 'The teacher had put a new idea into his head and he almost felt he was a veteran of the party' (23). His drift into the Mahatma's hut shows how full of instincts and impulses this scion of an ancient Kabir Street family is. 'The door of Mahatmaji's hut was half open. Light streamed out through the gap. Sriram went towards it like a charmed moth. [...] He peeped in like a clown' (43).

First 'a charmed moth', and then a 'clown': the images aptly represent this scion of a Kabir Street; but unlike many others of the species this creature is exceptionally fortunate: Sriram has stumbled into a house of benediction. Sriram's intellectual grasp of the Mahatma is negligible; but he feels comforted in the 'presence', in the 'Great Presence'. Later he hopes that Mahatma will become the Emperor of India (85); like his fellow prisoners. At this stage, Sriram feels Gandhi's presence, but understands little of his message. Sriram fails in his satyagraha move: '[A] satyagraha struggle is impossible without capital in the shape of character' (Andrews 1930: 204). Gandhi writes to him: 'Your work should be a matter of inner faith. It cannot depend upon what you see or understand. Your conscience should be your guide in every action. Consult it and you won't go wrong. Don't guide yourself by what you see. You should do your duty because your inner voice drives you to do it' (Narayan 1955: 86).[6]

Slade quotes Gandhi: 'You have to love humanity in spite of itself' (90). Sriram just cannot reach this level of self-discipline, spiritual progression; even towards the end Bharati is forced to tell him: 'You have not changed at all' (165). A cry of impatience; for Sriram, too, progresses in the course of the novel. After the departure of the Mahatma whose influence moved him from 'an age old somnolence', he slips back; when even Bharati moves away from him, he plumbs the pit; and the novel's action, too, grinds to a halt. Sriram has such weak will power that he is yoked by a character like Jagadish, who himself later shocks Srinivas with his lack of depth. Aptly it is a ruined shrine that harbours the two young men as they indulge in terrorist activities. However, redemption cannot be far; Bharati advises him: 'It is your duty to risk your life to see [Granny]' (116). And Sriram leaves 'the underground', risks arrest and incarceration, and visits his grandmother. Later still he passes another test when he turns down an offer of amnesty from his jailor; because, 'If he met Bharati she'd probably say, "You sneak out of prison, do you? You have degraded yourself beyond description. Get out of my sight"' (146). Under Bharati's Gandhian influence Sriram achieves enough moral strength to acknowledge in utter humility: '[S]he seemed too magnificent to be his wife' (167). Bharati guides this frail vessel through its choppy career. 'Bharati gave his whole life a new meaning and a new dimension [...]' (162).

To begin with, Sriram's perception of Bharati is characteristic: 'She looked different from the beauty in Kanni's shop' (13). Her strength of character, courage of conviction, simplicity of conduct and bearing; above all, her femininity: she is true to her name. The contrast makes a romance of their love story; even on the simplest level the tale appeals to us with its charm. However, its true significance lies in her moral influence on him. To Sriram, Bharati is the guru. 'Mahatmaji added: "Remember that she is your Guru, and think of her with reverence and respect and you will be all right and she will be all right"' (62). This is not the first time in Narayan's novels that the beloved becomes the teacher, the guru; we recall Krishna and Rajam in *The English Teacher*. For Bharati is also the New Woman who emerged during the national struggle against the British under the inspiration of the Mahatma. For the most remarkable feature of Bharati's personality is the utter lack of self-consciousness: 'How confidently she faced the crowd!' (19). Bharati is brought up by Gandhi (19);[7] she understands, accepts, and practises what Gandhi stands for. She accepts and takes charge of thirty refugee children; the Bride is also the Mother. Thus, in the climactic scene when Narayan raises the story to the level of a myth, when Gandhi blesses the union of Sriram and Bharati, we know that he is blessing a rejuvenated India; Gandhi is blessing a New India, which is of his making, which he has initiated into a path of self-discipline, sacrifice, and unconditional love; which has, in spite of itself, something of him ingrained in her. It is a different matter that the Gandhian spirit evaporates too soon: and Narayan draws our attention to the spiritual depletion in the novels to come.[8]

Like Raja Rao's *Kanthapura*, Narayan's novel is also inspired by the Gita: the Indian tradition holds with the Gita that from time to time God descends on the earth to root out evil and protect the meek. When Sriram comes out of the prison he wonders if independent India is 'independent'; Jagadish's version of independence bores him. For Sriram independence is the Gandhian version of it: it is inner emancipation. 'Gandhi craved for his country a psychological metamorphosis which would give it inner freedom and, then, inevitably, outer freedom, for once the people acquired individual dignity they would insist on better living and nobody would hold them in bondage' (Fischer 1954: 54).

Sriram raises the question, and within a year after the Mahatma's passing: post Gandhi, how good is India's 'independence'? Narayan's *Waiting for the Mahatma* is a story of one generation in India interrogating others to come.[9]

12

Grateful to Love and Death
The Guide

Raju rises from a petty shopkeeper to a 'man of consequence'. Like Margayya in *The Financial Expert* he is also a man possessed: 'I was a man with a mission.' When he crashes Raju redeems himself more spectacularly than Margayya.

The first novel in English to win India's Sahitya Akademi Award, *The Guide* is a novel with brisk pace, a story told with much verve. It is also a fine psychological study of a fraud, a charlatan; 'I will fix it with the gods' (Narayan 1958: 94); as a con artist Raju's portrait is a singular success. We are now mid-stream in the post-Independence period; what developed in *Mr. Sampath* as a subplot is centre stage here. Raju is an 'evolved' descendant of Sampath. Graham Greene had decided on the ending even before his friend started writing the novel: 'Kill him.'

Narayan's art triumphs in *The Guide* in retaining the reader's sympathy for his susceptible hero. He achieves this through a convincing development of Raju's character. '[I]t was in his nature to get involved in other people's interests and activities' (9). Raju shares his creator's zest for life: '[T]he panorama of life enchanted me' (14). And it is 'so good to be alive and feeling all that' (228); Raju's rajasic craving for food continues almost to the end: '[A]ll villagers should combine to help him eat *bonda* for fifteen days without a break' (110). The direct narrative part, in Raju's own voice, completely humanizes this typical rajasic character; the sensitive, elaborate description of the rains comes through Raju: 'Raju loved this season, for its greenness everywhere, for the variety of cloud-play in the sky, which he could watch through the columned halls' (91). Narayan's post-independence charlatans in *The Financial Expert* and *The Guide* also share their creator's own childhood: their loneliness is relieved by the devotion of a mother figure. Raju's tongue-in-cheek humour, too, is vintage Narayan: '[I]f this was prison life, why didn't more people take to it?' (202–3).

The post-Independence heroes suffer each from a vice; in Margayya it is avarice; in *Waiting for the Mahatma*, Sriram's sloth. With Raju, as with Sampath earlier, it is lust: 'The only reality in my life and consciousness was Rosie' (118). The novel is a study of illicit passion. In comparison with Sriram's crush in *Waiting for the Mahatma* Raju suffers blinding passion: 'It was a natural obsession' (138). *The Guide* dramatizes desperate desire: 'I made love to her constantly and was steeped in an all-absorbing romanticism' (175). The power of sex is presented, however, with the refinement we associate with Narayan: under its power, Raju acts 'as under chloroform'. The seduction itself is done with sophistication: 'I knew I had placed her in my debt' (88). He is candid: '[W]hat I watched were the curves' (145). Before long, Raju is a rajasic creature brought to bay.

Rural India, for a Narayan hero, is moral India; the villagers reform a young man of his sentimentalism in *The Bachelor of Arts* and reorient him. Villagers once again play a major role in *The Guide*. Their earnestness is contrasted with Raju's sham. Narayan of course does not romanticize these rustics: Raju notes with clarity that they lead a limited existence caught 'between irrigation and litigation'; and he concludes saying 'anything seemed possible in this village' (97). These villagers of Mangala, with their faith reformatory, are realized unsentimentally; violence is just below the surface. All the same, for the Narayan hero, they are the rural dynamic, recalling *The Bachelor of Arts*: '[T]hey loved to bring him gifts.' Raju realizes he 'must play the role that Velan gave him' (33). Gradually, thanks to the villagers, '[t]he pillared hall was bright with the lanterns the villagers had brought with them' (50); and '[h]is life had lost its personal limitations' (53); and 'he seemed to belong to the world now [... he] could hardly afford a private life now' (54). Sublimation follows.

Raju is headed for renewal of faith, as his creator was two decades earlier; for Narayan, after his post-Rajam psychic experience, what matters ultimately is the 'cosmic scheme'. At the back of all these post-Independence books is one philosophical priority of post-Rajam experience: Reality according to God. The ritual fast at the end climaxes the transformation of a very human hero.

The morning sun was out by now; *a great shaft of light* illuminated the surroundings. It was difficult to hold Raju on his feet, as he had a tendency to flop down. They held him *as if he were a baby.* Raju opened his eyes, looked about, and said, 'Velan, it's raining in the hills. I can feel it coming up under my feet, up my legs ...' and with that he sagged down. (247; emphasis mine)

That great shaft of light, having dawned ever so unobtrusively with *The Financial Expert*, shines again in Narayan's later novels; 'baby' suggests a new birth.

Brisk shuttling between past and present, opportune shifts of point of view, a natural ease to the dialogue, the pull and power of detail, the highs and lows of action, a well-charted crisis—these are other narrative elements contributing to the novelist's success in *The Guide*. Raju's preparation for his role as a *vadhyar* (teacher) in the jail is done early: while vending sundry eats, magazines, etc., on the Malgudi railway platform, before launching on his fateful career, he has already done much reading. 'I learned much from scrap' (49).

The casual introduction of Rosie is in character: her artistic temperament and interest as well as marital disharmony are presented with unobtrusive art. Raju realizes rather too late: '[Rosie] had seemed such a happy creature in our old house, even when my uncle was bullying her.' She yearns for a normal life: 'How I wish I could go into a crowd, walk about, take a seat in the auditorium, and start out for an evening without having to make up or dress for the stage!' (194). Rosie retains her dignity, her grace to the end. She realizes her lapse, that she 'committed an enormous sin' (150). Her reaction to the discovery of Raju's crime is typically Indian: 'This is *karma.* What can we do?' (216). Raju's concluding comments do credit to his nascent wisdom: 'Neither Marco nor I had any place in her life, which had its own sustaining vitality and which she herself had underestimated all along' (223). Rosie's final acts are in character: 'Before her departure she had methodically drawn up a list of all our various debts and discharged them fully [...]. The only article that she carried out of the house was the book [...]' (230). Marco's book.

Some of Narayan's memorable women characters are each associated with a fragrance, general or particular: Susila in *The English Teacher* with jasmine; Bharati of *Waiting for the Mahatma* with sandalwood; in a much later novel, *The Painter of Signs*, the heroine Daisy has her own fragrance. Here in *The Guide* Rosie's 'scent-filled presence' works magic on Raju.[1]

Marco's fixation for vouchers, the critical trait, is highlighted early. 'He would not yield an anna without a voucher, whereas if you gave him a slip of paper you could probably get him to write off his entire fortune' (75). Raju can still be objective: '[Marco] was a good man, completely preoccupied, probably a man with an abnormal capacity for trust' (115). A cuckold in the hands of a lesser writer could have yielded a caricature.

The Guide also can be viewed as a drama in five acts.[2] The first act consists of Raju's childhood and boyhood and his emergence as 'Railway Raju'. The second opens with the arrival of Marco and Rosie at Malgudi and ends with Marco's return to Madras abandoning Rosie in Malgudi. The third is entirely devoted to Raju and Rosie: their design for living; their lifestyle after Rosie becomes Nalini, the famous dancer; Raju's fall; and Rosie's exit from his life. The fourth act presents Raju's 'rebirth' after his release from jail, and his arrival and emergence as a 'swami' at Mangala. The final act covers Raju's fast and redemption.

The title of the novel sums up the hero's career and life. '"Tell me about it," Raju said, the old, old habit of affording guidance to others asserting itself' (8). For, '[i]t was in his nature to get involved in other people's interests and activities' (9). The first three acts mark the first phase of Raju's guidehood, while the final two acts, the second phase, as guru: 'His visitors sat patiently on a lower step, waiting for him to attend to them, like patients in a doctor's room' (21). Raju in the first phase is a tourist guide, then is in the metaphorical sense, and finally in the spiritual path. In fact two earlier heroes Sampath and Margayya, too, are 'guides', self-appointed. The title of the novel is ironical, like *The Financial Expert*: the guide is guided. Now, however, Raju has his mantle, his guidehood, thrust on him. 'Have I been in a prison or in some sort of transmigration?' (22).

The humour moderates any sentimentalism: 'He decided to look as brilliant as he could manage, let drop gems of thought from his lips, assume all the radiance available, and afford them all the guidance they required without stint' (34). The novelist charts the dramatic development. 'Raju felt cornered. "I have to play the part expected of me; there is no escape"' (51). For, 'the essence of sainthood seemed to lie in one's ability to utter mystifying statements' (52). In a way it is his temperament: 'I never said, "I don't know." Not in my nature, I suppose. [...] It was not because I wanted to utter a falsehood, but only because I wanted to be pleasant' (55). The guide needs to guide himself: is guided by the villagers, then, ultimately, by his inner voice, climactically in Raju's opting for an honest fast.

The Guide marks the end of the first phase of Narayan's post-Independence novels. Malgudi, post-Independence, presents self-seekers and impresarios. Sampath is responsible for the misery of his own family, a faithful wife, and children, the distress of Ravi's family and the failure of Shanti and the loss at the studios; only Srinivas, though fallible himself, emerges chastened. While Sampath zooms out at the end, Margayya, after his jerry-built financial project collapses, ruining all and sundry including his own family, is back with the knobby trunk; he may be materially ruined, but he remains unvanquished, and goes back to enjoying his family. The first phase of Raju's story sees him rise irrepressibly, to the popular status of 'Railway Raju'; then, like Sampath again, Raju surrenders to desire (kama), lands Rosie in trouble with her husband. In his reckless passion for Rosie Raju lets his infatuation ruin his business and his own home, and ends up in jail.

Rosie is the main influence in the second phase of Raju's life. Narayan's success in Rosie's portrayal is second only to his achievement in Raju. Rosie is at once conventional and modern. 'Don't imagine on hearing her name that she wore a short skirt or cropped her hair. She looked just the orthodox dancer that she was' (9). She is a master's degree holder, and 'was not very glamorous if that is what you expect, but she did have a figure [...]' (58). The name itself is calculated to represent a romantic dreamer: '[T]his girl herself was a dreamer if ever there was one' (100). Raju knows her; he knows too well this aspect of Rosie. Rosie is trusting: it is significant that after Raju's clever initial advances she only says: 'You are a brother to me' (74). But Raju knows she is vulnerable: for, her husband Marco, 'I disliked this man' (64), is the ineffectual angel. Marco proclaims: 'If a man has to have peace of mind it is best that he forget the fair sex' (71). Rosie pines for one 'real, live husband' (85), and Raju, with his bounce and knack, succeeds where Marco has only created a void. '"I'd have preferred any kind of mother-in-law, if it had meant one real, live husband," she said' (85). Raju observes: '[P]erhaps he married out of a desire to have someone care for his practical life [...]' (113). Later Raju realizes that Marco would have been happier with Joseph the caretaker, rather than a wife.

Rosie is haunted by her infidelity. 'After all, he is my husband. I have to respect him. I cannot leave him there' (105). When Marco comes to know of the perfidy through her own talk, 'the look of despair and shock in his face haunted me' (133). She confesses to Raju: 'I didn't want anything more in life than to make my peace with him [...]. I sincerely hoped you would leave us and go away and that we could be peaceful among ourselves [...]' (133). That is not to be, however. A month of ordeal follows for Rosie. When she confronts him he tells her: 'You are a woman who will go to bed with anyone that flatters your antics' (152). It is hard to ignore the truth in Marco's judgement. Rosie's vocation has been her weakness.

The affair is carried on at Raju's own home, but in his mother's absence. 'Her joy at finding shops, cinemas, and caresses made her forget for a while her primary obsession. But not for long' (107). Classical dance is her primary obsession; dancing, her vocation. Her fervour baffles Raju, while her dreams amuse him. Everything is funnelled towards fulfilment of her art. Specially, nature. For Rosie nature is the source of all art. 'Oh, see those birds! What colours! You know, there is a small piece about a parrot on a maiden's arm' (111). At the Peak House she is delighted with the rich vegetation. 'She ran like a child from plant to plant with cries of joy [...]' (67). Her aesthetic sense is revealed in her arrangements for receiving the two gentlemen from the college. The skilful way in which she handles the collegiate connoisseurs gives a foretaste of her success in managing her own affairs after Raju's forced exit from her life. Marco has cautioned Raju: 'She has enough sense to look after herself' (71). Resilience is this artiste's strong point. When, after the month of ordeal at the Peak House, Marco turns her out of his life she comes to Raju and looks 'slightly weak, but as if she hadn't a care in the world' (125). Later, as she starts her regular dance practice, Raju looks at her as she emerges after a bath 'fresh, and blooming. Looking at her, one would have thought that she had not a care in the world. She was quite happy to be doing what she was doing at the moment, was not in the least bothered about the past, and looked forward tremendously to the future' (136). (This sounds more like post-ordeal Narayan.) Raju can appreciate her gift. 'She was a born artiste, her passion for physical love was falling into place and had ceased to be a primary obsession with her' (146). The secret of Rosie's success is her extraordinary capacity for renewal—so like her creator.

Rosie belongs to a family of traditional dancers. Her approach to Bharata Natyam is purely traditional. 'She got up at five in the morning, bathed and prayed before the picture of a god [...] and began a practice session which went on for nearly three hours [...]. She ignored her surroundings completely, her attention being concentrated upon her movements and steps' (136). She is determined 'to keep the purity of the classical norms' (136): that sounds like R.K. Narayan about himself! She seeks out a dance master, 'a man who had steeped himself in the traditional dance for half a century' (166). She is Narayan's artiste, pure and simple; Raju is the commercial wizard, impresario. While the cheque is the most important item of a performance to Raju, she 'generally ignored everything except the flowers at the end' (188). There is a simplicity to Rosie's temperament and attitude; with emphasis on conventional womanhood. She delights in playing the middle-class housewife. In Raju's house, after her concentrated practice, she helps his mother, scrubs, washes, sweeps, and tidies up everything in the house. In that memorable scene (chapter 8), where Raju's mother and uncle try to break the spell of infatuation of these two young people for each other, Rosie is satisfied with Raju's protective assurances. 'My guidance was enough. She accepted it in absolutely unquestioning faith, and ignored everything else completely' (149). Raju recalls: 'It gave me a tremendous confidence in myself and seemed to enhance my own dimensions.' Rosie the artiste is grateful to Raju who is instrumental in the realization of her dreams for a life dedicated to her art. 'Even if I have seven rebirths I won't be able to repay my debt to you' (184), she tells Raju in her characteristic spontaneity and to his immense gratification. And towards that end, when Raju's defence by the star lawyer turns out to be a white elephant, she works harder than ever to supply the much-needed funds. Earlier she demurs at moving out from Raju's old house to which she is sentimentally attached. While Raju goes from vanity to vice to crime, Rosie continues with her dedication to her rehearsals; or just sitting around chatting quietly with fellow artistes who, she believes, 'have the blessings of goddess Saraswathi' (169). When Raju takes objection to her association with these humble folk who are her inferiors—less-well-to-do!—she ticks him off: 'I don't care much for that sort of superiority' (170). And in the early days of prosperity she tells Raju: 'I must not lose touch with my womanly duties' (164). That is Rajam of *The English Teacher* again! When the bubble bursts for Raju, her guide, her reaction is significant: 'I felt all along you were not doing right things' (193). After Raju's trial and conviction Rosie rises again. The novelist gives Rosie, too, the benefit of first-person narrative; she herself recounts her ordeal at the Peak House, winning the reader's sympathy. The novelist also gives Rosie a devadasi background; the term means literally 'maid dedicated to serving God', but carrying connotations of a courtesan: 'She knew only her mother and always spoke of her' (142). Rosie's extraordinary resilience and artistic fervour, drive and direction see her through her trials.

If Rosie moves in a curve that takes her down and up, Raju's mother goes steadily in a straight line. The portrait of the mother, too, is touched with grace; and Raju is her only child. Narayan himself has been developing a gallery: Krishna's mother, Mrs Sampath, Mrs Srinivas, Mrs Margayya—all unnamed most of the time, with some more to come later—all are specimens of womanhood and motherhood traditionally admired in India. Raju's mother has been toughened by life; enjoys quiet common sense, tact, with traditional moorings at the same time. Her efforts to bring round Raju to face reality offer an insight into her simple nature. She appeals to their good sense, coaxes them, cajoles Rosie; she then marks time before summoning 'the bolt from the blue' (164), her brother. When he fails she threatens to and does quit her own house from which her large steel trunk has not been moved for decades. 'My mother looked saddened rather than angry' (154). The scene ends on a poignant note: '"Don't fail to light the lamps in God's niche," said my mother, going down the steps. "Be careful with your health."[3] Soon they were at the end of the street and turned the corner. I stood on the step watching. At the threshold stood Rosie. I was afraid to turn round and face her, because I was crying' (185). That is as good an example as any of the novelist's skill in controlling the reader's sympathy for his hero through manoeuvring point of view.

Raju's mother keeps writing to Raju—in pencil and on yellow sheets of paper—forgoes her right in the house, though she would like to 'spend the rest of my days in my own house' (165).[4] Rosie, whom the old lady had called 'the snake-woman', is performing the snake dance at the time of Raju's arrest. Until Raju's trial and conviction his mother has never seen the inside of a law court and is 'overwhelmed with a feeling of her own daring' (207). Raju ends his reminiscences, understandably, with a reference to his mother. Even earlier Raju's mother has had to contend with the little vanities of Raju's father whose rise in business rockets Raju into his adventurist orbits; Raju seems to have inherited his vanity and fervour for showing off: the old man's jutka episode is an interlude after Narayan's heart. Raju's father, mother, and uncle together represent the traditional ways of living and values. Raju's mother and uncle retreat, after the inevitable clash, to their village; but the uncle has already given us an inkling of what to expect from the tough and enduring core of India, the village folk, 'guiding' their 'guide'.

Raju's confession to Velan wells up from within his psyche; he airs it to his first 'devotee', blending self-observation with authentic self-analysis. 'I felt vastly superior to everyone' (188); so he moves to a stylish house in the New Extension. 'Sitting in that hall and looking round, I had the satisfaction of feeling that I had arrived' (188). Narayan the social satirist grows relatively more direct (196–7): Raju's rise, like Margayya's, exposes the contemporary society. And we must remember this is part of the confessional statement Raju makes to the villagers of Mangala to open their eyes, disabuse their minds by exposing his true picaresque background, his real nature and stature. 'I liked to hobnob with them because they were men of money or influence' (189). Quite a range! His vices are reported towards eliciting an effect, a reaction. 'Although I myself cared very little for drink, I hugged a glass of whisky for hours. "Permit-holder" became a social title in our land and attracted men of importance around me [...]' (196). The confessional unveils his inner self: '[A]lways with a feeling that I was an interloper in that artistic group' (189). Introspection cleanses: 'I liked her to be happy, but only in my company' (190). It is not Raju speaking to Velan anymore; it is his inner voice on stream, asserting itself. Self-analysis cannot go farther: 'I liked to keep her in a citadel' (193). After making a clean confession of his crime in hiding Marco's book from Rosie, 'it was like hiding a corpse' (198), he makes a definitive discovery: 'I've come to the conclusion that nothing in this world can be hidden or suppressed. All such attempts are like holding an umbrella to conceal the sun' (198-9). Raju's perception of his follies goes with his self-assessment: 'She never spoke to me except as to a tramp she had salvaged [...]. After all, the mastery had passed to her [...]' (218). Raju's self-analysis goes deep: 'I could not bother to think of her own troubles, of the mess she had been led into, of the financial emptiness after all those months of dancing and working, of the surprise sprung upon her by my lack of—what we call it, judgement? No, it was something much lower than that. Lack of ordinary character! I see it all now clearly [...]' (219). Self-analysis cannot be more conclusive; prepares for the conclusion of the drama.

Commenting on his education Raju says: 'Now that I reflect upon it, I am convinced I was not such a dud after all. It seems to me that we generally do not have a correct measure of our own wisdom. I remember how I was equipping my mind all the time' (42). Craft-wise Narayan sandwiches Raju's self-education between his sessions with the villagers who are struck by his 'erudition'. 'Equipping': with enough material to satisfy the village folk to keep them engaged. In the two years that he spends in jail he is a model prisoner who engages in reading—'I gave them all a cursory look' (205)—and discourses to the fellow convicts on philosophy and what not. 'When there was a respite, I told them stories and philosophies and what not. They came to refer to me as *vadhyar*— that is, teacher' (203). This success as vadhyar during his jail term is expanded in Mangala now, where it attracts the simple village folk into developing an awesome—awful—faith in him, outdoing the prisoners. For Raju his tenure in jail is a period of reformation; he recalls to us Sriram's term in the jail after his terrorist stint.

In prison, too, Raju reveals his sensitivity to nature. He enjoys horticulture. 'I grew huge brinjals and beans, and cabbages. When they appeared on their stalks as tiny buds, I was filled with excitement. I watched them develop, acquire shape, change colour, shed the early parts' (203). Not just Nature, but life around him: 'Men and vehicles, hogs and boys—the panorama of life enchanted me' (13). 'Enchantment' is a phenomenon natural to Narayan's heroes. For Raju imprisonment is not incarceration; it is a course in spiritual regeneration: '[T]he blue sky and sunshine, and the shade of the house in which I sat and worked, the feel of cold water; it produced in me a luxurious sensation. Oh, it seemed to be so good to be alive and feeling all this—the smell of freshly turned earth filled me with the greatest delight' (228). This kind of experience is available even to a tamasic–rajasic 'hero' in *A Tiger for Malgudi* (Narayan 1983: 165–6).

Out of an assertion of life and its revels arises an affirmation of faith in God, not in spite of it. Coomaraswamy (1918: 28–9) says: 'But we need not on that account condemn the Self-assertion of the ignorant as sin; for could Self-Realization be where self-assertion had never been?' Thus, Raju would willingly and happily continue, away from the world. With the exit of the two women, his mother and Rosie, from his life, he enters a life of forced sanyasa; and here is an opportunity for him to turn over a new leaf in his life. It is rebirth for Raju. His passions under check, even partly sublimated, Raju in Mangala is a wiser person. Granting permission to Velan for bringing his difficult sister to him, he muses: 'Hope she is uninteresting. I have had enough trouble in life' (16). Jail life has mellowed him; he remains human still, with human weaknesses, and to keep him human is the novelist's purpose and success. Narayan's definition of 'human' offers infinite, progressive possibilities.

Raju's drift to swamihood is as fluent as his progress from Railway Raju to 'danger's back-stage boy'. Coming out of the jail Raju still hopes to become a guide—a star guide this time. In contrast to his passion for showing off earlier, now 'this jail-bird' desperately tries to go unnoticed. At Mangala when 'he could not open his lips without provoking admiration', he realizes that 'this was a dangerous state of affairs' (29). Unfortunately, 'there was a greater danger in silence' (30). The images signify it: 'Raju's heart palpitated as he crouched there like an animal at bay' (31). In the end, 'all this prudence did not save him'. In spite of himself Raju discovers he is becoming a swami. Food—'in return for just waiting for it' (33)—shelter, and what is more, people to guide—what else does Raju need? So he starts playing the role given to him. The novelist observes wryly: 'No one was more impressed with the grandeur of the whole thing than Raju himself.' Not just this: 'He was surprised at the amount of wisdom welling from the depths of his being' (47). The unseen power is pulling the strings and the puppet plays its destined role: 'The Lord abides in the hearts of all beings, O Arjuna, causing them to turn round by His power as if they were mounted on a machine' (Gita: XVIII.61).

Prayers, discourses, lectures, dispensations of justice or dispensing medicine; or 'hitting upon aphorisms', saying things 'grandly' and 'on inspiration' with 'a lot of authority', or 'because it sounded nice'; or 'dragging those innocent men deeper and deeper into the bog of unclear thoughts' (52) is all in a day's work. Before he knows what, things go out of his control: 'By the time he arrived at the stage of stroking his beard thoughtfully, his prestige had grown beyond his wildest dreams' (47). After all, '[i]t was a strain. He sighed a deep sigh of relief and turned to be himself, eat like an ordinary human being, shout and sleep like a normal man, after the voices on the river had ceased for the night' (48). Those 'voices', strident, soft, or silent, are more powerful than he can imagine. The transformation of Raju in Mangala is accomplished even before the invasion of the drought: '[H]is eyes shone with softness and compassion, the light of wisdom emanated from them' (79).

But the onset of drought poses a different level of challenge: 'Something was happening on a different plane over which one had no control or choice, and where a philosophical attitude made no difference' (93). That 'different plane' matters in Narayan, makes all the difference. During the drought when Velan's idiot-brother distorts his message to proclaim that the swami is going to undertake a purificatory fast, a fast to bring down rain, the villagers rush to him to pour out their gratitude; and our unsuspecting hero is just meditating on the taste of a bonda. Narayan's irony contributes to the rhetoric of the fiction, his control of the reader's sympathy for his hero. By the end of the novel Raju, unaware, is slowly subverted and converted by the innate innocence of the villagers. He benefits far more from their spiritual simplicity and stability.

The villagers are true to themselves and their ambience. They express their admiration, gratitude, and reverence effusively by touching his feet in the traditional style. 'He felt it ridiculous playing hide and seek with his feet. [A]nd they seemed ready to tickle his sides, if it would only give them his feet' (106). Raju does not as yet know the reason behind this sudden and alarming outpouring of reverence. The ironic tone keeps things in perspective. 'There was so much warmth in their approach that he began to feel it was but right they should touch his feet; as a matter of fact, it seemed possible that he himself might bow low, take the dust of his own feet and press it to his eyes. He began to think that his personality radiated a glory [...]' (107). This sardonic treatment continues till Raju, towards the end, takes that momentous decision to fast honestly. Now the irony shifts to a serious play on two planes: the impact of Raju's decision on himself is juxtaposed with scenes of festivity at the fair-like venue producing comic relief.

There have been other signs of change in Raju. He loses count of time; and he 'lost interest in accumulation' of the gifts now showered on him by the villagers. 'The villagers kept bringing in so many things for him that he lost interest in accumulation. [...] He gave them all back to the women and children' (90). He now leads, for all practical purposes, the life of a renunciant; and thanks to him the old shrine once again becomes the centre of village life at Mangala. 'The voices on the river' make all the difference to at least one man. The craft-wise novelist has so managed the reader's sympathy for Raju that we know Raju on the eve of the fast has already been, to some degree, self-reformed; he is far from the uninhibited entrepreneur of the earlier phase. Yet he remains credibly human; he resents this fast thrust on him.

And then it happens. The definitive transformation comes on the third day after the commencement of the fast; in contempt of his own instincts, in sympathy for Velan, who 'was of the stuff disciples are made of' (19), Raju decides to fast in the true spirit of the rite. Now positive feelings regain their hold: 'He felt moved by the thought of their gratitude' (111). He recalls his mother's faith that if there is one good man anywhere, the rains will come. The critical decision gives him joy. 'For the first time in his life he was making an earnest effort, for the first time he was learning the thrill of full application, outside money and love; for the first time he was doing a thing in which he was not personally interested [...] the fourth day of his fast found him quite sprightly' (238).

This is the high point of Raju's career; the novelist has been working steadily towards this transformation. Raju has confessed to Velan: 'I am no saint' (112). Ultimately, however, like the whisky priest in Greene's *The Power and the Glory* (1971: 209), Raju also realizes that 'at the end there was only one thing that counted—to be a saint'.

Raju's decision, for once, does not waver because it is a decision made in an effort towards self-abnegation, towards service to his fellow men. Raju experiences the joy of selflessness. 'Death' for Raju is culmination of Life.[5]

13

For God, Country—and Comedy!
The Man-Eater of Malgudi

The Man-Eater of Malgudi is Narayan's major novel in the post-Independence phase. First published in 1961, the author's ninth novel is dedicated to Graham Greene 'to mark (more than) a quarter century of friendship'.

The peace of Nataraj, a printer of Malgudi, and of his community, is disturbed by the arrival of Vasu, a taxidermist from the city; even as the outsider grows into a deadly menace, he self-destructs. Normalcy is restored.

After *Mr. Sampath*, Narayan turns once again to a printer, Nataraj, the citizen-hero of *The Man-Eater of Malgudi*. He is pitted against the tamasic Vasu—the 'man-eater'—the adversary absolute, a rakshasa, who sets himself against Nataraj, the citizen, his town, and, terminally, nature itself. The fascinating aspect of the drama is Vasu's extraordinary impact on the hero Nataraj and his friends, his vice-fection, an induction, sort of extro-susception of degenerate nature, landing Nataraj in unprecedented imbalance, distortion of personality; thus, the focus is substantively on Nataraj, the narrator, though the title represents a major character, Vasu.

Craft Wisdom

But first let us sample Narayan's craft wisdom.

Chapter 1 of *The Man-Eater of Malgudi* presents two 'movements'.

The first para, of less than sixteen lines, opens with the 'I' of the narrator: the tale is offered to us through the eyes of the central character. The passage fluently presents the key data. The hero's business premises on Market Road, the commercial artery of Malgudi, is privileged 'with a view of the fountain': this 'view' figures significantly in the climax of the novel. The narrator himself is considered 'a fool' for not renting out his spare front room; he would not yield. 'But I could not explain myself to sordid and calculating people' (Narayan 1961: 7): value grouping is suggested at the very outset; besides, Nataraj's hospice is in place for Vasu to move in, the setting for Vasu havoc. All the same Nataraj, non-sordid, non-calculating, hangs up a picture of the Goddess of Wealth. In the same passage the novelist takes us on smoothly to introduce the hero's family—his little son Babu and his wife—in that order—with Nataraj's middle-class male crack about the extravagance of his wife. The final detail of the first para puts the wife—and himself—in his hoary community: 'continuing the traditions of our ancient home in Kabir Street'. The first para thus presents not just 'a local habitation and a name' (7): besides a moral profile and the social status of the narrator, a whole ethos is evoked ('glittering with lace' and 'traditions of our ancient home in Kabir Street').

Narayan strikes a rich vein for some of his best post-1947 work: Kabir Street 'aristocracy'. Nataraj is not the first hero of Narayan's post-Independence novels hailing from Kabir Street nor is he going to be the last: Sriram of *Waiting for the Mahatma* is the first; the narrator-hero of *Talkative Man* (besides the short stories narrated by him[1]) and the hero of *The World of Nagaraj*, besides the guru in *A Tiger for Malgudi*, are some more of the same provenance. Now these ancient homes and families in Kabir Street can do with some illumination. In a novella to come much later, *Talkative Man*, the eponymous narrator offers us witty insight into this vanishing species, the declining Brahmin gentry of Kabir Street.

I belonged to one of those Kabir Street families which flourished on the labours of an earlier generation. We were about twenty unrelated families in Kabir Street, each inheriting a huge rambling house stretching from the street to the river at the back. All that one did was to lounge on the pyol, watch the street and wait for the harvest from our village lands and cash from the tenants. We were a vanishing race, however, about twenty families in Kabir Street and an equal number in Ellamman Street, two spots where village landlords had settled and built houses nearly a century back in order to seek the comforts of urban life and to educate their children at Albert Mission. Their descendants so comfortably placed, were mainly occupied in eating, breeding, celebrating festivals and spending the afternoon in a prolonged siesta on the pyol, and playing cards all evening. The women rarely came out, being most of the time occupied in the kitchen or in the safe-room scrutinizing their collection of diamonds and silks. This sort of existence did not appeal to me. (Narayan 1977: 4–5)

Our hero Nataraj also throws some light on the mores of the Kabir Street Brahmins.

I remembered a boy, a brilliant fellow, who had strode up and down Kabir Street singing all Tyagaraja's compositions for three days and nights continuously and had covered most of the compositions of that inspired saint. If he had been left alone for another day, he would have completed the repertory, but they seized and bundled him off by the five o'clock express to Madras [to its asylum for the insane]. He came back a year later with a shaven head, but sober and quiet in all other respects. He was a friend of mine in my school-days, and he confessed that he had sung Tyagaraja's compositions only because he was keen on letting the public get an idea of the versatility of that great composer, but now he was afraid even to hum the tunes in his bath. Our Kabir Street citizens had exacting standards of sanity. [...] (Narayan 1961: 158–9)

For a natural culmination of this Kabir Street sociological phenomenon we must wait until *The World of Nagaraj* (1990).

By the end of the first para we get, besides practical data, a hint of the narrator's value system: there are more things in the world than materialistic values. The earlier statement of not looking for money-making is confirmed presently in the opening of the third para: 'Anyone who found his feet aching as he passed down Market Road was welcome to rest in my parlour on any seat that happened to be vacant' (7): this hospitality is a key trigger in the plot. Taking advantage of it, Vasu enters his attic as non-rent-paying 'tenant' and makes a menace of himself in the novel. At the same time Nataraj's sense of community is going to play a central role in the projection of the poet and his epic in a climactic religious procession towards the end. Besides, altruism pays! 'While they rested there, people got ideas for bill forms, visiting cards, or wedding invitations which they asked me to print, but many others came whose visits did not mean a paisa to me' (7).

So the novelist opens with Nataraj's workplace: that makes sense because all planning and action by Nataraj and friends, besides their diurnal activity, takes place here. Incidentally the Queen Anne chair in Nataraj's parlour and the Heidelberg printing machine of Nataraj's neighbour across the road are given a little extra attention in the opening passage: these pieces of wooden furniture and business equipment figure again and again throughout the novel, to create a sort of still-life humour. Besides, the fact is also mentioned that even with the latest machinery Nataraj's neighbour, his 'competition', has few customers: reflecting something of the personal charm of Nataraj with 'an assortment of chairs' and 'a word of welcome' (8) in his business premises. The opening movement also introduces the group of characters that gather every day in Nataraj's parlour—Nataraj's friends—and he begins with the poet. With mention of the poet's monosyllabic verse-epic in progress the plot, too, is initiated; its launch, synchronized with the marriage of the god at the temple, makes for a memorable climax.

The presentation of the poet is typical Nataraj:

My admiration for him was unbounded. I was thrilled to hear such clear lines as 'Girls with girls did dance in trance' and I felt equally excited when I had to infer the meaning of certain lines; that happened when he totally failed to find a monosyllable and achieved his end by ruthlessly carving up a polysyllable. On such occasions even the most familiar term took on the mysterious quality of a private code. (8)

The comment—especially that last line—carries the hallmark of our novelist: Narayan could never reconcile himself to excesses of any kind.

The second opening movement of chapter 1 begins with 'I lived in Kabir Street, which ran behind Market Road' (9). This part further falls into three sections: the first, Nataraj's experiences with people and places on his way to his daily ritual bathe in the river; the second, his experience at the river; and the third, his return home. His encounters and observations on his way to and from his ritual bathe in the river effortlessly conjure up his society while revealing more of Nataraj himself. At the river Nataraj mentions the toddy palm that rises high with its liquor oozing into pots above and its stench. He says, 'I never looked up at the palmyra without a shudder' (9), revealing his traditional Brahminical upbringing. Toddy extraction also adds another detail to the picture of Nataraj's society: 'revellers fighting or rolling in the gutters' (9)—a stark contrast, we are going to see, to 'exacting standards' (158) of Kabir Street citizenry: completing a rapid sketch of Nataraj's ambience.

On Nataraj's way back, the disaffected cousin is a reminder of Nataraj's fragmented joint family and its emotional debris. The unpleasant reminiscence recalls for us at once the past 'glory' and the present state of householder Nataraj's Kabir Street family. We learn later, however, the temple, too, is part of Kabir Street heritage and of the town as well (138); in performing its deity's marriage Nataraj and the town celebrate their common tradition.

Nataraj comes across the adjournment lawyer next: adept at subverting the judicial system, the legal bird plays a more direct role in Nataraj's life later. Now Nataraj makes it a point to avoid the man. Finally the only fellow citizen Nataraj willingly lends his ear to during his ritualistic early outing is the septuagenarian 'living in a dilapidated outhouse in Adam's Lane, who owned a dozen houses in our locality' (10). For Nataraj, the old man affirms, even as the joint family system is falling apart, family life and attachments act as positives. This gerontic citizen appears again at a delicate stage of the Vasu drama and contributes his share of comic anxiety to the hassled Nataraj. The final section returns to householder Nataraj's memories of the feuds and division of the joint family: reflecting Nataraj's own lack of bitterness: 'I was content to live in our house as it had been left by my father' (11).

The mention of his father's love for his brothers is balanced by Nataraj's own difficulty as a child in receiving his father's attention: yet another case of parental failure in Narayan's post-Independence novels. Nataraj's admiration for his grandmother reflects his own value base: 'It was my father's old mother who had kept them together, acting as a cohesive element among members of the family' (11–12). Nataraj himself turns out to be the 'cohesive element' in his immediate 'parlour' group; and later in the entire town.

These encounters—brief or fleeting—the way Nataraj responds to each on the way to and from the river—besides the ritualistic bathe and meditation—build up, stitch by stitch, the social and moral profile of the narrator Nataraj as well as his matrix: Nataraj's good-humoured wit; his lack of bitterness, especially, at the division of property, besides, distinguishes him as an extraordinary scion of Kabir Street aristocracy with warmth for fellow townsmen.

Other features of the novel, aspects of its 'dramaturgy', are equally engaging: particularly from chapter 2 onwards. The dialogue in *The Man-Eater of Malgudi* is profuse, fluent, racy, crisp, and dramatic: revealing character, and building up tempo and action, particularly in the scenes with Nataraj and Vasu. Then there is the novel's pace: chapter 1 presents the hero and his ensemble and ambience; the very next chapter introduces Vasu, the adversary extraordinaire; and chapter 3 brings the two into conflicting proximity. Vasu moves into the attic above Nataraj's press: 'No human being has set foot in the attic for years' (23); infested with vermin: impressively, mosquitoes, Vasu's nemesis ('Night or day, I run when a mosquito is mentioned' [25]), thus preparing for the climax of the novel when a mere mosquito causes Vasu's self-destruction.

The novelist shows more of his 'craftiness' in the episode where Vasu 'kidnaps' Nataraj. So casual is the way Vasu manages to 'snatch' Nataraj and, against his wish, drives the busy printer away towards Mempi forest, drops him unceremoniously on the way at Mempi village. In this critical episode the novelist introduces Muthu, one of the more energetic minor characters, sort of rural Nataraj, besides the elephant Kumar and other bit players in the drama of the temple celebration to come; the episode also yields, to the delight of the reader, its harvest of a Narayan staple, wit and humour. This Mempi adventure confirms that Nataraj is one of Narayan's most engaging heroes; in this episode R.K. Narayan is authenticity on stream. At the climactic temple ceremony the novelist creates the celebratory atmosphere with verve, a gala in which the entire community participates joyously (136–7). At the same time Narayan also builds up—with the suspense of a Hitchcock—to Vasu's self-destruction (141–2) in the attic; and later when Nataraj discovers Vasu's body.[2]

The novelist brings in early the massive weapon of self-destruction: Vasu's fist. 'He gave me a hard grip. My entire hand disappeared into his fist [...]' (16). The novelist keeps focusing briefly on the extraordinary weapon from time to time. Vasu boasts: '[W]hen I banged my fist on a century-old door of a house in

Lucknow, the three-inch panel of seasoned teak splintered' (18). In his confrontation with Sen: 'He raised his fist and flourished it. "If I hit you with it, it will be the end of you"' (27). Again, at the opening of chapter 6, Nataraj could hear Vasu's jeep and 'that mighty fist pulling at the brake' (67). Earlier he boasts prophetically: 'I could settle many problems with this, but I don't' (27); for at the end Vasu does exactly that: settles all *his* problems and of Nataraj and his friends and the citizenry of Malgudi.

Nataraj the Householder

Like any middle-class householder Nataraj is very much domesticated; and a Kabir Street Brahmin at that. Consider his food habits. When hunger mitigates his Kabir Street abhorrence of 'fly-blown buns and tea in unwashed tumblers', he is generously fed by Muthu, the tea-shop owner in Mempi village. Yet Nataraj confesses: 'I might eat all the buns in the world, but without a handful of rice and the sauce my wife made, I could never feel convinced that I had taken any nourishment' (40–1). That sounds more like Narayan himself—(of Kabir Street heritage!). More of this later.

Though Rangi, the prostitute, risks her life to come to him and warns him about Vasu's secret plan to destroy the elephant Kumar, Nataraj feels: 'It seemed vulgar to share a secret with her' (137); that 'vulgar' proclaims his Kabir Street upbringing. Nataraj is hurt by little omissions and commissions in etiquette, which to Vasu are not worth any notice. When he eagerly carries food cooked by his wife and offers it to Vasu to appease him and make him change his murderous plan, Vasu does not praise her cooking: 'I was a little upset to see him take it so casually and critically, and was especially hurt to think that he couldn't pay a compliment to my wife even for courtesy's sake' (131–2). Nataraj's wife is all concerned after his collapse in the midst of the crowd at the temple; she prepares a feast for him: for, the unnamed housewife 'had decided to play the hostess and serve me ceremoniously' (153). The middle-class hero observes: 'The house was fragrant with the frying in the kitchen' (152). Nataraj welcomes these attractions and consolations of his middle-class home and family: for not often one is so fortunate: 'I enjoyed the status of being more important than god's wedding procession. To be fussed over like this came only once in a decade when one fell ill or down a ladder; it was a nice change, from protecting and guiding others and running the household at its head' (152). A middle-class husband has also defined his duties: the duties of a grihastha, householder.

Middle-class family life cannot be complete without domestic quarrels. In a brilliant move the novelist gives a twist to this idyllic interlude: Rangi's inconvenient visit to him at his house—though urgent—deflates the domestic euphoria. Rangi's timing is explosive. 'All the fine moments of the evening, the taste of exquisite food, everything was turning to gall on my tongue. Although I had had no occasion to test it, I knew she [his wife] could be fiercely jealous' (154). The furious wife flounces out of the house and heads for the procession; and Nataraj comes up with a classic plaint: 'She had not given me a chance even to pick a quarrel with her' (157). Now the peeved middle-class husband seethes with soliloquies inspired by self-pity. 'The trouble with me was that I was not able to say "no" to anyone and that got me into complications with everyone, from a temple prostitute to a taxidermist. [...] I should have behaved like one of my ancestors [...]' (158). That is, he should have asserted the macho ego in the classic style of Kabir Street aristocracy at the pinnacle of their mirasidar glory! 'I should have instantly said, "I want to seduce Rangi or be seduced by her." [...] "Yes, of course, you are blinded by jealousy. No doubt she chews tobacco and looks rugged, but she has it, it comes through even when she whispers to you. How can any man resist her? I am sorry for you. You should take more trouble to keep me in good humour"' (158). The impassioned soliloquy is evidence, as we are going to see later, of the Vasu vice-fection.

Self-pity only gives his predicament an amusing edge; and it is fancy at a trot again: if Vasu kills him, '[n]o one was going to miss me. My wife was separated from me, there was none to bemoan my loss; true, and Babu was likely to miss me for a few days [...]' (163). Nataraj's speculations, the various would-be retorts, and repartees only confirm the distance that this scion of Kabir Street has travelled on the sattvic trajectory since the days of his macho forebears. The backdrop to this semi-comic episode is the temple procession; the domestic scene comes as an interlude in the midst of God's wedding.[3] Better sense prevails: the worst is over; by this time, unknown to Nataraj, Vasu also has done himself in, self-destructed. 'Life had become normal again at the temple' (141). As though heralding relief, '[t]he moon came over the roof-tiles of the opposite row of houses, full and brilliant' (158). Vasu's death clears the domestic air. 'Our friendly relations were resumed the moment she heard that there was a dead body in the press and that the police assembled in my office. [...] I was very humbled now, and very pleased that at least over Vasu's dead body we were shaking hands again' (176). The loyalty and concern of the unnamed spouse get the better of her hurt.

Citizen Nataraj

Narayan was very much pleased with John Updike's review of his memoir *My Days*. 'It made me feel good to know that Updike understands my involvement with people—as individuals and as a community' (Krishnan 1975: 42).

Nataraj, too, is at his best as Citizen Nataraj in his involvement with people—as fellow citizens in a democratic polity.

Nataraj the citizen knows his limitations; that is his strong point. He confesses: 'My sincerity was unquestionable, but my resources were poor' (82). Self-knowledge makes for common man as hero in a democratic polity. It makes him practical and flexible in his interactions with fellow citizens: 'Now that I was at his mercy, I thought I might as well abandon myself to the situation' (32-3). This Malgudi citizen is equally concerned about his community and himself: '[W]hat was to happen to me and to my neighbourhood?' (51). Nataraj's commitment to the elephant Kumar is just one more example of his civic awareness. 'I felt genuinely concerned about poor Kumar now' (90). Duty, dharma, is a value for him: 'But duty impelled me on' (92). And its extension, as we shall see later, Nataraj's duty to his country. Vasu's uncivil ways bother Citizen Nataraj: 'I was appalled at his notion of democracy as being a common acceptance of bad odours' (52). Nataraj's last-minute attempt to persuade Vasu from his adventurism fails: 'The interview knocked out all the joy I had felt in the festival' (135). Even after he makes a spectacle of himself by shouting a prayer to God and collapsing in the midst of the crowded temple celebration, he is duty bound: 'My duty was now clear. [...] There was no use lying here and cogitating while every minute a vast assembly was moving towards its doom. I had to do something about it' (162). Duty is a key concept in the democratic world of citizen Nataraj.

Citizen Nataraj is resolved to stop Vasu, though the novelist makes it sound rather grandiose: '[B]ut it gave me a feeling of shedding my blood for a worthy cause' (93). In a desperate last-ditch attempt he enters the attic, Vasu's den. 'I was going to stop him from disturbing the procession; that was certain. [...] I was prepared to lose my life in the process. [...] I started crawling like one of those panthers of the Mempi jungle. [...] My knees were sore, but I felt that it was for a good cause that I was skinning them' (164). The playfulness apart, this is Citizen Nataraj's daredevilry at its best and in the service of his town.

Citizen Nataraj is also aware of his own professional competence: '(I prided myself on the excellence of my colour printing)' he says parenthetically at the beginning of chapter 2. '[Vasu] might pulverize granite, smash his guru with a slicing stroke, but where printing work was concerned I was not going to be pushed' (19). Nataraj proves it: witness the way he tackles difficult customers, even Vasu (21). Two episodes attest our printer's expertise in customer care: he outflanks Vasu in the episode of the forest officer's offer of a manuscript; before Vasu knows what is happening the aspiring 'friend' has voluntarily withdrawn his manuscript. Nataraj claims, justly, 'I was a seasoned printer' (31).

Nataraj's confrontation with the tight-fisted K.J. makes for one of the most amusing episodes in the novel. After subduing K.J. the tight-fisted customer—'I felt satisfied that I had cowed him' (107)—Nataraj formulates his professional wisdom for us: 'Initiative was half the victory in a battle, and so before he could open his mouth I remarked, wearing a look of grievance, "What's the use of my friends losing their temper here? I never delay anyone's business without a reason"' (107). He dismisses the colour supplied by K.J. with impressive rhetoric: 'Do you know what it looks like when it dries? It assumes the pink of an old paper kite picked out of a gutter' (108). And the astute printer draws satisfaction from his success: '[T]his was good, as it made K.J. look so ignorant, wrong, and presumptuous that he remained dumb' (108). Nataraj goes on playing with K.J., 'as if I were a god speaking to a sinner' (108). He handles the tight-fisted customer with great relish and verve. When Nataraj raises the topic of donations to the temple committee: '[K.J.] was afraid to ask further questions for fear of involvement. [...] He felt sorry that he had walked into this trap. I practically held him down and enjoyed it immensely' (109). The episode concludes triumphantly: 'He got up suddenly and dashed out, muttering that he would see me again' (110).

Later Citizen Nataraj's campaign to collect funds for the temple celebration turns out to be more difficult than expected: '[A]s every one of our citizens had the same temperament as KJ—affluent, afraid to reject an appeal, but unwilling to open the purse' (111). In the first meeting with Muthu, the humble tea vendor in Mempi village, Nataraj again reveals his professional tact. 'I wanted to do and say anything I could to please this man, whom at normal times I'd have passed as just another man selling tea in unwashed tumblers' (41).

Yet with their selfless involvement and effort, this unlikely hero and his motley band do manage to bring the town together in the temple celebration. For Citizen Nataraj is good to the helpless and deserving—compare his attitude to the poet—good to the good, wily to the tight-fisted.[4] For, Nataraj's value system all along is humanly comprehensive; for, it is inspired by God and country: 'My heart swelled with pride; I was performing a mighty sacrifice on behalf of God and country. By approaching him and humbling myself I would be saving humanity from destruction [...]' (129).

Did Nataraj presage the upswing in India's national fortunes?

That hyperbolic elevation effects comic self-deflation: not just God and country: to comedy as well. After all for Nataraj and his friends, God, the eternal collaborator, is at work! As ever it is God versus his adversary! The lamb against the man-eater: in the cause of God, country, and comedy! Here is a good contrast between the democratic approach to life and society and the anarchist way of life; between a full-life view and a 'still-life' view. Vasu's still-life view stands finally rejected.

The seasoned citizen knows the ways of the law: 'My desire to search for Vasu's purse and read the blue letter in it was really great, but I didn't want the police to conclude that I had killed him and taken his purse' (168). What interests businessman Nataraj is 'more than the mystery of his death, the mystery of the festival accounts' (169); but Citizen Nataraj has the final say: 'I folded my arms across my chest, remembering that I had better not touch anything and leave a fingerprint' (170). When death in mysterious circumstances brings the bureaucracy swarming in the attic above Nataraj's press—'Vasu dead proved a greater nuisance than Vasu alive' (170)—Nataraj's playful mind mulls possibilities of exploiting lacunae in the law: 'An excellent chance to confuse things by making the nearest restaurant busy defending their innocence [...]' (172). However, Citizen Nataraj's value system asserts itself: 'I dismissed the thought as unworthy [...]' (172).

After all, Citizen R.K. Narayan has given so much of himself to his hero, Citizen Nataraj.

Nataraj is fancy at a trot. 'I was struck with a sudden fear that this man was perhaps abducting me and was going to demand a ransom for releasing me, from some tiger cave [...]' (35). Nataraj's wild fancy recalls Narayan's own passing perturbations during his American sojourn: in his rejection of a place called 'Haste and Telegraph' for fear his letters will miscarry; later a drop of blood mars the day for our novelist. Nataraj can be self-analytical, self-critical: '[B]ut my nature would not permit it. I always had to get into complications' (90). The self-criticism recalls the novelist's memoir, *My Days*, besides his travelogue, *My Dateless Diary*. Nataraj observes in passing: 'I didn't like the idea of writing off anything' (74). The waggish comment sounds like Narayan! The novelist also gives his own choosy dining habits to his hero.[5] *The Man-Eater of Malgudi* also shows preoccupation with astrology (110–11). Though in the session with the astrologer Nataraj confesses that he is 'a veritable ignoramus among the stars' (106), he gives much of his precious time to his conference with Sastri and the astrologer, annoying a lucrative customer. Nataraj's shared faith in astrology recalls Narayan's own interest in the arcane subject. Nataraj is a kindred soul. Above all, the novelist gives his own evolved taste in music to his Citizen Nataraj. Nataraj claps in appreciation of 'Kalyani Rag', smacks his lips, metaphorically, 'a lovely melody at this hour' (138). Nataraj also reports critically: '[T]he story of Krishna and Radha was now being recited in song-form by a group of men, incoherently and cacophonously' (138). Narayan enjoyed the reputation of a severe and exacting music critic.[6]

Nataraj offers appreciation of another Raga, though he is not present on the scene with the musicians.

> I followed it, visualizing all the stages of its progress. [...] And the piper had saved his breath for his masterpiece—'bhairavi'. He was beginning an elaborate, intricate rendering of this melody, and that means the crowd would gather round him, the God would repose in his chariot, the elephant would stand ahead of the procession with the mahout asleep on his back. People would crowd around the piper and behave as if they had no further way to go. [...] 'Bhairavi' could be heard as well here half asleep as anywhere, and so I allowed myself to be lulled by it, my favourite melody in any case. It brought to my mind my childhood, when visiting musicians used to come as our guests; there was a room in our house known as the musician's room, for we always had some musician or other staying with us, as my father was very proud of his familiarity with all the musicians in South India and organized their recitals in our town. (161)

The childhood reminiscence is a direct import from Narayan's life.

Nataraj and Vasu: Inspired Morbidity

'I don't envy your luck in getting a man like that to live with' (81), says Sen to Nataraj. But Nataraj is seen in all his moods only in his complex and troubled and troublesome relationship with Vasu, the 'man-eater'; from Vasu's arrival to his destruction and aftermath, Vasu is the principal preoccupation as well as the engine of change in Nataraj and his friends. Nataraj's social activism, too, finds fulfilment in his evolving association with the 'man-eater'. Nataraj comes to realize that Vasu is born that way: '[H]is nature would not let him leave anyone in peace' (27); it is nature perverted, like that of a man-eater, swerving from its dharma: that is the significance of the title. A creature that has taken to unnatural ways: distanced from his own true self, denatured. And not just in 'your office', but at your 'home' as well: the Vasu 'presence'—this gnawing anxiety haunts Nataraj everywhere. At the same time, 'this man-eater softened, snivelled and purred, and tried to be agreeable only in the presence of an official' (28); otherwise, he conducts himself as though he 'was the lord of the universe [...]' (33).

Vasu is yet another orphan, after Sriram of *Waiting for the Mahatma*. Without the benefit of good family upbringing, 'this frightful man with the dark halo over his head [...] was a self-made man' (36). A lawless man himself, Vasu has little patience with lawlessness on the road. 'More people will have to die on the roads, if our nation is to develop any road sense at all!' (33). Vasu talks of the nation more than once: he and Sen bring in a national perspective to this clash of 'values'. '[W]hen one or other of the cartmen turned round with a frown or a swear-word, he was delighted, and he nudged me and confided, "That is how I like to see my countrymen. They must show better spirit; they are spineless, no wonder our country has been a prey to every invader who passed this way"' (102). Prevented from poaching animals in the wild, Vasu turns to womanizing: 'Vasu had turned his tracking instinct in another direction. I had had no notion that our town possessed such a varied supply of women' (86). Nataraj, however, is all professional admiration for Vasu: 'I admired him for his capacity for work, for all the dreadful things he was able to accomplish single-handed' (73). That kind of self-reliance, too, is unimaginable in Malgudi.

Soon enough Nataraj realizes that this 'man with a gun' (88) is a modern demon. Rangi analyses him to Nataraj: '[H]e is afraid of nothing on earth or in heaven or in hell' (156). Who better than a rakshasa to embody such avidya, Ignorance? Prolonged exposure to black halo radiance of 'a perfect enemy' affects our hero (73). For, who can be a man's 'perfect enemy'? Nataraj gets vice-fected.

Citizen Nataraj's involuntary association with Vasu turns out to be a complex relationship: the small townsman is repelled; yet unable, or even unwilling, to release himself from the Vasu entanglement, involution, infection. Clinical pathologists may have missed the malady; but creative writers have dealt with it: memorably, our patent omnibus, Shakespeare; for whom it is a fascinating psycho-moral sickness inspired by evil in man. And curiously, it is not Shakespearean comedy but the tragedies that substantiate our hypothesis here. Brutus and Hamlet—the two intellectuals of Shakespearean tragedy; 'readers' shown reading books in hand—are both affected by infusion of evil: Brutus directly, and Hamlet not so directly. And Iago affects the noblest of warriors, Othello; the witches, Macbeth: all outstanding men, they are affected by evil induction, they are vice-fected. By the time they realize what has happened it is too late; the tragedies conclude on a note of self-enlightenment, though. For Nataraj the source of the deadly radiation is the creature with the tell-tale black halo: producing in Nataraj a sort of extro-susception, morbidity, inspired by Vasu, with marked symptoms and unprecedented side effects.

God help him![7] He does.

The Man-Eater of Malgudi dramatizes yet another encounter with a force from outside. In an earlier novel, *Waiting for the Mahatma*, of the early post-Independence period, the benign Mahatma Gandhi inspires moral transformation in Sriram. In *The Man-Eater of Malgudi*, the later novel, the extraneous power is a malevolent force that 'inspires'—a species of morbidity in the hero; it shakes up even Nataraj's friends. Thus, Vasu's advent is appropriately theatrical: '[P]ractically tearing aside the curtain, an act which violated the sacred traditions of my press' (15).

Narayan gives depth to Vasu; he is a former 'Gandhian', one more in Narayan's post-Independence novels.[8] In less than a decade after *Waiting for the Mahatma*, Vasu, the first of 'Gandhians' in Narayan's late period, moves radically away from the Mahatma. And he is not the only one: earlier in *Waiting for the Mahatma*, Sriram finds it difficult to practise Gandhian principles, suffers instinctual relapse, before his beloved, a true Gandhian, puts him back on his feet. In the next novel, *The Vendor of Sweets*, Jagan, a Gandhian with a creditable record of Satyagraha, drifts away from Gandhian principles to become a thriving businessman—before he realizes his folly and returns to a life of values. For Vasu, a former Gandhian, there is no return to the Mahatma. Vasu recalls his early life to Nataraj: 'I was educated in the Presidency College. I took my Master's degree in History, economics and Literature.' Sound credentials! Then he joins the civil disobedience movement against the British rulers, breaks their laws, marches, demonstrates, and ends up in jail. He goes repeatedly to prison and once after his release finds himself in the streets of Nagpur (18). The postgraduate degree—with specialization in those subjects—also qualifies him as one more 'intellectual' in Narayan's post-Independence novels.

Beginning with Dr Pal of *The Financial Expert*, the very first novel of his post-Independence period, we get intellectuals infamous: later, marking the lowest depths, we will have the obnoxious Dr Rann of *Talkative Man*. Now it is hard to believe that Vasu has participated in the Non-Cooperation Movement led by the Mahatma, Father of the Nation. Vasu, with his 'tanned face, large powerful eyes under thick eyebrows, a large forehead and a shock of unkempt hair, like a black halo' (15), has transformed into Anti-Gandhi. Vasu's 'highlight,' his 'black halo', signifies radiance of Ignorance, 'evil'. Far from being any follower of the Mahatma and his philosophy—'his bull-neck and hammer-fist revealed his true stature' (16): for Vasu professes total faith in sheer physical strength. Might is right. With pugnacious Vasu, 'every other sentence was likely to prove provocative' (17). And Vasu is conscious of his superiority: 'I was stronger than he' (19). Vasu 'recognised no proprieties' (22): to Nataraj's horror he boasts of his murderous attack on his own guru. Vasu, predictably, boasts: 'I never read poetry; no time' (21). Presently in evil evolution, Vasu 'seemed to practise few restraints [...]' (34): earlier 'no proprieties'; now, 'few restraints'. Vasu's bloated individualism—inflated egotism—is of course pronounced: 'I can get on very well by myself' (113). Practically, though, for self-sufficient Vasu 'time is money' (130). Vasu's anti-social philosophy—and that for a former Gandhian!—contrasts starkly with the civilities and proprieties so natural to his democratic contrast—the self-effacing Nataraj. It is no longer the law of the jungle for Vasu, but the chaos of a lawless jungle; for he is a 'man-eater'.

Thanks to Vasu we get an adversarial view of Nataraj and friends. 'You know nothing, you have not seen the world. You know only what happens in this miserable little place' (19). He elaborates later: 'Your whole crowd sickens me! You are a fellow without any sense. Why you are so enthusiastic about a poetaster obsessed with monosyllables I don't know' (131). Still later Vasu tells Nataraj bluntly again: 'You are sentimental. I feel sickened when I see a man talking sentimentally like an old widow. I admire people with a scientific outlook' (134). Here is another set of opposites: Vasu's scientism and the religious fervour of Nataraj and friends. Providence seems at work already. 'Considering his enormous strength, it was surprising that he did not do more damage to his surroundings' (40). Vasu pontificates and just to irritate Nataraj: 'That's an unphilosophical way of looking at things. Money is only a medium of exchange and has no value by itself, and there can be no such thing as your money and my money. It's like the air, common to mankind' (114). And this from a man who cleans out the Mempi forest through savage poaching.

For, Vasu takes to poaching in the Mempi forest with a vengeance: '[H]e had been surrounding himself with carcasses' (50); not unnatural for a demon: 'I couldn't imagine any human being living in this atmosphere' (50). Vasu's goal is familiar to moderns: 'We have to constantly be rivalling Nature at her own game [...].' Not surprising, though; demons and even a great rishi Viswamitra, prompted by their egos, practised the same motto—and came to grief. Nataraj is disturbed: 'This man had set himself as a rival to Nature and was carrying on a relentless fight' (52-3). Nataraj is shaken. 'I shivered slightly at the thought and the way his mind worked. Nothing seemed to touch him. No creature was safe [...]' (53): a fairly accurate description of the standard demon. 'His presence defiled my precincts' (53). Thanks to Vasu, 'anything seemed possible in my press these days' (72). For, 'short of creating animals he did everything' (73).

Later, looking at all the stuffed creatures, big or small in the attic, 'all alike in death' (128), Nataraj is convinced: Vasu has gone demoniacal; with a passion for slaughter, pure and simple: relishing the power to take life. Nataraj's concern for the safety of the temple elephant elicits appropriate response from Vasu. Now Vasu offers a peep into his own upbringing: 'At one time I was squeamish like you. It was Hussein who broadened my outlook. He used to tell me the way to be broad-minded is to begin to like a thing you don't like. It makes for a very scientific outlook' (134). In contrast Nataraj represents not just an 'Indian' way of life—he upholds universal values: human values.

In simple contrast with Vasu the malcontent, the 'demon', Nataraj is happily and culturally conjugated, with a fulfilling family, a satisfying profession, and the congenial company of his friends; and the Malgudi 'society'; his background comprehends not only Gandhi, but the Buddha and Jesus. He realizes that Vasu's mores are starkly, blatantly, odd, out of sync with his own ethos, the way of living of the vast majority of his townsmen. Man–woman relationship, for one, is sacramental to Nataraj—as to his culture. Vasu's definition of marriage shocks Nataraj: 'If the man is willing and the woman is willing—there is a marriage [...]' (33). And the interloper explicates: '"If you like a woman have her by all means. You don't have to own a coffee estate because you like a cup of coffee" and he smiled, more and more pleased with his own wit' (33–4). Vasu shows scant respect for women: 'Modern women are no good at anything when you come to think of it' (132). More alarming, Vasu has no love lost for children: 'Knowing his attitude to children, I did not want to risk a meeting between them' (82). The fear is not unfounded: looking at the tiger cub in Vasu's collection in the attic, 'I shivered slightly at the thought of anyone taking so young a life' (129–30). Age no bar for the man-eater! Nor species! For Vasu an elephant is just right for slaughter: that is, every part has commercial value: in his opinion, 'it's a perfect animal in that way' (132). Buying over a member of the Mempi temple committee, the unethical village tailor, Vasu boasts: 'The elephant has been promised me when it's dead. I have it in writing here' (133). Vasu violates every norm of not just any civilized society, but a democratic polity; he breaks written and unwritten laws, civilities. Gandhian philosophy inspires Nataraj's response to Vasu—at least initially. 'Mahatma Gandhi had enjoined on us absolute non-violence in thought and speech, if for no better reason than to short-circuit violent speech and prevent it from propagating itself' (5).

Vice-fection overwhelms Gandhism. 'Somehow this man's presence roused in me a sort of pugnacity' (20). Nataraj, a typical representative of the staid community of Malgudi, cannot escape the Vasu effect. Nataraj, cheerful and charitable by temperament, self-sufficient businessman—'a seasoned printer'—is reduced to helplessness: 'I had resigned myself to anything [...]' (28).

The initial effect of vice-fection—Vasufection—creates confusion and bitterness. 'Having always lived within the shelter of my press, I had probably grown up in complete ignorance of human nature, which seemed to be vicious, vile, vindictive and needlessly unfriendly everywhere' (42). In the midst of all those stuffed animals lying about in Vasu's attic room Nataraj is convulsed with loathing: 'I couldn't imagine any human being living in this atmosphere' (50).

But, at the same time, 'as far as possible, I tried to shut my eyes' (53). He offers an explanation for his abject helplessness.

I had been brought up in a house where we were taught never to kill. When we swatted flies, we had to do it without the knowledge of our elders. I remember particularly one of my grand-uncles, who used the little room on the pyol and who gave me a coin every morning to buy sugar for the ants, and kept an eye on me to see that I delivered the sugar to the ants in various corners of our house. [...] You must never scare away the crows and sparrows that come to share our food; they have as much right as we to the corn that grows in the fields. And he watched with rapture squirrels, mice, and birds busily depleting the granary in our house. [...] That was in the days before my uncles quarrelled and decided to separate. (54)

Paternal failure also has done its bit. 'It was like waiting for my father in my childhood. I often had to spend days and days hoping to catch my father in a happy mood to ask him for a favour [...]' (56). An element of filial 'fear' also surfaces in Nataraj under Vasu's impact: 'My heart sank at the sight of him. There was a frown on his terrible brow' (56). Or just pusillanimity aggravated by Vasufection: 'I would be grateful if he left me alone and did not think of bringing that terrific fist of his against my chin' (59). Nataraj—middle-class, upper-caste—recalls his childhood home again: 'It used to have a red glass pane when we were young, and made me sick when the evening sun threw a blood-red patch on the wall' (142). And in that final scene he reaches out to grab Vasu's gun: 'I had never touched a gun before and felt scared' (165).

That background has shaped Nataraj's sensibility and philosophy of life: just right and ripe for Vasufection; this alien is an utterly new form, invisible radiation; Nataraj's immune system is unable to neutralize the black halo. The gregarious Nataraj, the confidant of his group, finds no one to share his problem with: 'After all one should learn to bear one's burdens' (55). Unused to this species of motiveless hostility he is unable to tackle it. Forbearance slips one notch to surrender. 'Abnormal' is the word. The victim analyses the consequence: 'I was getting into an abnormal frame of mind' (55). 'Abnormal' has become normal. The feeling haunts him: 'I had become abnormal' (56). Vasu is pathogenic. Vasu's lethal presence goes on to take its toll. Gandhi cannot help. 'I was, I suppose, getting into a state of abnormal watchfulness myself [...]' (73). Nataraj's staid background makes him more vulnerable. 'I did not want to do anything that might madden him further and worsen our relationship' (74); because 'I could never be a successful enemy to anyone. Any enmity worried me night and day.' And this is not the first time he has suffered: 'As a schoolboy I persistently shadowed around the one person with whom I was supposed to be on terms of hate and hostility. [...] It bothered me like a toothache' (74). A psycho-pathological condition, beyond his capacity for self-diagnosis—'in this state of mental confusion' (74)—affects Nataraj, so predisposed to Gandhian non-violence. Nataraj grows more bewildered by the subtle and the noxious: Nataraj is down with amoral extro-susception.

I stood like a child at the treadle, hoping he would look at me and nod and that all would be well again. He was a terrible specimen of human being no doubt, but I wanted to be on talking terms with him. This was a complex mood. I couldn't say that I liked him or approved of anything he said or did, but I didn't want to be repulsed by him. [...] I was in this state of mental confusion. (74)

The centre, Gandhian philosophy, cannot hold. 'I was very happy that he was no longer liked by Muthu. My enemy should be the enemy of other people too, according to age-old practice' (89). Vasufection goes terminal: 'I suddenly felt that I sounded like Vasu' [...] (118).

Under Vasu's sway Nataraj's sexuality, too, surfaces in rajasic–tamasic style: 'My mind was busy following the fleshy image of Rangi' (86). He is now willing to 'seduce or be seduced [...]' by Rangi because 'she has it' (157). Such sentiments are unimaginable in the pre-Vasu era; as in Narayan's pre-Independence novels. Not just Nataraj: an amoral condition has affected other sheltered small-town citizens and unnoticed. '[T]he idea of Vasu provoked Sen into incoherent unpredictable statements' (55).

The confrontation scene between Vasu and the temple group escorted by the police inspector (148ff), a showdown between demos and the demon, is at first look a flop show. The episode shows Vasu in typical demonic arrogance. As they knock on his door, 'Vasu's head appeared with its dark halo of hair, set off by the light from his room' (148). After breaking the wrist of the police inspector, '[h]e mocked the man in pain' (151). Fatefully the 'demon' follows up with another ego show: Vasu breaks his bed—preparing, unaware, for his own self-destruction. Providence comes to the rescue of the demos.

But Vasufection's ultimate damage is more disturbing; some effects of the inspired malady linger. 'I saw myself as others saw me, and was revolted by the picture' (177). The genial Nataraj is deserted by his friends: 'There was not a soul with whom I could discuss the question. Sen avoided me. The poet was not to be seen. [...] During my morning trip to the river and back no one stopped to have a word with me' (178). Nataraj is conscious of the effect of Vasufection on his personality. 'A touch of aggression was creeping into my speech nowadays. [...] I hardened myself [...] and suffered at the same time' (179). He has received the full blast of Vasufection. The worst of this man-eater's devastation is experienced only after Vasu's exit: '[H]e had destroyed my name, my friendships, and my world. [...] I burst into tears' (186). That moment, act, finally, comedically, brings absolution; as on cue Sastri returns and gives him the true story, the manner of Vasu's death; he assures Nataraj that Vasu had killed himself. Divine intervention, execution, has saved Nataraj from Vasufection, the black malady, inspired morbidity, vice-fection.

Nataraj and the Supporting Cast

It takes a great lot to bring down a 'demon'.

The Nataraj–Vasu drama is acted out with support from a delightful range of minor characters, a cast of common humanity. They are ambience characters as well as action characters: they contribute to the plot and they represent the small town society as well as the country around Malgudi, build up the 'commoner' solidity of Nataraj's world. Nataraj's missions, meetings, and encounters with these fellow citizens offer a comic feast. With his creative energy in full play in his handling of adjournment lawyer, K.J. and Vasu himself; and his abundant warmth for fellows like the eccentric poet and Muthu, and others, Nataraj holds the group together.

Group 1: Parlour Mates

Vasu styles them—not without reason—'friends who treat the place as a club lounge' (80), or 'those chair-fixtures in your press' (103)—they draw his censure: 'Your whole crowd sickens me!' (131).[9] Nataraj's immediate circle represents, however, a range of aspiration and interests alien to Vasu.

The Poet

On the very first page the novelist presents the 'permanent pair' (27): the teacher-poet and the journalist Sen, his 'constant companions'. Among the regulars and friends in the parlour the aesthetic interest of Nataraj's society is represented in comic-serious style by the poet. This humble creature—a schoolteacher, who teaches 'well, history, geography, science, English—anything the boys must know' (20)—like a pyol schoolteacher—reveals unsuspected strength and resilience. 'He had developed the art of surviving Vasu's presence' (28): as does Sastri!—both escape Vasufection. Nataraj is at his amusing best in his admiration for the poet: '[A]n implacable foe of all disyllables. […] He was a man of few words, probably because most expressions are poly-syllabic […]' (118). At the same time: 'I found it strangely irritating to think of the pink-coated poet and all the trouble he had caused me' (137). This prosodic fanatic creates strange problems for Nataraj and Sastri as they print his monosyllabic epic: they run out of types and they mark each omission with a star: the result is a star-filled galley. Nataraj observes with pardonable malice: 'When I threw on the poet's lap a particularly complicated star-filled galley, I watched him from my chair with calm satisfaction for a while' (117).

Nataraj finds the poet is incompetent to advise him on the problem created by Vasu; the waggish printer remarks: 'I feared that he might suggest reading poetry aloud as a possible step towards driving out the killer' (55). In the course of that hectic night of dramatic developments, the poet receives an epiphany from the novelist: 'A radiant light gathered around him and isolated him as if he were within an illuminated capsule or cocoon. His frayed jibba and dhoti, and the silly jute bag on his lap in which he carried his papers, were no longer there; they became smudgy and vague. I could see only his face—unshaven (he was saving up a blade for the great day); the light fell on his nose-tip and the rest receded in shadow' (118).[10] From this aesthetic—spiritual—experience the novelist takes us boldly to the earthy sexual comedy of the scene with Rangi—a startling shift of scene and mood. It is the poet's epic poem that initiates the climactic celebrations in the temple—bringing the whole town together.

Sen

Sen, the other regular—along with the poet—in Nataraj's parlour, 'came to read the newspapers on my table, and [...] held forth on the mistakes Nehru was making' (8). Sen facilitates constructive action by the little group; with his cyclopaedic knowledge of public affairs, the journalist ferrets out from his archives Dr Joshi's address for Nataraj. Sen is the intellectual of the group. Sen also represents the public domain; he provides the political background and the historical context: the Nataraj–Vasu drama is enacted against the macro backdrop of the nation. Sen's 'fixation' offers comic appeal: 'The journalist was frankly dumbfounded when he realized that there was no aspect of this particular problem which he could blame directly on the Government' (55).[11] Though comically obsessed Sen represents the democratic voice of Nataraj's society and epitomizes dissent in a democratic polity; Sen is the only one among the parlour group who stands up to Vasu (26–7). His name suggests that he is from east India, perhaps a Bengali; he—and Dr Joshi—gives the Nataraj–Vasu confrontation a national character.

Nataraj assigns to Sen the job of drafting the notice to the public on the forthcoming literary-religious event and celebration and inviting donations. This offers an irresistible opportunity to Narayan-Nataraj. 'He wrote a few hundred words, beginning with the origin of the world; then he went on to the writer's duty to society, the greatness of the tale of Krishna and our cultural traditions, the merits of monosyllabic verse, concluding with spicy remarks on the Nehru government's attitude to creative writing' (111). Happily for Nataraj: 'These were totally erased by Sastri himself before he set up type. "Let Sen write a separate book on Nehru, if he chooses. Why should he try to display his wisdom at our cost?"' (112). During the run-up to the temple celebration Sen, too, immerses himself in his community action: he 'never left the temple precincts for seven days, working at it night and day' (126); and on that big day of the celebration and procession Sen 'was nearly unrecognizable in his holy make-up' (135). After Nataraj's breakdown during the temple celebration, quips Sen: 'You really gave a shout which could have gone to heaven, you know' (144). It has!

Lacking Sen's social awareness and passion for public affairs, Vasu heaps derision on Sen; he nicknames him 'local Nehru': despotic contempt for a democratic citizen.

Today, in retrospect, it is not hard to imagine the magnitude of contribution of millions of 'local Nehrus' to India's development. *The Man-Eater of Malgudi* had invalidated Naipaul's early India books even before they were written.

Sastri

The novelist helps the reader along with this soft-spoken but steadfast chorus, Nataraj's assistant, Sastri, 'an orthodox-minded Sanskrit semi-scholar' (75). Though Sastri is Nataraj's employee—his entire 'staff' in the press—he turns out to be friend, pundit, and guard to his employer. Sastri is Nataraj's foil. 'Wife, children. Absurd. Such encumbrances were not necessary for Sastri, I felt. They were for lesser men like me' (15). Sastri is cleanliness personified: he tells Nataraj, 'all my life I have tried to keep this press so clean!' (75). That makes it more difficult for Nataraj to accommodate Vasu, the taxidermist. Nataraj loves to rally orthodox Sastri. The first time Sastri reports Rangi is spotted in the premises, Nataraj presses him mischievously: '"Who is Rangi?" [Sastri] looked desperate, shy, and angry. I was enjoying his discomfiture immensely' (84).

Nataraj adds: 'His deep and comprehensive knowledge of the dancer's family was disconcerting' (85).

But when things get desperate with Vasu-fection: 'I felt completely helpless. Sastri alone grasped the situation and now and then threw in a word of cheer such as "These things cannot go on forever like this, can they?"' (58). In contrast to Nataraj: 'Sastri himself seemed to take a detached, synoptic view of the hyena and other creatures on the other side of the grille' (77). His autocratic sagacity apart—a self-appointed censor of Sen's draft—Sastri is a spiritual counsellor to Nataraj. Sastri, the 'Sanskrit semi-scholar' that he is, plays the clarifying and consoling chorus on Vasu and his depredations: 'He shows all the definitions of a *rakshasa*', persisted Sastri and went on to define the make-up of a rakshasa. [...] He said: 'Every *rakshasa* gets swollen with his ego. He thinks he is invincible, beyond every law. But sooner or later something or other will destroy him' (58). Sastri glosses the myth of the demon Bhasmasura for Nataraj—and the non-Indian reader. 'He made humanity suffer. [...] Every man can think that he is great and will live forever, but no one can guess from which quarter his doom will come' (76).[12] That consoles Nataraj; and proves prophetic.

After Vasu's mysterious death: 'Sastri proved to be the shrewdest. The minute he heard of the corpse upstairs he planned his retreat. [...] He just put his work away, wiped his hand on a rag, and took off his apron; I watched him silently. He went through the process of retreat methodically' (170). That is 'the imperturbable Sastri': 'with a clarity of logic rare under the circumstances' (170–1). Sastri is the smartest of the dodgers in the novel; Nataraj, no mean player of the game himself is no match to Sastri. 'While all of us were running around him, Sastri alone had maintained a haughty aloofness' (171). Now Sastri leaves the town 'to attend a wedding'; he extends his absence by going on a pilgrimage, a tactical detour. Returns. Quietly; after the Vasu affair is sorted out. And briefs his boss on what has actually happened. Sastri has received the whole episode of Vasu's self-destruction from Rangi, the only witness to the accident. Thus, the well-connected Sastri unravels the mystery of Vasu's death for Nataraj; and brings total, conclusive relief to him; helps Nataraj's recuperation from the Vasu vice-fection. Sastri gets the curtain line. 'Yet the universe has survived all the *rakshasas* that were ever born. Every demon carries within him, unknown to himself, a tiny seed of self-destruction, and goes up in thin air at the most unexpected moment. Otherwise, what is to happen to humanity?' (183).

Otherwise what is to happen to democracy?
'In God we trust!'[13]

Group 2: Bureaucracy

Three officials represent bureaucracy in this democratic set-up.

First, we have the sanitary inspector with his pith helmet: '(I think he was the only one in the whole town who had such headgear, having picked it up at an army disposal store)' (68). Nataraj assesses him nicely: 'I could not say he was a friend, but a friendly man' (68). The official is unique in Malgudi: '[H]e was the most parched and dehydrated man I had ever seen in my life' (68). A cartoon clown he may be for looks; but this official's visit and goodwill alerts Nataraj that the nefarious activity in his attic above had accelerated; a reminder to Nataraj that he cannot close his eyes any longer.

Next we have the forest officer. On his second visit to the press, Nataraj is surprised at the change in this official's attitude: 'He had seemed such a timid moralistic man some months ago when he visited me' (77). But now the printer discovers that '[t]his thin cadaverous man, whose neck shot straight out of his khaki like a thin cylindrical water-pipe, was tough' (77). An official who, in spite of his authorial ambitions, is clear in his mind: 'Any man who violates the game laws is my enemy. I wouldn't hesitate to shoot him if I had a chance' (77–8). When Nataraj tries to humour him with his jokes: 'He recovered his composure, as if he realized that he ought not to spoil me by smiling too much, and suddenly compressed his lips into a tight narrow line and became grim' (78). This guardian of the wild is aware of ground realities: 'Some of our guards are none too honest' (78). The forest official goes on to try and beard the wolf in its den: 'Well, we may not get the taxidermist's services, but the taxidermist himself' (79).

Though the portrayals also carry a caricatural edge Nataraj's encounters with these two minor officials, offer the reader a couple of comic interludes. More to the point, each official does his duty; collectively such officials make a major difference to their nation. Following this dutiful forest official's inquiry the vigil in the Mempi forest is tightened against poachers: Vasu becomes 'jobless'; in desperation the idle taxidermist plots to get an easier quarry, Kumar the elephant—inviting his own destruction.

A third official, a humble police officer, the circle inspector of police of the rural jurisdiction, is presented in a cameo with crisp wit. 'I was overwhelmed by the proximity of this eminent person, who smelt of the sun, sweat and leather' (44): a capsule portrait of a conscientious police officer, he is an ambience character. If the 'circle' is not given the seat of honour, on the first seat, next to the driver, the erratic rural bus runs the risk of being impounded (43)! His very presence induces some discipline in the temperamental driver (44–5).

Group 3: Poor Folk

The scene with the junk dealer early in the novel (23) presents an ambience character: the lowly Muslim junk dealer has all the time in the world for a deal not worth more than a few rupees of profit; the man engages in, not small business, but wee business. The scene throws light on the provincial Nataraj: 'It was an ideal hour for a transaction in junk' (24). That remark conveys the peace of placid ambience before Vasu's intrusion. This prolonged 'negotiation', this delay in striking a deal also leads to a crucial development in the plot: Vasu arrives on the scene and moves into the attic, above Nataraj's press.

Another humble citizen, the postman, Thanappa, is presented by the novelist with palpable affection. 'Our postman, Thanappa, whom we had known as children, old enough to have retired twice over but somehow still in service. [...] He was a timeless being [...]' (166). This ancient, an institution by himself, is more than an ambience character; he is another cohesive element in the civil society and a humble cog in the plot of the novel as well: for, it is dutiful Thanappa that first discovers Vasu's death—alerts Nataraj.

Group 4: Business Class

The business class in this democratic society is positively represented by Nataraj himself and the chairman of the municipal council. The novelist presents the small-town business interests more amusingly and satirically in K.J. 'He was an old-type orthodox, who wore a red caste-mark on his forehead' (107). The novelist builds, as we have seen, an especially amusing scene around this tight-fisted drink-maker. The chairman and K.J. blend to give us Jagan (*The Vendor of Sweets*).

The Adjournment Lawyer

'[H]abituated to rambling on until the court rose for lunch' (61), the adjournment lawyer is one more in the series of tight-fisted characters in Narayan; the novelist delights in playing their ventriloquist: as in *The Dark Room*, *Mr. Sampath*, and in later novels. Now here is a home-brewed (not just bred) lawyer subverting the system. One more dodger of the novel, he is the most comical. In the opening chapter, during his morning routine Nataraj avoids this native lawyer; that aversion reflects the peaceable temper of a law-abiding citizen. In the first meeting with the wily lawyer (48) Nataraj dictates things; in the second, after the veteran dodger has failed to pay for his daughter's wedding invitations, Nataraj gives a polite hearing to the defaulter's long list of expenses; Nataraj assesses the slippery customer accurately: '"And you have to manage all this," I thought, "by securing endless adjournments". [...] But I said aloud, "Yes, life today is most expensive"' (48).

The third meeting is forced on Nataraj by Vasu's plaint in the local court; Nataraj is left with no other option: he is forced to go to the adjournment lawyer for legal counsel. For this meeting (60ff), Nataraj's third, the novelist chooses the adjournment lawyer's office. It is a hilarious encounter with the adjournment lawyer's devious ways and methodologies on view. The ambience reflects the rot in Nataraj's provincial society; the man is more of an ambience character. The first-time litigant studies the setting closely: the country lawyer's office is situated right above a cotton merchant's: 'I went sneezing up the wooden stairs' (63). Nataraj, the latest victim of the legalist, adds: 'He seemed to delight in punishing people who came to see him. I could hardly recognize my own voice, it sounded so thick with cotton dust' (64).

Nataraj keeps standing throughout the meeting, for the miserly lawyer has not provided any space in the cubby hole for a visitor/ client to sit; a psychological ploy to subdue the prospective client: 'I felt like a pauper petitioning for help' (66). The lawyer's table and office room present a dismal tableau: '[C]overed with dusty paper bundles, old copies of law reports, a dry ink-well, an abandoned pen, and his black alpaca coat, going moss-green with age, hung by a nail on the wall' (63). As he handles another tight-fisted character,

K.J. later, in this meeting, too, Wily Nataraj finally diverts the old man's attention to Vasu's highhandedness: 'You remember that day when you came to have the wedding invitations printed. [...] That prejudiced him' (65). Even after Vasu's death, with the intimidating 'halo' of a 'murderer' around Nataraj's head, the seasoned printer is unable to collect his dues from the devious lawyer. At the inquest Nataraj practises one lesson learnt from the adjournment lawyer: 'I bore in mind our adjournment lawyer's dictum, "Don't say more than you are asked for"' (174).

Group 5: Civil Society

Even anarchic Vasu, the 'destroyer', in a certain mood, gives due importance to society: 'We are members of a society, and there is no point in living like a recluse, shutting oneself away from all the people around' (103). To Nataraj's credit he seeks out and gathers around himself, besides Sen and the poet, other people with values: Muthu and Dr Joshi; Rangi herself teams up—uninvited, spontaneously and courageously—with Nataraj and against Vasu.

Muthu

No one among Nataraj's friends is more remarkable than the humble villager Muthu. 'He was a self-made man' (37): but a complete contrast to another self-made man: Vasu. This owner of a small tea shop in Mempi village is a disciplined professional: 'I never eat anywhere outside, when I travel, and it keeps me fit. I like and enjoy a good meal when I go home.' (88) That sounds more like the novelist himself.

Muthu knows his man. He brings the problem of the elephant's sickness to Nataraj and Nataraj responds honestly: 'The enormity of the problem oppressed me. This was not something I could evade by suggesting that they looked over the Heidelberg' (90). Muthu's sincerity and selflessness impress Nataraj: 'I felt genuinely concerned about poor Kumar now' (90). The Nataraj–Vasu confrontation is replicated in the country through Muthu, the wise commoner neutralizing the collusion of a countryman, the village tailor, with Vasu. While Nataraj takes interest in the poet's epic and its consecration at the temple in Malgudi, Muthu, a great believer, 'began to take interest in the shrine at the confluence of the mountain and the plains' (37). Setting out for Malgudi for the elephant's medical treatment, he 'suddenly remembered that he had come out without thanking the Goddess. He ran back to the temple, lit a piece of camphor before the Goddess and rejoined the procession' (100). Muthu is more than a man of faith; Muthu is a man of action: 'I rebuilt the temple with my own funds' (38). He is generosity itself in comparison with the adjournment lawyer and K.J. With four children and a daughter to marry, he plays host to the stranded Nataraj: 'This is my treat. You don't have to pay for this cup' (39). No extro-susception works on him, no inspired morbidity affects him.[14]

When Muthu comes calling on his friend Nataraj he is at his dignified best. 'He had dressed himself to come to town [...]' (88). Nataraj sheepishly offers to pay for the treat of buns and tea Muthu has given him in his village during the 'kidnap' episode; Muthu quietly spurns the offer. Muthu's conclusive query (88) reflects his values—in stark contrast to tight-fisted townsmen like K.J. and the adjournment lawyer—shames printer Nataraj. And this is the second upper-class citizen Muthu reprimands. In the curious gathering around the ailing elephant in Mempi village (95-6), a schoolmaster ('who was not sure what he wanted to say but kept interrupting everyone with his reminiscences') utters an inauspicious remark, Muthu pulls him up calmly and firmly: '"Should I teach a wise one like you what to speak and when, and what not to speak?" He looked sadly at the teacher.' The comment followed by the gesture confirms the balance of mind and sense of propriety and proportion of this villager. The unassuming villager has read Vasu and his problem early and better than Nataraj: '"He is a man with a gun," he said. [...] He has other people, who are more suitable to his temperament [...]' (88-9).

Here is another man engaged, like Dr Joshi, in selfless service. Muthu inspires Nataraj: 'I had to overlook the responsibilities on hand. Kumar's welfare became an all-important issue. The visiting cards that I was printing could wait, but not Kumar' (91).

Muthu also comes through as a man of progressive ideas; he has definite views about his daughter's marriage: 'My wife is scheming to marry her off to her own brother's son, but I have other ideas. I want the girl to marry a boy who is educated' (39). Muthu makes sense even on family matters, a spring of native wisdom: 'It's best to listen to the advice of one's wife—because sooner or later that's what everyone does, even the worst bully' (143). When Vasufection builds up and Nataraj suffers a breakdown in the midst of the celebration, Muthu is among the friends that rush to him.

Muthu is a country Nataraj: better still, a refined Nataraj: another missionary with a piety project of his own. 'Muthu hoped by hiring out the elephant for processions to earn enough money to build a tower for the temple of Goddess, which would be visible for fifty miles around' (159). Muthu, this rural Indian, initiates action that also culminates towards the end in the critical scene of the temple procession.

Dr Joshi

Anti-social Vasu and his mischief in the novel are countered and neutralized by humble citizens, 'small men', educated or uneducated, who just believe in carrying out their local duties. After Muthu Joshi is another outstanding example.

As Nataraj goes looking for Dr Joshi, on the other bank of the Sarayu he discovers that the vet's setting is already promising; and such a relief from the Vasu-hassled town: 'The mango-trees cast a soft shade and the air was thick with the scent of blooms. The river flowed on with a soft swish. It was so restful that I could have set my bicycle against the trunk of a tree and gone to sleep on the mud under the shade of a tree. But duty impelled me on' (92).

An appropriate setting for the vet engaged in animal welfare. The vet halloos to the visitor to come through the fence. 'I slipped through the fence, the barbed wire slightly gashing my forearm and tearing my dhoti. I swore at it, but it gave me a feeling of shedding my blood for a worthy cause' (93). 'Duty' a minute ago; and 'worthy cause' now—though grandiloquent they prepare us for the able and amiable Dr Joshi. The very first look at the doctor's humble camp dwelling convinces Nataraj: 'Here definitely was a man with a mission' (93). Dr Joshi is yet another home-grown 'missionary', true to the soil; he represents the positive ballast of civil society:

balances Vasu cynicism. Dr Joshi is also another citizen preoccupied with animals: 'He was a man completely serious, living in a world of animals and their ailments and diseases' (95).

In the classic confrontation building up now between the citizen and the denizen the self-effacing vet offers illuminating relief again to Vasu's demonics. This animal doctor is a kindred soul to both Nataraj and Muthu; and, 'with the characteristic patience of a doctor' (93). Later Dr Joshi joins the indignant group of Nataraj's friends that bravely confronts the man-eater in its den. Dr Joshi is the second north Indian, after Sen: both give this Malgudi of *The Man-Eater of Malgudi* a pan-Indian character and strength.

The vet confides to Nataraj: 'I have a hope that things will be O.K. some time. I'm not allowing things to rust, you know' (94). That remark recalls to us Nataraj's comment on the journalist Sen (91); Sen, too, is an optimist and believes firmly in the future of his nation. Now these small men, with their small schemes—and without 'big talk'—represent a burgeoning democracy's vitality; their sense of duty, dedication to social causes—'small schemes'—steadily fuel the nation's progress. R.K. Narayan's faith in sustainable sanguinity is the very life spring of democracy.

Muthu and Dr Joshi and Sen, and Nataraj are the foot soldiers of a democratic polity—in their struggle against a lethal foe, an anarchic invasion, they respond and act like the Americans when, struggling against the atheistic USSR, they declared 'In God We Trust'.

Rangi

'Rangi was a notorious character of the town' (84). The first time Rangi is spotted leaving Vasu's place, Sastri testifies: '[S]he was the worst woman who had ever come back to Malgudi' (85). Now, Rangi 'live[s] in the shadows of Abu Lane' (84); Abu Lane is adjacent to Kabir Street, the hotbed of Malgudi 'aristocracy': who had sent that youthful singer of Tyagaraja bhajans to an asylum in Madras. Rangi is one more victim of this decadent culture. The Vasu effect—inspired morbidity, dark radiance—inflames Nataraj into 'speculations on the theme of lust'. Thanks to Rangi—and Vasu-fection—we have sexual comedy for the first time in Narayan's novels; and in the very first novel of his final phase. 'My mind was busy following the fleshy image of Rangi and perhaps I resented the intrusion' (86). Viewed through Nataraj's nightful eyes Rangi is somewhat less forbidding: 'Anyway whatever might be the hour, every inch of her proclaimed her what she was—a perfect female animal [...]' (85). Nataraj is terrified by the 'vision': 'My hair stood on end. Rangi! The woman to avoid [...] the awful fleshy creature whom Sastri considered it a sin to look at!' (119). Nataraj fails. The novelist takes his treatment of illicit sexuality a step further. After his vision of the 'poet', Nataraj, the Kabir Street scion of a community which prided itself on 'strict morals' is rewarded with another epiphany.

Not bad, not bad. Her breasts are billowy, like those one sees in temple sculptures. Her hips are also classical. [...] My blood tingled with an unholy thrill. [...] I was an adolescent lost in dreams over a nude photograph. [...] To dissolve within the embrace of her mighty arms all the monogamous chastity I had practised a whole lifetime [...] a goddess carved out of cinder. (120)

In sattvic Nataraj this is evidence of inspired morbidity!

At the same time Nataraj is rewarded with another epiphany: 'The shadows cast by the low-powered lamp were tricky and created a halo around her' (120). After the unshaven poet yet another apotheosis with Rangi! The hour of the flesh is here: the middle-class moralist capitulates, promoting sparkling comedy. 'In my fevered state I wanted to ask her if she was aware that the grille was locked and the key was where Sastri was sleeping' (122).

The crisis passes. Nataraj is abashed: 'Even at that mad hour, I am glad to think, I kept my head and tongue' (123).

In a critical scene later with Nataraj, Rangi's strength of character asserts itself. 'Sir, I am only a public woman, following what is my *dharma*. I may be a sinner to you, but I do nothing worse than what some of the so-called family women are doing. I observe our rules [...]' (121). At the same time Rangi is touchingly realistic: 'In a year or two who will care to have me?' (123).

'Duty' is a key motivator in the story of a developing nation. Here is Rangi rising to the occasion: 'It will be my duty' (122). And

Rangi declares with pride that 'no man so far has stopped my doing what I like' (122). Rangi is determined: '[Vasu] may kill me for speaking, but I don't care. I want to save poor Kumar' (123). Here is a lowly citizen rising to meet a threat to her community. Rangi is as integral to her society's autoimmune system as Muthu, Dr Joshi, and Nataraj. The decision is not at all easy for Rangi; she takes, and knowingly, by far the greatest risk among the mobilized force of common citizens; and Rangi knows Vasu better than anyone else and knows who she is dealing with: 'He may come to my house and set fire to it. Only my old mother is there—deaf and blind. [...] [Vasu] is afraid of nothing' (156). She knows the adversary. 'He is afraid of nothing on earth or in heaven or hell. [...] He is so strong and obstinate. If he thinks of something, he has to do it; no one on earth can change his mind' (156). That is perhaps the best lay description—as opposed to Sastri's—of the nature of a 'demon'. Rangi also knows Nataraj does not know: 'You don't know him well enough' (156). Yet Rangi works towards neutralizing Vasu's evil. In a final act of social service it is Rangi, the only witness to Vasu's self-destruction, who unravels the mystery of Vasu's death to Sastri: helps rescue Nataraj from the worst crisis of his life. More than any other citizen of Malgudi, man or woman, it is Rangi the prostitute who offers the reader reassuring experience of the human spirit. Rangi, more than anyone else, restores our faith and confidence in humanity and democracy.

These little people—'small men of R.K. Narayan'!—are the nuclei of civil society, each a minuscule reactor of social commitment. Little folk with small missions: this is the India that R.K. Narayan— and even my generation—grew up with; and Vidia Naipaul missed.

Nataraj's Wife

The first of Nataraj's supporting cast, mentioned on the very first page as 'my wife', this sensitive woman remains that—'my wife'—all through the novel: unnamed. She is the second unnamed wife of a hero in Narayan's novels after Sampath's wife. Margayya's wife, too, is unnamed most of the time. Perhaps the novelist is underscoring their selfless anonymity, their unstinted, spontaneous service to their husbands, their children, their families—and the failure of the men folk to give them due recognition and dignity, their space and place. Are these unnamed but certainly not faceless, self-respecting women representative of their class—the Indian middle-class woman? Even later the two husband hunters in *Talkative Man* and *Grandmother's Tale* outshine their husbands; heroically, because they get nothing more precious in return than their worthless husbands. Mrs Nataraj, the simple-minded housewife, leaves the moment Rangi arrives for an interview with her husband; once the news of the dead body in the press reaches her, however, she is back by her husband's side. Mrs Srinivas, Mrs Margayya, Rosie, and Selvi of the story in *Malgudi Days*: there can be no doubt who is holding up human values, keeping afloat the traditional Indian family—the Indian society. Towards the end of his career Narayan presents Daisy, who hates the very idea of the family: representing the changing mores of post-Independence India. Narayan's women characters, particularly in the post-Independence phase, outdo the men in sheer strength of character—share, unmistakably, the heritage of the novelist's grandmother Ammani and his mother Gnanambal; but none more memorably than plucky Rangi.[15]

Group 6: Nataraj and Friends, 'for God and Country'

Nataraj says: 'I wanted to stretch my capacity for patience to the utmost in the cause of God and country' (131). Once the decision is taken to celebrate the release of the poet's epic at the temple, '[e]normous preparations began. Once again, my normal work of composing and printing was pushed to the background' (105). Citizen Nataraj, non-sordid, non-profiteering, immerses himself in this voluntary social service project, combining it with a piety mission.

I had to send people to be served by Heidelberg, as neither myself nor Sastri had any leisure to attend to our profession. [...] Sastri and I had a hundred things to do, morning till night. I kept walking in and out of my office. I saw very little of my wife and child. I went home for dinner late every night. (111)

When the day arrives, 'Every hour of that day was like a tenth of a second to me, it was so compressed and so fleeting [...]' (124).

Nataraj manages to get the best specialists to decorate God's chariot, and the best florist—'a man amenable only to my influence' (125); and the best piper and the best drummer—'they had condescended to accept a local engagement because it was the first of its kind in our town' (125). And Nataraj and his band of humble comrades achieve complete success: 'The whole town was at it' (126). Nataraj justly boasts later of his managerial competency: '[T]here was not a single person in that whole throng who could organize and guide a procession as I could' (158). In the midst of the colourful and noisy procession Nataraj muses:

> Vasu was like an irrelevant thought. He should have no place in my scheme of things. [...] The sight of the God, the sound of music, the rhythm of cymbals and the scent of jasmine and incense induced in me a temporary indifference to everything. [...] When the time came the elephant would find the needed strength. The priest was circling the camphor light before the golden images, and the reflections on the faces made them vibrate with a living quality. God Krishna was really an incarnation of Vishnu, who had saved Gajendra; he would again come to the rescue of the same animal on whose behalf I was [...]. (138)

Nataraj's inspired malady has abated in divine presence and service.

Towards the same end Citizen Nataraj risks his life in the attic next to Vasu in his chair: 'I was prepared to lose my life in the process' (164). When he finds Vasu shows no movement, he muses: 'He was obviously a sound sleeper, thank God' (164). Looking back, God is more than an expletive here; for faith is a force in the world of R.K. Narayan. God is the invisible player among Nataraj's team of humble citizens: 'In God we trust.'

Both terms, 'democracy' and 'country' in the sense of 'nation', are mentioned a number of times in the novel. For Nataraj and his friends the two terms are interchangeable.

Now the term 'democracy' is used the first time by a patriot and Gandhian visiting Nataraj's parlour: he is a 'Congressman who had gone to prison fourteen times since the day Mahatma Gandhi arrived in India from South Africa' (14). He counters Sen: 'You think democracy means that if there is no sugar in the shops, Government is responsible' (14). Democracy demands clarification, definition.

Later Nataraj handles a customer, the wily adjournment lawyer, who threatens to have his work done at another press. He says coolly: 'Oh, no trouble whatever. This is a free country, you are a free man. Our constitution gives us fundamental rights [...]' (47). Vasu himself reminds Nataraj: '[T]hese are days of democracy, remember.' Nataraj is appalled at Vasu's 'notion of democracy as being a common acceptance of bad odours' (52). The novel goes on to prove quietly, wittily, what it takes to make a democratic nation.

Nataraj, though a scion of the Kabir Street aristocracy, is among those citizens who form the bedrock of a democracy—though he is an unlikely and—at first sight—unequal adversary to the lawless 'man-eater'. [...] Citizen Nataraj experiences his moments of doubt, second thoughts: from the elephant to the poet, and even about the god in the temple. 'There were moments when I wondered why I had involved myself in all this, when I could have spent the time profitably printing K.J.'s fruit-juice labels' (117). All through, however, we see Nataraj in action—'for God and country!'

Citizen Nataraj manages to collect a band of common citizens from the town and the countryside who, individually and collectively, defend and promote values that are indispensable for the conduct of a democratic polity: they are peaceable, respectful of the law, and tolerant of the different views of other groups and individuals. They are able to bring the whole town together in a celebration, 'the whole town was at it' (126). And not just Nataraj. When Kumar the elephant falls ill, Nataraj's quest for a vet takes him to Sen. '[Sen] sat on a rush mat and worked by a small kerosene light. [...] Part of his equipment was knowing what was going on in the town' (91). Here in brief is ambition, aspiration of a developing country, underlying democracy, sustained by optimism of humanism, faith in man. The dual celebration at the temple is actually a quiet triumph of the spirit of democracy at the grassroots level. *The Man-Eater of Malgudi* is an allegory of democracy in action; of micro units—'little men'—rushing to control and repel an alien invasion. This band of honest citizens has to contend with whiners like K.J. and the adjournment lawyer. When things get too tough for the good citizens of the land, Providence takes a hand: Nataraj and friends can claim with the American people: 'In God we trust.' They had better: He alone makes the difference between a totalitarian regime and a democracy; so as E.M. Forster put it, 'Two cheers for democracy!' R.K. Narayan gives his nascent polity a joyous thumbs-up.

When R.K. Narayan wrote the book in the late 1950s—the novel was first published in 1961—India was in bad shape; when Naipaul quotes Narayan in *An Area of Darkness* Narayan was not just savouring the success of his major novel, but also of his nation's democracy: 'Whatever happens, India will go on.' Naipaul is proved wrong in his dismal misdiagnosis of India; while Narayan's faith in democracy—and Providence, God's scheme of things has been vindicated. For the Indian novelist democracy is deocracy.

The loss of innocence in *The Man-Eater of Malgudi* deserves celebration; it also makes us rather sad especially the way friends desert Nagaraj after Vasu's 'mysterious' death. But after the clarification and reaffirmation from Sastri, Nataraj returns—not to pre-Vasu innocence, but to service. If Nataraj has been anything he has been serviceable. That is the significance of the brilliant closing line: 'Yes, Sastri, I am at your service, I said.'

And for Comedy as Well!

The Man-Eater of Malgudi is soused in wit and humour. We experience the engaging appeal of a born humorist, with his instinct for laughter. *The Man-Eater of Malgudi* offers first-rate comedy: of intrigue, conspiracy and rumour! And humour! All in the normal course of things; underplayed.[16]

There is this simple way in which Narayan is able to create humour centred on inanimate objects. Still-life humour, making material things wink and glow: 'The poet would transfer himself without fuss from the high-backed Queen Anne chair to a poorer seat' (27). Or the cross-country bus (41), a truly Indian—even Third World asset—such as young Mohun Biswas who rides as a conductor in Naipaul's *A House for Mr Biswas*. Or the old timepiece: '[I]t was so brown that I could hardly make out the numerals on it' (40). Nataraj mentions the original Heidelberg more than once and to witty effect. Or K.J.'s drink (105). The fun with the adjournment lawyer begins with the signboards: 'There you saw his signboard, bleached by time and weather [...] nailed to a pillar on which a more aggressive board announced Nandi Cotton Corporation' (63). The scene with Rangi at Nataraj's home (154) is Narayan's domestic comedy at its best. Sexual humour also finds a prominent place in the very first novel of Narayan's late post-Independence phase: 'Sastri darkly hinted that he knew who fathered her into this world, and I hoped it was not himself' (85). The comedy develops bolder notes: '[E]ven in the dark I could see the emphatic curves of her body. I stood away from her, at a safe distance, right by the inner doorway, and asked rather loudly [...]' (155). There is also humour of common humanity, normality humour: following Vasu's death the members of the group suspect each other. 'I knew that they were all unanimous in suspecting me when I was not there' (175). Not to speak of Narayan's societal humour: a jibe at the municipality (159). Sombre sarcasm, too, is part of Narayan's broad spectrum humour: 'Our Kabir Street citizens had exacting standards of sanity' (158–9). Nataraj's experiences in his Mempi episode and his witticisms light up the serious theme (41). Not just for God and country—for comedy as well!

After a struggle between a citizen and a denizen in a democracy, violence and non-violence, small-town mores versus metro methods, 'East' versus 'West', finally the conclusion of *The Man-Eater of Malgudi* is typical of Narayan's religious optimism in the later novels. On return from Mempi village, with the normal routine on the market road re-established, Nataraj experiences—far from the placidity of the opening scene—that 'great feeling of security and stability' (47). *The Man-Eater of Malgudi* breathes the spirit of the Indian epic tradition; a modernized myth of Bhasmasura, the demon who after winning a deadly boon from Lord Shiva wishes to test it on the Lord Himself; but with opportune intervention from Lord Vishnu, the demon destroys himself. 'Yet the universe has survived all the *rakshasas* that were ever born' (183). Otherwise what is to happen to democracy? Deocracy?

14

Private Sorrows, Indian Remedy

*The Vendor of Sweets**

Jagan achieves great success as a sweet vendor: fails dismally as a husband and as a father. He recovers from his private sorrows and moves on.

After Vasu, the archetypal recusant of Mahatma, lesser renegades attract the novelist's attention. Indian politics and society may have turned away from the Mahatma; the 'Great Soul' keeps making his presence felt in Narayan's novels—and dramatically.

As a satyagrahi Jagan had attempted audaciously to pull down the Union Jack from the collector's bungalow: '[T]hey had to beat him and crack open his skull in order to make him let go his hold' (Narayan 1967: 138). Now: 'His training was always there, but somehow had dimmed inexplicably' (138). The results of the distancing, gradual, steady, pronounced, have been striking in Jagan's life since; as in his nation's life.

In *The Vendor of Sweets* Jagan, the eponymous hero, recalls the Mahatma often:

When he remembered the word 'service', any activity became touched with significance. 'Service' intoxicated him, sent a thrill through his whole being and explained everything. The first time he had heard the word was in 1937 when Mahatma Gandhi visited Malgudi and had addressed a vast gathering on the sands of the river. He spoke of 'service', explaining how every human action acquired a meaning when it was performed as a service. (47)

---

* This chapter was published in the *Hindu*, Chennai, on 5 October 2013. Reprinted here with permission from the *Hindu*.

Jagan has problems with his wife; his 'non-violent' footwear (5); 'his theories of sound living' (26); his 'theory of keeping a thing for seven years' (81); his 'theories of sane living' (120); or health-giving activities are hard to bear for anyone in the family. Jagan's wife 'hated his theories and lived her own life' (27). A faddist hero can try the reader as much as he does his dear ones. For an advanced version of Jagan, the terminal avatar, we will have to wait until Nagaraj of *The World of Nagaraj*.

Over the decades since the Mahatma Jagan has evolved a 'delicate balance': an intricate alliance in equal measure of cash and scripture; of *iham* and *param* (this world and the next). Jagan's attitude to the scripture is ambiguous. The novelist comments wryly: 'He had the outlook of a soul disembodied, floating above the grime of this earth' (14). His cousin, too, pays him an enigmatic compliment: 'You have perfected the art of living on nothing' (16). Jagan's materialistic philosophy is patent now:

As long as the frying and sizzling noise in the kitchen continued and the trays passed, Jagan noticed nothing, his gaze unflinchingly fixed on the Sanskrit lines in a red bound copy of the Bhagavad Gita, but if there was the slightest pause in the sizzling, he cried out, without lifting his eyes from the sacred text, 'What is happening?' (18)

Jagan also recalls Gandhi selectively: to justify his unaccounted, hence untaxed, income of 'immaculate conception!' (20)—'immaculate cash'; more adorably, 'black money'. '"Money is an evil," he added with great feeling' (87). But 'he could no more help it than he could the weeds flourishing in his backyard' (116–17). After all: 'Gandhi made no reference to the sales tax anywhere to Jagan's knowledge' (117).

What the novelist also achieves in the novel, among other things, is a timely and well-warranted parody of Gandhian philosophy as practised in post-Gandhi India. Jagan's perversions are microcosmic; represent the larger distortions in post-Gandhi India, presented by our novelists, from Jhabvala and Khushwant Singh to Vikram Seth and other novelists of the 1980s.

In the post-Independence period beginning with *The Financial Expert*, Narayan is also fascinated by the theme of generation gap; a feature of the disintegrating joint family.[1] Jagan's attachment to his son, his only child, too, is a higher priority, like unaccounted money: 'As long as his son Mali's blue airmail letters had been the theme, the Gita had receded into the background. Now it was coming back, which showed that Jagan was becoming mentally disturbed again' (67). Progressively, for our hero, 'prayer was a sound way of isolating oneself' (89).

The conflict is central to *The Vendor of Sweets*: '[Young men] are a problem everywhere' (32). Jagan's observation is just right to send the next generation away from the Mahatma: 'It's not like my generation; we came under the spell of Gandhi and could do no wrong' (45). His son's reaction is predictable. With the force of his American experience behind him, Mali, Jagan's only child, ticks off his father: 'Oh, these are not the days of your ancestors' (84). Ominously for Jagan the American sojourn also seems to have had a strange effect on the young man: 'He seemed to cower back and recoil from the bright Indian sunlight' (150).

Margayya fails as a father; Jagan fares no better. Jagan's 'zeal for education' recalls Margayya's travails with his son's schooling. Jagan himself realizes his failure; he resolves piously to 'give him more time' (23), as he talks glibly of his social concern. '"For twenty years," Jagan reflected, "he has grown up with me, under the same roof, but how little I have known him"' (41–2): sentiments with universal appeal, though. Secretly Jagan's mind is bothered by 'an invisible barrier' (42) between him and his son. And '[p]eace reigned at home, with speech reduced to a minimum between father and son' (47); and '[t]hough they lived under one roof, they might be in two different worlds' (48). The cousin, Jagan's confidant, makes the point, and with astute candour: 'That means you have carried things to a point where you cannot speak to him at all' (50).

Jagan's grandiloquent response to the vagrant eating the leftovers in the leaf plates thrown out by the citizens of Malgudi is typically post-Gandhi hypocrisy: '[H]is head throbbed with several national and human problems and their ramifications' (22). At the same time the novelist is preparing the reader for Jagan's self-development later. As Jagan returns home: 'He stood for a moment gazing at the stars, enthralled at the spectacle of the firmament. […] And feeling proud that he was also a part of the same creation' (24).

The genesis of the barrier between Jagan and his son Mali may be traced to an early trauma of the boy. Full of affection for his ailing and suffering mother, '[Mali] came running home from school in order to feed her, rarely going out to play with his friends' (43). Little Mali watched his mother suffer helplessly, while his father neglected her, let her suffer alone: 'From that day, the barrier had come into being. The boy had ceased to speak to him normally' (44). Jagan was 'aghast at the transformations that had come with time' (81), unaware of his own contribution. The old man pities his paternal self: 'He can't speak even two sentences without upsetting me' (136). Unlike in *The Financial Expert* the mother–son–father equilibrium is disturbed beyond repair in this novel. The novelist sums up Jagan's plight variously, pithily: 'private sorrows' (32); 'the serious burden of life' (33); and 'inside he was all torn up' (39). Following the discovery of his son's live-in relationship with Grace, Jagan is overcome by the universal anguish: 'Though at one time Jagan had sighed for a word from his son, he now wished that the thaw had not occurred' (88). After his refusal to support Mali's proposal for a commercial venture Jagan realizes that his son 'didn't want him if he did not claim to be a wealthy father!' (96). A startling image drives home the changed relationship: 'He felt shy and reserved about talking of his son—like one not wishing to exhibit his sores' (126). But then for us Indians there is the ultimate refuge: 'Fate seemed to decree that there should be no communication between them' (132). As a result: 'A tremendous stillness reigned over the house' (134). It no longer feels like a home. 'This looks like somebody else's home' (138); for, '[Mali and his partner, Grace] had tainted his ancient home' (141).

Jagan has done poorly with Mali partly because '[h]e was a cowardly father' (30); in the crisis later we see 'Jagan did not have the courage to stay and face him' (96). His cousin, playing the chorus in this domestic tragedy, tells him: 'You have beaten about the bush and practically lost contact with your son […]' (139).

The setting for this drama, this disintegration, is once again an 'ancient house' (24): '[E]verything in this home had the sanctity of usage' (25). Jagan wails helplessly: 'I don't know how I can live in that house without him. The very thought depresses me' (55). He fondly recalls: 'Theirs had been the brightest home in those days. That was long before the birth of Mali, years even before his marriage' (154). The joint family is falling apart; the cause, from Jagan's point of view, is the younger generation: '[T]hey are not the sort to make a home bright' (181); the sentiment anticipates *The Painter of Signs* and *The World of Nagaraj*.

Certain signs of recuperation are inevitable at some stage in Narayan's heroes. Even with such a hero as Jagan, self-analysis leads to self-development. The novelist has already prepared us, and early: that his hero carried 'a vestige of conscience from his days of public service' (31). The clash of generations is the engine of critical change in Jagan now. Jagan throws up his hands: 'I have had enough' (98). He hints to his cousin: 'Some changes are coming. [...] I have left things to drift too long' (99). Drawing from his prolonged acquaintance with the Gita he declares: 'No good has been achieved without a fight at the proper time' (103).

Now realizes that '[f]or years his fixed orbit had been between the statue and the shop, his mental operations confined to Mali, the cousin and frying' (112). Now Jagan yearns for the river: as much as Market Road, the river Sarayu is a soothing presence in the world of R.K. Narayan. The river calls up other value associations for Jagan, like friendships lost for want of cultivation—'hardly uttering four syllables in twenty years' (112); recalling *The Bachelor of Arts* and the novelist's own observations on friendship to Susan Ram (see Ram and Ram 1996a: xxiv–xxv).

Jagan's movement towards self-reform is signalled by his return to the Mahatma. Jagan returns to Mahatma Gandhi with genuine warmth: he 'had felt his whole life change when he heard that voice' (112). Now he claims proudly that 'Gandhi was my master' (112).

When the time is ripe Narayan introduces a catalyst, a creative agent, into the life of the protagonist; villagers, rural India, in *The Bachelor of Arts* and *The Guide*. Here in *The Vendor of Sweets* the instrument of regeneration is the religious sculptor, an idol maker: who, like the headmaster in the pre-Independence novel *The English Teacher*, touches a chord of tradition and culture in Jagan, with a hoary value system.

Watching him in this setting, it was difficult for Jagan, as he mutely followed him, to believe that he was in the twentieth century. Sweetmeat vending, money and his son's problems seemed remote and unrelated to him. The edge of reality itself was beginning to blur; this man from the previous millennium seemed to be the only object worth notice; he looked like one possessed. (118)

As in *The Man-Eater of Malgudi* and *The Guide*, we have here another 'piety project' offering a way out to the hero.

Narayan charts Jagan's transformation. 'He went on talking and Jagan listened agape as if a new world had flashed into view. He suddenly realized how narrow his whole existence had been—between the Lawley Statue and the frying shop; Mali's antics seemed to matter naught. "Am I on the verge of a new janma?" he wondered' (119). That new janma, new birth, recalls *The Guide*. Nothing seemed really to matter. '"Such things are common in ordinary existence and always passing," he said aloud' (120). Jagan 'felt a sense of elevation—it would be such a wonderful moment to die, leaving the perennial problems of life to solve themselves' (121–2). Jagan longs for '[a]nything but a money-making sweet-maker with a spoilt son' (122).

The retrieval of the block of stone marked for carving the statue of a goddess marks yet another stage in Jagan's life. Though his son Mali disturbs him still, at the same time he had a feeling that his [own] identity was undergoing a change:

[H]e was a different man at this moment. An internal transformation had taken place; although he still cared for the shop and house this latest contact had affected him profoundly. The gods must have taken pity on his isolated, floundering condition and sent this white-bearded saviour [...] his mind analyzed everything with the utmost clarity. [...] The man had really communicated a thrilling vision when he described the goddess with five heads. [...] An internal transformation had taken place. (127)

Jagan goes back to his charkha-spinning, so dear to the Mahatma. 'One enters a new life at the appointed time and it's foolish to resist' (129): Jagan is alluding to the asramas, socio-spiritual stages of the Hindu way of life. Once he appreciates that 'circumstances pushed one across the threshold of a new personality' (130), he discovers within himself a new strength: 'He was beginning to shed the awe in which he had held his son' (130). He is surprised: 'In a few hours, I have undergone a lot of change, but the boy doesn't know it' (130). It follows: 'He was not scared, as he would have been forty-eight hours ago' (130). For: 'I am a new personality and have to speak a new tongue' (130). Now he is convinced: '[H]e was no longer his old self' (138): no longer the money-making machine with a spoilt son, that is.

The cousin, unnamed (like the hero's wife in *Mr. Sampath*), is several entities in one; confidant; a sort of lay psychiatrist and legal counsel; and a home-made business consultant to merchants; 'a man about town' (13). 'Flattery was his accredited business in life; even when he joked and disparaged it was all a part of his flattery' (76); he is factotum to many: 'I have to do various things for various persons' (79); and 'the peace-maker' (99); wise counsellor to Jagan: '[T]he cousin now brought the matter down to a practical level, as he always did' (144); and his 'role was to help Jagan crystallize his attitudes in a crisis' (144); a friend in need: 'The cousin was extremely practical and knew exactly what should be done' (186). A fixer! (188). '"No wonder he was in such demand," thought Jagan, "all over the town"' (186); he is the informant, emissary, and ersatz uncle to Jagan's son, Mali. And clown: witness his flying frantically on his bike, 'his tuft flying in the wind' (184). And, Jagan and the cousin are made for each other: Jagan 'explained the situation in a round-about way without letting the cousin know too much' (137).

Jagan has not taken sanyasa; not abnegating his worldly duties. When Mali is arrested under anti-prohibition laws, Jagan arranges for his bail; and hands over the management of his business to his cousin. 'Jagan's mind had attained extraordinary clarity now' (190). We recall that is what Margayya, too, achieves on the last page of *The Financial Expert*: *The Vendor of Sweets* takes *The Financial Expert* one step further.

Not just the sattvic heroes of the pre-Independence novels, even the rajasic characters of the post-Independence period seek 'clarity' in life, a proper perspective: 'I will seek a new interest—different from the set of repetitions performed for sixty years' (190). It is never too late to seek moral drive, spiritual direction, to one's life. 'I am off to a retreat. I'm sixty and in a new janma' (184). And 'I don't care. [...] I am going to watch a goddess come out of a stone' (191).

Naturally, the 'cousin was amazed at the transformation in Jagan' (192).

Jagan carries his chequebook into his 'retirement'; after all, our hero is not taking sanyasa, he is going into vanaprasthya ('retiring to the forests'), the penultimate stage before sanyasa. '[R]etirement. What a magic word!' (182). Later retreating from active life— even more so since 'this was going to be a kind of death actually, although he'd breathe, watch, and occasionally keep in touch, but the withdrawal would not be different from death' (184).

Jagan's response, remedy, to his 'private sorrows' (32) is central to the Indian tradition. After all as the Talkative Man says in one of Narayan's short stories, 'Around a Temple' (included in *A Story-Teller's World* [1989: 131–3]): '[I]t is very simple to please a god.' Easier than indulging a spoilt son.

15
First Love Again!
The Painter of Signs

The Painter of Signs is the biggest surprise from Narayan. In the parlance of our film fraternity this is Narayan's 'A' (Adults Only) novel. And by the novelist in his late sixties.

A modern young man, swearing by rationalism and anti-love, lands in love and trouble, until released by his beloved.

After his success with middle-aged Jagan, Narayan creates a young man, but an off-beat young man, an idealist sign painter. As a story of first love, comparison with *The Bachelor of Arts* is in order; the structure of this late novel, too, is tidy: in four parts. Young Narayan had written *The Bachelor of Arts*; now late in life, a grandfather, he performs a sort of metempsychosis and gets inside a young man: a rajasic young man at that, and 'modern', besides.

Raman is R.K. Narayan's romantic hero. 'You are everything a girl dreams of' (Narayan 1976: 180), Daisy, his beloved, tells him when it is all over. Raman is also intellectually inclined: like his maker he has engaged in reading extensively, 'Plato to *Pickwick Papers*' (17). And he is on a mission: to establish the Age of Reason in the world, nothing less. '"I want a rational explanation for everything", he cried' (5). He preaches rationality: 'Be scientific'; for 'how could the Age of Reason be established if people were like this! Impossible!' (20). His idealism borders on the Utopian: 'Ultimately he would evolve a scheme for doing without money' (13). Not just this. Raman subscribes to definite views on man–woman relationship; the young man is a staunch celibate, a rare young man, 'a fellow whose outlook is to place sex in its place' (33). For: 'He wished to establish that the man–woman relationship was not inevitable and that there were other more important things to do in life than marrying' (45). Raman, like his maker, also pities the status women are consigned to in our society: '[T]hat is the tragedy of womanhood—utility articles whether in bed or out' (46). Raman is also clear in his mind—about his mind, its role: '[D]isciplining my mind against sex—obsessive sex' (16). That reference to 'mind' is familiar to us by now.

It happens. Raman falls in love. *The Painter of Signs* is the comedy of a self-declared rationalist, falling in love and behaving predictably, irrationally.

Raman in love recalls to our mind Chandran: '[T]here she stood like a vision [...] saw her in a mist.' And: '[H]e hopped over the short wall and reached her side. He was completely self-forgetful. [...] Her invitation cast a spell on him. [...] Daisy was here and he was back in her favour—that was all that mattered' (125). We recall Narayan's advice to his typist in *My Dateless Diary*: 'But don't you love each other? If you do, it should blindly sweep aside all other considerations, you know' (184). Narayan, the love-sage!

The handsome young hero of *The Painter of Signs*, this self-appointed rationalist and champion of the Age of Reason, whose outlook is to place 'sex in its place' falls headlong in passionate love with an attractive and strong-minded young woman. The crux of the comedy stems from this reversal of the young man. 'I used to be the most sensible person known at one time. Full of good sense, logic, reason' (144). In love Raman is overcome with wonder as he comes up against 'all those strange ways' (49). With the kind of gentle banter we have savoured in the early novel *The Bachelor of Arts*, the novelist has fun at his hero's expense: '[Raman] would wear coloured glasses so that she might not know where he was looking' (41). Soon emotional chaos reigns: 'An edifice of self-discipline laboriously raised in a lifetime seemed to be crumbling down' (45). The author knows better than anyone else: 'In darkness he confessed to himself. This is true love-sickness' (46); though, even when Raman falls in love, he strives 'to retain his sobriety' (54).

The Painter of Signs stands out among Narayan's books for its frank treatment of sexuality. For the novelist—who wrote it in his late sixties—the tale is an imaginative feat; youthful passion is captured with lively realism; what is more, the sex instinct is paid due, decent homage. We witness in this novel a sexual surge, the power of a life impulse, with a new explicitness, a new idiom, which aptly jells with the 'modern' rajasic hero: '[B]ut the female figure, water-soaked, is enchanting' (14): Raman goes 'judging her nether half' (31) with 'her bodice nearly bursting!' (50), while she talks of 'sawing off of the organs of generation' (57). Raman is a later gunas hero: 'His imagination wallowed in speculation of all that she might do in the privacy of a room, dressing or washing' (85). Later: 'His whole being was convulsed with waves of desire.' Raman speaks to himself while observing her: 'I know you are wearing nothing inside' (95). After his attempt to take her by force: 'He was appalled at the potentialities that lay buried within him' (96). He acknowledges 'the drive and pressure that he had felt last night' (98). The sexual revolution in Narayan's post-Independence phase, beginning with *The Financial Expert*, reaches its finale in *The Painter of Signs*.

Narayan presents for the first time a love-making scene; and premarital sex at that. Earlier, in *The Guide*, where adultery plays a key role, the lovers 'locked the door on the world'. Perhaps at some stage a novelist is taken over by his own characters.

He was overcome with tenderness. He stroked her gently, letting his hand rest on her breasts; as he watched, her face wore a serenity he had not noticed before. Her angularities and self-assertiveness were gone. He was struck by the elegance of her form and features, suddenly saw her as an abstraction—perhaps a goddess to be worshipped, not to be disturbed or defiled with coarse fingers. Very gently he withdrew his hand and edged away. But she suddenly turned over on her side and with her eyes still closed, threw her arms around his neck and drew him nearer and lay unmindful as his fingers fumbled with her clothes. He was overwhelmed by her surrender and essayed to whisper, 'this is our true moment of consummation. No need to feel stealthy or guilty anymore [...].' (175)

With such finesse—ease, economy, grace—there certainly is little need to feel stealthy or guilty any more.[1] At the same time, just earlier Raman has observed his beloved clinically: '[H]er feet were unattractive and the skin had cracked at the heels' (173).

Earlier in *The Man-Eater of Malgudi* it was the Bhasmasura myth; now in *The Painter of Signs* Narayan brings in the Ganga–Santanu myth of the Mahabharata and creates an engagingly modern update. King Santanu falls in love with Ganga, a beautiful maiden (in reality, she is the goddess of the sacred river and the daughter of the creator Brahma), and comes to earth on divine dispensation. Ganga consents to marry Santanu on one condition: that he will never question her actions. Santanu agrees. They marry. Ganga drowns each one of her children soon after their birth in the river. As she is about to drown their eighth son Santanu cannot take it anymore and asks her why she has been committing this sin. Ganga discloses to Santanu the secret: both of them have been living out a curse; in the previous life, in the court of Indra (King of the gods), Santanu looked at her with desire and she did not discourage him. Indra did not approve of their conduct and sent them to the earth to marry and beget. She reveals that their eight children were the eight vasus (minor gods) serving the curse of a great sage; she has released seven of them from their mortal life by drowning. Obviously their eighth son is yet to complete his time on earth. She tells Santanu that the infant needs his mother more than his father till he grows up, and assures the king that his heir will be returned to him at the appropriate time. With these words she goes back to her celestial home with the child, who grows up to later play a significant role in the Mahabharata, as Bhishma.

The novelist adapts the myth notionally: in Narayan's reworking of the epic story, a young man and a young woman fall in love; the 'weaker' one lands in trouble: romantic love is pitted against the family. Once again the family is a key concern of the novelist in *The Painter of Signs*. The hero discovers that for his beloved Daisy: 'Home was a secondary matter, the primary one was work' (167). The hapless young man reports: 'A home, in Daisy's view, was only a retreat from sun and rain, and for sleeping, washing, and depositing one's trunk. Her possessions were limited to this ideal—in some ways, very much like Aunt' (167). Daisy, the 'missionary' propagating birth control, hates the very idea of a joint family. Raman is disturbed: '[I]t shook all his notions of a life of "togetherness"' (167). But he consoles himself: 'Such things do not matter in love' (167). In his late phase R.K. Narayan has created the definitive 'New Woman' in Daisy. After all, 'Malgudi was changing in 1972' (12). (In fact, Malgudi had been changing since 1936.)

Narayan establishes this New Indian Woman fairly early in the story. 'She seemed to know her mind and its "limits"' (35). Daisy's rural origins, too, are significant: 'I did not see a chair till

I was eighteen' (55). Daisy the professional surprises Raman: 'Such missionary zeal!' Raman is convinced soon: 'He realised he had been mistaken in taking her to be just a suave bureaucrat [...] while within she seemed to carry a furnace of conviction' (57). Her boondocks origins make her idealism more credible: 'Why should we live differently from a million others?' (167). Daisy's professionalism and her spirit of service impress Raman. Though not a Gandhian Daisy is as spartan as Bharati of *Waiting for the Mahatma*. After its initial parody in Jagan of *The Vendor of Sweets* we experience authentic Gandhian austerity in Daisy, without a mention of the Mahatma.

Like Sriram of *Waiting for the Mahatma* Raman now teams up with a stronger personality; and he prepares to adapt himself to the fact: 'All the world's workers who had any results to show were fanatics, he reminded himself' (56). Unable to decode her, he wonders: 'Some madness must have got into her head quite early in life and stayed on there' (67). That makes Daisy the second 'mad woman' in Narayan after Savitri; decades after of *The Dark Room* the 'madness' is more successful. This is a changed Malgudi.

Daisy is more than a committed professional: '[S]he was like a yogi with his eyes fixed on the centre of his nose, seeing nothing else in life' (85). She becomes inaccessible; she is someone out of Raman's reach, 'cold and aloof like an eagle circling high up in the skies' (175). The images, yogi and eagle, make Raman's admiration patent. Daisy concludes: 'Married life is not for me. [...] I can't live except alone. [...] I cannot afford to have a personal life' (178–9). After Rangi of *The Man-Eater of Malgudi* Daisy is the most selfless and liberated of Narayan's post-Independence women.

In Narayan's later novels generation gap is a prominent theme. Now Raman, too, mulls: '[W]hy couldn't Aunt be like Daisy—so easy to deal with!' (149). Raman's elderly aunt, his 'foster' mother-father, is yet another woman of strength and complexity in this exceptional novel. Raman cannot think of any other woman who could be Daisy's opposite. Raman's aunt reveals unsuspected resilience. The young man admires his aunt for a familiar reason: 'Raman wished he had her stability of mind' (108). Once again like Granny in *Waiting for the Mahatma* Raman's aunt meets rebellion with understanding: 'You must live your life, that is all' (152).

Following a hoary Indian custom she retires to Banaras with a sense of fulfilment. Her parting words to Raman are in character: 'I have done my duty, it was mainly seeing that you didn't miss anything in life.' For Raman's aunt, 'the prospect of pilgrimage seemed to have given her poise' (156). She clinches her argument for Banaras: 'But who will want greater shelter than the temple and the River Ganga?' (156), recalling, again, Granny of *Waiting for the Mahatma*. Though Aunt is a woman of limited literacy, 'she spoke with the cold efficiency of Daisy' (157). Yet Raman cannot let the old lady go easily: 'He sobbed like a child' (152). At the same time Raman shows rare appreciation of the older generation: '[H]er way of life was a revelation to him. [...] It'd been a lifetime of dedication for another being, actually' (165). Once she leaves for the holy city of Banaras he experiences 'a feeling of loss'. Raman reconciles himself: 'Anyway, my aunt has complete trust in the gods and possesses greater serenity than anyone else I have known' (171).

In Narayan's post-Independence novels generation gap finds resolution in two parallel movements: members of the older generation also find their own way out; the self-sufficiency of the older generation is a distinctive feature of these novels. When the time comes these old people in Narayan's post-Independence novels can think of withdrawing from active society, go into vanaprasthya, like Raman's aunt 'planning so thoroughly her exit from home, town, and even life' (158).

Daisy describes her young man as 'the prowling tiger'. Raman is a predator: '[H]is only aim being to seize his prey, whatever the consequences' (93). R.K. Narayan's post-Independence novels present potential for gunas evolution: from 'prowling tiger' to 'contemplative tiger'.[2]

16

Caution! Masterful Male!

Talkative Man*

As amusing as Narayan's *The Man-Eater of Malgudi* his *Talkative Man* presents the career of a compulsive womanizer, Dr Rann: yet another 'rogue' in Narayan's post-Independence gallery.

Talkative Man, the narrator, clarifies: 'Dr Rann was actually, as I discovered later, Rangan, a hardy Indian name, which he had trimmed and tailored to sound foreign; and the double "N" at the end was a stroke of pure genius' (Narayan 1977: 3). Rann is a PhD, no less, an intellectual with a book in the making: he is the apotheosis of Narayan's intellectuals and academics: recall the first of the series, Dr Pal, the purveyor of filth in *The Financial Expert*. Talkative Man is affected by 'this man's presumptuous presence in our town' (10); for, unlike in Vasu, we have a relatively low-calibre inductance; and we have a seasoned reporter playing host to him. From the havoc Rann creates, however, it is almost like the return of the man-eater, in the avatar of a specialist woman-eater. Rann is 'a regular lady-killer' (67). He is 'like a feline coming upon its unsuspecting prey' (94). Now we have a 'lecherous demon' (95), with 'an after-shave lotion and hair cream which, I suspected, made him irresistible to women' (95). Rann works on unwary women 'as if playing on a musical instrument' (96). He is 'the wolf of the fairy tales' (96).

Dr Rann himself can be self-perceptive: 'Again and again I seem to fall into the same trap like a brainless rat' (104). There cannot be a better image to describe this post-Independence gunas character.

* The chapter was published as part of the essay 'Three Novellas' in *The Book Review*, New Delhi, in December 2013. Reprinted here with permission from *The Book Review*.

Towards the end Rann delivers a talk on a topic he is best qualified for: a pest, the Giant Weed. The latter period of Narayan's post-Independence novels is the season of pests; mosquitoes and bugs, too, are a presence. Rann grumbles about the bed bugs in the waiting room of the Malgudi railway station: responds the narrator, 'they are service bugs actually' (20).

If '[t]he spruce tailor-dummy called Rann' (64), the 'slippery Rann' (66), is 'a regular lady-killer' (67), his wife is a New Woman of Narayan's post-Independence era: she is 'the Delhi woman' (86). She is a police officer who grapples with an unofficial case assigned to her by fate: tracking down a promiscuous husband: 'Husband-hunting is a fatiguing business' (69). For, as Talkative Man observes sardonically, Rann, the confidence man, is 'like our gods [...] to have a thousand names' (102). The lady officer comments on Rann's intellectual profile: 'All wrong ideas and misleading notions. I tell you he had unsuspected depths of duplicity' (142); she has no doubt that he is 'an expert really in the art of deception' (143).

Even in this sombre world of evil the novelist keeps affirming the salvation of love. The charming episode of youthful romance of Rann and his beloved—*The Painter of Signs* again!—relieves the Rann horror. His wife recalls those early love-filled days: '[W]hile we stayed in the pleasure of each other's company—listening to the waves splashing on the shore, blue sea and blue sky and birds diving in and the breeze' (77). The allusion to the elements and the birds in the context is suggestive of love as a natural phenomenon. The lovers lead a lovers' life, 'a beautiful existence' (82). R.K. Narayan knew love's logic: recall again Raman in love; also how Narayan counselled a young American woman on love (Narayan, in *My Dateless Diary* 1960: 184).

Rann is also given redemption of perspective; his present depredations are balanced by his past purity: his wife discloses the shameful injury to his psyche caused by her parents; when in the legal battle to prove that she is too young to marry, her parents extracted from her under coercion a false affidavit. After that Rann 'seemed to have undergone a change of personality' (85).

This tale narrated by Talkative Man himself is filtered through his sensibility.[1] Now Talkative Man belongs, like the guru in *A Tiger for Malgudi*, to a vanishing species, the declining upper-class

Brahmin gentry of Kabir Street, which figures prominently in the novels of Narayan's final phase. In this novella we have a fairly good case sheet on this breed (4–5, quoted in Chapter 13 in this book).

Talkative Man, the insider–outsider, returns to the subject again later: 'I belonged to the Kabir Street aristocracy, which was well known for its lofty, patronising hospitality, cost what it may' (32); for, it is the Talkative Man who gives shelter to Dr Rann in Malgudi. Sambu, Talkative Man's neighbour, is another Kabir Street specimen: he 'spent more and more of his time reading'.[2] Ramu, yet another of the endangered species,

> had grown so fat and immobile that he could do nothing more than sit on the pyol leaning on a pillar morning till night enjoying the spectacle of arrivals and departures in Kabir Street. I looked on him more as a sort of vegetation or a geological specimen than a human being—he loved to play rummy provided the company assembled around him. (25)

But as Talkative Man, the narrator, confesses: 'This sort of existence did not appeal to me' (5). Later he offers asylum to Dr Rann 'for no clear reason [...] out of an idiotic kindness' (53). But Talkative Man, the bachelor that he is, adds as an afterthought: 'I decided to protect him from wifely intrusions' (63). Narayan also shares with Talkative Man his own exquisite sensitivity to feminine charm. Besides, Talkative Man, a journalist, 'acts as the eye for humanity' (39); and cherishes within himself, like Nataraj (in *The Man-Eater of Malgudi*), its heart.

Narayan directs the narrative in *Talkative Man* with economy; develops tempo with precise steps; as in his seduction story of the period, 'A Breath of Lucifer' (included in *A Horse and Two Goats* [1970: 109–30]). The novelist smoothly builds up anticipation—'I'll come to it later' (64); and suspense: as the reader waits to see what happens when the couple meet again, the narrator introduces an interruption. The brief prologue of *Talkative Man* is an invocation: it also introduces the narrator, a 'monologist', and his audience, as well as hints at the developments to come through a casual mention of Mahishasura, a demon who is suppressed by Goddess Durga. Rann's particular aversion to photographs is mentioned early and intriguingly. As his wife recounts her experiences with Rann,

Talkative Man is held in 'a spell of narrative' (80). Equally hypnotic is this novella. In the postscript the novelist defends the length of the novella. *Talkative Man* needs no apology.

17
Guru and Chela
*A Tiger for Malgudi**

The 'hero' of this slender novella is a tiger. Trapped by a sadistic circus owner, the harassed beast kills him accidentally and escapes; its presence terrifies Malgudi until a sage adopts him as his chela, disciple.

Narayan's novellas belong to the late post-Independence period, the novelist's final phase. Soon after sending off the manuscript of *The Painter of Signs* to his American publisher Narayan confided to his friend, S. Krishnan (1975: 42):

'Whatever the joys of creation might be, it is really a nuisance writing a novel! It ties you down so completely for a year or two. [...] I have a contract with Viking and this is the last novel I owe them. What a time-consuming business writing a novel is!' he said again. 'I am tempted to make my next contracts for collections of short stories, say four or five at a time, each of about 20,000 words or so. Then I will be rid of this tyranny. In fact, you know I think I shall give up writing novels altogether.' I laughed and he also laughed [...].

Hardly surprising, when the novelist was close to seventy.

Six years after *The Painter of Signs*, we have *A Tiger for Malgudi*. While there is relatively little of it in Narayan's pre-Independence phase violence in the early post-Independence novels extends into the late phase and grows virulent: in the verbal and psychological clash in *The Vendor of Sweets* (1967); in the hero's attempt, though comically unsuccessful, to surprise his beloved in the dark of the

---

* The chapter was published as part of the essay 'Three Novellas' in *The Book Review*, New Delhi, in December 2013. Reprinted here with permission from *The Book Review*.

night in *The Painter of Signs* (1976); and now in *A Tiger for Malgudi* in the brutality of the Captain—'who wielded his chair and whip like a maniac' (Narayan 1983: 49); 'alternating between occasional sanity and general madness' (54); for 'it was his will that counted' (113), as he is 'drunk with his authority' (114)—all unmistakable features of a rampant rajasic character—ending in his decapitation.

A Tiger for Malgudi charts the extraordinary spiritual transformation of a tiger, 'an unmitigated animal' (24), into a spiritual adept. For, says the novelist in his Introduction: '[D]eep within, the core of personality is the same in spite of differing appearances and categories, and with the right approach you could expect the same response from a tiger as from any normal human being' (10). The tiger itself makes it more than clear at the very outset: 'I can think, analyse, judge, remember and do everything that you do, perhaps with greater subtlety and sense. I lack only the faculty of speech' (11–12). For, this Narayan 'hero' is no ordinary run-of-the-mill beast; he is a tiger 'almost human in understanding' (65) who is trapped by a man: 'I had let myself into ultimate slavery' (28). 'Beast' for the hermit 'is an ugly, uncharitable expression' (125); for this tiger 'is no brute' (130); the guru assures visitors that 'inside he is no different from you and me' (146). Later the sage claims: '[My] tiger is godly' (156).[1]

The spiritual progress of the tiger under the sage's guidance seems to have been patterned after the novelist's own experience following the death of his beloved wife (see Chapter 7 in this book). The tiger recalls: 'There were the stages of knowing attained through suffering [...].' Suffering as a means of wisdom! Narayan has gone through it. The tiger goes on: 'I can hardly describe that kind of suffering, an emptiness, a helplessness, and a hopelessness behind the bars' (47). Narayan's humanism also comprehends one's karma: 'That's the natural law of life, as inevitable as the ripening of a mango in its season or the fall of a withered leaf.'[2] The guru talks to 'him' every evening 'on life and existence and death [...]' (157); and God, 'the Great Spirit pervading every creature, every rock and tree and the sky and the stars; a source of power and strength' (157–8). Under the guidance of the yogi the tiger evolves. 'We cannot understand God's intentions. All growth takes place in its own time. If you brood on your improvements rather than your shortcomings, you will be happier' (160). Finally the sage is able to 'calm his turbulent soul' (172).

Now the chela can appreciate life's felicities, recalling the heightened sensuousness of Raju 'trapped' into guru-hood. 'My sight became clearer; if I lifted my gaze to the horizon, the sun shining on the land filled me with joy; the leaves of the mighty banyan trees sparkling like gems, the bamboos swaying their golden stems with their filigreed leaves—I felt I could ask for nothing more in life' (165–6).[3]

The guru is satisfied with the progress of his chela and hands him over to a zoo: 'He is a sensitive soul who understands life and its problems exactly as we do' (175).

The novelist anticipates and parallels the tiger's spiritual development with the sage's own transformation from a full-blooded rajasic character with enormous appetites to a renunciant. Marital strife, another prominent theme, especially of Narayan's post-1947 novels, also figures in the guru's personal background; besides the novelist places him in Ellamman–Kabir Street 'aristocracy', a decadent section of Malgudi we are already familiar with.

After the vanaprasthya of *The Vendor of Sweets* we have in this novel finally sanyasa in total spirit and content: time to 'shed purpose of every kind' (162); move from time to timelessness. Don't move away from life—accept and experience life, all life, and passage of Time, and old age: 'Beautiful old age, when faculties are dimmed one by one, so that we may be restful, very much like extinguishing lights in a home, one by one, before one goes to sleep' (174).

Q. 'What would you rather be in your next birth?'
A. 'Contemplative tiger.'[4]

18

Mettle Fatigue
The World of Nagaraj[1]

The title.

The title says it all. Nagaraj's world is Narayan's main focus. '[Nagaraj] sometimes wondered at the transformations time brings about' (Narayan 1990: 24). Jagan had experienced it earlier: Nagaraj's world is changing and this is the late post-Independence period.

Nagaraj is childless. His brother's son rebels, quits his parents and home in the village, and comes to Malgudi and lives with Nagaraj. This guardian, however, can neither guard nor guide his new-found ward and his wife. Narayan presents Kabir Street community microcosmically: in the plight of one family.

The World of Nagaraj focuses once again on Kabir Street residents as 'people who were considered aristocratic inheritors of vast rice fields in the village' (25). Marked by 'supreme contentment' (5), mirasidar forebears of the novelist show that their degeneration is more patent now than ever. The jutka driver, on being underpaid, offers a general comment on the whole lot, perhaps representing the perception of the general public of Malgudi: '[He] declared the general meanness of Kabir Street dwellers' (158). And Nagaraj himself recounts the ultimate anathema: '[W]hen Mahatma Gandhi came this way, they could not find anyone to offer him flowers from Kabir Street' (158).

The kind of domestic charm we experienced in the pre-Independence novels of Narayan is now remote, like the sun viewed from Pluto. Nagaraj's family shows ample evidence of bitter divisions and loss. Jagan's wife in *The Vendor of Sweets* and Nagaraj's wife Sita in this novel are sisters in suffering. Nagaraj conveys something of this terminal state when he alludes to 'the tightrope walking called domestic harmony' (4). A maidservant for Nagaraj's mother is a 'dependable ally against the daughter-in-law' (7). Nagaraj's wife Sita was 'too timid and bashful' in the early days: '[T]he girl meekly accepted the role of a lackey at home' (25). Nagaraj admires his neighbour, the Talkative Man: 'Blessed fellow, never married, unlike me, a prisoner of domesticity' (5). He preferred as far as possible to go out, 'otherwise he might have to arbitrate between his mother and Sita all day' (24). For: 'He could not make any demand on her or anyone. Not in his nature' (26). The sister-in-law learns quickly: 'After the first few days she ignored all queries and communicated only when it pleased her' (30). She sets up a separate kitchen fire: effects undeclared partition: 'It was a state within the state' (30). Worse, 'the family ate in general silence' (31). His mother now hobbles about 'like a frail ghost asking inane questions' (31). The old mother—'routine wandering' (37)—is the image of terminal senescence: distressing enough to send several Siddharthas on the path to Buddha-hood; we have come far from the fetching portrayal of Granny in *Swami and Friends*. Nagaraj inhabits and represents a degenerative community: 'the world of Nagaraj.'

Narayan's later novels also present vices comedy. More than Sriram (*Waiting for the Mahatma*), Nagaraj is sloth embodied: '[T]oo much of thinking is no good, rather fatiguing' (9). He takes 'to the pyol habit, to sitting there and watching the street' (25). The dynamism of his friend Coomar, 'a self-made man' (16), strikes a contrast. Jagan of *The Vendor of Sweets* turns to thoughts of renunciation and opts for the less extreme vanaprasthya; though just 'past fifty' Nagaraj obtains an ochre robe from an itinerant sadhu: after that it is 'as if he ceased to exist' (12). And his goal is set, 'a haven of peace, silence, isolation' (13). Jagan looks for peace only towards the end of the novel; Nagaraj hankers for it much earlier. For: 'Nagaraj's nature had no resistance of any kind' (111). Even midway we realize Narayan has created an extraordinary character: the superlative non-doer, perfectly feckless.[2]

Nagaraj's brother does not mince his words: 'You exist from day to day like a cow chewing the cud and staring at space' (41). The elder brother is resolved: '[W]e do not want another Nagaraj in the family' (42). He goes further, bestows a title on Nagaraj: '[Y]ou are Narada, mischief-maker' (44). But as Nagaraj himself realizes he is so unlike Narada, the best loved singing sage of our epics, who 'was a unique personality, the god of music' (44).

The trouble is just that Nagaraj is 'a smiler at all times' (143). When his elder brother demands an explanation from him for not asking Tim, his wayward ward, and his wife where they were going, he says: '[B]ut I was wearing the ochre robe.' The enraged brother rounds on him: '[T]hat's another thing in your mad scheme' (148). Not much later the elder brother is 'in tears from the strain of talking to Nagaraj' (152). He is convinced that 'Nagaraj was wishy-washy and dreamy—a view he held to the last' (25): a view the reader, too, might hold to the last. Nagaraj proves to be an incompetent ersatz father; his own elder brother, the father of Tim, is a failed father himself—yet another such in Narayan's post-Independence novels. The two brothers in this novel are among the breed of inept elders so prominent in the later novels; and they are members of 'Kabir Street aristocracy'. Nagaraj withdraws like a tortoise into its shell.

How can there be a later gunas hero without an obsession? In Nagaraj's case it is an intellectual preoccupation though; his *mission*: to write a book on Narada.

Kavu Pundit, whom Nagaraj approaches for Sanskrit lessons to help with his book, outdoes any Kabir Street specimen. With this pundit holy readings and playing cards go together; for, this scholar 'has spent a whole lifetime playing cards. [...] While his evenings were spent in holy readings his days were spent at cards' (112). Cards and snuff are this Sanskrit scholar's first love. Naturally his Sanskrit classes for Nagaraj face 'starting trouble': Kavu Pundit has to look for an 'auspicious moment to seek an auspicious moment' to start the lessons for Nagaraj.

Jagan begets a child; Nagaraj is childless. Barrenness is an apt image in *The World of Nagaraj*. The main door of Nagaraj's ancient home, described elaborately, may still remain solid; but the family's mettle fatigue—moral and spiritual exhaustion—is blatant. The drunkard in the last house of Kabir Street, a former executive engineer, makes startling appearances ('good morning, good brothers' [87]) like the vagrant in *The Vendor of Sweets*.

But of course as a Narayan hero, Nagaraj has his heart in the right place. In spite of his brother's condemnation: 'He continued to be a devoted younger brother' (27). After his father's death Nagaraj notices his mother's plight: '[F]elt deeply moved by her withdrawal and from time to time went near her to whisper a word of comfort or philosophy' (32–3). Narayan also gives Nagaraj something of his own libido: '[C]hewing the pan, lips red with betel juice. You could not find a more contented soul in Malgudi at that moment' (16). The river, too, redeems Nagaraj, just as it does Narayan's later heroes. 'He contemplated the flowing river and all his doubts vanished' (100).

Nagaraj is barren, but not sterile.

Nagaraj is also touched up through his love for Tim, 'sharing his joy and wonder [...] enjoying fully every moment with Tim and through Tim' (48). After *The Financial Expert* and *The Vendor of Sweets* where the heroes suffer acutely from filial shenanigans we have another example of mutinous offspring in this novel: Tim, the son of Nagaraj's elder brother. Tim himself gains in stature with his pure warmth: 'He was fond of his grandmother and was seen now and then sitting on her bed chatting.' After an accident she is bedridden, 'with Tim nursing her, without leaving her side even for a moment' (50). We recall that early in *The Vendor of Sweets* Jagan's son, Mali, supports his mother in her illness, physically and emotionally. Like Margayya and Jagan before him Nagaraj dreams about Tim's academic progress: '[T]o watch the young man in his room bent over his studies—a vision which stirred him deeply' (49). Like the novelist Narayan Nagaraj has his own views about the upbringing of a child; he hates child-beating and child-beaters.

There are other autobiographical details in the novel. 'He called me a donkey' (37), says Tim; that recall is a direct lift from Narayan's wife Rajam's early school experience. Later in the story Narayan returns to the same episode in his personal life and completes it: 'Some day he is going to hit back, he has already retorted, "What is a donkey's father?"' (116). Yet another landmark from the novelist's life also is added to Nagaraj's portrait: 'No wonder I failed in BA and scraped through with a third class later' (49). Coming towards the end of a long, self-made fulfilling career, R.K. Narayan's *The World of Nagaraj* suggests self-parody. Nagaraj's antecedents and placidity seem to hint at a self-mocking novelist. The mood is reflected in an interview by Geeta Doctor (1992: n.p.):

Did he realize on that morning so long ago that he might one day become the grand old man of Indian literature?

'Neither grand nor old,' replies Narayan, with what sounds suspiciously like a snort. 'Probably mad.'

But self-knowledge is what we expect of any hero of Narayan's novels; and Nagaraj is one of the family. 'There is an evil half of me which floats to the surface at unexpected moments and provokes sinful thoughts' (182). Nagaraj also comments intriguingly on himself: 'I am stationary like a milestone. The procession passes. Why can't I also pass instead of being a milestone? People take advantage of my milestone nature' (160). Nagaraj comes back to this rooted image, with a touch of conclusive satisfaction: 'I am only a milestone. [...] I must only watch, not ask questions' (183).

Is Nagaraj an idler or a genuine seeker of self-realization, surrendering all action? Has Narayan given us finally a 'sanyasin', who has shed all purpose? A mere spectator, a witness? With his dreams of authorship is Nagaraj claiming the stillness and calm of a creative spirit at the centre of his society?

19

Gunas Horror

Grandmother's Tale*

The novelist's last work, *Grandmother's Tale*, tells the story of a determined young woman who goes searching for her husband missing for years; she succeeds in her mission, with unexpected subsequences.

The novelist remarked to Susan Ram and N. Ram that as writers grow older, their novels get shorter: 'It's like the Indian goldsmith at the end of the day. […] He sweeps in the dust carefully to retrieve the gold particles he thinks can be found in the dust' (1996b: 17). Narayan's final book is a good example.

This novella, incidentally, complements Narayan's *My Days*: for example, we get more about the occupations and interests of Narayan's maternal uncles, especially the colourful junior uncle; and details of the music lessons Narayan's grandmother Ammani taught him (Narayan 1992: 2); we note a new detail in Ammani's homely syllabus for her grandson: folk songs. Of particular interest is the Sanskrit sloka which enjoins women on their various roles (5); that Ammani thought of teaching this sloka to 'Kunjappa' is rather mystifying, but the sloka has immediate relevance to the story of Bala, especially after her return to her village, and her sudden transformation—regression, some might say—into a docile housewife. We also find in this novella a nostalgic harking back to little Swami of *Swami and Friends* in the 'stone-technique' of getting mangoes. And for those looking for more autobiographical trivia after *My Days* there is confirmation that Narayan was a premature

---

* The chapter was published as part of the essay 'Three Novellas' in *The Book Review*, New Delhi, in December 2013. Reprinted here with permission from *The Book Review*.

baby; and that his grandfather, Swaminathan—after whom Narayan named his first fictional character—was simply venal; 'money just poured in' (78).

Narayan's 'telling' strategy here strikes us. *Grandmother's Tale* is his contribution to self-reflexive fiction. Towards the end of his decades-long career as novelist and storyteller, Narayan attempts to reconstruct in this book the story narrated by his own maternal grandmother Ammani, and in fits and starts about *her* mother. With the novelist's 'explanation' at the beginning, a sort of preface, Narayan prepares us for his extraordinary performance. 'The borderline between fact and fiction, between biography and tale wears thin in the following chronicle.' At the same time, 'it might not all be imaginary'. Later the novelist confesses: 'It is not possible for me to fix the historical background by any clue or internal evidence' (8). However: 'One has to assume an arbitrary period—that is the later period of the East India Company, before the Mutiny' (8); and during the Mutiny, 'I hear sepoys are killing white officers' (27); and beyond still, into the later decades of the nineteenth century.

India was entering the modern period. The novella reflects a sociological churning—'They decided to move to a nearby town' (73)—and the 'village seemed to have been deserted by all the old families' (73); marking the urban shift—from village to town—of Narayan's forebears, with Brahmins taking up 'Kumpini' jobs; the migrants also included the ancestors of 'Kabir Street Aristocracy' who figure prominently in Narayan's final phase. In south India the first of Indians qualified for the medical profession in the first Medical College in Madras (77).

The ethos of the novella is completely and quietly of a south-Indian (Tamil) Brahmin vintage; in such features as 'a [Brahmin] bachelor's three-stranded thread' (13); 'an elegant little tuft on top' (49); a community in which 'a wife could not utter her husband's name' (23). The child groom Viswa's teacher says on marriage: 'It's all arranged by the God in that Temple. Who are we to say anything against His will?' (14). When Bala goes out in search of her husband she carries in her bundle 'above all a knife in case she had to protect her honour and end her life' (34). But Narayan does not romanticize the village ambience: '[M]ounds of garbage here and there, a temple tower looming over it all' (9). We also get to know the dark side of village India: a nearby 'village notorious for its evil practices, such as fostering family intrigues, creating mischief and practising black magic' (90), the village from which the woman who cooks for Bala and Viswa comes; the same village supplies the poison mixed in Viswa's favourite payasam which the designing woman administers to him, 'a confirmed glutton these days' (93).

Nothing evokes the milieu better than the manner of Bala's marriage: 'My mother told me that she was playing in the street with her friends one evening when her father came up and said, "You are going to be married today next week"' (9). Narayan comments: 'The girl's life changed after her marriage' (14).

The novelist takes his reader further into confidence on the writing of this novella: 'Day after day, I sat up with her [Ammani] listening to the account, and at night developed it as a cogent narrative [...] but this is mainly a story-writer's version of a hearsay biography of a great-grandmother' (8). Narayan is aware that the exploits of his great-grandparents are not very pleasant; nor are the social customs of that period in India. So Narayan enters his own narrative, not to neutralize the inequity, but to endorse her account; and uniquely for a Narayan novella, the 'chronicle' part is also supported by authorial soliloquies presenting historical evidence: autobiographical asides, linking the historical with the fictional. 'One morning, two years ago, I had a desire to revisit Number One Vellala Street in Purasawalkam, where all of us were born in one particular room' (79). Or:

My—this writer's—mother, Ammani's second daughter, who was ninety-three at the time of her death in 1974, used to maintain that she had a hazy recollection of being carried on the arms of her mother at Kumbakonam and witnessing a lot of hustle and bustle following a funeral, people passing in and out of the house and some boxes being locked and sealed by the police and a motley crowd milling around. (94)

The venal ancestor had come to grief.

Another feature of the narrative is the interruptions: the grandmother breaks off her narrative. Each such intermission is filled with auto-reportage: 'Anyway it is none of our business' (50); 'left in a huff' (51): or for whatever other reason; or it can develop into a colloquy on missing details; or it may mark the end of a phase in the life of Bala and Viswa. As a result grandmother herself develops into a character in the novella. 'At this point Ammani interrupted herself' (70), for Ammani is a bit like her own mother Bala: 'I was eleven and followed my parents' (74). At the same time Ammani enjoys a tender relationship with her grandson, 'Kunjappa' (Narayan): 'I realized that she knew it was Kumbakonam but was only teasing me' (75). Ammani gradually develops into a character by herself—and she is offering us a motivated recall; for, the grandmother's purpose in narrating her own mother's story is to show 'how strong and bold she was at one time'. Narayan's grandmother is a chip off the old block.

The Narayan flavour touches up the novella: as when the father is grilled; at the same time there is no attempt to touch up or romanticize Bala: '[R]ather stocky with no pretensions to any special beauty except the natural charm of full-blown womanhood, she could not pass down the *agraharam* street without people staring at her and whispering comments behind her back' (28). The novelist also plays the chorus: '[U]p to this point my grandmother remembered her mother's narration' (33); or, 'many gaps from this point onward' (34); or, 'these questions never got an answer' (34). The chorus offers moral judgements as well: 'Your mother was too deep and devious for the poor lady, who had shown so much trust in her' (65). This is shot down by the grandmother: 'Don't talk ill of your ancestors. Not right' (65). Narayan brands Bala's actions as 'your mother's coercive tactics' (65). And he is reminded by Ammani: 'To a woman, her husband is everything' (65).

The writer is edified by his grandmother on the constraints of the fictional form he has not handled before: '[Y]ou cannot manipulate people in real life as you do in a story' (67). Grandmother's rejoinders raise questions relevant to the narrative artist and his problems. 'Am I a Wizard to see the past?' (34); she dismisses his queries offhand as 'all sorts of useless information' (34). She justifies her own mother's account of her life (35). She chides him on his insistent probing into aspects of her story: '[B]ut you question me as if I could see the past' (74). There are problems in sticking close to the details of a life lost in the deep space of history. But the novelist's magic eye can see what is impossible for the mundane organ.

The scenes between the children, Bala and Viswa, 'husband and wife', and their discussion on the relevance of prayer (20–1) are relevant to the ethos. 'After that they discovered an interest in each other's company' (15–16). Man–woman relationship is positive in Narayan.

The novelist finds sufficient motivation for Viswa's and Bala's departures from the village. On being charged with throwing cow dung on his teacher, '[Viswa] denied it and became violent' (13), already confirming the rajasic–tamasic nature. The juvenile's reaction anticipates his flouncing out his son's household towards the end for an imagined slight and neglect.

Bala, the girl, in contrast is justified in quitting the place; when the villagers want her to consider herself as a widow and confine herself to her home, and the temple priest insists on her shaving her head and wear the widow's cloth, she opts for the challenge of going in search of her absconding husband: 'Bala rushed out like a storm' (30). And she swears an oath: 'I'll not rest until I come back with him some day and shame you all' (33). When she goes to her mother-in-law in that fit of rage, the elder says: 'You look like Kali' (33).

Bala reaches Poona a year later! When face to face with the man she suspects to be Viswa, '[s]he invoked the God in their village. "Guide me, Oh Lord! I don't know what to do"' (41). And God does! At the same time Bala 'had the shrewdness to conceal her purpose' (43). And she gathers 'much information' (44). For: 'She had worked out the details of the campaign with care, timing it in minute detail' (55). She deceives the Poona couple, Viswa and Surma, completely: 'Bala assumed an air of extreme gloom to match Surma's mood in sympathy' (58). Bala is a perfect example of a rajasic character in action; besides, Bala and her husband are made for each other. Though Bala's retrieval of her husband may parallel the Savitri legend in the Mahabharata, Narayan's story is but a parody, in the spirit of the later comedy; like the legend of Sage Narada in *The World of Nagaraj*.[1] Bala is not averse to using coercive tactics: her ruthless pressure on Viswa in Poona rattles Viswa and he falls sick (57). Bala is domineering, devious, aggressive; she belongs properly to the post-Independence world of Narayan's novels. But once she gets back her husband she becomes 'docile'.

The novelist brings out Surma's own love affair in her own words, winning the reader's sympathy. 'There was something about his person that touched my heart' (46). Surma marries Viswa against her father's wishes; but in the worst crisis of her life she shows a relatively gentle sattvic spirit: 'Let me also drown with you' (62). Surma is no match and does not suspect that Bala is her co-wife leading her into a trap.

Bala's transformation to orthodox Hindu wife, too, was pre-planned by her! Perhaps Bala is not confident otherwise of holding Viswa. How can she retain her husband from thinking of his gentle Surma in Poona? 'You only see me as a cook at home, feeding you and pampering your father's whims and moods but at one time I could do other things which, petted and spoilt children, could never even imagine' (35).

Soon after their return to the village the transformed Bala wields considerable influence on Viswa. She sets the barber on hirsute Viswa and admires the result: 'Whatever made you hide such a fine face behind a wilderness of hair!' (70). Viswa changes for the worse only after Bala's death.

For Viswa, too, is an unmistakable rajasic character of the later novels: 'What mad rage drove him to that extent no one could say' (89); but his marriage to a much younger woman after Bala's death is 'a culmination of his rage against his son' (90). Though '[h]e had a sturdy constitution which withstood all the Gluttony he was indulging in' (90). Viswa is ultimately consumed by gluttony.

Grandmother's Tale reads like a folk tale. The period of the tale—the later days of John Kumpini—was a rough season in Indian history. The novelist brings a close-up focus to his narrative dealing exclusively with the designing woman. When at one point the lady vents her anger at a security guard—'Don't touch me, I will reduce to ashes' (43)—she is echoing Kannagi of the ancient Tamil classic *Silappadigaram*.

The art of the veteran novelist is evident in other ways. Narayan makes no attempts to romanticize his forebears or even his grandmother. Besides, the first few pages of this novella are only apparently a rehash of *My Days*; actually they serve the novelist's purpose by linking the recent past to the distant, besides highlighting the family likeness and ambience: the grandmother recounting the story is as self-willed as *her* mother or father. The only time the child-wife touches her boy-husband she feels the black patch under his ear; it is this birthmark which, decades later, and in an alien region, helps her identify her truant husband. Yet another narrative feature, the dialogue in the novella is, as can be expected from a seasoned raconteur, brisk-paced in character; witness the scene between Bala and Viswa in Poona (51–7).

Both central characters—Narayan's forebears—are typically rajasic; Narayan continues to present the havoc caused by rajasic, the ruthless self-centrism of the protagonists of the final phase of his fiction. 'He felt nervous to remain alone with Bala and was terrified of her tactics' (56). Bala just delivers the ultimatum: 'I am taking you back even if you kill me' (56).

When Bala and her husband manage to return to their village after decades they find the whole place is completely changed; just two landmarks—no more—have withstood the hand of Time. 'Only the river was there and the temple stood solidly as ever.' Even after the last wave has battered the shore Narayan seems certain that, even in this era of dying rivers and dissolving poles, the emblems of his pure Hinduism will endure.

Gluttony kills. Viswa, too, is vice-fected. The payasam brings to a close with a gunas finale R.K. Narayan's vices comedy of the post-Independence novels. R.K. Narayan had always enjoyed himself, enjoyed life and people, always enjoyed his work. He has, in *Grandmother's Tale*, ceased to be conscious of his Western audience: the book is spiced liberally with Indianisms: *sumangali, thali, kotwal, janma*....[2]

It is time now for a tribute. The first time we take this slim book into our hands what strikes us is the illustrations. R.K. Laxman's contribution to his elder brother Narayan's success is unique. Though there had been only one book claiming official collaboration between the two talented brothers: *The Emerald Route* (1977), a sponsored project, the younger brother, a great cartoonist—and a writer in his own right—R.K. Laxman has been the sole illustrator of his elder brother R.K. Narayan's books.

Greene wrote to Narayan in 1945 about his new book, *The English Teacher*: 'Your book will always probably have greater sales in England than it will have in India' (Ram and Ram 1996a: 402).

That perception led Greene to reject R.K. Laxman's illustrations for his brother Narayan's novels. Looking back it was Laxman's sketches of humble Mysoreans—and crows!—which in part had probably inspired Narayan to think of 'Malgudi'; one cannot think of Narayan today without Laxman's illustrations. Like Cruikshank and Dickens. 'Who else can feel his work like I do? He used to be amazed by the way my drawing meshed with his own idea of the situation' (Philipose 1990: n.p.).

The very profusion of Laxman's work in this novella strikes us—as many as fourteen drawings, not counting the cover picture. We also note with delight Laxman's masterly attention to detail; for example, the typically south-Indian coffee cup and glass on the floor behind the grandmother who is comfortably perched on the swing. Notice also the crown of curly hair of the child absorbed in his grandmother's tale: we recall little Narayan, 'Kunjappa' ('Little Fellow'), with 'such large eyes and all those curls falling down to [his] cheeks!' (Narayan 1996: 2). Laxman's pen invariably picked up telling details. Laxman himself is a novelist; he selects the key scenes and moments in *Grandmother's Tale*; we have to merely thumb through the illustrations from the first to the last, to get, as in a bi-scope, all the key events in the novella. Laxman also records the march of time, the panorama from childhood to old age, of the couple in the story with instinctive precision. Laxman's choice of a key moment for his final illustration is outstanding: the old man Viswa, the glutton, is pouring the payasam down his throat, unsuspecting it is poisoned. Curtains!

Now let us sum up the critical developments in Narayan's post-Independence phase.

As quoted in *The Vendor of Sweets*: '[Jagan is] aghast at the transformation that had come with time' (1967: 81).

From Narayan's early comedy to his post-Independence novels there is a significant shift, from sattvic to rajasic–tamasic comedy, from the 'genteel' to the 'rumbustious'. The post-Independence Narayan—post-professional struggle, post-Rajam realization—a different personality, gives us novels which also reflect remarkably the career of the postcolonial Indian nation. Gifted writers have their ears to the ground; the haunting echoes of the axe blows on the cherry trees in Chekhov's play at the dawn of the twentieth century anticipated the cataclysm looming large in Russia.

Narayan's fifteen novels and novellas broadly fall into three groups. First, the pre-Independence novels: the final novel of the group, *Mr. Sampath* (1949), also inaugurates the second phase comprising four novels, namely, *The Financial Expert* (1952), *Waiting for the Mahatma* (1955), *The Guide* (1958), and *The Man-Eater of Malgudi* (1961); the last novel of this series stands out, like the first phase, as a watershed. In contrast with the heroes of the first phase who are sattvic—conscionable, 'truth-seeking'— Narayan's later protagonists are rajasic–tamasic: passionate, restless, tending to be obsessive ('*It was a natural obsession* with Raju' [Narayan 1958: 138; emphasis mine]). And these heroes of the second phase succumb each to a vice: for example, cupidity in *The Financial Expert*; sloth in *Waiting for the Mahatma* ('[D]o something instead of wasting my life' [1955: 38]); and lust in *The Guide* ('Hope she is uninteresting' [1958: 15]). The vices comedy of the second phase climaxes in the drama of Vasu in *The Man-Eater of Malgudi*, an embodiment of excess and anarchism, a rakshasa of the Hindu epics. During his psychic training Narayan had discovered that even 'simple vices' could be effective blocks; 'a very small stone is enough to block an entire pipeline' (Ram and Ram 1996a: 376–7).

Narayan produced in the succeeding decades six more novels and novellas: *The Vendor of Sweets* (1967), *The Painter of Signs* (1976), *Talkative Man* (1977), *A Tiger for Malgudi* (1983), *The World of Nagaraj* (1990), and *Grandmother's Tale* (1992). Taking up some themes of earlier phases for fresh treatment, these novels and novellas form the third and final group. Even this late phase reveals some of the spirit of the middle phase: 'People are moved by strange, inexplicable drives' (Narayan 1976: 64). The heroes of *The Painter of Signs, The Vendor of Sweets,* and *Talkative Man* are faddist or compulsive. Things get worse presently; in *A Tiger for Malgudi*, a truly late novel, we have the Captain 'alternating between occasional sanity and general madness' (1983: 54); the narrator mentions the Captain's 'energy and power', recalling Vasu of *The Man-Eater of Malgudi*; the Captain is also 'such a determined man' (1961: 59), and with him 'will counted' (1961: 113): unmistakable configuration of rajasic–tamasic traits, placing this man firmly in the different generic cast of the novelist's post-Independence period.

The later heroes practise deviousness. 'By habit, his nature avoided a direct and bald truth,' says the novelist of his hero Raju in *The Guide* (1958: 112). This is equally true of Margayya, the financial wizard; even a much later hero Jagan (*The Vendor of Sweets*) betrays this trait: 'Jagan said neither yes nor no; there was danger in either statement' (1967: 94). In *The World of Nagaraj*, Nagaraj is so successful that his brother is 'in tears for the strain of talking to Nagaraj' (1990: 152). Most of the post-Independence heroes are also little educated; God be praised!—for the most 'educated' of them all, the most learned, the scholarly Dr Rann (*Talkative Man*), is a pest: a 'regular lady-killer' (1977: 67), 'a lecherous demon' (1977: 95), 'the wolf of the fairy tales' (1977: 96), and, conclusively, 'a brainless rat' (1977: 104).

If there is any doubt about the trend of the late post-Independence phase, just *The World of Nagaraj* should dispel it. To begin with, though, Nagaraj recalls the sattvic heroes of the early novels, Srinivas of *Mr. Sampath*, for example; but soon enough we realize that this hero is a different sort altogether: a man who has 'no resistance of any kind' (1990: 111); and Nagaraj shows it in rearing Tim and in writing a book on the divine sage Narada. He knows it: 'I am only a milestone. I stay and others come and pass' (1990: 183). Nagaraj betrays, besides, a streak of anti-feminism: 'Women are an impediment' (1990: 178); and 'You must never listen to women. They will not let you do anything worthwhile, nothing more important than buying brinjals and cucumber, and mustard and rice, and caressing whenever a chance occurred' (1990: 184). Let us put the statement in the perspective of Narayan's feminist salvo in *The Dark Room*; and Narayan's wholesome tribute to his grandmother and his mother as well as his sensitivity to feminine charm in his memoir *My Days*; and his homage to womanhood in his post-Rajam journal. The feminine warmth and wisdom of the early 'autobiographical' novels is already a distant memory. With this reversal goes disillusionment with young people: 'Young people of these days are different' (1974: 113). The degeneration in the post-Independence world of Narayan is best revealed by the Sanskrit scholar, Kavu Pundit in *The World of Nagaraj*. Nagaraj muses on 'this slippery pundit and his devious ways' (1990: 116).

The later novels present a different Malgudi, a darker world. The post-1947 Malgudi of the novels is progressively a country of 'unexpected depths of duplicity'. It is possible for Malgudi now to be a humanscape of 'a hundred evil possibilities'; with an ambience of 'a thousand other sins' we might find ourselves now 'neckdeep in a cesspool'. There is no mistaking; it is a picaroon world now. Aptly law courts appear in the later novels and jails as well. This, too, is Malgudi, but a town so unmistakably, definitively distanced from the idealism and aspiration of the first phase heroes; beginning its career as a semi-rural town in the heart of colonial south India of the late 1920s, Narayan's fictive setting has subtly and steadily reflected the development of the novelist's environment.

Take the family. Let us recall Narayan's claim: 'To be a good writer anywhere, you must have roots, both in religion and in family. [...] I have these things' (Mehta 1962: 148). As a social institution the family was dear to Narayan. He had presented it in his early novels as a prime source of moral sustenance; family harmonies account for the extraordinary charm of the pre-Independence novels. Even in *Mr. Sampath*, a turning point in this aspect as in much else, the hero Srinivas's failure is in part domestic. Now in the later novels, too, attachments prevail, though fitfully. In the midst of his worries Margayya (*The Financial Expert*) thinks of his wife and still feels 'the tenderness that he had felt for her as a virginal bride' (1952: 44). In a much later novel, *A Tiger for Malgudi*, the spiritually adept tiger comments on the turbulence in the marital life of her captor and adds: '[But] God who sees everything must be aware of their thoughts and the secret ecstasies of companionship of even that Captain and his wife' (1983: 69). Even much later, in *The World of Nagaraj*, Narayan's hero is still attached to his old and ailing mother, 'a frail ghost'; and her grandson, the postmodern Indian Tim, too, is 'fond of his grandmother' (1990: 49).

The decline of the family, all the same, is evident in the post-Independence period and imparts to the later novels elegiac undertones. The disintegration is witnessed at the very beginning of the second phase: in *The Financial Expert*. 'After the death of the old man the brothers fell out, their wives fell out, and their children fell out. They could not tolerate the idea of even breathing the same air or being enclosed by the same walls' (1952: 8). The narrator reports in *The Man-Eater of Malgudi*: 'My cousin [...] hated me for staying in our ancestral home, my father having received it as his share after the division of property among his brothers' (1961: 5). In *The Vendor of Sweets*, young Jagan's wife gets a rough tongue from her mother-in-law until she gives birth to a child; Jagan fails even as a husband. The novelist uses family relationships, now in decline, to realize both Margayya and Jagan: Narayan's preoccupation with the family and the bad blood it generates extends prominently into his last novel, *The World of Nagaraj*. The later heroes of Narayan appear to be incapable of holding up the family as an institution. Raju's uncle in *The Guide* accuses his flighty nephew darkly of having 'no respect for family traditions' (1958: 154). In these novels, more often than not, fathers founder. Nataraj in *The Man-Eater of Malgudi* recalls that as a child: 'I often had to spend days and days hoping to catch my father in a happy mood to ask for a favour' (1961: 69); when Nataraj grows up he, too, fails to take care of his son: his wife complains: 'You see so little of him' (1961: 103). Father–child relationship, memorably presented in *The Bachelor of Arts*, is in decline in the later novels. The problem becomes the central theme of *The Vendor of Sweets*, the first novel of the third phase; the son is mentioned rather late in the novel when Jagan resolves that he 'must give him more time' (1967: 23); Jagan's problem is made explicit soon after: 'He was a cowardly father' (1967: 30). While Mali's attachment to his mother is just noted (1967: 43) his estrangement with his father Jagan is progressively charted. In contrast Margayya in the first post-'Independence' novel errs by spoiling his son with too much love and cash. All too late, Jagan is 'aghast at the transformation that had come with time' (1967: 81). And that is now Narayan's concern and interest too. Nagaraj of *The World of Nagaraj* marks a terminal decline; he manages to spoil his brother's son through a total lack of engagement. The 'invisible barrier' (1990: 42) that Jagan mulls over becomes a regular feature of the besieged and barricaded lives of the later novels. In comparison with the early, pre-Independence novels, a sombre loneliness is a recurrent note in the post-Independence novels of R.K. Narayan. The vagrant who appears from time to time in *The Vendor of Sweets* offers us a leitmotif in this world of declining homes. The problem reaches critical proportions in the third phase. Before we know what is happening we move from the family, however battered, to beyond the family itself. The father–son struggle as in *The Vendor of Sweets* at least presupposes a family; the very possibility is ruled out in the next novel, *The Painter of Signs*; Raman, the youthful hero of this novel, cannot establish a family; Daisy, his beloved, does not believe in marriage or a *family* of her own. It is now work for Daisy, not wifehood; no *home* for her, no *togetherness*: husband–wife relationship does not appeal to her. Courting such a heroine we have a hero who has been orphaned early; and Raman is the second orphan hero in the later novels, after Sriram of *Waiting for the Mahatma*; later Vasu in *The Man-Eater of Malgudi* and Captain in *A Tiger for Malgudi*, both orphans, create enough havoc around them. After the failure of the family in *The Painter of Signs* the Swami in *A Tiger for Malgudi* abandons his family and becomes a sanyasin; the narrator of *Talkative Man* is a confirmed bachelor; and his story of Dr Rann—the woman-eater of Malgudi—makes mockery of the institution of marriage. And in Narayan's last book, a novella, *Grandmother's Tale*, the young woman's epic search for her missing husband takes us on a nostalgic time machine to the past when the family was a central value. The conclusive rejection of the joint family and the family itself is a disquieting finale to Narayan's attachment to the family and family relationships from *Swami and Friends* and *Talkative Man*—a pointer to radical changes in the world of R.K. Narayan, the post-Independence India.

Another development in Narayan's post-Independence world is more alarming. Violence, even verbal, is unnatural to the 'heroes' of Narayan's early novels. In the odd novel of the period, *The Dark Room*, Savitri's husband indulges in outrageous verbal and physical violence; and the hero of *Mr. Sampath* surprises us with occasional harshness and domestic 'unconcern'; but that novel is already a turning point. The different human type at the centre of the second phase novels is forcefully confirmed for us by the very first post-Independence novel, *The Financial Expert*. Margayya beats up Dr Paul—a critical and cathartic act on his part. Sriram of *Waiting for the Mahatma* follows with his temper; when provoked by a fellow convict in the jail he 'wanted to get up and hit him' (1955: 134). The jail in this novel offers more than a glimpse of the underworld, as much as Kismet, the dubious tavern in *The World of Nagaraj*. Sriram's attempt in *Waiting for the Mahatma* to take his beloved by force is a definitive act of the later novels—unimaginable in the pre-Independence period. If Sriram restrains himself from attacking a fellow prisoner for fear of losing his beloved, Raju in *The Guide* goes that one step further. When frustrated in love and cheated in business: 'I grew desperate and angry. […] I slapped the boy on the cheek and he cried […]' (1958: 138). Raju presently finds the new showman who has usurped his place on the station platform is a different proposition: 'He repelled me with a back-stroke of his left hand as if swatting a fly, and I fell back, and knocked against my mother—who had come running on to the platform a thing she had never done in her life' (1958: 157). The mother's reaction—her very presence—underscores the gross violation of pre-Independence norms; the image of the fly squares with the level of post-Independence culture. The violence of the second phase peaks in the savagery of Vasu of *The Man-Eater of Malgudi*. The narrator sums him up: 'He made humanity suffer' (1961: 96); Vasu makes other forms of life suffer more. Vasu is the culmination of the instinctual egotism, the rajasic–tamasic nature of the middle-phase heroes. He is 'the prince of darkness' (1961: 163). Naturally.

Violence is not exclusive to the middle phase; it extends into the late phase: in the verbal and psychological violence Jagan (*The Vendor of Sweets*) inflicts on his wife, with the son reciprocating; and, climactically, in the extreme cruelty of the Captain and his decapitation (*A Tiger for Malgudi*).

R.K. Narayan's later phase springs another startling surprise. Narayan had an unmodern reputation for keeping sexuality away from his books. The restraint is actually a sort of 'maidenliness'; it does not preclude wholesome sexuality. The early novels present charming first love, felicitous conjugal love, but not overt sexuality let alone erotic episodes. Now Narayan surprises us—and himself— in his post-Independence novels with changing sexual mores.[3] Narayan's openness to sexuality is inaugurated by Margayya of *The Financial Expert*; it progresses through *Waiting for the Mahatma*, *The Guide*, *The Man-Eater of Malgudi*, and—skipping *The Vendor of Sweets*, its theme and aesthetic focus precludes any possibility for such openness—it peaks in *The Painter of Signs*. But sex cannot be an end in itself in Narayan's social or ethical perspective; sexual attraction that does not lead to an abiding human relationship is sterile. In *The Painter of Signs* the young, unconventional lovers get going a sexual affair without founding a durable relationship, let alone setting up a family.

Things fall apart? Not quite. On the contrary, looked at from another angle, Narayan's world is also growing more spiritual; the stark sociological and moral trends are paralleled by a thriving life of the spirit. In his journal Narayan had arrived at certain philosophic conclusions which gave him peace of mind. While 'a final understanding' would bring greater joy, personal tragedies would keep a person 'in trim in the relations between himself and God' and during the journey through several lives towards 'a final understanding' (Ram and Ram 1996a: 360). In other words faith in God. Narayan's later novels are more openly, even spectacularly spiritual, even 'Hindu', none more than *The Guide* and *A Tiger for Malgudi*, the two salvation novels of the later phase. The writer is celebrating his discovery of heritage. The Hindu posits that there is no lost soul; all of us are pilgrims at various stages of progress ('journey through several lives' [Ram and Ram 1996a: 360]): towards self-realization. Narayan presents the Hindu view in his introduction to *Gods, Demons, and Others* (1964a: 5): '[T]here is no tragedy in the Greek sense. The sufferings of the meek and the saintly are temporary, even as the triumph of the demon is; everyone knows this. Everything is bound to come out right in the end; if not immediately, at least in a thousand or ten thousand years; if not in this world, at least in other worlds.' *The Guide* dramatizes this philosophical truth; it makes sense that the rajasic hero of the middle phase, obsessive, instinct-ridden, discovers the joy of selflessness, and here and now, in this *life*. In the next novel, *The Man-Eater of Malgudi*, the temple elephant is saved at the end and continues to carry the god in his wedding procession: it is Vasu who self-destructs; the triumph of the *demon* is temporary, the eternal struggle between faith and reason, devotion and egotism, is resolved once again. The Hindu also believes in the fundamental unity of all life; this cosmic view is presented, climactically, in the second salvation novel, *A Tiger for Malgudi*; the 'hero', a tiger, popularly believed a true representative of benighted existence, turns out to be as spiritually eligible and apt to achieve Self-Realization as any sattvic soul. Spiritual potential is not the monopoly of a few. *A Tiger for Malgudi* establishes definitively a spiritual optimism, first dramatized in *The Guide*. Societal degeneration and increasing spiritual possibilities are not mutually exclusive. The greater the degeneration, the greater the scope for regeneration—and the artist's opportunity. And grace. It is probably one more reason why Graham Greene admired Narayan's work.

Narayan had throughout affirmed his Indian integrity; he prized his roots in *family and religion*. The family is the matrix of the pre-Independence novels; when it declined progressively as a social structure in the later novels, religion developed a stable tectonic. What strikes us is the fullness of creative development: from the charming humanism of *Swami and Friends* and the early pre-Independence novels, through the wholesome spiritual comedy of *Mr. Sampath*; and after India's Independence, the vices comedy, the moralities, and the miracles of the middle period, culminating in the religious humanism of *The Guide*; and Narayan's pure Hinduism of *A Tiger for Malgudi* followed by the self-parody of *The World of Nagaraj*.

When David Davidar asked the novelist in 1988 to mention his favourite novel Narayan replied: *A Tiger for Malgudi*. And what would he rather be in his next birth? *A Contemplative Tiger*.

IV
SUMMING UP

20

Cosmic Comedy

R.K. Narayan's Gunas Comedy

> [T]ill the cosmic process ends, the multiplicity of individuals with their distinctive qualitative contents persists. The multiplicity is not separable from the cosmos.
> — S. Radhakrishnan (1993: 104)
>
> [Narayan is] one of the few profoundly humanistic writers of our time.
> —Warren French, in Atma Ram (1981: xv)

R.K. Narayan was no theoretician. As Graham Greene (1937: 240) discovered early on, Narayan was simply that rare creative writer who 'stake[d] everything on his creative power'. Under invitation, though, Narayan did comment on his own fiction and fictional practice (see 'The Man-Eater of Malgudi' in Amirthanayagam 1982; and Narayan 1964b, 1965a); it will, however, be too much to suggest that in his novels Narayan offered explicitly a specific conception of comedy as, say, Ben Jonson had on his species of drama.[1] All the same, from our reading of Narayan's works, it seems to me that Narayan's imagination had struck early a new vein of comedy which he cultivated—not consciously—but consistently and progressively. Narayan's interest in people—a wide range of characters—leads me to believe that we have a conceptual possibility here of a different species of comedy, the gunas comedy.

The Background

The three gunas or qualities bear the names of sattva, rajas, and tamas. In common Indian parlance—which is what matters in Narayan's context—they denote three personality types: in Telugu, for example, the lay man knows that 'sattvic' means 'gentle, mild, kindly, amiable', as in Brown's dictionary in the nineteenth century: confirmed a century later by Gwynn. Similarly, 'rajasic' in Gwynn is a person of 'domineering spirit, haughty, arrogant' which he has taken from Brown, not finding any need to change the sense of the word over a century and more; and 'tamasic' is 'angry, wicked'; the average Indian even talks of sattvic/tamasic food; as he talks of tamasic worship, with animal sacrifice.

In his article published in the *Hindu* on 18 October 1998, renowned neurosurgeon Dr B. Ramamurthy observed:

The three gunas, which people in India have been talking about for centuries, are being talked about in the West only for the past 50 or 60 years. There are people with satva guna, tamo guna, and rajo guna. The brain activities of these people are entirely different. In satvic people, the alpha waves are ten cycles per second. These waves are prominent throughout the brain. In rajasic people, who are very active, the beta waves and theta waves are much more prominent. Whereas in dull people, the slow waves of the brain, what are called the delta waves, are often predominant. These days magnetic activity can measure these waves.

The popular glossary alone will do to represent the cast of Narayan's novels from *Swami and Friends* to *Grandmother's Tale*. These terms in everyday speech have, however, descended from a religio-philosophical source, the Bhagavad Gita. On the gunas the Gita, Radhakrishnan's 1993 translation, says: 'And whatever states of being there may be, be they harmonious (sattvika), passionate (rajasa), slothful (tamasa)—know thou that they are all from Me alone' (12:VII.217).

Radhakrishnan clarifies:

[T]he evil-doers cannot attain to the supreme, for their mind and will are not instruments of the spirit but of the ego. They do not seek to master their rude impulses, but are a prey to the rajas and tamas in them. If we control them by the sattva in us, our action becomes ordered and enlightened and ceases to be the result of passion and ignorance. (15:VII.218)[2]

Radhakrishnan further expounds the concept: 'Sattva is perfect purity and luminosity while rajas is impurity which leads to activity and tamas is darkness and inertia. As the main application of the gunas in the Gita is ethical, we use goodness for sattva, passion for rajas and dullness for tamas. [...] When the soul identifies itself with the modes of nature, it forgets its own eternity and uses mind, life and body for egoistic satisfaction. To rise above bondage, we must rise above the modes of nature' (5:XIV.317).

For our purpose the ethical and psychological connotations alone matter. Certain verses in the Gita are explicit: 'Greed, activity, the undertaking of actions, unrest and craving—these spring [...] when rajas increases' (12:XIV). Dominance of rajas is revealed in a life of passion and activity. Similarly on tamas: 'Unillumination, inactivity, negligence and mere delusion—these arise [...] when dullness increases' (13:XIV). While illumination is the effect of sattva, non-illumination is the result of tamas. Error, misunderstanding, negligence, and inaction are the characteristic marks of a tamasic temperament. The ethical implications are significant: '[T]he fruit of good action is said to be of the nature of "goodness" and pure; while the fruit of passion is pain, the fruit of dullness is ignorance' (16:XIV). Radhakrishnan (1993: 363) comments: 'Happiness is the universal aim of life. Only it is of different kinds according to the modes which dominate our nature. If the tamas predominates in us, we are satisfied with violence and inertia, blindness and error. If rajas prevails, wealth and power, pride and glory give us happiness.' To get beyond the three gunas we have to attain first the rule of sattva. *Be ethical before you can be spiritual.*

Two aspects must be underscored: there are no pure categories. There is only predominance and, more significant, whatever the karmic make-up evolution runs its course, there is hope for everyone, for success is inevitable. One cannot expect to obtain the reward until one has sounded well the depths of experience in its varied complexity. One may have to go through many lives before reaching the destination; however, *no effort is wasted.* 'Human nature cannot be hurried' (Radhakrishnan 1993: 37, 36).

Here is Narayan on karmic progress (1964a: 5):

[T]here is no tragedy in the Greek sense. The sufferings of the meek and the saintly are temporary, even as the triumph of the demon is; everyone knows this. Everything is bound to come out right in the end; if not immediately, at least in a thousand or ten thousand years; if not in this world, at least in other worlds.[3]

Narayan's own world view had developed during the post-Rajam psychic training; and found immediate expression in the very first novel written after his recovery, *The English Teacher*. The hero Krishna says: 'I felt I had discharged a duty assigned to me in some eternal scheme' (1945: 8). And for the hero of *Mr. Sampath*: '[T]he possibilities of perfection seemed infinite, though mysterious' (1949: 6). Srinivas's vision of evolution in *Mr. Sampath* makes sense.

Mr. Sampath dramatizes another insight of the Gita. 'The gateway of this hell leading to the ruin of the soul is threefold, lust, anger and greed' (Radhakrishnan 1993: 340). Ravi, the old landlord, and Sampath, in various degrees, exemplify this truth. In the post-Independence phase Raju's career in *The Guide*, too, makes better sense: 'The Lord abides in the hearts of all beings, O Arjuna, causing them to turn round by His power as if they were mounted on a machine' (XVIII.61).

The Gita offers to us more than a conceptual base to appreciate Narayan's comedy. With the gunas comedy we are in an ambience of R.K. Narayan's humanism. For Narayan's humanism offers an inclusive point of view; the larger vision inspires Narayan's comedy. For a symbolic presentation of Narayan's humanism in Narayan's gunas comedy we may recall the episode of the dolls in Narayan's *The Dark Room* (1938: 39–40). The inclusiveness and tranquillity of Narayan's humanism are clearly suggested in this description of the navaratri dolls: a whole world view—God's eye view—is offered through them, with a place for everyone, all God's creatures. That is the central tradition of Hinduism as propounded and practised by humanists like Swami Vivekananda, Tagore, Mahatma Gandhi, and Bhagavan Sathya Sai Baba. That of course is Narayan's world view too. William Walsh (1982: 167) was ahead of his time: 'What one can say about Narayan without qualification is that he embodies the pure spirit of Hinduism. [...] Again, one must say that there is deeply in Narayan the profound Hindu conviction, or instinct for, the fundamental oneness of existence.'

Narayan's religious belief is a quiet, cultured kind. He affirms: 'Religion is not a thing that anyone can openly avow—it's like one's underwear' (1960: 118).[4] Radhakrishnan also cites Lucretius (1993: 124; see the epigraph to this chapter). Narayan had always been a believer; more so in the period following the death of his wife.[5] In one of the seances Susila sums it up: 'Worshipping and wondering, how much life's journey is made easier for one who can see nature and God every moment!' (1945: 175). This togetherness of nature and God, the acceptance has vital implications for the here and the now. 'He who sees Me everywhere and sees all in Me; I am not lost to him nor is he lost to Me' (Radhakrishnan 1993: VI.30). The Eternal is the same in all (Radhakrishnan 1993: 181), in animals, as in men, in learned Brahmins as in outcastes. See with an equal eye: *samadarsinah*, that is a cardinal spiritual ideal; sages see with an equal eye, a learned Brahmin or an outcaste; a cow, an elephant, or even a dog. The vision of the gunas comedy is germane to such a generous, underplayed preoccupation with the cosmos and the human personality, such 'a total view of oneself and others' (1974: 194); besides a cherished universal goal: self-development.

For once again of interest to our study, especially of Narayan's pre-Independence comedy, is what Narayan says in *My Days* (see the epigraph to Chapter 7 in this book). How central the mind is in Narayan's early comedy!—as it was in the writer's life. To 'still the restless mind and understand one's real self' is the central theme of Narayan's gunas comedy; of the five novels, however, *The English Teacher* and *Mr. Sampath* are remarkable for preoccupation with the self.

'Any fetish, fanaticism, rigidity or rigour, by their very nature make living harsh, hard and dried up, while the positive values of existence all along lie in *suppleness, harmony and joy*. This is, according to my outlook, what God intends it to be' (Ram and Ram 1996a: 378; emphasis mine). 'Harmony' is the hallmark of Narayan's vision in the sattvic early comedy; in the later rajasic and tamasic phases, 'harmony' is a natural and wholesome evolution, and more spectacularly. The question of right vocation, too, is crucial; as well as, over all, a growth in sensibility, personality: self-development. Even the young man Chandran (*The Bachelor of Arts*) attempts mind training: 'He felt that his greatest striving ought to be for a life freed from distracting illusions and hysterics' (1937: 132); and young Chandran achieves some success. It is the same goal Krishna (*The English Teacher*) and Srinivas (*Mr. Sampath*) aspire for in the two novels Narayan wrote after overcoming the trauma of his wife's death; both heroes progress towards higher levels of self-understanding and spiritual perspective: aiming at a fine balance of the here and the hereafter. Krishna and Srinivas are on track, towards the goal of *sthithaprajna*: 'He whose mind is untroubled in the midst of sorrows and is free from eager desire amid pleasures, he from whom passion, fear, and rage have passed away, he is called a sage of settled intelligence' (Radhakrishnan 1993: II.56). For social man, says Radhakrishnan, sthithaprajna is the ultimate in spiritual evolution.

However, when the mind surrenders to the senses it carries away the understanding, 'even as a wind carries away a ship on the waters' (Radhakrishnan 1993: II.67); Sampath, the old landlord, and Ravi in *Mr. Sampath*—all three make sense; while sthithaprajna relates to Srinivas's goal. Sthithaprajna also links Narayan's gunas comedy to a significant tradition in the Indian novel in English: the theme of higher awareness, beginning with probably the very first novelist in English in south India, Rajam Iyer in his—unfinished—novel, *Vasudeva Sastry*; followed by Madhavaiah's Thillai *Govindan*, through K.S.Venkataramani's *Kandan the Patriot*, to Raja Rao's *Kanthapura*.

Karma Yoga

Doesn't all this lead to 'withdrawal', 'Hindu calm', 'the killer'? Not necessarily. With Narayan a further ethical ideal of the Gita holds the key. For the sattvic hero the Gita offers an attractive socio-spiritual goal: karma yoga, the path of works: reaching God through service to mankind.

Marx's criticism, that philosophers interpret the world while the real task is to change it, does not apply to the author of the *Gita*, who gives us not only a philosophical interpretation, brahmavidya, but also a practical programme, yogasastra. Our world is not a spectacle to contemplate, it is a field of battle. Only for the *Gita* improvement in the individual nature is the way to social betterment. (Radhakrishnan 1993: 96)

Radhakrishnan glosses karma yoga: 'The path of works is a means of liberation quite as efficient as that of knowledge. [...] The teacher points out that jnana or wisdom is not incompatible with karma or action' (1993: 132).

What about sanyasa? 'He who does the work which he ought to do without seeking its fruit he is the sanyasin, he is the yogin, not he who does not light the sacred fire, and performs no rites' (Radhakrishnan 1993: VI.1.187). Radhakrishnan further comments: '[Renunciation] consists in the accomplishment of the necessary action without an inward striving for reward. This is true yoga, firm control over oneself, complete self-possession.' And 'disciplined activity (yoga) is just as good as renunciation'. Not withdrawal. 'For the Gita teaches not renunciation of works but conversion of all works into nishkamakarma or desireless action. What is demanded is not renunciation of action, but renunciation of selfish desire. [...] Nishkamakarma is the spiritual as well the social essence of karma yoga' (Radhakrishnan 1993: 133). The Lord says in the Gita: 'Do thou thy allotted work, for action is better than inaction; even the maintenance of thy physical life cannot be effected without action' (Radhakrishnan 1993: III.8). 'Withdrawal'—'Hindu calm, the killer'—is not supported by the Gita. R.K. Narayan belongs to this pure Hinduism of Vivekananda, Tagore as well as Gandhi, all inspired by the Gita.[6]

That ought to set at rest the populist 'killer' theory.

Radhakrishnan (1993: 167) has commented earlier: '[E]very form of self-control, where we surrender the egoistic enjoyment for the higher delight, where we give up lower impulses, is said to be a sacrifice (yajnam); the renunciation of works and their unselfish performance both lead to the soul's salvation. But of the two, the unselfish performance of works is better than their renunciation.' That puts Raju (*The Guide*) again in the perspective of the gunas comedy; this unlikely hero makes amends for his expedient renunciation with a selfless act. Then of relevance, in particular for *Mr. Sampath*, are the two sides of religion, the personal and the social, both emphasized by the Gita. 'Man has not only to ascend to the world of spirit *but also descend to the world of creatures*' (Radhakrishnan 1993: 167; emphasis mine). A social ethic is enjoined: no 'withdrawal'! Srinivas's guardianship of Ravi in *Mr. Sampath* makes spiritual sense to a Gandhi, or a Vivekananda, or a Sai Baba. Srinivas's commitment to his journal, *The Banner*, is also conclusive evidence of his socio-religious orientation.

At the same time R.K. Narayan savoured life. 'More than all else, do I cherish at heart that love which makes me to live a limitless life in this world,' said Kabir. Narayan's extraordinary zest for life, here and now, is evident in his fiction as well as non-fiction. Here is a 'song':

It is not right to call it a habit. The word 'habit' like the word 'addict' has a disparaging sense. One might call smoking a habit, one might call almost everything else a habit, but not coffee. It is not a habit; it is a stabilizing force in human existence achieved through a long evolutionary process. The good coffee, brown and fragrant, is not a product achieved in a day. It is something attained after laborious trials and errors [...]. (Narayan 1988: 55)

And cloves too get a eulogy:

But I preferred to wait: the cloves of this shop were reputed to be genuine 'Zanzibars'—any connoisseur of spices knows what it means, cloves of ebonite shade, sheeny with oil, and each perfectly designed in miniature like a Greek column supporting a four-pointed cupola. A quarter of this pristine specimen placed on the tip of the tongue would be enough to sting and to tingle the nervous system. At other shops cloves looked anaemic, enfeebled, and tasted like match-stick. (Narayan 1964b: 70)

The fine team-up of body and mind and spirit in Narayan's novels contributes overall to a paean to the here and the now: the senses are at their legitimate job in early gunas comedy! The sense of smell, for example, in *The English Teacher*. The heroes of Narayan's novels are also close to nature; they cherish the river: even Raju (*The Guide*) and Raman (*The Painter of Signs*). No other novel of Narayan's presents enchantment with nature as *The English Teacher*; but soon the concept gets an extension, a new definition, by the end of the novel: nature comprehends supra-nature.

In the post-Independence novels, presenting comedy of the more earthy gunas, the moral effort is more impressive, especially in *The Guide*; but even Margayya (*The Financial Expert*), after a life of hectic rajasic activity, reaches at the end for his grandchild. If optimism is the life breath of comedy, gunas comedy is 'inspired' optimism. Spiritual evolution is not the prerogative of the few. Narayan's gunas comedy also presents other thematic preoccupations, for example, of the family and family relationships; of a context of refined relationships. Narayan is our poet of personal relationships, of the family and of friendship. The fine plexus of familial warmth is charmingly foregrounded in *The Bachelor Arts*. There is, at the same time, a disturbing share of anti-family sentiment as well in the post-Rajam novels, *The English Teacher* and *Mr. Sampath*; and more strikingly in the post-Independence novels.

Gunas Comedy and Humours Comedy

Narayan's gunas comedy is not an Indian form of humours comedy. The humours of the Jonsonian kind are no doubt very much part of our indigenous systems of medicine even today. The humours, however, have not given rise to an Indian species of humours comedy. Humours are physio-psychological; the gunas are psychic-moral. Jonsonian humours give rise to comedy of 'excesses': of 'morbidity'; Jonsonian humours comedy presents abnormality humour. Narayan's gunas comedy offers normality humour. In the world of Narayan's novels the singular comedic enjoyment—'a humour strange to our fiction'—and its refined integrity can best be explained by positing a new species of comedy. For, the three gunas are not, as we have seen, aberrations of human nature, but states or stages or phases—totally this-worldly—in the inevitable progress of the human spirit. Narayan's novels offer humane comedy in a higher perspective, milieu, of serene optimism.

The gunas comedy at its best arises out of the attitudes and actions even of the higher human type, the sattvic—see, for example, the flower-thief episode in *The Bachelor of Arts*, where almost the entire family, including the father—otherwise so sober, 'elderly'—are turned to butts of sophisticated laughter, sane laughter, and little satire. *Vis comica* in Narayan is also *vis sanitas*. Its characteristic dignity arises from the sattvic nature of the hero; though practically no mortal is purely sattvic (only God is sattva), or purely rajasic or tamasic—it is ever a blend—the contribution of the sattvic type to the comedy of the pre-Independence novels carries a singular appeal.

Unlike the humours comedy again, the gunas comedy enacts the dynamic of the human self, dramatizing the possibilities of spiritual evolution, as in *The English Teacher*. The post-Rajam novels of the early gunas comedy especially make Narayan's characteristic preoccupation amply clear; the ethical ballast of the gunas comedy is already evident in the philosophic aptitude of Krishna and Srinivas. The joyous, celebratory, life-affirming 'happy ending' of conventional comedy becomes also a fulfilment of the self: consider the conclusions even of *The Financial Expert* and *The Guide*. This ordained predisposition for introspection and self-development, more than any other feature, gives homogeneity to Narayan's gunas comedy.

Narayan's Humour

'Strange,' said Greene.

Humour is a cardinal value for Narayan. He privileges a few select characters with it. Samuel the Pea in *Swami and Friends*, for example. Narayan presents comic sense as a premium social merit. Chandran and Ramu in *The Bachelor of Arts* and Savitri and Gangu in *The Dark Room*, too, bond in humour. Even in Narayan's non-fictional prose we witness the same equipoise. See 'In the Confessional' in *A Writer's Nightmare*.[7] Or the concluding passage in *The Writerly Life*. Thirty-six years later see Narayan on Narayan again, on his being rumoured to have been shortlisted for the Nobel, but denied.[8]

Humour in Narayan's novels rises naturally out of their very ground: all three gunas are a source of humour, of comic enjoyment; the gunas comedy is a universal feast provided by the gunas of nature. Take first the sattvic protagonists in comic light: 'He liked the way she sat; he liked the way she played with her sister; he liked the way she dug her hands into the sand and threw it in the air' (1937: 59). Conscionability, too, can yield, like any moral feature, subtle humour especially in a sattvic hero; it leads us to the comedy of human resolves and resolutions, as in *The Bachelor of Arts*. 'He also resolved not to smoke because it was bad for the heart, and a very sound heart was necessary for the examination' (1937: 19). Even in *The Dark Room*, Narayan's shock novel, Savitri's moral struggle is presented against a moving backdrop of stark humanity, meshing just adequately—and comically—with the world of the heroine; humour and humble humanity go hand in hand: for both are provided by the fringe world, the have-nots, who, while playing a crucial role in the development of the plot, also provide the novel's ballast of human values. The gunas comedy attains considerable extension in *Mr. Sampath*. This watershed novel is a blend of the sublime and the ridiculous; even the sattvic Srinivas contributes his bit to the fun.

Narayan's fullness of philosophic poise and his flair for comedy go together. Grounded in extraordinary physical energy, it has grown into comic enjoyment of spiritual equilibrium. Narayan's comedy contemplates human nature and ethics and morality with detachment and delight. Narayan's temperament also rules out the tragic perspective. Few modern writers can declare: 'If I had to live again, I would want nothing different. I live from moment to moment. [...] Nothing really has gone wrong with me. I am deeply interested in life as a writer. That is perhaps why I have not gone mad.'[9] Narayan has gone on record that he cannot write unless he is at peace with himself.[10]

From charmed smile to muffled guffaw, that is the rare breadth of Narayan's laughter: an impressive bandwidth of humour, from the puckish to the sage. Narayan recalls Chaucer—a secularist within a matrix of faith. 'Strange,' said Graham Greene; for Narayan's humour is, most of the time, that extraordinary breed: good humour, that is, humour of optimism, religious Humanism. And something else besides: humour of animal spirits, expression of the sheer joy of life—the life-spirit; humour of equilibrium, serenity. Narayan's comedy is marked by humour of assurance, of a timeless perspective.

Narayan seems to have enjoyed at least one other form of humour in real life; which he mostly kept out of his fiction: and that is sharp sarcasm. The boundaries of Narayan's humour are self-imposed by a combination of moderated temperament (in wit and humour, a natural) and self-training; like the rest of his art it is discipline of exclusion, artistic rigour. Never coarse: well-mannered, in good taste, with a good sense of timing. There is no creed in Narayan's humour, not creed, but a human interest, fascination for people for just what they are, engaging with people for themselves. Narayan's humour goes with his full participation in life and society—his 'social immersion'. R.K. Narayan is the insider humorist. Two other humorists, G.V. Desani (*All About H. Hatterr*) and Anantanarayanan (*The Silver Pilgrimage*), I am sure, will bear this out. M.K. Naik and Shyamala A. Narayan share with their readers a telling quote from an unpublished paper by Desani: 'In my *All About H. Hatterr* [my hero's] view was to accept all situations, events, creatures, including the devil, as well within God's laws, and get on with the business of living' (Naik 1982: 227).

For the Western readers the parallels can only come from medieval Europe: 'The medieval sense of the grotesque and the strong Medieval laugh may be further adduced as evidence for a certain hearty wholeness of world view or a resilient and full awareness of both the heavenly and the earthly' (Wimsatt 1969: 18). Vasu in *The Man-Eater of Malgudi*, as well as his puranic analogue the demon Bhasmasura, belongs to the same spirit which has given us Satan in early British drama—'evil ranting in a context of unfailing Providence'.

Narayan read Chekhov only after Greene had compared him to the Russian writer in his introduction to *The Bachelor of Arts* in 1937. Though there are similarities between Chekhov and Narayan it is time we reviewed Greene's seminal analogy. No doubt both Chekhov and Narayan are outstanding for their moral strength, without a trace of self-pity; between the two writers separated by continents and cultures there is still a fraternity of humour; yet the Indian novelist is unlike Chekhov, in social and political attitudes; with Narayan's Hindu world view the Malgudi blend is unique. Chekhov does not limit himself at all; he exploits even the penumbral width. Chekhov's *Marriage Proposal* is out of the question for Narayan.

Does Narayan have any Indian models? It does not appear he does. His examples, if any, are more likely British; Narayan had widely and methodically read in the literature of Great Britain. He says in his introduction to *Gods, Demons, and Others* (1964a): '[L]aughter should be dignified and refreshing rather than demonstrative' (5): that sounds closer to the 'British' species.[11] Narayan may have been put off by Chaucer's Middle English: that poet of seminal importance, however, offers a parallel in the wide range of humour, though Narayan fights shy until late in his career of sexual humour—his Brahminism keeps him from doing, say, a 'Miller's Tale'; Narayan's spirit in the later period is closer to 'The Pardoner's Tale'. In the post-Independence novels where the heroes are more obviously rajasic or tamasic, the comedy develops 'bolder' tints, wilder possibilities. In a word there is a revolution of sorts in Narayan's post-Independence work; this is accompanied by growing violence and the progressive disintegration of the Indian joint family. Towards the end of his career Narayan's religious temper finds explicit expression in a novel like *A Tiger for Malgudi*.[12] Narayan's achievement might suggest that comedy ought to come naturally to a Hindu. It has not; the outstanding exceptions are G.V. Desani and Anantanarayanan.

In his interview with Davidar, Narayan was not being facetious:

Q. 'What would you rather be in your next birth?'
A. 'Contemplative tiger.'

Narayan! Narayan!

Over the decades R.K. Narayan underwent a natural transformation: from styling himself 'a realistic fiction writer in English' to viewing for himself a definite role in his own community. He is also clear in his mind about his matrix.

Traditionally, India is the Ramayana, the Mahabharata and the Puranas. The values remain the same in every village, town or city. [...] *The Silappadhikaram*, Kalidasa's works—they are all there. We have perhaps lost touch with the terminology, but the philosophy, the values, they are all there in the heritage, the vast store-house. [...] Narayan reflects fully the India that was, is, and will ever be. (S.V.V. 1963: 45)[13]

Narayan's image of the storyteller and his audience under the banyan tree in his introduction to *Gods, Demons, and Others* (1964a: 1–10; emphasis mine) is familiar to us by now.

[S]omewhat isolated from the main stream of modern life [...] *but actually they* [the villagers] *have no sense of missing much; on the contrary, they give an impression of living* in *a state of secret enchantment. The source of enchantment is the story-teller in their midst,* a grand old man who seldom stirs from his ancestral home on the edge of the village [that's Narayan self-romanticized?] [...] [C]ontinuing *in his habits and deportment the traditions of a thousand years.* [...] *He is completely at peace with himself and his surroundings.* [...] He has unquestioned faith in the validity of the *Vedas.* [...] Even the legends and myths [...] are mere illustrations of the moral and spiritual truths enunciated in the *Vedas.* [...] *Everything is interrelated.* [...] [E]ach forms part and parcel of a total life and is indispensable for the attainment of a *four-square understanding of existence* [...] *a comprehensive and artistic medium of expression to benefit the literate and the illiterate alike.* [...] Over an enormous expanse of time and space events fall into *proper perspective* [...] destroyed by the tempo of his own misdeeds. Evil has in it, buried subtly, the infallible seeds of its own destruction. [...] [A] *profoundly happy and sustaining philosophy which unfailingly appeals to our people* [...] *an ever-deepening understanding of life, death, and destiny.*

Like the raconteur he admires above Narayan in retrospect is a narrative artist in his own ambience. Every word of this applies to Narayan himself and to his global readership today. Our 'storyteller' has held his world in open enchantment.

Notes

Introduction

1. Against this backdrop of the dynamic decades, consider the following observations: '[A] literature which has yet to achieve itself' (Rajan 1966: 84). And 'Whether a truly Indian novel [in English] is at all possible' (McCutchion 1969: 84). Also see Meenakshi Mukherjee's quotation from Chaudhuri's address at a conference in 1983 (Mukherjee 2000: 48).
2. The first critical essay on Narayan available to me at the Andhra University library, the back of beyond in those days, was by William Walsh, 'The Intricate Alliance' (1960), and thanks to Professor Iyengar's drive and direction.
   Narayan was first published in the USA through the enterprise of a university press. The first doctoral thesis ever on Narayan, Nirmal Mukherji's 'The World of Malgudi', was submitted at Louisiana State University in 1960.
3. Also see *Frontline* (Ram and Ram 1996b: 16): 'Among others, Somerset Maugham, E.M. Forster, H.E. Bates, Elizabeth Bowen, Malcolm Muggeridge, Compton Mackenzie and Paul Scott were Narayan enthusiasts in their time.'
4. Richard Greene (2007: xiv) observed: 'Throughout his career, Narayan was venerated by critics but ignored by readers in Britain.' In the same book, Graham Greene suggests one possible reason for the poor sales: 'Hamish Hamilton published his first book right back in the depression years' (272–3, 281).
5. 'If a writer's readership and appeal survived his death by some years that would be worth celebrating.' See Narayan in Ram (2006: 6).
6. 'His international standing is expressed in the fact that his novels, short stories, and retellings of Indian epics and myths can be read in most of the world's major languages. [...] He was, in fact, modern India's first successful professional writer in English' (Ram and Ram 1996b: 5). 'Living locally, thinking globally is as much Tagore's way as it is Narayan's' (Ramanan 2013: 187).

7. Williams and Thieme, however, consider that the first four books constitute the first phase.
8. 'The exception is *Mr. Sampath*, a treatment of the zany Indian film industry, which is both uncertain in intention and queerly humpbacked in shape' (Walsh 1973: 11–12).
9. Inspired by Vidia's avid interest in cricket (as reported by Theroux 1998). See my essay 'Naipaul's Nobel Poise?' (2003) and Chapter 9 in this book.
10. See my essay 'Book(er) of the Year' (1997), on Roy's novel.

    See also: 'A man who does not lick his lips, can he blame the harmattan for drying them?' (Achebe 1995: 60).
11. Harrex (1977: 51–2, vol. 1) observed: '[Narayan] relates the complex fate of the individual not to an Indian negation of life but rather to an Indian affirmation of life.'
12. 'Tell me about yourself,' Narayan said to Geeta Doctor (1992: n.p.) in an interview.

    'Earlier I used to walk eight to ten miles a day; now it is along the garden path up to the gate' (Narayan 1996: v).

    T.S. Satyan (2006: iv) notes: 'He observed people and their ways with pleasure. He confidently interacted with all strata of society—hawkers, lawyers, clerks, printers, shopkeepers, students and professors and was curious to know all about them and their daily problems. He would even linger on the fringe of the crowd during a street brawl, attentively listening to every word spoken.'

    Narayan told Mehta (1962: 142) in New York: 'I like travelling underground because the people there remind me of the crowds in our bazaars.'

    Compare with Naipaul (Theroux 1998: 245) where he could be addressing Narayan.
13. The exception so far is John Thieme's *R.K. Narayan* (2008) that carries thirty-five pages of notes at the end. Thieme has also written a book on Naipaul.

Chapter 1

1. 'I don't think you should bother very much about the writer behind the book—books are more important than writers' (Croft 1983: 25).
2. On the popularity of university education in the formative period of modern India, see H.S. Maine quoted by O'Malley (1941). See also Williams (1976: 3); King (1974: 2); Narayan on Macaulay's *Minute* in Gowri Ramnarayan (1990: ix): '[E]very book, once written, acquired

a value and integrity of its own, an organic substance and meaning, for which the author was not responsible!'; and Narayan in 'When India Was a Colony', in *A Writer's Nightmare* (1998: 222).

For another angle, see Anand's *The King-Emperor's English* (1948: 14); and V.S. Naipaul in *An Area of Darkness* (1964: 228–9): 'The Indo-British encounter was abortive; it ended in a double fantasy.'

3. Anand (1948: 9) notes 'that great bombast, Macaulay, and the favourite fool of Mr. Kipling's lucubrations'.
4. See comments by Krishnaswami's friends in Narayan (1974: 100–1). See also H.Y. Sharada Prasad (1996: n.p.): 'There were some people who recalled Narayan's father who was such a disciplinarian that he even caned the younger teachers if they came late to school—or so the story went.'

Has there been a father deprivation in the novelist's life? 'When my father came home we stopped playing and shouting and became restrained' (Narayan 1974: 34). Grandmother Ammani and uncles compensated the loss? Contrast the endearing portrait of the father in *The Bachelor of Arts* (1973).

5. See *Grandmother's Tale* (1992) for more on this man.
6. Narayan reminisces particularly about his grandmother's gardening (1974: 3–4, 36). How important gardening—and by extension nature—is to the protagonists of the early gunas comedy! Narayan tried his own hand at horticulture and failed (Narayan 1974: 234ff). See Narayan's reflections on the subject in 'Gardening without Tears' (Narayan 1988).
7. The grand lady gets her book: *Grandmother Tale*, Narayan's last book.
8. As noted by Ram and Ram (1996b: 17):

> Narayan, a great walker until his eighties, has been a campaigner for a clean environment and for the preservation of parks and wide open spaces as the 'lungs' of urban centres. He is pained to witness the phenomenon of urban decay and deterioration of the environment. He wonders what civic authorities and the government can really do if people themselves are not more aware of the costs and the implications and continue the present tendencies.

And as S. Krishnan (1975: 42) has noted:

> He was particularly pleased by John Updike's recent review of his autobiography in the New Yorker: 'I thought it one of the best things written about me. Or for that matter about the writer's vocation. I was particularly interested by the point Updike makes about the writer as citizen since I feel exactly the same way. It made me feel good to know that Updike understands my involvement with people—as individuals and as a community.'

9. 'From his grandmother, the child Narayan absorbed folk-tales, a fluent narrative tradition, and an appreciation of Carnatic music' (Ram and Ram 1996b: 6). See *Grandmother's Tale* (1992) for more on Ammani's non-formal syllabus for her grandson. Also see Thieme (2008: 216, n. 23) who noted: 'Surprisingly, music as a theme and musicians as characters do not figure in Narayan's novels, rues our common friend, H.Y. Sharada Prasad [...].'
10. 'He possessed as many as four tape-recorders and used them regularly to tape bits of music picked up here and there [...]' (*Hindustan Times* 1968: 9). Two decades later David Davidar (1988b: 75) noted: 'Every winter he goes to Madras for a couple of weeks to attend the Madras Music Festival, something he has been doing for nearly four decades.'
11. 'I was rather alone,' said Narayan in *My Days* (1974: 31). Child specialists are of the belief that children in the company of pets grow to be caring adults (*The Hindu*, 17 January 1999, p. iv).
12. H.Y. Sharada Prasad in a letter to me dated 14 February 1992 wrote: 'You can spend hours with Narayan as long as you talk about people and life's little ironies and not expect him to hold forth on how to set the world right. He is not an oracle.' He also mentioned (1996: 27): 'After every meeting I leave with a feeling of wonder that a man so wise about the world is so free of the urge to play guru. Perhaps he fears that if he set the world right and people ran out of foibles, he would run out of themes to write about.' See also Narayan's comment on 'reforming the world' in his praise for Vikram Seth: 'The Vikram Seth type of writer is very rare, one who has no desire to change the world' (Davidar 1988a: 75). A scholar says about K.S. Venkataramani, a precursor to Narayan: '[H]e set himself to set the world right' (Ramaswami 1988: n.p.).
13. 'My full name with all the honours I aspired for' (Narayan 1992: 75).
14. See Narayan (1974: 35–6).
15. Even his elder maternal uncle Seshachalam was talented, 'he was a good raconteur' (Narayan 1974: 6).
16. R.K. Laxman noted: 'Mother was a lively influence on all of us. Father was like a Roman senator, aloof [...]. We seem to have inherited our discipline from our father and our sense of the light-hearted from mother' (Philipose 1990: n.p.).

   For notes on his mother, see Narayan (1974: 113). And in a lighter vein, see Narayan's paean to coffee and his mother's 'coffee ideals' (Narayan 1960: 9).

   Now see T.S. Satyan (2006: iv): 'He was a strict vegetarian and, when invited for a meal, would often tell my wife not to prepare many dishes. "I am happy with curd rice and lime pickle," he would tell her. He thought, "the sound of curds falling on a heap of rice is the loveliest sound in the world."'

17. 'Narayan lives happily with his mother and brothers in Mysore city. [...] His chief relaxation is playing with his nephews and nieces. He is greatly devoted to his daughter Hema, who is practically the first person to read his manuscripts these days' (Libra 1952: 27). See also Mehta (1962: 146). Several other interviewers confirm Narayan's attachment to his family (see the list of interviews and profiles in the bibliography).

    However, I sympathize with Vidia Naipaul; Narayan to some readers can be trying: 'Indians are more serene perhaps because of their background of religion' (Kalhan 1973: 1).

18. Problematic: Narayan's attitude to some classic Western writers, see Mehta (1962: 149). Also: 'For the writer in India, the ancient classics and legends are an indispensable background to his own writing. They are not merely historical curios, but form the very stuff of his cultural outlook. They stimulate his thinking and outlook, and give him facility of language' (Amirthanayagam 1982: 99).

19. But see *Frontline*, 18 October 1996. And also *My Days* (Narayan 1974: 126). During his early struggle to find his feet, Narayan visited this uncle.

20. Narayan put them in Kabir Street and turned his attention to them in some of his later novels: especially, *The World of Nagaraj*.

21. But see H.Y. Sharada Prasad (1996: 27):

    > To me as a young student of literature it was fascinating to see how real-life people became characters at his hands and how Narayan fitted Mysore into Malgudi by stripping it of its veneer of feudal sophistication. It is noteworthy that the Malgudi of *Swami and Friends* is a Tamil town, for Narayan had his schooling in the old Madras presidency, while the Malgudi of *The Bachelor of Arts* is Mysore, where Narayan did his B.A. The Malgudi of later novels takes on some new aspect of Mysore.

22. Mysore also nurtured Narayan's aesthetic sensibility. See Narayan (1974: 92).

23. The early years of 'good reviews, poor sales, and a family to support' (Ram and Ram 1996b: 5).

24. 'Narayan may not care much for fame but he cares for friendships' (Sharada Prasad 1996: n.p.). And Satyan (2006: iv): 'Though there was a difference of seventeen years between us, he was frank and outspoken while talking to me about his personal life and his early years as a writer. "Writing in the beginning was like going uphill.

Absolutely terrible. It was all frustration and struggle for more than fifteen years [...]."' Narayan's financial problems ended only after his novel *The Guide* was published in 1959. Narayan sustained hope and himself over three decades!

25. Friends in Mysore made the difference (Ram and Ram 1996a: 233). Satyan told me that they had had to go around from school to school and to college in Mysore, offering to donate a copy each of *Swami and Friends* that had been remaindered.

    M.N. Srinivas further stated: 'I moved to Bombay in 1936 for higher studies in Sociology. [...] But even while in Bombay I was active on Narayan's behalf; I met editors and tried to tell them that Narayan was willing to write for them, if only they had the good sense to invite him. [...] But Bombay was not ready to welcome Narayan: I was two decades ahead of my time' (Ram and Ram 1996b: 24).

    R.K. Narayan was a people's man. In his letter to me dated 14 February 1992, Sharada Prasad wrote: For 'Narayan's strength comes from his strong family ties and the simple delight he derives from knowing people—not the famous but the ordinary.' 'Incidentally, once I meet a person I always like to keep in touch' (Mehta 1962: 152).

    See also M.N. Srinivas (1996: 24–6).

26. R.K. Laxman said: 'Nobody noticed success or failure in our home. We all failed in our various classes, but nobody was too perturbed. I failed in SSC. Narayan failed in Inter in English. My parents regarded it as part of education' (Philipose 1990: n.p.). On Narayan's scholastic career, see Narayan (1974: 69).

    The young man who felt anything but comfortable in the Indian classroom went on to become Very Distinguished Professor who taught in various colleges and universities in the USA—his favourite country, next only to India—and he enjoyed the experience.

27. See Narayan (1974: 76). See also 'Sketches from Life', in *Indian Thought* (1997: 209). The making of a writer! See Anand (1948: 17).

28. '[A]nd if I am bogged down in letters, I become desperate for fear that I may miss my day's schedule. [... I] was sustained by the gambler's inexhaustible hope and a Micawberish anticipation of something turning up' (Narayan 1974: 174, 153).

29. Narayan tells Mehta (1962: 144):

    While I was standing at the carner [sic] of the equivalent of a big-city mall there [in Coimbatore], I saw a girl about eighteen. She was tall and slim and had classical features; her face had the finish and perfection of sculpture. She walked past me as in a dance. I kept looking for a gargoyle or some such imperfection, but there was none. It was spring and I was twenty-eight [Rajam, seventeen]. I suppose that had something to do with my falling completely and instantly in love with her.

30. Narayan found an outlet for his mood and feelings by writing a melodramatic and 'highly philosophical play examining the ideas of love, resignation and death'; the play titled *The Home of Thunder* was never published (Ram and Ram 1996a: 122).
31. Yet when it came to writing fiction, Narayan mentioned: 'I wished to attack the tyranny of Love and see if Life could offer other values than the inevitable Man-Woman relationship to a writer' (1974: 125).
32. Vimala Anandaram, Narayan's niece, shared a radio talk with me, whose transcript, undated but approved by Narayan with an autograph, is as follows:

    And to a very large extent, Narayan my uncle, helped in creating this wonderful world for us children. [...] Narayan would make sudden, surprise visits to the summer school Hema [Narayan's daughter] and I attended—just to ensure that the school staff was not torturing us! [...] [A]nd one day, I remember, he came full of righteous anger against the establishment and marched us off home in the middle of classes! [...] They were a closely-knit family, and we children loved nothing more than to curl up near our grandmother and listen to our elders' conversation, as they talked far into the night. [...] Uncle Narayan would regale us with anecdotes from his youth and keep us laughing with his droll sense of humour. [...] I remember the long walks I took with him and Hema. Often, on the way, he would stop and talk to people, or pause by a wayside shop, or on the fringe of a crowd—listening, observing. [...] Narayan's expressions matched his moods—a wicked sparkle in his eyes when he was amused—a steely look when he was not, and a fierce scowl when he was annoyed—we used to call it the bull-dog expression! [...] Narayan's inner strength, I believe, came from his sincere belief in God. Not for him the rituals and the fanfare but the firm and simple faith in Divinity.

33. Rajam's exact words were: 'What is the connexion between writing stories and not taking up a job?' In Ram and Ram (1996a: 128), the authors add: 'But her approach was generally indirect; she did not want to join the ranks of Narayan's naggers.'
34. '[M]y horoscope showed that I would be either a polygamist or a widower' (Mehta 1962: 145).
35. See also Narayan (1974: 193). And M.N. Srinivas (1996: 26): '[H]is preoccupations expressed themselves in a few ghost stories.' Which ones? M.N. Srinivas recalled to Ram in 1995 that his friend Narayan had become interested in the concept of time after his wife's death (Ram and Ram 1996a: 374–5).

36. A Margayya (*The Financial Expert*) or a Jagan (*The Vendor of Sweets*) of the later gunas comedy, too, reveals this resilience.
37. Davidar comments on this development in 'A Writer's Trials' (1988b: 81–2).
38. Narayan was more fortunate in his director, Nagabharana, on TV; with little Manjunath living the role of Swami, Narayan's first hero, the series was an outstanding success: another Kannadiga contribution to the writer's success. Earlier *The Financial Expert* had been made into a movie in Kannada as *Banker Margayya*. Much earlier the movie mogul Vasan, who had given him a slot in his story department during the War, had made *Mr. Sampath* into a film.
39. Narayan's frugal habits are shared by some of his characters, for example, the granny in *Waiting for the Mahatma*.
40. 'Every practical transaction for me is a painful ordeal', as quoted in 'Better Late', in *Reluctant Guru* (Narayan 1964b: 41).
41. Narayan gave me his sales figures in the late 1960s (Rao 1971: 79):

> Polish: five hundred thousand; Russian, two hundred thousand; middling in Italian, French, and Dutch; Hebrew: twenty thousand an edition; U.S. paperbacks: one hundred thousand each. Indian: on an average, two thousand a month; one edition of Lawley Road sold thirteen thousand; his own (Indian Thought) edition of *The Guide* sold over thirty thousand; and the Hindi translation of *The Guide* sold over thirty thousand.

I cannot believe it! Not the magnitude of commercial success for an Indian writer of those days, but that Narayan gave these figures to me! Except for that acerbic quip about the Indian poet, Narayan did not propose any changes in my transcript.

On the matter of Nobel speculation, see 'R.K. Narayan on R.K. Narayan' (*Frontline*, 15–28 November 1986; included as 'Reflections on Frankfurt', in *Salt and Sawdust* [1993: 119–24]) and 'Nobel Prize and All That', in *A Writer's Nightmare* (1988).

'One must set about one's work, whether producing a film or a book or whatever it may be, with an eye on one's own standards and purposes rather than on the pulse of an imaginary being called the average man' (Narayan 1997: 228).

42. 'Off the record and in daily conversation, he offers pithy comments or pungent, ironic insights on the ways of politicians and public figures. He deplores the phenomenon of communalism and the way women are still mistreated in different sections of Indian society' (Ram and Ram 1996b: 18).
43. 'I wish they would leave me and my books alone' (Mehta 1962: 151).

44. An insight remarkably anticipated by a Tamilian as early as 1937, B. Appasamy, reviewing *The Bachelor of Arts* in the *Hindu* (25 April 1937) said: 'Narayan wrote an English which was not incorrect, except from a pedantic point of view and which managed in a remarkable and mysterious way, to convey the flavour of the Tamil mind of his hero, that Tamil temperament which is tinged with irony and whimsy and yet contrives to be orthodox and conventional' (Ram and Ram 1996a: 92).

On Narayan's prose, see A.N. Kaul in Meenakshi Mukherjee (1977).

Mojtabai (1981: 25) said: 'At rare moments lumps occur, which may or may not reflect idiomatic Tamil usage, or, perhaps, only impatience with high style. It is entirely possible, however, that the few but inevitable moments of clumsiness found in each book represent deliberate policy.' See also Jhumpa Lahiri's introduction to *Malgudi Days* (2006) and Narayan on Indian English in 'A Literary Alchemy', in *A Writer's Nightmare* (1988).

45. 'One of my classmates was even warned not to waste his time reading Narayan's writings' (Satyan 2006: iv). Chinua Achebe (1995: 60) observes: 'But strange though it may sound some of [Europe's] ideas and precepts do exert an influence on our writers, for it is a fact of our contemporary world that Europe's powers of persuasion can be far in excess of the merit and value of her case.'

46. Later I read Rajagopal (1987: n.p.): '[Narayan] is dismissive of most other writers, and authors in the English language, whatever their success, barely concealing his contempt [...].' Narayan declined to participate in the reception in Mysore for Golding. 'But, you see, I don't read William Golding.'

However, Gowri Ramnarayan (2001: 20) offers a different view:

> This was one of Narayan's endearing qualities. He could be, and often was, very generous in praising others. But he was never guilty of sentimental effusions. He kept in touch with Indian writing in English, and had good things to say about several writers, particularly Vikram Seth. But I have heard him trounce pretension [...] once he said that modern writers mistook documentation for writing [...] ready to talk with undimmed insouciance, especially about yesteryear musicians. [...] He had an irreverent way of talking about people. There was mischief, but no malice.

See Croft's (1983: 32) interview: 'Narayan had very much enjoyed reading *Kanthapura* [...] he said he read "whatever comes my way".'

Now see also the acerbity of the conclusion to 'On Funny Encounters', in *A Writer's Nightmare* (1988): Narayan was a member of the Indian Parliament at the time.

47. See also my 'Arrival in Malgudi' (1990).
48. The brothers, so creative, were so different. 'The only serious disagreement between them arose during the Emergency. One supported it, while for the other, it was a tragedy. Later, when it was over, Narayan wrote a charming piece on their disagreement' (Philipose 1990: n.p.).

    See also 'Permitted Laughter', included in *Salt and Sawdust* (1993)—written in 1977, presumably after the Emergency had been lifted. See Indira Gandhi's observation on Laxman and Narayan's response to it in 'Indira Gandhi' (Narayan 1988).
49. Narayan observed to Susan Ram: 'When fifty years end, you find it just the same—the illusion of time, you know' (Ram and Ram 1996a: 52).
50. Satyan (2006: iv) noted: 'In one of his letters to me he [Narayan] wrote [from Chennai/Madras]: "I spend a lot of time reclining in my easy chair and thinking of Mysore, which now has become a sort of emotional landscape, which is quite satisfying! [...]".' He added: 'Whenever I went to Madras I used to find Narayan constantly talking to friends on a cordless telephone. "Without this I cannot survive," he would tell me.'

    R.K. Narayan, the people man; and into his nineties.
51. Ram and Ram (1996b: 18; italics mine) note:

    In a wistful little piece titled 'Eighty Plus' [...] he turns to the bright side: It takes time and practice to understand your potentialities and exert your inner strength. You must reach a minimum of eighty years to mellow down and realise your potentialities. [...] With hope, 'potent in earlier life', finding its area diminishing in later life, 'more mental space is usurped by memory', which is pleasant and sustaining only up to a stage. Beyond that stage, recollection becomes painful for most people. 'To forget the past and live in the present,' Narayan concludes, 'relishing the quality of every moment as it comes and letting it also pass, without regret, realising *the inevitability of the Eternal Flux* is the practical way to exist in peace'.

52. Ram reports: 'This writer's mind was extraordinarily clear until the last' (Ram and Ram 1996b: 10). The novelist discussed, in spite of the physician's warning not to strain himself, his next writing project of about '35,000 words'.

    See Croft (1983: 33): 'He has proved extremely adept at managing the lot Fate gave him.'
53. See Chapter 43 of *Yogananda*.

Chapter 2

1. B. Rajam Iyer (1973: 426) writes in his unfinished novel *Rambles in Vedanta*: 'Reader! This is a religious novel, but wait, you will have enough and more of it later on. Look at our Upanishads, how many stories they contain! So excuse me and wait. "They also serve who stand and wait."'

    On Madhaviah's fiction, see K.S. Ramamurti (1987: 189).

    As early as 1937, B. Appasamy said that the Indian authors writing in English were handicapped at times by 'their obviously propagandist motives' (Ram and Ram 1996a: 193). Iyengar (1962: 317) quotes Annada Sankar Ray: 'When Bankim wrote, the chief question was how to restore the national self-respect. In Rabindranath's time, it was how to bridge the East and the West. In this dynamic age, it is how to identify ourselves with the common people.' M.K. Naik (1985: 236) also confirms this aspect of the early Indian novel in English.

    See also T.W. Clark (1970: 16), Krishna Kripalani (1982 [1968]: 49), and Meenakshi Mukherjee (1971: 19). Holmström, however, offers a different insight on style (1973: 23, 27, 33).

2. 'All of India's energies were directed to the freeing of the country from foreign rule' (Narayan 1953: 119–20).

3. Narayan was not the first writer in India to aspire for a British imprint. Isvaran (1932) notes that Venkataramani's work was praised by *Times Literary Supplement* and E.V. Lucas.

    See also Williams (1973: xv, vol. 1): 'So small is the book-buying public in India and so specialized the English book market that most Indians who use English write consciously for readers in England, America, Australia and Canada.'

    V.S. Naipaul in *India: A Wounded Civilization* (1979: 19; emphasis mine) mentions: 'Narayan is one of the earliest and best of Indian novelists who wrote in English *for first publication in London*.'

4. Krishna Kripalani (1982 [1968]: 92) notes:

    It is doubtful if Sanskrit, as Panini standardized it, could ever have been the tongue in which Kalidasa or Jayadeva lisped to their mothers. Many distinguished writers of Hindi and Urdu—Premchand and Iqbal are illustrious examples—had to discard the dialects or speeches which were their mother tongues and adopted as their literary vehicles languages consciously cultivated for the purpose. Of late there are a number of noted poets and writers, Kaka Kalelkar in Gujarati, Bendre in Kannada, Yashpal, Balakrishna Rao and many others in Hindi, Kishan Chander and Bedi in Urdu, born to one language and writing successfully in another of their adoption.

5. T.S. Satyan (2006: iv) quotes 'our close friend and well-known sociologist Dr M.N. Srinivas': 'It must have required enormous courage and self-confidence to decide on creative writing in English as a source of livelihood. Somewhere in Narayan's gentle personality there is a steely layer which enabled him to face the tragedies which came his way—the death of his wife Rajam and daughter Hema.'

Here is another take on Narayan's achievement in his immediate context:

> The era in which R.K. Narayan was climbing the ladder of success as a writer [in Mysore], more importantly struggling in the mundane world of earning a decent livelihood, giants ruled the Kannada literary world. Names of B.M. Sri, Pu.Thi.Na [...] and others held sway. To carve out a local readership for his writings in English must be rated as a distinct part of R.K. Narayan's greatest achievement. (BRS 2006: ii)

6. This cosmopolitan awareness may have influenced his work in theme and style. See my essay 'Pounding Greene' (2002: 1, 4).

The support to Narayan came from a small number of young people: see Narayan (1974: 71); Ram and Ram (1996a: 110–11) for M.N. Srinivas's reminiscence; and Narayan (1974: 91) for his recall of Purna's reading *Swami and Friends* while it was being written.

7. 'I found out later that [Narayan] thought Kalki [a reputed writer in Tamil] wasted his talent on causes and movements instead of concentrating on the actual business of writing' (Ramnarayan 2001: xi).

'This career, with its utter frustration, has always seemed to me very tragic. And this type of anticlimax seems to be peculiar to our country' (Narayan 1997: 222). In this piece Narayan indicated the range of discouraging responses to his work during the early phase. See Ram and Ram (1996a: 110): 'Narayan was no "Gopal", however' [Gopal of the fictional sketch ends up taking a bank job]; and T.S. Satyan (2006: iv): 'He used to get upset when interviewers asked him if he was an inspired writer. "Please don't talk about inspiration and all that. It's a hard task to make one's writing readable."'

8. **A Professional at Work**

'In order to stabilize my income I became a newspaper reporter. [...] But I enjoyed this occupation, as I came in close contact with a variety of men and their activities, which was educative' (Narayan 1974: 145, 149).

And much later, in collaboration with his younger brother Laxman, Narayan updated *Mysore* (1939) as *The Emerald Route* (1977)—'our joint travelogue, *The Emerald Route*' (Philipose 1990: n.p.). Narayan also accepted an assignment to write the biography of the late Magsaysay, the famous Philippine president in 'Looking for Magsaysay' in his 1993 book *Salt and Sawdust*. See *My Dateless Diary* (Narayan 1960: 105); also 'Sketches from Life', in *Indian Thought: A Miscellany* (1997: 213, 219): 'But Gopal has in him the stuff of a literary workman. [...] But Gopal has grand faith in himself and idealism.' See Narayan in 'Junk', in *A Writer's Nightmare* (1988). And in Mehta (1962: 150): 'You must allow me my contradictions. I contradict myself all the time.'

9. Narayan had been successful in placing a piece with *Punch* and been paid six guineas for it (Ram and Ram 1996a: 118); that, probably, gave him the confidence to try his luck in London again. Now see *Frontline* (18 October 1996) for more on Narayan's writing and publishing success.

10. '[T]he author acquired an impressive collection of rejection slips in various colours and styles, "cold, callous ... impersonal and mocking"' (Ram and Ram 1996b: 7).

11. Greene concludes his first letter to Narayan: 'I hope this [*Swami and Friends*] will be only the first of a long series of books' (see Richard Greene 2007: 69). Incidentally, Greene also discovered Nabokov and Muriel Spark, among others.

12. And in the thick of his early battles, Kittu Purna, another Mysorean friend, 'advised him not to despair because, although "as a mood it is human [...] as an inspiration you will make your life a lie. And you will not lie"' (Ram and Ram 1996a: 200). In a letter to Graham Greene in 1935, Narayan wrote: 'Deluged under rejection slips I should have given up writing years ago and destroyed all my manuscripts but for Purna's persistence. He put a lot of stubbornness in me!' (Ram and Ram 1996a: 200). Purna was an interesting man in himself; for more on this man, see M.N. Srinivas (1996: 24–6).

Purna, however, died prematurely of alcoholism (Ram and Ram 1996a: 145).

13. Greene, in a letter dated 23 August 1934 that blends tact with candour, advised Narayan to trim his name, quoting the example of a writer who had not clicked with the British audience because he had a foreign-sounding name (Ram and Ram 1996a: 155).

14. See Desmond Hawkins in Ram and Ram (1996a: 407); and Ram and Ram (1996a: 162ff, 183) for more reviews.

15. Even before writing it, Narayan had dedicated it to his friend and called it 'Graham Greene's novel'.
16. On *The Bachelor of Arts*, see Narayan's letter to Greene in Ram and Ram (1996a: 176). See also Ram and Ram (1996a: 186).
17. See Ram and Ram (1996a: 319), and on what Narayan had to say in a letter to Greene on his celluloid experience, see Ram and Ram (1996a: 267). Narayan did not seem to remember this when he went ahead and signed a contract for the filming of *The Guide* (see 'The Misguided Guide', in *A Writer's Nightmare* 1988: 206).
18. Narayan said in a radio talk on 'The Business of Authorship':

    > I have often wondered [...] I chose to be a writer mainly because it's the only career which guarantees absolute freedom to live as one pleases, stay or go where one pleases, without waiting for anyone's approval or sanction—freedom to sleep, read, walk, and above all turn to one's work only at one's pleasure. This indeed is the meaning of the word 'freedom'; but there is a price to be paid for it. (Ram and Ram 1996a: 98)

    Narayan's early heroes care for 'freedom'!
19. In 'Meet R.K. Narayan' Vinaya Kumari (1949: 33) notes: 'Even now he always makes it a point to spare some time for *The Hindu* for he feels that he can never repay the initial encouragement extended to him by that paper [...].'
20. See Greene's letter to Narayan: 'I am anxious to see you published in Sweden as a possible Nobel prize-winner one day!' And again, conclusively: 'Nothing alters my opinion that you are one of the finest living novelists [...].' And the decency: 'Would it be possible for me to buy a copy of your *Mysore*? I want to add it to the collection of your books on my shelf' (Greene 2007: 228, 283, 330). See also my 2002 essay 'Pounding Greene'.
21. Again Narayan wrote to Greene on 10 June 1936: 'I hate to trouble you with my financial worries, but I shall be obliged to you if you can let me know if I can get freelance work (worth about 3 or 4 pounds a month) from any literary weekly there. If not, will no editor take at least a dozen of my short stories? No editor in this country wants any of my pot-boiling' (Ram and Ram 1996a: 176).

    Greene played the guru! 'Don't on any account be discouraged. You are far too good a writer to let a temporary setback affect you' (Ram and Ram 1996a: 176). See also Ram and Ram (1996a: 178). Again Narayan talks of his 'hollow finances' (Ram and Ram 1996a: 184).

    This was not all. After finding a publisher for *Swami and Friends*, Greene wrote to Narayan: 'It is a real joy to be of use to a new writer of your quality.' And it must have been a really satisfied Greene, who wrote to Narayan on 19 November 1953 after the American success of Narayan's novels: 'It's taken a long time for your genius to come through to the public, but at last it really seems to be making itself felt.' Ram quotes from Greene's last letter to Narayan on 2 July 1990: 'Do take care of yourself. Literature demands it.' Greene passed away on 3 April 1991. He was only a couple of years older than Narayan. Vivien Greene did not lag behind her husband (Ram and Ram 1996a: 186–7). For more on the Narayan–Greene relationship, see Ram and Ram (1996b: 18–19); and my 2002 essay 'Pounding Greene'. See also Ram and Ram (1996b: 17):

> Two American educational institutions, Boston University and the University of Texas at Austin, now house Narayan's manuscripts and private papers, making them accessible to researchers. The letters he received from Greene are with a private collector in New York while his letters to his British writer-friend are part of the splendid Greene Archive acquired by Boston College in the mid-1990s.

22. Thanks to Greene, by July 1936 Narayan, too, had engaged an agent: Pearn, Pollinger & Higham Ltd (Ram and Ram 1996a: 177).
23. From the three brief introductions Greene wrote, we can see what he valued in R.K. Narayan. Chekhov and Narayan each knew exactly what he wanted. Narayan said to his friend T.S. Satyan (2006: iv): 'I am a story teller and not a commentator.' Chekhov could not have agreed more.
24. **Writer at Work**
'I like to shut myself in for three or four hours at a stretch whenever I am in the mood for writing' (Kumari 1949: 33; emphasis mine). Kewlian Sio (1961: 44) notes: 'He never reads his own work, he told us later. After he finishes a book, he loses interest in it and turns to something new [...] he puts in four hours of desk work daily when writing a novel and he never thinks of his work outside those hours. He does not spend a great deal of time planning. "I am a great believer in words as *movers*! he said"'.
Croft (1983: 30) notes further: 'I asked him if he spent a lot of time choosing *le mot juste*. "No, I just write and then revise a great deal. A change here, make-up something there. [...] I don't have a complete plan, just a broad outline, and the book simply grows."'
See also Narayan (1960: 34; 1974: 24–5; 1985: 10).

Narayan once pulled up his kid brother, Laxman (1992): 'But his sense of pathos was so delicate that he saw in his own injunction a theme for a story and wrote the "Regal Cricket Club", which was about the harassment a boy suffered from un-understanding adults in his search for a place to play cricket.'

Chapter 3

1. 'I cut out a portrait of her [the British novelist, Marie Corelli] from *Bookman* and mounted it on my bookshelf' (Narayan 1974: 82).
2. Narayan wrote to his agents about *Prince Yazid*: 'Kindly destroy Prince Yazid. It has been a bad shock for me to learn that it is still in existence' (Ram and Ram 1996a: 428).
3. The launching of *Indian Thought* had only added to Narayan's depression (Ram and Ram 1996a: 359). The journal folded up after a brief career and will be remembered best for its printer who inspired the novelist to create one of his most memorable characters, Mr Sampath.
4. In other words, R.K. Narayan, 'the creative non-victim'! See Henry Reed's BBC talk of 29 October 1945 (Ram and Ram 1996a: 405), who commended Narayan for combining the amusing and the profound in a way 'we can't find anywhere else in English writing'. Profundity with a light touch! T.S. Satyan (2006: iv) says: 'Reading his essays, I felt that Narayan was chatting with me and making me laugh. [...] I also felt that Narayan was writing about people who were familiar to me in my own quiet, uneventful town of Mysore. A very thin line seemed to divide fiction from fact.'
5. **Tangential Topic: Narayan as a Literary Critic?**
   The non-academic Narayan rarely engaged in critical forays.
   See Narayan on Narayan in the *Illustrated Weekly of India* (23 July 1950: n.p.): 'In any case I can't undertake it because I myself do not understand what is evil and what is good in my various characters. They interest me only as Individuals and not as symbols or embodiments of this and that. What they say or do or think within the limits of their own worlds, what they hope for, what they suffer [...].'
   Next, Narayan's Leeds paper is his 'literary manifesto'; for Narayan seems to be speaking about his own work. (Chinua Achebe made his equally famous declaration, a perfect counterpoint, at the same seminar at Leeds.)
   See 'Fifteen Years', in *A Writer's Nightmare* (1988), Mehta (1962: 149), my interview with Narayan (Rao 1971); and Guy Amirthanayagam (1982).
   See also Narayan on Shakespeare:

Shakespeare was endowed with a mind so transparent and clear that it never coloured or obstructed the thoughts and words of his characters [...] he himself must have pursued his vocation without self-consciousness or a feeling of self-importance. There is no evidence that he was ever preoccupied with the theories of drama or culture, or ever assumed a solemn pose for a possible career of immortality. He must have gone about his work in a businesslike manner, confining his attention to the day-to-day practicalities of his profession. [...]

R.K. Narayan was speaking from his own experience about R.K. Narayan!

See *My Dateless Diary* (Narayan 1960: 34) for Narayan's working style decades later, which remains unchanged.

On the writing of *The Guide*, see *My Dateless Diary* (1960: 106, 110, 167, 172, 174, 182, 190, 199). And *My Days* (Narayan 1974: 53, 65, 66).

Also see 'Reluctant Guru', in *A Writer's Nightmare* (1988), Susan Ram (Ram and Ram 1996a: xxxv), and Foreword to *Salt and Sawdust* (1993).

But see Narayan's observation on another novel in *My Dateless Diary* (1960: 49). And the author's introduction to *Malgudi Days* (the 1996 edition).

Narayan on *The Painter of Signs*:

You know, I think some of my regular readers might be a bit dismayed by some of the biological references. [...] I suppose I have moved along with the times. This girl in my new novel is quite different. [...] To show her complete independence and ability to stand by herself. [...] She is a very strong character. All the same, when you read the novel you will find she is very feminine also. There is a conflict. That is the whole point.' (Krishnan 1975: 42)

6. '[A] stylistic balance between the formal and the colloquial, a preference for quiet irony, understatement, realistic subject matter, and a concern with man in relation to society' (King 1974: 5)—which also describes, in part at least, Narayan's work. See Anand on Indian literature in English (1948: 16).
7. Narayan had said: 'We have been mainly concerned with the matrix and types' (see S.V.V. 1963: 44).
8. See Anand on his own writing in English (1948: 17–18).
9. Narayan did not mention any of his precursors here or in his memoir; he offers us in his work something that recalls them: Rajam Iyer's hero is a *sthithaprajna*, a person who has mastered his mind, a mastermind by principle and practice. Narayan's own heroes from Chandran to Srinivas tend towards this goal; while, Madhaviah's social reformism anticipates Narayan's own fervent 'feminism' in *The Dark Room*.

10. Richard Greene (2007: xxxi) gives an instance of Narayan's influence on Graham Greene's book *Monsignor Quixote* (1982), 'with the lightness of touch': 'He may have learned that particular set of narrative skills from many years of reading R.K. Narayan.'
11. Walsh (1973: 11) offers yet another insight into Narayan's style: 'R.K. Narayan's language is beautifully adapted to communicate a different, an Indian, sensibility.'
12. Narayan commented elsewhere on his approach to style: 'I'm very unconscious of style, and I wish to make the style as unnoticed as possible—style should not be noticed' (Croft 1983: 29). Perceptive readers agree. William Walsh (1973: 13) was the first to attest: 'Narayan's work is singularly free of pretentiousness.' Nearer home, an anonymous interviewer in the *Times of India*, New Delhi, 28 March 1961, had put his finger on Narayan's distinction: '[A] gentle wit and irony and real wisdom and profundity underlie its seemingly superficial approach to people and things.' Smart!

    Later Narayan extends the idea of 'Indian' English in 'Toasted English', in *Reluctant Guru* (1964).

    Now see Theroux (1998: 205) on Naipaul's style.
13. Narayan mentioned Manohar Malgonkar as a novelist he liked (see Rao 1971: 82).
14. Compare Anand's 'social realism' in his first novel *The Untouchable* and Raja Rao's lyrical realism in his first novel *Kanthapura*.
15. There were probably other models for Narayan: the Bible and Mahatma Gandhi. See Iyengar (1962: 272) on the Gandhian influence.

Chapter 4

1. For another angle on Greene's praise for *Swami and Friends*, see M.N. Srinivas (quoted in Ram and Ram 1996b: 25): 'Incidentally, Greene knew, as only an insider could, the difficulties inherent in writing about children, and he greatly admired those who had successfully written about—or even for—children. [...] It was this sensitivity of Greene's that made him an admirer of *Swami and Friends*, and perceive Narayan's potential as a writer.' Elsewhere, Graham Greene confirms this in passing: 'English literature has too little that is light, lucid, and witty' ('Henry James: The Private Universe', in Greene 1962: 24). Also see my 2002 essay 'Pounding Greene'.
2. The child was continually in his mind throughout his life. See Vimala Anandaram quoted earlier in note 32, Chapter 1. See also 'Children' and 'Glimpses of Thumbi', in *Reluctant Guru* (1964). In the same

volume, in 'Thumbi's Schooling', Narayan sums up the child: 'Impulse was action; desire was possession.' In this world, the only false note is the adult—the alien, says Narayan. See also Narayan's 'No School Today', in *A Writer's Nightmare* (1988): the Monday-morning-feeling is a solid reality.

And see his maiden speech in the Rajya Sabha, the upper house of Indian Parliament, on 27 April 1989.

Sundaram (1973: 167–8) quotes the headmaster in *The English Teacher*: 'A time at which the colours of things are different, their depths greater, their magnitude greater, a most balanced and joyous condition of life; there was a natural state of joy over nothing in particular.' Trailing clouds of glory? See Narayan reminiscing about his nursery class experience (Narayan 1974: 11)—over sixty-five years after the writing of *Swami and Friends*. R.K. Narayan carried his childhood—as well as his youth—into his old age; a sure sign of a creative spirit.

3. Even in a later novel like *The Guide*, the central character is spurred into selfless action by his conscience.
4. Narayan the schoolboy had himself flounced out of school in almost similar circumstances (Mehta 1962: 141).
5. But see Holmström (1973: 36): 'It is not a novel about childhood [...].'
6. **Malgudi**
See William Walsh (1973: 12): 'The details suggest, surely and economically, the special flavour of Malgudi, a blend of oriental and pre-1914 British, like an Edwardian mixture of sweet mangoes and malt vinegar.'

Mehta (1962: 156) says: 'Compared to Faulkner's spiritual home, Malgudi is quiet, dusty, and uneventful. [...] But the bland cosmos of Malgudi is blessed with grace, because its people are innocent and comic—copies of Narayan, with his dazzling smile fixed on their faces.'

Anthony Spaeth (1992: 51) notes: 'Malgudi is changeless, little different now than in *Swami and Friends* [...] has become a kind of ancestral village for the whole literate world [...] subtle and enormously funny.'

Now for Narayan on Malgudi, see 'Misguided Guide', in *A Writer's Nightmare* (1988). He would remark later in a 1995 conversation: 'Malgudi is absolutely central to his literary achievement. [...] I am a treacherous writer when I move out of Malgudi' (Ram and Ram 1996b: 7). See also Narayan in Croft's (1983: 30) interview: 'An Imaginary town like that has great possibilities [...].' John Thieme (2008: 3, 4) notes: 'vivid "false geography". [...] [T]he town is the product of a particular coming together of social, religious and above all psychic forces, which undergo transformations as they interact with one another. [...] Narayan's open endings are the logical conclusion to works written in a discursive mode that is as hard to place generically as Malgudi is cartographically.'

See also Thieme (2008: 198, n. 40), citing A. Hariprasanna (author of *The World of Malgudi*): 'Malgudi is Coimbatore which has many of the landmarks—a river on one side, forests on the other, the Mission School and College, and, all the extensions mentioned in the novels.'

See Jhumpa Lahiri's introduction to *Malgudi Days* (1996).

7. On Narayan's views on the joint family, see *My Dateless Diary* (1960: 72, 121).
8. Anand, Raja Rao, and Narayan lived and worked into their nineties.
9. Narayan admired Vikram Seth: 'The Vikram Seth type of writer is very rare, one who has no desire to change the world' (Davidar 1988a: 75). See also Narayan's comments later on Vikram Seth's bestselling novel, *The Golden Gate*, in 'A Literary Alchemy', in *A Writer's Nightmare* (1988). For more definitive observations by the novelist on politics and his own style of writing, see Susan Ram and N. Ram in *Frontline* (1996b: 22): 'Politics is the least interesting aspect of life, in my view. I don't attach too much importance to it as literary material. Because most politically inspired novels die in good time. They don't last. It's only the human elements which last, not the political concepts or the pressures. They become just insignificant.'
10. This was published in England and included in *Dodu and Other Stories* (1943).
11. Mahatma Gandhi was known for similar sternness of self-analysis. See Narayan (1974: 17).
12. Now see Cynthia Vanden Driesen: '*Swami and Friends*: Chronicle of an Indian Boyhood', in McLeod (1994).

Chapter 5

1. 'Renunciation is ever a desirable means of attaining a higher life, and at some stage every character of goodness adapts it' (Narayan in *Gods, Demons, and Others* 1964a: 9).
2. A self-aware reader offering unaware misreading of Narayan's pre-Independence novels.

    And misconceptions have a way of perpetuating themselves, like precious heirlooms; see Mojtabai (1981).
3. 'The food was very Indian and very enjoyable' (Narayan 1974: 104). Narayan admires the Vedanta Society of Hollywood on Vine for its vegetarian restaurant (1974: 151).

4. See Narayan's own paean to coffee at the beginning of *My Dateless Diary* (1960).
5. 'I live from moment to moment. [...] Nothing really has gone wrong with me. I am deeply interested in life as a writer. That is perhaps why I have not gone mad' (Kalhan 1973: 1).
6. 'My inseparable friend at the college was Ramachandra Rao' (Narayan 1974: 95).
7. See also Ram and Ram (1996b: 17): R.K. Narayan's lifelong friendships with his Mysorean friends and N. Ram are testimony to our author's emotional maturity. Narayan's friendships have covered an interesting range, encompassing literature, scholarship, music, journalism, politics, and mundane, everyday life. Those who have remained close to him over the decades include M.N. Srinivas, H.Y. Sharada Prasad, veena maestro V. Doreswamy [sic] Iyengar, M.S. Subbulakshmi and her nonagenarian husband Sadasivam, and K. Natwar Singh. They have been what he terms his 'constant friends'.
8. The same character reappears in Narayan's fourth novel, *The English Teacher*, and the portrait is palpably the same.
9. For Narayan's thoughts on the bane of parochialism, see 'Pride of Place', in *A Writer's Nightmare* (1988: 147): 'Prejudice is only the other side of the medal of pride.' See also his views on atheists and theists in 'God and the Atheist', in *A Writer's Nightmare* (1988: 164–6).
10. Is he a 'non-Brahmin'? And that too during a period when the Justice Party was striking roots in the Tamil country of south India.

    See the significant essay 'Caste in the Fiction of R.K. Narayan' by D.A. Shankar in McLeod (1994: 137–46); though Shankar seems to have missed Veeraswami. Narayan may have downplayed some castes in his work; but some of his most engaging characters are drawn from the downtrodden, the dalits; for example, Ponni and Mari in *The Dark Room*; and in some memorable short stories, such as 'Annamalai', 'The Edge', and 'A Horse and Two Goats'.

    See also Thieme (2008: 11–12) for caste in Narayan.
11. This is Narayan's 'junior' maternal uncle, Venkataraman. See *My Days* (1974: 126). Narayan says: 'I can't tell wine from beer; all alcohol seems poison to me' (Mehta 1962: 157). Well, then, witness a rare spectacle: Narayan suffering from hangover! In 'Crowded Day', in *Salt and Sawdust* (1993: 155–62).
12. The first time Narayan's hero leaves Malgudi: Madras is a poor human contrast to Malgudi.
13. The indulgent eye of the one and only Geoffrey Chaucer in *General Prologue to the Canterbury Tales* looks back at his own youth in the portrait of the Squire: 'So hote he lovede, that bi nightertale/ He sleep

namore than doth a nightingale.' The remarkable difference is that Chandran and his creator are more or less the same age group!

14. See the thinly veiled autobiography in 'Sketches from Life' (Narayan 1997: 213): '[B]ecause he is without peace of mind unless he studies for two hours his college texts.'
15. This kind of conflict becomes prominent in the post-Independence novels, in *The Financial Expert* and *The World of Nagaraj*, and central in *The Vendor of Sweets*. But see Walsh (1982: 41) on the Narayan hero and the family. Walsh's Hebrew parallel is well taken; perhaps even Narayan's humour can draw a Jewish analogy?
16. One of the sidelights of Narayan's relationship with Graham Greene was Greene's horoscope: our Indian author had got it cast and forwarded to him.
17. The family will be at the very centre of his next novel, *The Dark Room*. In the post-Independence novels, like *The Financial Expert, The Guide, The Vendor of Sweets*, and *The World of Nagaraj*, fathers fail; the institution of the Hindu joint family itself crumbles. (See the summing up of Part III in this book.)
18. This so remarkably anticipates a passage from the Psychic Journal Narayan maintained after his wife Rajam's death; it means the novelist had it in him; and the tragic experience and the psyhic training only strenghtned his moral and spiritual tendencies; on 'hysterics and illusions'; see Narayan's note in his journal years later (Ram and Ram 1996a: 364). See Narayan's quotation from a Tamil mystic in *My Days* (1974: 149). See also Walsh (1982: 37): '[T]he "distracting illusions" are in the Indian tradition; the freedom from "hysterics" is the cool qualification introduced by Narayan. The complete phrase suggests the subdued association of seriousness and comedy which distinguishes the tone of these novels. […] The serious and the comic flow in and out of one another throughout in an intricate, inseparable alliance.'

Chapter 6

1. *The Dark Room* was published within one year of *The Bachelor of Arts* on 11 October 1938, a day after Narayan's thirty-second birthday.
2. Graham Greene wrote to Narayan: 'The ending I think is triumphantly successful' (Greene 2007: 84).
3. *My Days* presents several other colourful portraits, so promising, which Narayan has not used in his novels. See Susan Ram's introduction in Ram and Ram (1996a: xvi). See also Updike (1975).

NOTES | 277

4. See Ram and Ram (1996a: 211) for Narayan's later comments on *The Dark Room*; see also Promilla Kalhan (1973) and my 1971 interview, 'Tea with R.K. Narayan'.
5. Read *Saguna* by Krupabai Satthianadhan, the first autobiographical novel in English by an Indian woman writer. I doubt Narayan had read it, or was even aware of it; the book had been out of print until resurrected by an enterprising scholar.
6. Harrex (1977: 56–7, vol. 1): '[I]t appears that the most accomplished novelists to date are essentially tradition-oriented sensibilities, and that even among the committed writers tradition, artistically speaking, need not be destructively incompatible with social realism.'

    Also Harrex (1977: 27, vol. 2): '[Narayan] indicates time and again that for the modern Indian the traditional way provides the best guarantee of happiness and fulfilment.'
7. That strategy, of course, is R.K. Narayan's golden mean.
8. The custom behind the dark room: in Tamil Brahmin homes of those days one small room was kept apart for women to retire during their monthlies; when hurt or offended, women entered it to register their protest.
9. Gardening seems to be another gift from Ammani, Narayan's grandmother. See *My Days*. And Chapter 1 in this book.
10. This, of course, reads like a translation! Colourful expression; and, Graham Greene let it through.
11. Decades later, Daisy, the heroine of *The Painter of Signs* too feels the same way; she views the joint family in the 'modern' spirit: a large family is 'a mad house' (1976: 128). The reason she gives is characteristic: 'All individuality was lost in this mass existence' (130). Now she is in good company: 'To grow up in a large extended family was to acquire a lasting distaste for family life', Naipaul told an interviewer in 1983 (Theroux 1998: 283). Read Naipaul's masterpiece, *A House for Mr Biswas*.
12. A phrase which carries with it the stamp of Narayan's restraint; his 'classicism'.
13. 'The questions that engaged the minds of some of these novelists [of the nineteenth-century Indian Renaissance] were the position of women, the plight of the peasants and the decay of the old aristocracy' (Naik 1985: 236).
14. After the success of *Swami and Friends* in Tamil, the Tamil weekly *Ananda Vikatan* arranged for the translation of the writer's third novel *The Dark Room* (Ram and Ram 1996a: 318). Narayan told me (in the 1971 interview) that many Tamil women had written to him in praise of the novel.

Had Tamilians not found *The Bachelor of Arts* good enough?
15. 'So, like a slave whose freedom had just been purchased, I was happy, deliriously happy' (Satthianadhan 1998b: 131).
16. 'We all know that Narayan had a healthy respect for women, some of his women are strong, wise, and pragmatic often in contrast to the dreamy ne'er-do-well men around them' (Ramnarayan 2001: xi).
17. In *India: A Wounded Civilization* (1979), Naipaul complained that Narayan's novels did not prepare him for the 'cruel reality' of India.

Chapter 7

1. See the Psychic Journal in Ram and Ram (1996a: 355ff). Keeping a journal was uncharacteristic; see Ram and Ram (1996a: 356). All quotes in this section have been taken from Ram and Ram (1996a: 353–95).
2. For more on theosophy, see Ram and Ram (1996a: 308, 376–7). The style of *The English Teacher*, with its imagery in untypical intensity and profusion, seems to show residual impact of the novelist's reading during the period of his psychic training.
3. Brunton disclosed to Narayan that 'this was really [Narayan's] three hundredth incarnation in India' (Ram and Ram 1996a: 374). An evolved Indian!
4. See also the letter to Greene quoted in Ram and Ram (1996a: 215). Compare Naipaul: 'He felt "a very great fatigue and a great anxiety about the future". He was thirty-nine' (Theroux 1998: 171).
5. **Glimpses of Narayan's Professionalism**
'There was little suspension of literary activities during this traumatic period. Narayan's first collection of short stories, *Malgudi Days*, came out in November 1942. He was now working full steam on his fourth novel' (Ram and Ram 1996a: 259). See also Thieme (2008: 215, n. 21): '[H]is manuscripts in the Mugar Memorial Library Boston University and the Harry Ransom Humanities Research Centre at the University of Texas in Austin often suggest careful revision.'
6. On Narayan's view on sex in his novels, see 'Love and Lovers', in *A Writer's Nightmare* (1988: 174).
7. Narayan practised this special version of the mantra throughout his life, even while on a tour of the USA (see Mehta 1962).
   The Gayatri mantra is part of the thrice-daily adoration of the supreme reality prescribed, along with the sacred thread, to upper-caste boys during their *upanayanam*, the thread ceremony; it is a prayer for intellectual and spiritual enlightenment.

(a) Vivekananda's simplified translation: 'We meditate on the glory of that Being who has produced this universe; may He enlighten our minds.'

(b) Bhagavan Sri Sathya Sai Baba's translation: 'Oh Mother, Who subsist at all the three kalas [time periods], in all the three lokas [worlds] and in all the three gunas, I pray to You, to illumine my intellect and dispel my ignorance just as the splendorous sunlight dispels all darkness. I pray to You to make my intellect serene and bright.' In the Gayatri mantra, there is description and extollation, there is prayer and dhyana. It richly embodies in itself, all these three.

8. This relates to 'True Perspective' and 'Some Eternal Scheme': the heroes of the gunas comedy strive for a comprehensive vision of life. See also Ram and Ram (1996a: 356).
9. See also Spaeth's 1992 interview.

Chapter 8

1. 'What Brunton said to the writer sometime in 1941–2 was as follows: "You will write a book which is within you, all ready now, and it is bound to come out sooner or later, when you give yourself a chance to write"' (Ram and Ram 1996a: 329). For the creative effort it had taken, *The English Teacher* is unique. See also Ram and Ram (1996a: 229). And also Ram and Ram (1996b: 26): 'Narayan had worries about how the novel would be received but was reassured when Graham Greene wrote to him that at worst it was a thumping good ghost story, or words to that effect.'

Narayan published *Cyclone and Other Stories*, his third collection of short stories, under the Indian Thought imprint in 1945. By this time, he had already republished *Swami and Friends* and his travelogue *Mysore* in inexpensive Indian editions.

See Desmond Hawkins in Ram and Ram (1996a: 407). Besides offering prescient insights, the British writer comments on Krishna's poetic sensibility, and so early! For more reviews of *The English Teacher*, see Ram and Ram (1996a: 402ff).

2. In the same letter Greene (2007: 97) writes: 'If you ever have a snapshot of yourself and your child, do send it to us.' To appreciate the rapport between the two writers, see another letter: 'It seems a very long time since I heard from you and I hope that you can spare the time one day to let me know how you are.' See also my 2002 essay 'Pounding Greene'.

3. The Irish writer Elizabeth Bowen confessed to have wept; see Ram and Ram (1996a: 402ff).
4. Narayan says: 'But now I think the critics and readers are able to see my point of view. And they get a lot more out of the stories than I would have suspected. Because a piece of writing is not a thing a writer can judge fully himself. It's for others—the impact, what it stirs up in your mind. It's all very different' (Ram and Ram 1996b: 20).
5. '[U]nlike Narayan, Krishna keeps the seances a secret from his family' (Ram and Ram 1996a: 275, 285).
6. 'The title I originally thought of for *The English Teacher*—"Jasmine Home"' (Narayan in Ram and Ram 1996b: 21).
7. This is a limitation of the novel; the novelist cannot convince the reader of his hero's merit as a practising poet without specific examples. However, the novelist has established Krishna's poetic sensibility.
8. 'Religion does not consist in turning unceasingly towards the veiled stone, nor in approaching all the altars, nor in throwing oneself prostrate on the ground, nor in raising the hands before the habitations of gods, nor in deluging the temples with the blood of beasts, nor in heaping vows upon vows; but in beholding all with a peaceful soul' (Lucretius quoted in Radhakrishnan 1993: 124).
9. Experience Narayan's ecstasy on sighting the Grand Canyon in *My Dateless Diary* (1960: 154).
10. In *The English Teacher*, Krishna's feelings are 'an alchemy of inexplicable joy'. The phrase could have come from Narayan's early verse which he never published. Or, it is probably one more contribution from Paul Brunton and the theosophists.
11. 'Over the decades Narayan has carefully kept letters relating to both his literary and personal life. The Rajam letters are conspicuously missing' (Ram and Ram 1996a: 437, fn. 1).
12. But Krishna also reveals contempt for academic histories and academic criticism, which goes with his general attitude to work. Krishna the English teacher reads, and realizes the importance of reading ['I realized that I used to read better when I was in the hostel and had not become the head of a family' (73)]. But he cannot stand critics and commentators—so like Narayan!—the present company always exempted! See also page 73 of *The English Teacher*.

Narayan as a critic: For Narayan, Tolstoy, Joyce, and Faulkner were all 'bores' (Mehta 1962). See also my 1971 interview 'Tea with R.K. Narayan'. And: 'Those authors who have lost their significance were all

deliberate in their expression, they were all seeking effects—and these effects mean nothing at all today' (S.V.V. 1963: 45).
13. Such 'characters' act in some novels, such as *The Financial Expert* and *The Vendor of Sweets*, for better or for worse, as catalysts of critical change. The most spectacular interventionist, the role raised to mythic proportions, is Vasu in *The Man-Eater of Malgudi*.
14. 'Innermost self' and 'innermost aspiration': Krishna is the closest representation of an extraordinary man called R.K. Narayan: Srinivas, too, talks and behaves like his creator did: 'The question of a career seemed to him as embarrassing as a physiological detail' (11).
15. Is the family-and-home theme significant for Indians everywhere? In Naipaul's *A House for Mr Biswas* the family is a central theme. Mr Biswas resents his sojourn with his in-laws at Short Hills because he is lodged away from his family: '[I]t is a hotel-like arrangement'. A 'house' of his own to Mr Biswas is a family of his own.
16. See Ram and Ram (1996a: 244). The tolerant response of the modern medical practitioner is also predictable.
17. Behind the image of the 'mother' in Narayan's novels are happy memories of his own mother and his grandmother; but none behind the image of the 'father' in *The Bachelor of Arts*.
18. Compare other 'grannies' in *Waiting for the Mahatma* and *The Vendor of Sweets*; and Narayan's own native inclination for thrift established by his early struggle, when a half-rupee mattered.
19. Family relationships: the wife. Rare in modern literature! Romancing wedded love.
20. 'Narayan in this novel is the poet of Indian domestic life [...]' (Walsh 1982: 51). We also admire the novelist's restraint, detachment, when he wrote that scene, composed that monologue, from recent memories.
21. See also Narayan (1974: 144).
22. Krishna later prays: 'God bless this child and protect her' (Narayan 1945: 70).
23. Maugham confirms Narayan's appeal to the West; see Ram and Ram (1996a: 409).
    A good family is a good family anywhere in the world: see Narayan's experience in an American home (1960: 58ff).
24. See also Narayan (1974: 18).
25. 'Only remember that the planet you live in with its problems is just a speck compared to the rest of the Universe I have to mind. Good Bye. Are you now convinced of my existence?' ('God and the Atheist', in *A Writer's Nightmare* 1988: 164–6). Yahweh in *Job*!

26. *Amor vincit omnia*: Love conquers all.

Chapter 9

1. The first of Narayan's novels to be serialized in the *Illustrated Weekly of India*, Bombay; the novelist had arrived even in India.
2. **Real Life Model for Srinivas as Editor**
Narayan's senior uncle 'had given up all lucrative activities on principle and was [among other things] dedicated to bringing out a literary weekly to revive Tamil classics, and all his resources were utilised for it' (Narayan 1974: 128, 132).
3. Of particular interest is Narayan's search, Ram and Ram (1996a: 369, 370). See Narayan's advice to an American in *My Dateless Diary* (1960: 35).
4. '[H]e would invariably spend some time at his favourite port of call—the City Power Press—owned by his dear friend Cheluva Iyengar—Sampath to his friends. He was the earliest printer of Narayan's paperback titles and the short-lived sturdy [sic] journal *Indian Thought*. Sampath turned up in several incarnations in Narayan's books' (Satyan 2006: iv). Narayan seems to have excelled in depicting characters modelled on real-life people; see also the short story 'Annamalai' based on his own gardener.
5. See Thieme's 2002 editorial on Naipaul's reputation among academics.
6. Narayan's description of the creative moment! Sounds so authentic, as does what follows in the next observation: 'taking dictation'.
7. If a species of 'Orientalism' affected the thinking of colonial intellectuals, Naipaul's 'Karmism', India ideology, held critics and academics in thrall for about five decades. Now see my 2003 essay 'Naipaul's Nobel Poise?'.
8. 'Narayan disliked anything extravagant, sentimental, "artificial"' (Ram 2006).
9. The period produced a good number of 'India experts'; the 'new' nation was doing badly; and its postcolonial plight made for good 'copy', especially in the West.
10. And this attack Nicholas Grene terms (2011: 2), accurately, 'an extremely influential critique'.
11. Here is Naipaul (1979: 26) on how attentively—obsessively—he had read *Mr. Sampath*:

> Now, reading *Mr Sampath* again in snatches on afternoons of rain during this prolonged monsoon, which went on and on like the Emergency itself—reading

in Bombay, looking down at the choppy sea, and the 1911 Imperial rhetoric of the British-built Gateway of India that dwarfed the white-clad crowd; in suburban and secretive New Delhi, looking out across the hotel's sodden tennis court to the encampment of Sikh taxi-drivers below the dripping trees; on the top veranda of the Circuit House in Kotah, considering the garden, and seeing in mango tree and banana tree the originals of the stylized vegetation in the miniatures done for Rajput princes, their glory now extinguished, their great forts now abandoned and empty, protecting nothing, their land now only a land of peasants; in Bangalore in the south, a former British army town, looking across the parade ground, now the polo ground, with Indian army polo teams—reading during the Emergency, which was more than political, I saw in *Mr Sampath* a foreshadowing of the tensions that had to come to India, philosophically prepared for defeat and withdrawal (each man an island) rather than independence and action, and torn now between the wish to preserve and be psychologically secure, and the need to undo.

'Our master of the English Sentence'! Select details here connote India's feudal and colonial past (the 'wonders'), and aggravates Naipaul's 'Emergency' depression, already convinced that he had before him a 'wounded' nation: 'wounded' is his favourite concept (see Diana Athill's 2001 book *Stet* for a balanced portrait of the 'wounded' writer). The 'India' before him—the India of his 'perception'—'the background', may have overwhelmed the sensitive writer engaged in reading *Mr. Sampath*; add to this 'reading in snatches'.

Incidentally that passage is remarkable, one paragraph of over 200 words; and the syntax—one long period—must be unique in Naipaul. The prosecution counsel building his case?

Now see Thieme (2008: 209, n.13): 'Narayan admired *Mr Biswas*, referring to it as "a very charming novel" and "almost like Malgudi" in an interview with Andrew Robinson, *The Independent*, 24 October 1986, 14.'

12. Part autobiography, part fiction: a decent blend!
13. In a much later novel, sex is recognized as the 'normal drive of a force which kept the whole world spinning' (Narayan 1976: 98).
14. Clarity of vision is a top priority to the protagonists of Narayan's gunas comedy.
15. Next, Naipaul picks up Narayan's *The Vendor of Sweets* for his critical analysis (1979: 38–41) and seeks to convince the reader that the 'other-worldliness' of Narayan's heroes had not changed: Srinivas had abandoned his friend, and Jagan abandons his son; the latter novel is 'a confused book'. The 'confusion', Naipaul does not realize, lies nearer home: apart from the authorial distancing made obvious throughout the book, Naipaul seems unaware of the difference between

vanaprasthya and sanyasa, the final asrama, stage in life. Naipaul also plays down the practical instructions Jagan gives to his cousin about his son and his live-in mate and his own business. And Naipaul ignores the evidence of the chequebook Jagan carries with him to carry out his piety project: renunciants have no use for cheques.

We have here a classic case of the impressions of an 'outsider' (however creative) failing to perceive the authentic—ear-to-the-ground—experience of a creative insider. The year 1961 is significant; Narayan had just published *The Man-Eater of Malgudi*; Vasu or no Vasu, Malgudi-India goes on, and Narayan tells Naipaul 'India will go on!' And India has gone on.

16. The last time darkness flowed out was in *The Dark Room* (1938: 179–80).
17. This recalls the ending of *Swami and Friends*. The ruby is known as the stone of royalty; it was believed that as long as a piece of ruby was around, wealth would be too (see 'Astrological Benefits of Ruby Stone'; available at http://www.sarnam.com/rubystone.asp, accessed on 23 February 2011). The colour red also represents rajas guna; white, sattva; and black, tamasa. The colour symbolism can also be seen in the 1953 Hollywood movie *Shane*.
18. The most eventful part of his life as it is reflected in Narayan's own memoir (Ram and Ram 1996a: xvii–xviii). See also Williams (1973: 15).
19. 'Mr. Sampath is the first of a line of comic eccentric villains to enliven Narayan's world' (Williams 1976: 57). See Walsh (1982: 61): '[A] passage from an enclosed, contemplative and personal art to a more strenuously imagined and external fiction.'

Chapter 10

1. A similar situation recurs in Narayan's final novel *The World of Nagaraj*.
2. See Narayan's short story 'Guru'.
3. Now see Fakrul Alam, 'Narrative Strategies in Two Narayan Novels', in McLeod (1994).

Chapter 11

1. For the novelist's preparatory research into the Mahatma and his comments on the Mahatma, see Ram and Ram (1996b: 21).
2. See Ram and Ram (1996a: 179), my interview with Narayan, and *My Days* (1974: 17). See also Croft (1983: 31): 'I liked Mahatma's

personality, and I wanted to somehow recount this. He was a very impressive person. I didn't know him personally but I went to many gatherings he addressed.'
3. See 'Emden' for yet another Kabir Street character.
4. See Jhabvala's *A Backward Place*, Vikram Seth's *A Suitable Boy*, Khushwant Singh's *I Shall Not Hear the Nightingale*, and Achebe's *A Man of the People*.
5. Madeleine Slade quotes Romain Rolland in her 1960 book *The Spirit's Pilgrimage*.
6. '[P]erformance of one's duty should be independent of public opinion', as quoted in Andrews (1930: 136).
7. 'It would be difficult to find in the East a freer and fuller life for young girls than that which can be seen and witnessed every day at Sabarmati' (Andrews 1930: 322).
8. Other novelists like Khushwant Singh, Jhabvala, and Vikram Seth, too, testify to the post-Gandhi degeneration.
9. Graham Greene (in Richard Greene 2007: 207) comments:

> I was fascinated by the portrait you have drawn of Gandhi and that period in India's history, the love story of Sriram and Bharati is charming, and the whole book will do you credit I am sure. I confess myself a little disappointed to find politics entering Malgudi if only because politics either date or become history, and I have always felt a kind of eternal quality in Malgudi.

Politics! Refer to Vidia Naipaul's comments on politics in Narayan's novels.

Chapter 12

1. Was the novelist familiar with the *Kamasutra*?
2. Narayan was a great admirer of Shakespeare. See his paper 'What Shakespeare Means to Me' presented at a seminar at Sahitya Akademi, New Delhi, in 1964. Was Narayan practising the five-act construction of Shakespearean drama?
3. The last time we heard this voice was in *The English Teacher*, as the hero Krishna's mother bids farewell to her bereaved son.
4. The old lady has made it clear already: 'After all, I wish to spend the rest of my days in my own house' (186).
5. 'But the novel is open-ended. We have only Graham Greene's comment that Raju dies,' Shyamala Narayan tells me in a personal e-mail. Experience also V.Y. Kantak's exasperation: 'Should we reduce

what is essentially a question to the banality of a facile affirmation?' (Srinath 2012: 30).

On Rosie–Nalini as well as on Raju, see Narayan's short story 'Selvi'. Which is earlier?—the short story!

Chapter 13

1. Such as: 'A Career', 'The Roman Image', 'Old man of the Temple', 'The Tiger's Claw', 'A Night of Cyclone', Uncle's Letters', 'Engine Trouble', 'Lawley Road', and 'Around a Temple'.
2. Narayan's experience in the film studios may have influenced his craft. See Part I of this book.
3. 'I am sure fiction will soon start going back to the original lofty notions of romance, to the dignity of the man–woman relationship [...]' (Krishnan 1975: 42).
4. As Sri Sathya Sai observed:

    If there is righteousness in the heart,
    There will be beauty in the character.

    If there is beauty in the character,
    There will be harmony in the home.

    When there is harmony in the home,
    There will be order in the nation.

    When there is order in the nation,
    There will be peace in the world. (Leslie-Chaden 1997: 490)

5. See Satyan (2006) on Narayan's dietary preferences, and Nicholas Grene (2011) for Satyan's criticism of Narayan.
6. For Narayan the music critic, see also Narayan's short story 'Selvi': 'Her voice possessed versatility and reach which never failed to transport her audience' (Narayan 1943a: 160).
7. Walsh calls it 'motiveless hostility'—after Bradley's 'motiveless malignity'?—which is closer to the reality of Shakespearean tragedy. Who reads Bradley today?
8. As mentioned earlier other post-Independence Indian novelists, too, present a dismal spectacle of Gandhi's countrymen abandoning the Mahatma's values within years of his assassination. However, this desertion may have taken place even during the Mahatma's lifetime: as suggested by the conclusion of Raja Rao's first novel *Kanthapura*—the hero drifts away from the Mahatma, and to Nehru. See also *Chronicles*

of *Kedaram* (1961) by K. Nagarajan. So what helped the Indian nation to get up and go ahead? The kind of introspection and values reflected in our novelists/writers and their work!
9. That sounds like someone we know: 'Small men, small schemes....'! (Naipaul 1979: 19).
10. That little detail about saving up a blade confirms the economic status of our schoolteachers even today, especially in rural India.
11. Narayan admired Nehru, Sen's bête noir.
12. See also Amirthanayagam (1982: 99).
13. 'An education bereft of culture is worthless like a counterfeit coin. What is meant by culture? It is the realization of the inherent Divinity in man and making it manifest in one's way of life' (Sri Sathya Sai Baba 2002; discourses delivered in 2001).
14. 'I must be absolutely certain about the psychology of the character I am writing about, and I must be equally sure of the background' (Krishnan 1975: 42).
15. 'I do not have much time for women characters. Men generally crowd them out. There is more variety among men. Women in this country are conventional and true to type. However I created a dancer in *The Guide*' (Kalhan 1973: 1). 'I find women uninteresting' (Davidar 1988b: 79).

    Now see Britta Olinder's 'The Power of Women in R.K. Narayan's Novels', in McCleod (1994: 96–104).
16. See Forster's tribute quoted in the introduction to this book. See also Croft (1983: 30): 'The best word to describe Narayan would probably be "simplicity".'

Chapter 14

1. Narayan sings praises of the joint family in *My Dateless Diary* (1960: 72–3).

Chapter 15

1. See Narayan's letter to me reproduced on page ii of this book.
2. Now see Narayan's short story, 'The Edge' (*Malgudi Days* 1996). Also in the same collection the extraordinary short story 'The Hungry Child', a fascinating piece, perhaps unique, sort of postscript to *The Painter of Signs*: the Daisy-wife dream of the novel is succeeded now by a child he dreams of.

Chapter 16

1. 'Where some incredible experience has to be narrated, it is the Talkative Man who talks. He's a good link, he can link people up, he's a man who goes through the city like a breeze everywhere, who knows lots of people. He links up a lot of background and personalities and landmarks very convincingly. Everybody is his friend. And he's a generous man' (Narayan in Ram and Ram 1996b: 22).
2. See Narayan's long story 'Second Opinion', in *Malgudi Days*.

Chapter 17

1. 'This anthropomorphic tale was the culmination of the writer's longstanding interest in animal behaviour and psychology' (Ram and Ram 1996b: 16).
2. This is more than 'high-class comedy': this is philosophical comedy.
3. Perhaps acceptance of old age is tougher than accepting death.
4. Given Narayan there could be other possible reincarnations: '[A]nd probably in the next janma, I will be not an author, but a publisher' (Narayan in Mehta 1962: 155). And puckish Narayan in Davidar (1988a: 81) interview: 'I'll probably be a Tamil writer in my next janma. A fourth-rate Tamil writer.'

Chapter 18

1. Narayan dedicated this book to Susan Ram and N. Ram 'whose involvement with Nagaraj at every stage, since inception, helped [him] no end'.
2. Vidia Naipaul had been too hasty by a half-century: the non-doers jostle each other in Nagaraj's world.

Chapter 19

1. Compare the novelist's use of the same epic legend in *The Dark Room*, of the pre-Independence phase.
2. Or, his friend Greene was no longer there to edit the manuscript.
3. See the letter reproduced on page ii of this book; also my 1992 review, 'R.K. Narayan's Mutable World'.

Chapter 20

1. 'As an artist, he was not interested in the theory of fiction and elaborate concepts structured by literary critics. As a novelist, he

NOTES | 289

wanted his stories to be read. As an essayist, he was content to chat. He read widely and had clear views on the quality of the writings of the younger generation' (Satyan 2006: iv).
2. Ruth Prawer Jhabvala, more insightful on matters Indian than many Indian writers, has titled one of her novels *The Nature of Passion*.
3. This might help us appreciate that one remark of Narayan's which outraged Naipaul in *An Area of Darkness* (1964: 227): 'Whatever happens India will go on.' See R.K. Laxman to Pamela Philipose (1990: n.p.): 'Actually, I envy Narayan. He is an optimist. I am a pessimist. He's always looking forward with hope—even at 84.'
4. See 'India and America', in *A Writer's Nightmare* (1988: 233–40).
5. On the author's social equation Kohli (1970: n.p.) notes:

> The author is both a spokesman of the community in which he lives and of himself. The problem is that absolute freedom of spirit matters most to a writer. He must be free from himself, even from his own previous standards, in order to be able to be a good creative writer. At the same time he is also a product of the society in which he lives and has to keep a very tricky balance between the two. So I would say to be a good creative writer one needs to be a combination, a perfect combination of the two.

See also Croft (1983: 31):

> He valued his privacy and autonomy, and these seemed central to his personality. [...] I just started writing with no definite views on what I should be doing. I probably preferred to be a writer because it leaves you free to travel, to go from place to place and not to have to apply for leave. It leaves you absolutely free.

6. **R.K. Narayan and Humanism**
Narayan's spiritual philosophy as represented by Srinivas belongs to the central tradition of the Hindus—affirmed by Swami Vivekananda, Mahatma Gandhi, Bhagavan Sathya Sai Baba, as well as by all major religions! The following quotes might help the reader understand Narayan and *Mr. Sampath* better as well as Narayan's pure Humanism—and any major religion for that matter.

Swami Vivekananda writes:

> [The real Dharma] is doing good to others. [...] Injuring others is sin. [...] Loving others is virtue; hating others is sin. [...] Dedication to selfless unattached work is a cardinal principle of Hinduism. One must grow and expand beyond the limits of one's own faith. Love all beings as the temple of God. One must have a firm faith in the brotherhood of a universal life. Fanaticism, bigotry and intolerance of other faiths and beliefs have no place in life. (Bose 1994: 84)

Mahatma Gandhi also represents the same centrality:

I want to find God, and because I want to find God, I have to find God along with other people. I don't believe I can find God alone. If I did, I would be running to the Himalayas to find God in some cave there. But since I believe that nobody can find God alone, I have to work with people. I have to take them with me. Alone I can't come to Him. (Mandela 1999: n.p.)

Bhagavan Sri Sathya Sai has also offered the same route to spiritual fulfilment: 'Serving hands are holier than lips that pray' (Orefjaerd 1995: 45).

Narayan's spiritual philosophy as represented by Srinivas belongs to this central tradition of the Hindus.

7. See 'In the Confessional', in *A Writer's Nightmare* (1988: 41–2). Also: 'I prefer a reader who picks up a book casually. I write a story or a sketch primarily because it is my habit and profession and I enjoy doing it. I'm not out to enlighten the world or improve it' ('The Writerly Life', in *A Writer's Nightmare* 1988: 199–201).

8. See *Frontline*, 15–28 November 1986; also as 'Reflections on Frankfurt', in *Salt and Sawdust*. See Narayan's psychic journal in Ram and Ram (1996a) where the writer accepts even his wife's death as part of the larger divine scheme; and this is post ordeal!

9. As quoted in *Hindustan Times*, 9 December 1973. '[D]elivered a long discourse on joint-family living in India' (Narayan 1960: 49). See also Mehta (1962: 158).

10. Here's a handy overview, a simplified ready-reckoner, for what it's worth, of Narayan's range of humour.

- First, the species that is a matter of sensibility, an expression of personality, comic intelligence. In Meredith's words: Narayan enjoys 'predisposition towards comedy'; he enjoys 'an esteem for common-sense'—it is humour of commonsense—and it precludes sentimentalism. This species lights up his non-creative work, his essays, causeries, etc.
- Humour as a social grace, for amusement or entertainment; load every rift with wit and humour: the professionalism of a humourist, with witticisms, etc. 'So difficult to convince others that I'm not myself' (Narayan 1988: 68–71).
- Deflatory humour (opposite of the self-important/sardonic)—inherited perhaps from his grandmother Ammani and his mother Gnanambal. Krishna in *The English Teacher* addressing himself in the mirror.
- Rally humour: light raillery. In *Mr. Sampath* the delicious comment on Somu's abortive bridge speech: '[M]asterly declamation [...] as old as humanity [...]' (1949: 71).

- Rough-and-tumble humour: slapstick. The studio scene in *Mr. Sampath*.
- Humour of social satire: 'It is difficult to get any money, even of living people, out of the Post Office Savings bank!'
- Equalitarian humour: of the comedy of family relationships in Narayan's pre-Independence novels, as in the flower-thief episode of *The Bachelor of Arts*.
- Humour of sexual comedy: a remarkable development in the post-Independence period and goes with it. But not until *The Man-Eater of Malgudi*: the delicious midnight scene when Rangi, the prostitute, accosts Nataraj.
- Still-life humour: using a material object as a provenance of fun; for example, Queen Anne chair and the Heidelberg printing machine in *The Man-Eater of Malgudi*; and the harmonium in *The World of Nagaraj*, 'pains of composition and the harmonium music of Saroja' (1990: 134). And finally, as vision—vis comica—a philosophic feature: humour is an integral aspect of Narayan's vision. Narayan's humour is inalienable from the seriousness and assurance of his vision, Narayan's humour is a structural attribute of Narayan's vision ('intricate alliance', as Walsh discovered so early); it flows from Narayan's gunas comedy: 'A wholeness of world view'—resulting in a quiet, refined, assured restraint—'pure, terse, proper'. And hearty laughter, inaugurated by *Mr. Sampath*, in the post-Independence novels, where 'evil' is a palpable presence and Narayan realizes an 'incredible relation between mud and God'.

11. See Dyson's introduction to *The Idea of Comedy* for comments on Western comedy (Wimsatt 1969: 15).
12. See my 1992 review 'R.K. Narayan's Mutable World'.
13. H.Y. Sharada Prasad wrote in the *Hindu*, 29 August 1988:

    Two of Narayan's books do bear out the theory of his being an export-oriented writer—his *Ramayana* and *Mahabharata*. He wrote them at his foreign publisher's instance. And his mother, a remarkable person from any measure, confessed that she was grateful to the Americans, for without them Kunjappa (Narayan's pet name at home) would not have studied the epics. Narayan spent months with scholars having the Sanskrit originals read out and interpreted.

    But see Croft's (1983: 27) interview: 'No, I wrote them for myself. I don't have any audience in mind at all, at any time.'
    See Indira Gandhi's opinion: 'Your *Ramayana* is very readable, of course, but one misses in it details and the poetic grandeur of the epic' (Narayan 1988: 218–21).

Bibliography

Works by R.K. Narayan

(in chronological order)

'How to Write an Indian Novel'. 1933. *Punch*, Narayan's first article published abroad without a by-line, 27 September, n.p. Reprinted in the *Sunday Economic Times*, Bangalore, on 29 May 1994, n.p.

Swami and Friends. 1935. London: Hamish Hamilton. Also published by Indian Thought Publications, Mysore, in 1971.

The Bachelor of Arts. 1937. With an introduction by Graham Greene. London: Nelson. Also published by Indian Thought Publications, Mysore, in 1965; reprinted in 1985.

The Dark Room. 1938. London: Macmillan. Also published by Indian Thought Publications, Mysore, in 1960, and Mandarin Paperbacks, London, in 1990.

Mysore: A Travel Record. 1939. Mysore: Government of Mysore; reprinted in 1968.

Malgudi Days. 1943a. Mysore: Indian Thought Publications. Also published by Viking Books, New York, in 1982; reprinted in 1996. A different edition, with an introduction by Jhumpa Lahiri, was published by Viking Books and Heinemann, New York, and London, respectively, in 1982.

Dodu and Other Stories. 1943b. Mysore: Indian Thought Publications.

Cyclone and Other Stories. 1944. Madras: Rockhouse & Sons.

The English Teacher. 1945. London: Eyre and Spottiswoode. Also published as *Grateful to Life and Death* by Michigan State College Press, East Lansing, in 1953; and Indian Thought Publications, Mysore, in 1955; reprinted in 1968.

An Astrologer's Day and Other Stories. 1947. London: Eyre and Spottiswoode.

Mr. Sampath. 1949. London: Eyre and Spottiswoode. Also published by Indian Thought Publications, Mysore, in 1956; reprinted in 1971. Published in the USA as *The Printer of Malgudi* in 1957, and serialized in the *Illustrated Weekly of India* in 1949.

'Obituary'. 1950. *The Illustrated Weekly of India*, Bombay, 23 July, p. 23.

The Financial Expert. 1952. London: Methuen. Also published by Indian Thought Publications, Mysore, in 1970.

'The Fiction Writer in India: His Tradition and His Problems'. 1953. *The Atlantic Monthly,* vol. 192, no. IV, pp. 119–20.

Waiting for the Mahatma. 1955. London: Methuen. Also published by Indian Thought Publications, Mysore, in 1969.

Lawley Road and Other Stories. 1956a. Mysore: Indian Thought Publications.

Next Sunday: Sketches and Essays. 1956b. Mysore: Indian Thought Publications.

The Guide. 1958. New York: Viking Books; and London: Methuen. Also published by Indian Thought Publications, Mysore, in 1963; reprinted in 1970.

My Dateless Diary. 1960. Mysore: Indian Thought Publications. Previously serialized in the *Illustrated Weekly of India* in 1958.

The Man-Eater of Malgudi. 1961. New York: Viking Books. Also published by Heinemann, London, in 1962; Indian Thought Publications, Mysore, in 1968; reprinted in 1994. Also serialized in the *Illustrated Weekly of India* in 1961.

Gods, Demons, and Others. 1964a. Illustrated by R.K. Laxman. New York: Viking Books. Also published by Heinemann, London, in 1965.

Reluctant Guru. 1964b. Mysore: Indian Thought Publications. Also published by Orient Paperbacks, New Delhi, in 1974.

'English in India'. 1965a. In John Press (ed.), *Commonwealth Literature: Unity and Diversity in a Common Culture,* pp. 120–4. London: Heinemann.

'What Shakespeare Means to Me'. 1965b. *Indian Literature,* vol. 8, no. 1, pp. 19–22.

The Vendor of Sweets. 1967. Mysore: Indian Thought Publications; and New York: Viking Books. Also published as *The Sweet-Vendor* by Bodley Head, London, in 1967.

A Horse and Two Goats. 1970. New York: Viking Books; and Mysore: Indian Thought Publications; reprinted in 1986.

The Ramayana. 1972. Delhi: Hind Pocket Books.

My Days: A Memoir. 1974. New York: Viking Books. Also published by Chatto & Windus, London, in 1975; and serialized in the *Illustrated Weekly of India* in 1974.

The Painter of Signs. 1976. New York: Viking Books. Also published by Heinemann, London, in 1977; Indian Thought Publications, Mysore, in 1978; and serialized in the *Illustrated Weekly of India* in 1976.

Talkative Man. 1977. Mysore: Indian Thought Publications. Also published by Heinemann, London, in 1986.

The Emerald Route. 1978a. Bangalore: Government of Karnataka.

The Mahabharata. 1978b. Illustrated by R.K. Laxman. New York: Viking Books; and London: Heinemann. Also published by Indian Thought Publications, Mysore, in 1979.

A Tiger for Malgudi. 1983. New York: Viking Books; London: Heinemann; and Mysore: Indian Thought Publications; reprinted in 1993.

Under the Banyan Tree and Other Stories. 1985. London: Heinemann.

'R.K. Narayan on R.K. Narayan'. 1986. *Frontline*, Madras, 15–28 November, n.p.

A Writer's Nightmare: Selected Essays, 1958–1988. 1988. New Delhi: Penguin Books.

A Story-Teller's World. 1989. With an introduction by Syd Harrex. New Delhi: Penguin Books; reprinted in 1990.

The World of Nagaraj. 1990. London: Heinemann; and Madras: Indian Thought Publications.

Grandmother's Tale. 1992. Mysore: Indian Thought Publications.

Salt and Sawdust: Stories and Table Talk. 1993. New Delhi: Penguin Books.

The Indian Epics Retold. 1995. New Delhi: Penguin Books. (Omnibus edition including *Gods, Demons, and Others*, *The Ramayana*, and *The Mahabharata*, illustrated by R.K. Laxman, and an introduction by S. Krishnan.)

My Days: A Memoir. 1996. Special commemorative edition, with a Foreword by R.K. Narayan. New Delhi: Viking Books.

Indian Thought: A Miscellany. 1997. With an introduction by S. Krishnan. New Delhi: Penguin Books.

The Writerly Life: Selected Non-Fiction. 2001. New Delhi: Viking Books.

Interviews/profiles

(in chronological order)

(For interviews abroad, see John Thieme's *R.K. Narayan* [2008].)

Caution by H.Y. Sharada Prasad as in his article in *The Hindu* (29 August 1988: 9): 'With journalists, especially interviewers, he likes to play little games.'

Kumari, Vinaya. 1949. 'Meet R.K. Narayan', *The Illustrated Weekly of India*, 23 January, p. 33.

Libra. 1952. 'R.K. Narayan: A Writer of Distinction', *The Illustrated Weekly of India*, 5 October, p. 27.

The Times of India. 1957a. 'Indian Theme Holds Glamour in West: Mr R.K. Narayan's Tour Impressions', Bombay, 20 June, n.p.

The Times of India. 1957b. 'The Bombayman's Diary', Bombay, 24 June, n.p.

Rosenthal, H.M. 1958. 'A Talk with R.K. Narayan', *The New York Times Book Review*, 23 March, p. 5.

Sio, Kewlian. 1961. 'Meeting R.K. Narayan', *The Miscellany (Writers Workshop)*, no. 5, March–April, p. 44.

The Times of India. 1961. 'Mr. Sampath in Town', Delhi, 28 March, n.p.

The Miscellany (Writers Workshop). 1961. 'Interview with R.K. Narayan', no. 8, September–October, p. 50. Transcript of the interview on All India Radio.

Mehta, Ved. 1962. 'The Train Had Just Arrived at Malgudi Station', *The New Yorker*, 15 September, pp. 135–72. Also included in Ved Mehta. 1971. *John Is Easy to Please*. London: Secker and Warburg.

S.V.V. 1963. 'A Visitor from Malgudi', interview with R.K. Narayan, *The Illustrated Weekly of India*, Bombay, 23 June, pp. 44–5.

Hindustan Times. 1968. 'City People Have Forgotten How to Live, Laments Author', Delhi, 2 December, p. 9.

Kohli, Suresh. 1970. Interview with R.K. Narayan, *Indian and Foreign Review*, 15 May, pp. 13–20.

Jagannathan, N.S. 1970. 'Deepest Things Are Same Everywhere', interview with R.K. Narayan, *Hindustan Times*, August, pp. 7–8. Reprinted in the *Sunday Economic Times*. 1994, Bangalore, 29 May, pp. 7–8.

Mehta, Ved. 1972. 'R.K. Narayan', extracted from an essay in *John Is Easy to Please*, *The Illustrated Weekly of India*, 23 January, pp. 34–5, 37.

Kalhan, Promilla. 1973. 'The Legend of Malgudi', *Hindustan Times*, Delhi, 9 December, p. 1.

Krishnan, S. 1975. 'A Day with R.K. Narayan', *Span*, New Delhi, April, pp. 42–3.

Croft, Susan E. 1983. 'Interview with R.K. Narayan', in Bhagwat S. Goyal (ed.), *R.K. Narayan: A Critical Spectrum*. Meerut: Shalabh Book House, pp. 25–33.

Rajagopal, D.R. 1987. 'The Genius from Malgudi', *The Statesman*, Delhi, 27 October, n.p.

Davidar, David. 1988a. 'I Have Written Enough', interview with R.K. Narayan, *Sunday*, Calcutta, 3–9 January, pp. 75–81.

———. 1988b. 'A Writer's Trials', *Sunday*, Calcutta, 3–9 January, p. 80.

Sharada Prasad, H.Y. 1988. 'A Reluctant Guru', *The Hindu*, Madras, 29 August, p. 8.

Murari, T.N. 1990. 'R.K. Narayan', *The India Magazine*, Delhi, April, pp. 40–7.

Philipose, Pamela. 1990. 'My Brother, Myself', interview with R.K. Laxman, *Sunday Observer*, Delhi, 28 October, n.p.

BIBLIOGRAPHY | 297

Ramnarayan, Gowri. 1990. 'An Experience in Self-Discovery', *The Hindu*, Madras, 26 January, p. ix.
Doctor, Geeta. 1992. 'The Indian Summer of R.K. Narayan', *The Illustrated Weekly of India*, 19–25 September, n.p.
Ram, Susan and N. Ram. 1996a. 'Narayan of Malgudi Sixty-Five Years of Story-Telling', *Frontline*, Madras, 18 October, pp. 4–27.
———. 1996b. 'R.K. Narayan in First Person', excerpts from interviews by Ram's 'Over the Past Decade', *Frontline*, Madras, 18 October, pp. 1–4.
Sharada Prasad, H.Y. 1996. 'Portrait of a Novelist as a Young Man', *Frontline*, Madras, 18 October, pp. 26–7.
Srinivas, M.N. 1996. 'A Writer's World: A Long-Time Friend Reminisces', *Frontline*, Madras, 18 October, pp. 24–6.
Davidar, David. 2001. 'Remembering a Literary Wizard', *The Hindu*, 20 May, p. 3. Available at http://www.thehindu.com/thehindu/2001/05/20/stories/13200676.htm, accessed on 27 September 2016.
Ram, Susan and N. Ram. 2001. 'Living Memories: R.K. Narayan's Mysore Years, A Neighbour's Memories', *Frontline*, Madras, 26 May–8 June, n.p.
Ramnarayan, Gowri. 2001. 'Glimpses of a Private Person', *The Hindu*, Madras, 3 June, p. 20.
O'Yeah, Zac. 2006. 'Meeting Mr. Narayan', *The Hindu*, Madras, 3 December, p. 3.
Ram, Susan and N. Ram. 2006. 'The Reluctant Centenarian', *The Hindu*, Chennai, 8 October, pp. 1–11.
Anandaram, Vimala. n.d. 'R.K. Narayan, As I Knew Him', n.p., transcript of a radio talk autographed by Narayan, copy made available by Mrs Anandaram.

Books and Articles on R.K. Narayan

(in alphabetical order)

(For a complementary Bibliography see John Thieme's *R.K. Narayan* [2008].)

Amirthanayagam, Guy (ed.). 1982. *Writers in East-West Encounter: New Cultural Bearings*. London: Macmillan.
Andrews, C.F. 1930. *Mahatma Gandhi's Ideas, Including Selections from His Writings*. London: Macmillan.
Balachandran, P.K. 1996. 'Malgudi's Very Own Swami', review of Ram and Ram's *R.K. Narayan*, *Hindustan Times*, 9 June, p. 4.

BRS. 2006. *The Star*, Special Supplement, Mysore, 10 October, pp. i–iv.
Chaudhuri, Amit. 2001. 'A Bottle of Ink, a Pen, and a Blotter', *London Review of Books*, vol. 23, no. 15, 9 August, pp. 21–2.
Chew, Shirley. 1973. 'A Proper Detachment: The Novels of R.K. Narayan', in William Walsh (ed.), *Readings in Commonwealth Literature*, pp. 58–74. Oxford: Clarendon Press.
Cronin, Richard. 1989. *Imagining India*. London: Macmillan.
Daily Telegraph. 2001. 'R.K. Narayan', obituary, 14 May, n.p.
Das, G.K. 2001. 'Here's God's Plenty', *The Pioneer*, 20 January, n.p.
Derrett, M.E. 1966. *The Modern Indian Novel in English: A Comparative Approach*. Brussels: Universite Libre de Bruxelles.
Deshpande, Shashi. 2001. 'Paved the Ways', obituary, 15 May. Available at www.outlookindia.com, accessed on 15 May 2001.
The Economist. 2001. 'Obituary: R.K. Narayan', London, 24 May, n.p.
Frontline. 1996. 'A Bibliography', Madras, 18 October, n.p.
Garebian, Keith. 1976. 'Narayan's Compromise in Comedy', *The Literary Half-Yearly*, Mysore, vol. 17, no. 1, pp. 70–81.
Gaur, June. 2001. 'Imaginary Homeland', *The Hindu*, Madras, 3 June, p. 9. Available at http://www.thehindu.com/thehindu/2001/06/03/stories/1303067s.htm, accessed on 27 September 2016.
Gerow, Edwin. 1977. 'The Quintessential Narayan', in Meenakshi Mukherjee (ed.), *Considerations*, pp. 66–83. New Delhi: Allied Publishers.
Ghosh, Amitav. 2001. 'On R.K. Narayan', obituary, May. Available at http://www.amitavghosh.com/essays/rknarayan.html, accessed on 29 June 2016.
Gooneratne, Yasmine. 1976. 'Traditional Elements in the Fiction of Kamala Markandaya, R.K. Narayan and R.P. Jhabvala', *World Literature Written in English*, vol. 16, no. 1, pp. 121–4.
Greene, Graham. 1937. 'Introduction', in *The Bachelor of Arts*, pp. v–x. London: William Heinemann. Also featured in the 1978 reprint edition of the same book.
Grene, Nicholas. 2011. *R.K. Narayan*. Horndon: Northcote, British Council.
Harrex, S.C. 1977. *The Fire and the Offering: The English Language Novel of India, 1935–1970*, 2 vols. Calcutta: Writers Workshop.
Hemenway, Stephen Ignatius. 1975. *The Anglo-Indian Novel*, vol. 1 and *The Novel of India: The Indo-Anglian Novel*, vol. 2. Calcutta: Writers Workshop.
Hindustan Times. 2001. 'Humanism, Harshness: R.K. Narayan Captured It All', 14 May, n.p.
Holmström, Lakshmi. 1973. *The Novels of R.K. Narayan*. Calcutta: Writers Workshop.

Iyengar, K.R. Srinivasa. 1962. *Indian Writing in English*. Bombay: Asia Publishing House; second edition (revised and enlarged) in 1973.
Kantak, V.Y. 1970. 'The Achievement of R.K. Narayan', in C.D. Narasimhaiah (ed.), *Indian Literature of the Past Fifty Years, 1917–1967*, pp. 133–46. Mysore: University of Mysore.
Kaul, A.N. 1972. 'R.K. Narayan and the East–West Theme', in A. Poddar (ed.), *Indian Literature*, pp. 233–79. Shimla: Indian Institute of Advanced Study. Reprinted in Meenakshi Mukherjee (ed.). 1977. *Considerations*. New Delhi: Allied Publishers.
Krishnan, S. 1996. 'Narayan at Ninety', *Outlook*, New Delhi, 16 October, n.p.
Lahiri, Jhumpa. 2006. 'Narayan Days', *Boston Review*, July/August, p. ix. Available at http://bostonreview.net/BR31.4/lahiri.html, accessed on 14 August 2006. Also included in the Penguin Classics edition of *Malgudi Days*, 2006.
Laxman, R.K. 1992. 'Oh Brother!' *Frontline*, Madras, 31 January, pp. 99–102.
———. 1996. 'My Brother, R.K. Narayan', *Sunday Times, The Times of India*, 1 December, n.p.
———. 1998. *The Tunnel of Time: An Autobiography*. New Delhi: Viking Books.
Madhavan, A. 2001. 'There's Mourning in Malgudi', *Indian Review of Books*, Chennai, 16 May, pp. 5–6.
Majumder, Piyali. 1992. 'Anachronistic', *The Illustrated Weekly of India*, 19–25 September, n.p.
Maugham, Somerset. 1938. '"Encourage Your Writers": Somerset Maugham's Advice, A Novelist's Impressions of South India', *The Hindu*, 18 January, p. 8.
McCutchion, David. 1969. *Indian Writing in English: Critical Essays*. Calcutta: Writers Workshop.
McLeod, A.L. (ed.). 1994. *R.K. Narayan Critical Perspectives*. New Delhi: Sterling Publishers.
Menon, Sadanand. 1994. 'How Will They Celebrate This in Malgudi's Streets?' *Sunday Economic Times*, Bangalore, 29 May, n.p.
Mishra, Pankaj. 2001. 'The Great Narayan', *The New York Review of Books*, 22 February, pp. 44–8.
Mohan, Ramesh (ed.). 1978. *Indian Writing in English*. Bombay: Orient Longman.
Mojtabai, A.G. 1981. 'India's Master of Comedy', *The New Republic*, 25 April, pp. 25–8.
Mukherjee, Meenakshi. 1971. *The Twice-Born Fiction*. New Delhi: Arnold-Heinemann.

Mukherjee, Meenakshi (ed.). 1977. *Considerations*. New Delhi: Allied Publishers.

———. 2000. *The Perishable Empire: Essays on Indian Writing in English*. New Delhi: Oxford University Press.

———. 2001. 'The Magician of Malgudi: A Personal Tribute to R.K. Narayan', *Gentleman*, Bombay, August, n.p.

Murthy, Sachidananda. 2001. 'The Forbidden Fruits of Malgudi', *The Week*, Kochi, 27 May, n.p.

Nagarajan, T.S. 2007. 'The Walk, The Talk', *Vijay Times*, Bangalore, 5 January, p. 9.

———. n.d. 'The R.K. Narayan Only I Knew'. Available at https://churumuri.wordpress.com/tag/n-ram, accessed on 12 November 2015.

Naik, M.K. 1982. *A History of Indian English Literature*. New Delhi: Sahitya Akademi.

———. 1983. *The Ironic Vision: A Study of the Fiction of R.K. Narayan*. New Delhi: Sterling Publishers.

——— (ed.). 1985. 'The Achievement of Indian Fiction in English', in *Perspectives on Indian Fiction in English*, pp. 235–52. New Delhi: Abhinav.

Naik, M.K. and Shyamala A. Narayan. 2001. *Indian English Literature 1980–2000: A Critical Survey*. Delhi: Pencraft International.

Naik, M.K., S.K. Desai, and G.S. Amur (eds). 1968. *Critical Essays on Indian Writing in English*. Dharwad: Karnataka University.

Naipaul, V.S. 1964. *An Area of Darkness*. London: Andre Deutsch.

———. 1979. *India: A Wounded Civilization*. Harmondsworth: Penguin Books.

———. 2001. 'The Master of Small Things', *Time Asia*, 9 June, p. 77.

Narasimhaiah, C.D. (ed.). 1967. *Fiction and the Reading Public in India*. Mysore: University of Mysore.

———. 1969. *The Swan and the Eagle*. Shimla: Indian Institute of Advanced Study.

———. 1970. *Indian Literature of the Past Fifty Years, 1917–1967*. Mysore: University of Mysore.

Narasimhan, C.V. 2001. 'Remembering R.K. Narayan', *Frontline*, Madras, 26 May–8 June, pp. 1–4.

Padmanabhan, Manjula. 1999. 'Rural India's Sole Chronicler', review of *A Town Called Malgudi: The Finest Fiction of R.K. Narayan*, *The Pioneer*, 4 September, n.p.

Paranjape, Makarand. 2001. 'Last Halt at Malgudi', obituary, *The Indian Express*, New Delhi, 14 May, p. 9.

Ram, Atma (ed.). 1981. *Perspectives on R.K. Narayan*, in Indo-English Writers Series No. 3. Ghaziabad: Vimal Prakashan.
Ram, N. 1991. 'A Literary Friendship: Graham Greene and R.K. Narayan', *Frontline*, Madras, 13–26 April, pp. 117–20.
———. 1996. 'A Rare Friendship', *Frontline*, Madras, 18 October, pp. 18–19.
———. 2001a. 'R.K. Narayan', *Guardian Unlimited*, London, 14 May, n.p.
———. 2001b. 'Writer's Writer R.K. Narayan, 1906–2001: Malgudi Will Live, Forever', *Hindustan Times*, Delhi, 20 May, n.p.
———. 2001c. 'Malgudi Will Live Forever: Writer's Writer, R.K. Narayan 1906–2001', *Hindustan Times*, New Delhi, 20 May, n.p.
———. 2001d. 'Malgudi's Creator: The Life and Art of R.K. Narayan (1906–2001)', *Frontline*, Madras, 26 May–8 June, pp. 1–13.
Ram, Susan. 2001. 'Narayan of Malgudi: In Homage and Celebration', *The Hindu*, 20 May, pp. 1–2.
Ram, Susan and N. Ram. 1996a. *R.K. Narayan: The Early Years, 1906–1945*. New Delhi: Viking Books.
———. 1996b. 'Narayan of Malgudi: Sixty-Five Years of Story-Telling', *Frontline*, Madras, 18 October, pp. 5–27.
Ramachander, S. 2007. 'The English Teacher', *The Hindu*, Chennai, 14 January, p. 3. Available at http://www.thehindu.com/todays-paper/tp-features/tp-sundaymagazine/the-english-teacher/article2274845.ece, accessed on 27 September 2016.
Ramanan, Mohan G. 2013. *R.K. Narayan: An Introduction*. Bengaluru: Foundation Books and Cambridge University Press.
Rao, A.V. Krishna. 1969. *The Indo-Anglian Novel and the Changing Traditions*. Mysore: Rao and Raghavan.
Rao, V. [Ranga Rao] Panduranga. 1970. 'The Art of R.K. Narayan', *Journal of Commonwealth Literature*, vol. 3, pp. 29–49.
———. 1971. 'Tea with R.K. Narayan', *Journal of Commonwealth Literature*, vol. 8, pp. 79–83.
———. 1978. 'The Cratsmanship of R.K. Narayan', in Ramesh Mohan (ed.), *Indian Writing in English*, pp. 57–64. Bombay: Orient Longman.
———. 1990a. 'Arrival in Malgudi', *Frontline*, Madras, 17 February–2 March, pp. 94–7.
———. 1990b. 'Contemplative Tiger', *London Magazine*, June/July, pp. 85–94.
———. 1992. 'R.K. Narayan's Mutable World', *The Sunday Times*, Bombay, 11 October, p. 7.
———. 1996a. 'A Contemplative Tiger', *Biblio*, New Delhi, October, n.p.

Rao, V. [Ranga Rao] Panduranga. 1996b. 'Satvic Sensitivity', *The Indian Express*, Delhi, 6 October, n.p.

———. 1998. 'R.K. Narayan Self-Aligned', in three parts, *The Hindu*, 21 June, 28 June, and 5 July, pp. xii–xiii, iv, iv.

———. 2001a. 'R.K. Narayan: An Indian Perspective', *The Journal of Commonwealth Literature*, vol. 36, no. 2, pp. 117–21.

———. 2001b. 'Realistic Fiction-Writer in English', *Indian Literature*, vol. 203, pp. 198–205.

———. 2001c. 'Area of Lightness', *Outlook*, New Delhi, 28 May, pp. 56, 58.

———. 2001d. 'Narayan's Unique Comedy', *The Hindu*, 7 October, pp. ix, xii.

———. 2002. 'Pounding Greene', *The Hindu*, Madras, 3 February, pp. 1, 4.

———. 2004. *R.K. Narayan*. New Delhi: Sahitya Akademi.

———. 2006. 'R.K. Narayan's Comedy', *Biblio*, September–October, pp. 10–11.

Rao Jr, Parsa Venkateswara. 2001. 'We Never Really Honoured Narayan', *Sunday Express Magazine*, 20 May, n.p.

Reddy, Sheela. 2001. 'Swami and Friends', *Outlook*, New Delhi, 28 May, p. 59.

Satyan, T.S. 2006. 'Remembering R.K. Narayan', *The Star*, Special Supplement, Mysore, 10 October, pp. i, iv.

Singh, Khushwant. 2001a. 'Modesty? Blasé!' *The Week*, Kochi, 27 May, n.p.

———. 2001b. 'Blue Hawaii Yoghurt', *Outlook*, 28 May, p. 60.

Singh, Natwar K. 1983. 'A Tiger for Malgudi', *The Times of India*, 7 August, n.p.

———. 1996. 'RKN: Evergreen at 90', *Hindustan Times*, New Delhi, 6 October, n.p.

———. 1997. 'My Man in Yadavagiri', *The Pioneer*, 29 November, p. 13.

———. 2001. 'Man from Malgudi', *The Asian Age*, Kolkata, 14 May, n.p.

Spencer, Dorothy. 1960. *Indian Fiction in English: An Annotated Bibliography*. Philadelphia: University of Pennsylvania Press.

Srinath, C.N. (ed.). 2012. *R.K. Narayan: An Anthology of Recent Criticism*. Delhi: Pencraft International.

Sundaram, P.S. 1973. *R.K. Narayan*, Indian Writers Series, vol. VI. New Delhi: Arnold-Heinemann.

Tharoor, Shashi. 2001. 'Comedies of Suffering', in 'The Shashi Tharoor Column', *The Hindu*, 8 July, p. 3.

Thieme, John. 1998. 'Letter from India', *The Literary Review*, March, pp. 42–3.

———. 2004. 'The Double Making of R.K. Narayan', in Satish C. Aikant (ed.), *Essays in Honour of Professor C.D. Narasimhaiah*, pp. 172–91. Delhi: Pencraft International.

———. 2008. *R.K. Narayan*. Manchester and New York: Manchester University Press.
The Times. 2001. 'R.K. Narayan', obituary, London, 14 May, n.p.
Times Literary Supplement. 1958. 'Well Met in Malgudi', 19 April, n.p.
Trivedi, Harish. 1990. 'Narayan, Narayan!' review, *The Times of India*, New Delhi, 13 May, n.p.
———. 1996. 'The Greeneing of Narayan', review, *The Pioneer*, New Delhi, 9 November, n.p.
Updike, John. 1975. 'R.K. Narayan: A Writer Immersed in His Material', *Span*, vol. 16, no. 4, pp. 38–9. Originally published in *The New Yorker*, 2 September 1974, pp. 80–2.
Varadarajan, Tunku. 2001. 'In Chennai Once, A Sweet Talk with Narayan', *The Indian Express*, New Delhi, 19 May, n.p.
Vedantam, Vatsala. 1997. 'A Celebrity at Home', *The Hindu*, Madras, 4 May, p. xvi.
Walsh, William. 1960. 'The Intricate Alliance: The Novels of R.K. Narayan', *Review of English Literature*, vol. 2, no. 4, pp. 91–9.
———. 1964. *A Human Idiom: Literature and Humanity*. London: Chatto & Windus.
———. 1973. *Commonwealth Literature*. London: Oxford University Press.
———. 1982. *R.K. Narayan: A Critical Appreciation*. New Delhi: Allied Publishers.
White, Ray Lewis (guest ed.). 1983. *R.K. Narayan: The American Reception, 1953–1970*, The Journal of Indian Writing in English, Special Number, vol. 12, no. 1.
Williams, Haydn Moore. 1973. *Studies in Modern Indian Fiction in English*, 2 vols. Calcutta: Writers Workshop.
———. 1976. *Indo-Anglian Literature, 1800–1970: A Survey*. Bombay: Orient Longman.

Miscellaneous

(in alphabetical order)

Abrahams, Peter. 1989. *Mine Boy*, African Writers Series. London: Longman Publishing Group.
Achebe, Chinua. 1958. *Things Fall Apart*. London: William Heinemann.
———. 1995. 'Colonialist Criticism', in Bill Ashcroft, Gareth Griffiths, and Helen Tiffin (eds), *The Post-Colonialist Studies Reader*, pp. 57–61. London: Routledge.
Ali, Ahmed. 1940. *Twilight in Delhi*. London: Oxford University Press.

Anand, Balwant Singh. 1961. *Cruel Interlude*. Bombay: Asia Publishing House.

Anand, Mulk Raj. 1947. *Untouchable*. London: Hutchinson International Authors.

———. 1948. *The King-Emperor's English; or, The Role of the English Language in the Free India*, with an afterword by Maulana Abul Kalam Azad. Bombay: Hind Kitabs.

Anantanarayanan, M. 1961. *The Silver Pilgrimage*. New York: Criterion Books.

Ashcroft, Bill, Gareth Griffiths, and Helen Tiffin (eds). 1995. *The Post-Colonial Studies Reader*. London: Routledge.

Athill, Diana. 2001. *Stet: An Editor's Life*. London: Granta Books.

Book of Job, Holy Bible New International Version. 1978 [1973]. Colorado: International Bible Society.

Bose, Nemai Sadhan. 1994. *Vivekananda*. New Delhi: Sahitya Akademi.

Brown, Charles Philip. 1992. *Telugu–English Dictionary*. New Delhi and Madras: Asian Educational Services.

Brunton, Paul. 2003 [1934]. *A Search in Secret India*. London: Ebury Press.

Butcher, Maggie (ed.). 1983. *The Eye of the Beholder: Indian Writing in English*. London: Commonwealth Institute.

Chatterjee, Bankim Chandra. 2008. *Rajmohan's Wife*. Delhi: Rupa & Co.

Chekhov, Anton. 1991. *The Steppe and Other Stories*. UK: Everyman's Library Classics.

———. 2004. *Ward No. 6 and Other Stories, 1892–1895*. New Delhi: Penguin Books.

Clark, T.W. (ed.). 1970. *The Novel in India*. London: George Allen & Unwin.

Contemporary Indian Literature, A Symposium. 1959 [1957]. New Delhi: Sahitya Akademi.

Coomaraswamy, A.K. 1918. *The Dance of Siva: Fourteen Indian Essays*. New York: The Sunwise Turn Inc. Also published by Munshiram Manoharlal, Delhi, in 1970; reprinted in 1982.

Das, S.K. 2000 [1991]. *A History of Indian Literature*, vol. VIII, *1800–1910: Western Impact and Indian Response*. New Delhi: Sahitya Akademi.

Desai, Anita. 1963. *Voices in the City*. London: Peter Owen.

———. 1965. *Cry, the Peacock*. London: Peter Owen.

Desani, G.V. 1972. *All About H. Hatterr*. Harmondsworth: Penguin Books.

Einstein, Albert. 1950. *Out of My Later Years*. New York: The Philosophical Library.

Fischer, Louis. 1954. *Gandhi: His Life and Message for the World*. New York: Signet Key Books.

Ghose, Sudhin. 1949. *And Gazelles Leaping*. London: Michael Joseph.

BIBLIOGRAPHY | 305

Gooneratne, Yasmine. 1991. *A Change of Skies*. Chippendale: Picador.
Gowda, H.H. Anniah. 1967. 'East–West Encounter in K.S. Venkataramani', in C.D. Narasimhaiah (ed.), *Fiction and the Reading Public in India*, pp. 52–9. Mysore: University of Mysore.
Greene, Graham. 1962. *The Lost Childhood and Other Essays*. Harmondsworth: Penguin Books.
———. 1971. *The Power and the Glory*. London: Heinemann.
———. 1990. *Reflections*. London: Reinhardt Books in association with Viking Books.
Greene, Richard (ed.). 2007. *Graham Greene: A Life in Letters*. New York: W.W. Norton & Company.
Gwynn, J.P.L. (assisted by J. Venkateswara Sastry). 1991. *A Telugu–English Dictionary*. New Delhi: Oxford University Press.
Hosain, Attia, 1961. *Sunlight on a Broken Column*. London: Chatto & Windus.
Hughes, Thomas. 1999 [1857]. *Tom Brown's Schooldays*. USA: Oxford University Press.
International Coloured Gem Association. n.d. 'Ruby'. Available at http://gemstone.org/index.php?option=com,content&view=article&id=85:ruby&catid=1:gem-by-gem&Itemid=14, accessed on 23 February 2011.
Isvaran, S. Manjeri. 1932. *Venkataramani, Writer and Thinker: An Appreciation*. Madras: The People's Printing and Publishing House Ltd.
Iyer, B. Rajam. 1973. *Rambles in Vedanta*. Madras: Ezhuthu Prachuram.
Jagadisan, S. and M.S. Nagarajan. 2006. 'Letting the Light In', *The Hindu*, Madras, 1 October, p. 3.
Jhabvala, Ruth Prawer. 1955. *Esmond in India*. London: George Allen & Unwin.
———. 1956. *The Nature of Passion*. London: George Allen & Unwin.
Jonson, Ben. 2007. *Every Man in His Humour*. Gloucester: Dodo Press.
King, Bruce (ed.). 1974. *Literatures of the World in English*. London: Routledge & Kegan Paul.
Kohli, Devindra. 1989. 'Indian English: A *Khichri* of Words', *Times Literary Supplement*, 1–7 December, n.p.
Kripalani, Krishna. 1982 [1968]. *Literature of Modern India*. New Delhi: National Book Trust.
Krishnan, S. 1996. 'The Definitive Biography', review of Ram and Ram's *R.K. Narayan*, *The Hindu*, 3 November, p. xviii.
Lal, P. 1967. 'Indian Writing in English since Independence', *The Illustrated Weekly of India*, 29 January, n.p.
Leslie-Chaden, Charlene. 1997. *A Compendium of the Teachings of Sathya Sai Baba*. Puttaparthi: Sri Sathya Sai Towers Pvt Ltd.

Lindsay, Jack. 1948. *Mulk Raj Anand: A Critical Essay*. Bombay: Hind Kitabs.
Linscott, Robert N. (ed.). 1922. *The Stories of Anton Chekhov*. New York: Modern Library.
——— (ed.). 1932. *Chekhov's Letters*. New York: Modern Library.
Llewellyn, Richard. 2001. *How Green Was My Valley*. Harmondsworth: Penguin Books.
Luce, Edward. 2006. *In Spite of the Gods: The Strange Rise of Modern India*. London: Little, Brown.
Madhaviah, A. 1916. *Thillai Govindan*. London: T. Fisher Unwin.
———. 1909. *Satyananda*. Bangalore: Mysore Review.
Malgonkar, Manohar. 1963. *A Bend in the Ganges*. London: Hamish Hamilton.
Mandela, Nelson. 1999. 'The Sacred Warrior', *Time*, 27 December, n.p.
Markandaya, Kamala. 1954. *Nectar in a Sieve*. London: Putnam.
McCutchion, David. 1969. *The Modern Indian Novel in English*. Calcutta: Writers Workshop.
Menon, Sadanand. 1998. 'The Truth Governs Writing', interview with V.S. Naipaul, *The Hindu*, Madras, 5 July, p. ix.
Mphahlele, Ezekiel. 1971. *Down Second Avenue*. New York: Anchor Books.
Mukherjee, Meenakshi. 2004. 'Conversation with Vikram Seth', XIII Triennial Conference of AICLALS, Hyderabad, 4–9 August, n.p.
Nagarajan, K. 1961. *Chronicles of Kedaram*. Bombay: Asia Publishing House.
Naipaul, V.S. 1961. *A House for Mr Biswas*. London: Andre Deutsch.
———. 2001. 'Nobel Acceptance Lecture', 7 December. Available at http://nobelprize.org/nobel_prizes/literature/laureates/2001, accessed on 6 December 2006.
Narasimhaiah, C.D. 1968. *The Swan and the Eagle*. Shimla: Indian Institute of Advanced Study; and Delhi: Motilal Banarsidass.
Narayan, Shyamala A. (ed.). 1988. *Non-Fictional Indian Prose in English (1960–90)*. New Delhi: Sahitya Akademi.
Neman, Beth S. 1983. *Writing Effectively*. Ohio: Charles E. Merrill.
Niven, Alastair. 1978. *The Yoke of Pity: The Fictional Writings of Mulk Raj Anand*. New Delhi: Arnold-Heinemann.
O'Malley, L.S.S. 1941. *Modern India and the West: A Study of the Interactions of Their Civilizations*. London: Oxford University Press.
Orefjaerd, Curth. 1995. *Bhagavan Sri Sathya Sai Baba: My Divine Teacher*. Delhi: Motilal Banarsidass.
Palmer, D.J. (ed.). 1984. *Comedy: Developments in Criticism*, Casebook Series. Houndmills, Basingstoke, Hampshire, and London: Macmillan.

Pontes, Hilda. 1983. *Bibliography of Indian Writing in English: R.K. Narayan*. New Delhi: Concept Publishers.

Radhakrishnan, S. (ed.). 1993. *The Bhagavadgita*. New Delhi: Indus, an imprint of HarperCollins Publishers.

Raghavan, V. 1980. *The Indian Heritage*, fourth edition. Bangalore: The Indian Institute of World Culture.

Rajan, Balachandra. 1962. *Too Long in the West*. New York: Athenaeum.

———. 1966. 'The Indian Virtue', *Journal of Commonwealth Literature*, no. 5, pp. 79–85.

Ramamurti, K.S. 1987. *Rise of the Indian Novel in English*. New Delhi: Sterling Publishers.

Ramaswami, N.S. 1988. *K.S. Venkataramani*. New Delhi: Sahitya Akademi.

Rao, D.S. 2006. *Five Decades: The National Academy of Letters, India*. New Delhi: Sahitya Akademi.

Rao, Raja. 1938. *Kanthapura*. Bombay: Oxford University Press.

———. 1960. *The Serpent and the Rope*. London: John Murray.

Rao, Ranga (V. Panduranga Rao). 1990. 'Between Exile and Engagement', Special Inaugural Issue, *The Times of India Review of Books*, August–September, n.p.

———. 1991a. 'From Chatterjee to Chatterjee', *Indian Literature*, no. 144, pp. 103–11. Also published in 1996 in *Creative Aspects of Indian English*, pp. 35–42. New Delhi: Sahitya Akademi.

———. 1993. 'The Book of the Year', review of Vikram Seth's *A Suitable Boy*, *The Hindu*, 19 December, p. 3.

———. 1997. 'Book(er) of the Year', a two-part essay on Arundhati Roy's *The God of Small Things*, *The Hindu*, 16 and 23 November, pp. 2, 3.

———. 2001. 'Iteration of Royals? A Letter to V.S. Naipaul', *The Hindu*, Chennai, 9 December, pp. 5, 6. Reprinted in Erika J. Waters (ed.). 2002. *Caribbean Writer*, vol. 16, pp. 198–203. St. Croix: University of Virgin Islands.

———. 2003. 'Naipaul's Nobel Poise?' *Indian Literature*, vol. 47, no. 3, May–June, pp. 199–210.

Rushdie, Salman. 1991a. *Imaginary Homelands: Essays and Criticism, 1981–1991*. London: Granta Books in association with Penguin Books.

———. 1991b. *Midnight's Children*. New York: Penguin Books.

———. 1997. 'There Is a Kind of Buzz around Indian Writing in English', interview, *India Today*, New Delhi, 14 July.

Robinson, Andrew. 1997. Review of *R.K. Narayan: The Early Years, 1906–45*, *Times Higher Education Supplement*, 2 May, n.p.

———. 2002. 'Bad Business but Good Art', review of two anthologies of essays by Naipaul, *The Asian Age*, Kolkata, 22 September.

Satchidanandan, K. 1999. *Indian Literature Positions and Propositions.* Delhi: Pencraft International.

Satthianadhan, Krupabai. 1998a. *Kamala the Story of a Hindu Child-Wife,* ed. Chandani Lokuge. New Delhi: Oxford University Press.

———. 1998b. *Saguna: The First Autobiographical Novel in English by an Indian Woman.* New Delhi: Oxford University Press.

Segal, Ronald. 1968 [1965]. *The Crisis of India.* Bombay: Jaico Publishing House.

Sheean, Vincent. 1949. *Lead, Kindly Light.* London: Cassell & Co.

Singh, Khushwant. 1956. *Train to Pakistan.* London: Chatto & Windus.

———. 2005. *I Shall Not Hear the Nightingale.* New Delhi: Penguin Books.

Slade, Madeleine. 1960. *The Spirit's Pilgrimage.* London: Orient Longman.

Spaeth, Anthony. 1991. 'Rushdie's Children', *Time,* 16 December, pp. 46–7.

———. 1992. 'Passages from India', *Time,* 24 August, pp. 50–1.

Sree Ramulu, G. 2001. *Telling Stories the Indian Way: A Study of R.K. Narayan, Anita Desai and G.V. Desani.* New Delhi: Sterling Publishers.

Sri Sathya Sai Baba. 2002. *Sathya Sai Speaks,* vol. 34. Prasanthi Nilayam: Sri Sathya Sai Books and Publications Trust.

———. 2005 [2002]. *Bhagavatha Vahini.* Prasanthi Nilayam: Sri Sathya Sai Books and Publications Trust.

Stevenson, Camille (tr.). 2000. *Brihadaranyaka Upanishad: With Comments Taken from the Writings of Bhagavan Sri Sathya Sai Baba.* California: Sathya Sai Book Center of America.

Theroux, Paul. 1998. *Sir Vidia's Shadow: A Friendship across Five Continents.* London: Hamish Hamilton.

Thieme, John. 1987. *The Web of Tradition: Uses of Allusion in V.S. Naipaul's Fiction.* London: Dangaroo Press.

———. 1998. 'Letter from India', *Literary Review,* March, n.p.

———. 2002. 'Naipaul's Nobel', *The Journal of Commonwealth Literature,* vol. 37, no. 1, pp. 1–7. Reprinted in 2002 in *The Atlantic Literary Review,* vol. 3, no. 1, pp. 1–8. Abridged version published in 2002 as 'V.S. Naipaul's Nobel Prize', *The Caribbean Writer,* no. 16, pp. 183–6.

Times Literary Supplement. 1958. 'England Abroad', London, 26 May, n.p.

Tolstoy, Lev. 1852. *Childhood, Boyhood, Youth.* Moscow: Foreign Languages Publishing House.

Vaidyanathan, T.G. 1999. 'The Writer's Writer', review of Theroux's *Sir Vidia's Shadow, The Hindu,* Chennai, 4 April, p. xiv.

Varadarajan, Mu. 1988. *A History of Tamil Literature.* New Delhi: Sahitya Akademi.

Venkataramani, K.S. 1927. *Murugan the Tiller.* London: Simpkin, Marshall, Hamilton, Kent & Co., Ltd.

———. 1934. *Kandan the Patriot*. Madras: Svetaranya Ashrama.
Verghese, C. Paul. 1971. *Problems of the Indian Creative Writer in English*. Bombay: Somaiya Publishers.
Walsh, William. 1972. 'Modern Indian Writing in English', *Indian and Foreign Review*, 15 November, pp. 17–21.
———. 1979. *Introduction to Commonwealth Literature*. London and Basingstoke: Macmillan.
Watson, Francis. 1945. 'What Is Indo-English?' *Listener*, London, 29 November.
Wimsatt, W.K. (ed.). 1969. *The Idea of Comedy: Essays in Prose and Verse, Ben Jonson to George Meredith*. Englewood Cliffs, New Jersey: Prentice-Hall.
Yogananda, Paramahamsa. 1975. *Autobiography of a Yogi*, second edition. Bombay: Yogoda Satsang Society of India and Jaico Publishing House.
Young, G.M. (ed.). 1862. *Speeches of Lord Macaulay with His Minute on Indian Education*. Oxford: Oxford University Press.

Index

Achebe, Chinua, xvii, 256n10, 263n45, 270n5, 285n4
Amirthanayagam, Guy, 241, 259n18, 270n5
Ammani/Parvati (Narayan's grandmother), 4–6, 23, 110, 137, 162, 192, 223–6, 233, 257n4, 258n9, 277n9, 290n10
  gardening as passion, 5, 257n6, 277n9
Anand, Mulk Raj, 15, 17, 25, 138, 257n3, 271n6, 271n8, 272n8
  Untouchable, 36, 272n14
Anandaram, Vimala, 11, 261n32
Anantanarayanan, xvii, 252–3
Andrews, C.F., on Gandhi, 142, 285n7
'Annamalai' (Narayan), 282n4
Arbuthnot and Company, collapse of, 7

The Bachelor of Arts (Narayan), 18, 31, 37–49, 55, 67, 72, 136, 205–6, 263n44, 281n17
  depiction of youth in, 38, 50
  father–mother relationship in, 54
  father–son relationship in, 44–6
  flower-thief episode in, 249, 291n10
  freedom in, 47–9
  images of parental concern, 46
  inner voice in, 43
  conscience and conscionability in, 43–4
  review by B. Appasamy of, 263n44
  rural India in, 48, 145
Bhuvaneswari (Narayan's granddaughter), 12
Book of Job, spiritual surrender in, 69
Bowen, Elizabeth, 55n3, 280n3
'A Breath of Lucifer' (Narayan), 213
BRS, on Narayan, 266n5
Brunton, Paul, psychic training by, 10, 66–7, 68–70, 89, 276n18, 278n3, 279n1

Chatterjee, Bankim Chandra, 3, 14, 15–16
  Rajmohan's Wife, 3
Chaucer, Geoffrey, 251–2, 275–6n13
Chekhov, Anton, similarity with Narayan, xx, 20, 252, 269n23
Childhood, Boyhood, Youth (Tolstoy), 29
Chronicles of Kedaram (Nagarajan), 286–7n8
Coomaraswamy, Ananda, 38, 108, 110, 154
Croft, Susan, 72, 256n1, 263n46, 264n52, 269n24, 273n6, 289n5, 291n13

quoting Narayan on Gandhi, 284–5n2
Cronin, Richard, xviii
Cry, the Peacock (Desai), xvii
Cyclone and Other Stories (Narayan), 279n1

The Dark Room (Narayan), 50–64, 78, 86, 113, 275n10, 276n1, 284n16
　adultery in, 50, 54
　dolls episode in, 244
　domestic discord in, 50, 99, 236
　economic independence in, 60–2
　as family drama, 55
　'fear' in, 62
　feminism in, 233, 271n9
　freedom in, 50, 59
　Greene on the ending of, 276n2
　humanity in, 64, 250–1
　psychological realism in, 58
　rajasic man in, 115–16
　rejection by publisher, 18
　Tamil translation of, 277n14
Davidar, David, 15, 238, 258n10, 262n37
Development of Maritime Laws in 17th-Century England, review by Narayan, 17
Doctor, Geeta, 8, 221–2, 256n12
Dyson, on Western comedy, 291n11

early comedy, 19, 33, 36, 39, 47–8, 50, 52, 58–9, 63, 66, 69, 73–4, 80–1, 86–7, 89, 98–100, 104, 112–13, 118–19, 231, 245. *See also* gunas comedy; humours comedy; vices comedy
'The Edge' (Narayan), 275n10, 287n2

Einstein, Albert, on Gandhi, 137
The Emerald Route (Narayan), 229, 267n8
The English Teacher (Narayan), 20, 71–88, 91, 95, 244, 273n2, 278n2, 280n10
　family in, 72, 80, 82
　Greene's praise for, 229–30
　house-keeping philosophy in, 81
　love in marriage in, 72, 80, 100
　middle-class life in, 84
　rebellion in, 73
　role of child in, 86
　'self' in, 245–6
　spiritualism in, 104, 107, 244

'Father's Help' (Narayan), 31–2
The Financial Expert (Narayan), 123–35, 173, 198, 211, 231, 234, 236, 248
　as a film (*Banker Margayya*), 262n39
　sexuality in, 237
　spirit of post-Independence in, 123
　vice-fection in, 126
Forster, E.M., xviii, 195, 255n3, 287n16
French, Warren, xviii–xix

Gandhi, Mahatma/Gandhianism, 173, 289–90n6. *See also* Einstein, Albert, on Gandhi; *Waiting for the Mahatma*
Gayatri mantra, 69
　translations by Swami Vivekananda and Bhagavan Sri Sathya Sai Baba, 278–9n7
Ghose, Sudhin, xvii

INDEX | 313

The Gita, 13, 67, 69, 118, 143, 198–9, 201, 242–4, 246–7
Gnanambal (Narayan's mother), 4–6, 18, 192, 258n16, 259n17, 281n17, 290
Gods, Demons, and Others (Narayan), 237, 252–3
'God and the Atheist' (Narayan), 275n9, 281n25
Grandmother's Tale (Narayan), 57, 192, 223–38
   dedicated to the Rams, 288n1 (ch. 18)
   based on and guided by Ammani's story, 223–6, 258n9
Greene, Graham, xv, 18, 19–20, 24, 29, 71, 144, 229–30, 241, 268n21, 272n1, 272n10, 276n2, 285n9
   on Narayan's portrayal of the Mahatma, 285n9
   The Power and the Glory, 157
Greene, Graham, horoscope sent by Narayan, 276n16
Greene, Richard, 255n4, 272n10
Grene, Nicholas, 282n10, 286n5
Garbo, Greta, Narayan's meeting with. See under Narayan, R.K.
The Guide (Narayan), x–xi, xvii, 39, 144–57, 202, 234, 236–8, 244, 247–8, 250, 273n3, 276n17
   adultery in, 207
   end of financial problems in, 260n24
   filming of, 268n17
   Hindi translation of, 262n41
   power of sex in, 145
   religious humanism in, 238
   rural India in, 201
   success of, 262n41
gunas (sattva, rajas, tamas), x, xx, 91–2, 94, 118, 125, 136, 210–11, 241–3, 248–50, 279n7, 284n17
gunas comedy, xx, 109, 241–54, 257n6, 262n36, 279n8, 283n14, 291n10. *See also* early comedy; humours comedy; vices comedy
'Guru' (Narayan), 132

Harrex, Syd, 15, 51, 82, 256n11, 277n6
Hemenway, Stephen Ignatius, xix
Hemingway, Ernest
   The Sun Also Rises, 140
Hinduism
   concept of, 37–8, 244, 289n6
   and marriage, 60–1
Holmström, Lakshmi, 51, 265n1, 273n5
The Home of Thunder (Narayan's play), 261n30
A House for Mr Biswas (Naipaul), xvii, 195, 277n11, 281n15. *See also under* Naipaul, V.S.
How Green Was My Valley (Llewellyn), 29
'How to Write an Indian Novel' (Narayan), 267n9
humour, range of, 290–1n10
humours comedy, 249–50. *See also* early comedy; gunas comedy; vices comedy
'The Hungry Child' (Narayan), 287n2

The Illustrated Weekly of India, 270n5, 282n1
India: A Wounded Civilization (Naipaul), xix, 265n3, 278n17

Indian Thought: A Miscellany (Narayan's journal), 19, 23, 98, 270n3, 282n4
'In the Confessional' (Narayan), 250, 290n7
Iyengar, Cheluva, 282n4
Iyengar, Doreswamy, 5, 275n7
  on Narayan's self-taught veena style, 5
Iyengar, Srinivasa K.R., 31, 71, 137, 265n1
Iyer, B. Rajam, 14, 23, 246, 271n9
  Rambles in Vedanta, 265n1
Iyer, Krishnaswami (Narayan's father), 3–4, 8–9, 16, 46, 257n4

James, Henry, admirers of, xviii, 29
Jeffares, Norman, critic of postcolonial literature, xviii
Jhabvala, Ruth Prawer, xvii, 198, 285n8, 289n2
Jonson, Ben, 241
Jonsonian humours, 249

Kabir, Sant, 38, 248
Kabir Street, mirasidar settlers in, 165
Kalhan, Promilla, xix, 5, 259n17, 275n5, 277n4, 287n15
Kalki, Narayan's views on, 266n7
Kohli, Suresh, interview with Narayan, 289n5
Kripalani, Krishna, 14–15, 265–6n4
Krishnan, S., xx, 12, 215, 257n8, 271n5, 286n3, 287n14
Kumari, Vinaya, 268n19, 269n24
Kunjappa, Narayan's pet name, 4–6, 223, 226, 230, 291n13

Lahiri, Jhumpa, on Narayan, xix, 263n44, 274n6

Laxman, R.K. (Narayan's brother) on Narayan 4, 10, 12, 16, 229–30, 258n16, 260n26, 267n8, 269–70n24
Libra, xx, 259n17
Lucretius, on religion, 280n8

Madhaviah, A., 14, 23, 265n1, 271n9
Malgonkar, Manohar, xvii, 272n13
Malgudi Days (Narayan), 192, 278n5
  critics' reviews of, 273–4n6
Mandela, Nelson, 137, 289–90n6
The Man-Eater of Malgudi (Narayan), 57, 158–96, 238
  Bhasmasura myth in, 182, 196, 207, 252
  bureaucracy in, 183–4
  business class in, 184–6
  citizen-hero in, 158
  civil society, 186–92
  craft wisdom in, 158–64
  features of, 163
  Gandhian past of Vasu, 172–7
  illicit sexuality in, 190
  parlour mates in, 179–82
  preoccupation with astrology in, 169
Maugham, Somerset, xvii–xviii, 255n3, 281n23
  on *The English Teacher*, 80
McCutchion, David, 255n1
Mehta, Ved, xx–xxi, 5–6, 9–10, 16, 24, 70–1, 233, 256n12, 259n17–18, 260–1n29, 261n34, 262n43, 267n8, 273n4, 273n6
Minute (Macaulay), Narayan on, 256–7n2
Miss Malini (Narayan's film script), 19

Mojtabai, A.G., xxi, 36, 263n44, 274n2
Monsignor Quixote (Greene), influenced by Narayan, 272n10
Mr. Sampath (Narayan), 89–119, 138, 144, 256n7, 282–3n11
  adverbial clauses in, 91
  importance of The Gita in, 244–5
  narrative style in, 90–2, 101, 105, 113
  critique by Naipaul. *See under* Naipaul, V.S.
  domestic discord in, 99, 236
Mukherjee, Meenakshi, 255n1, 263n44, 265n1
Mukherji, Nirmal, 'The World of Malgudi' (thesis), ix, 255n2
My Dateless Diary (Narayan), ix, 11, 169, 206, 271n5, 274n7, 275n4, 280n9, 282n3, 287n1
My Days (Narayan), ix, 3, 52, 72, 166, 169, 223, 228, 233, 245, 258n11, 276n3
Mysore: A Travel Record, 17, 267n8, 268n20, 279n1

Nadanta, dance of Siva, 110
Naik, M.K., xix, 68, 252, 265n1, 277n13
Naipaul, V.S., xvii, 64, 89, 181, 256n12, 259n17, 281n15, 282n5, 288n2
  account of reading *Mr. Sampath*, xix, 101–7, 113, 282–3n11
  critique of Narayan, xix, 7, 195, 265n3, 278n17, 283–4n15, 285n9, 289n3
  India: A Wounded Civilization, 278n17
  'Karmism' of, 282n7

  as an outsider, 284n15
Narayan, R.K.
  attending Madras Music Festival, 258n10
  balance in, xx, 48, 52–3, 59, 70, 187, 289n5
  career/professional life of, 14–21
  on celluloid experience, 268n17
  on cloves, 248
  on coffee, 248, 258n16, 275n4
  creative writing, as career, 16, 20, 180, 266n5
  critique by Naipaul. *See under* Naipaul, V.S.
  crucial period in life of, 65–70
  on curd rice and lemon pickle, 259n16
  first typewriter of, 16
  Garbo, Greta, meeting with, 13, 71
  Hinduism of, 57, 229, 238, 247
  hobby of music, 5, 223, 258n9
  humanism of, 61, 216, 244, 289–90n6
  humour in, xx, 290–1n10
  influence of Carnatic music on, 5
  influence on Graham Greene, 258n9
  on joint family, 34, 72, 98–9, 162, 198–9, 235, 253, 274n7, 290n9
  as a literary critic, 270–1n5
  on Manohar Malgonkar, 272n13
  mental and psychic training. *See* Brunton, Paul, psychic training by
  personal life of, 3–13
  on renunciation, 38–9, 219, 247, 274n1

radio talk by, 261n32, 268n18
reason to opt for a writing career, 290n7
relatives. *See individual relations*
on Shakespeare, 13, 171–2, 270–1n5, 285n2
social activism of, 5
on style, 272n12
style compared with his precursors in south India, xxi, 23–4
theosophy of, 66, 278n2
views on sex, ii, xi, 68, 237, 278n6, 283n13
'writer at work', 269–70n24
writing for *the Hindu*, 65, 98, 268n19
writing style of, 22–5
Narayan, R.K., comedy of. *See also individual terms*
Narayan, R.K., heroines associated with fragrance, 76–7, 82–3
Narayan, R.K., literary works. *See individual works*
charity in, 61–3, 107
conscience in, 31–2, 43, 59, 73, 75, 98, 112, 142, 201, 273n3
conscionability in, 32, 35, 43–4, 250
deflatory humour in, 290n10
disintegration of the family in, 270n6
enchantment in, 97, 111, 154, 248, 253
figure of granny in, 5, 33–5, 136–7, 140–2, 209–10, 219, 262n39
figure of wife in, 52–9, 61, 72–4, 76–7, 79–87, 96, 99–101, 105–7, 114, 125–9, 132, 134, 148–50, 164–5, 191–2, 198, 212–13, 218–19, 224, 228, 235–6
gardening in, 54–5, 77, 81, 282n4
inner voice in, 43, 142, 148, 153
sexual morality in, 68
Narayan, R.K., in love, x, 9, 116
Narayan, Shyamala A., 252
on the ending of *The Guide*, 285n5
Niven, Alastair, 'Why Can't Englishmen Write Like R.K. Narayan?', xix
'A Night of Cyclone' (Narayan), 23, 286n1

The Painter of Signs (Narayan), 147, 201, 205–10, 215, 232, 271n5
family in, 208, 235, 277n11
Ganga–Santanu myth in, 207–8
romance in, 212
sex-act in, 207
sex in, 205–7, 237
Pearn, Pollinger & Higham Ltd (Narayan's first agent), 269n22
'Permitted Laughter' (Narayan), 264n48
Philipose, Pamela, 12, 230, 258n16, 260n26, 264n48, 267n8, 289n3
pre-independence novels. *See The Bachelor of Arts; The Dark Room; The English Teacher; Mr. Sampath; Swami and Friends*
Prince Yazid (Narayan's play), 270n2
'The Psychic Journal' (Narayan's journal), 41, 66, 276n18, 278n1, 290n8
Purna, Kittu (Narayan's friend), xvii, 18, 266n6, 267n12

INDEX | 317

Rajagopal, D.R., 11, 263n46
Rajam (Narayan's wife), 9, 78, 221, 260–1n29, 261n33
Rajam, death of, 10, 266n5, 276n18
  Greene on, 71
  psychic training after, 13, 66, 68–9, 145–6, 244, 249–50
  writing after, x, 85, 231, 233
Ram, Susan, 40, 201, 264n49, 276n3
Ram, Susan and N. Ram, 13, 16, 65–6, 70, 223, 275n7
  on Narayan's professionalism, 278n5
Ramamurthy, B., 242
Ramayana (Narayan)
  affirmation to Croft, 291n13
  Indira Gandhi's reaction to, 291n13
  Sharada Prasad's reaction to. See under Sharada Prasad, H.Y.
Ramanan, Mohan G., 255n6
Ramnarayan, Gowri, 263n46
  emphasizing Narayan's respect for women, 278n16
Rao, Raja, 15, 25
  Kanthapura, 36, 138, 143, 272n14, 286n8
  The Serpent and the Rope, xvii
Reed, Henry, xviii
  BBC talk, 270n4
Reluctant Guru (Narayan), 262n40, 272n2
renunciation, concept of, 247
rough-and-tumble humour, 290n10
rural India, importance to Narayan, 48, 145, 201

S.V.V., on Narayan, 6–7, 71, 253, 271n7, 280–1n12

Salt and Sawdust (Narayan), 267n8
Satthianadhan, Krupabai, 278n15
  Saguna, 277n5
Sathya Sai Baba, Bhagavan Sri, 279n7
Satyan, T.S., 258n16, 265n5, 270n4
self-education, 42, 44, 48, 65, 153
self-knowledge, 101, 166, 222
self-pity, 165, 252
self-training, 66, 251
'Selvi' (Narayan), 286n5, 286n6
Seshachalam (Narayan's 'senior' uncle), 6, 258n15
Seth, Vikram, xviii, 15, 198, 285n8
  The Golden Gate, 274n9
  Narayan's views on, 258n12, 263n46, 274n9
Shankar, D.A., on caste in Narayan, 275n10
Sharada Prasad, H.Y., xi, 257n4, 258n12, 259n21
  on Narayan's *Ramayana* and *Mahabharata*, 291n13
Singh, Khushwant, xvii, 198, 285n8
Slade, Madeleine
  quoting Gandhi, 142
  quoting Rolland in *The Spirit's Pilgrimage*, 285n5
Spaeth, Anthony, on Narayan, xviii, xxi, 13, 273n6
Srinivas, M.N., on Narayan, 7, 260n25, 261n35
  on Greene's praise for *Swami and Friends*, 272n1
Srinivasan, Gemini 19
  Gemini Studios, 85
Srinivasan, Kasturi, support to Narayan, 19
Stet (Athill), 283n11
Sundaram, P.S., 273n2

Swami and Friends (Narayan), 18, 19, 29–36, 41, 219, 250, 272n1
   conscience in, 31–2
   critical difference with 'Father's Help', 31–2
   freedom and discipline as theme in, 33
   humanism in, 238
   Tamil translation of, 19
   televization of, 262n38
   virtues of the first novel, 35

Tagore, Rabindranath, xix, 244, 247, 255n6
Talkative Man (Narayan), 159, 173, 211–13, 232
   Brahmin gentry of Kabir Street, 159–60, 164, 212–13
   family in, 235
   prologue of, 213
Theroux, Paul, 256n9, 256n12, 272n12, 277n11, 278n4
Thieme, John, 58, 256n7, 256n13, 258n9, 273–4n6, 275n10, 278n5, 282n5, 283n11
   on Narayan's professionalism, 278n5
   R.K. Narayan, 256n13
Things Fall Apart (Achebe), xvii
'Thumbi's Schooling' (Narayan), views on the child, 272–3n2
A Tiger for Malgudi (Narayan), 212–13, 215–17, 235, 238
   guru in, 159, 212–13
   hero in, 154
   spiritual transformation in, 216, 232, 233–4
Tom Brown's School Days (Hughes), 29

Updike, John, xviii, xxi, 5, 166, 257n8

The Vendor of Sweets (Narayan), 197–204, 215, 231, 237, 276n15, 283n15
   family in 218, 221, 234–5
   Gandhian influence on the hero, 198–9, 201
   sanyasa in, 217, 219, 231
   shift from Gandhism, 172, 197
   vanaprasthya in, 217, 219, 283–4n15
   violence in, 236
Venkataraman (Narayan's 'junior' uncle), 7, 275n11
Venkataramani, K.S., 14, 23, 258n12, 265n3
   Kandan the Patriot, 246
   Murugan the Tiller, 24
vices comedy, 219, 229, 231, 238. *See also* early comedy; gunas comedy; humours comedy
Vivekananda, Swami, 244, 247, 279n7, 289n6

Waiting for the Mahatma (Narayan), 136–43, 145, 171, 172, 236
Walsh, William, xviii, xix, 11, 57, 244, 255n2, 256n8, 272n11–12, 273n6, 276n15, 276n18, 281n20, 284n19, 286n7
   on *Mr. Sampath*, 291n10
Williams, Haydn Moore, xix, 256n7, 265n3
   on Mr Sampath, 284n19
'Women's Lib' movement, 50, 52, 61–2

'The World of Malgudi'
(Hariprasanna), 274n6
The World of Nagaraj (Narayan),
159–60, 198, 218–22, 227,
291n10
  decline of a Kabir Street family
  in, 234–5

Kavu Pundit in, 220, 233
post-Independence world in,
232–3, 276n15
self-parody in, 221, 227, 238
success in, 232
A Writer's Nightmare (Narayan),
263n46, 274n9

About the Author

Ranga Rao grew up in the coastal districts of the Indian state of Andhra Pradesh, and shifted base to New Delhi in 1964. After teaching in the Department of English, Sri Venkateswara College, University of Delhi, for thirty-seven years, he returned to his home town; at present he is a visiting faculty at the Department of English, Sri Sathya Sai Institute of Higher Learning, Puttaparthi, Andhra Pradesh. His career as a critic of postcolonial literatures predates his success as a novelist. Besides creative and critical works, he has also compiled, edited, and translated anthologies. As part of the Indo-Australian cultural exchange programme, he has represented India at Wordfest, a literary festival held in Canberra, Australia, in 1989.

From among the gamut of his published works, some are: among novels, *Fowl-Filcher* (1985), *The Drunk Tantra* (1994), and *The River Is Three Quarters Full* (2001); a collection of short stories titled *An Indian Idyll and Other Stories* (1989); two translated anthologies, *Classic Telugu Short Stories* (1995) and *That Man on the Road: Contemporary Telugu Short Fiction* (2006); two monographs, *R.K. Narayan* (2004) and *Bal Vikas for Lok Vikas* (2011); and two edited volumes, *Full-Flame: Infinite Scenarios* (2010) and *Full-Flame: Volume II, Unconditional Love* (2015).